Understanding the Active Economy and Emerging Research on the Value of Sports, Recreation, and Wellness

David J. Finch
Mount Royal University, Canada

David Legg
Mount Royal University, Canada

A volume in the Advances in Finance, Accounting, and Economics (AFAE) Book Series

IGI Global
PUBLISHER of TIMELY KNOWLEDGE

Published in the United States of America by
IGI Global
Business Science Reference (an imprint of IGI Global)
701 E. Chocolate Avenue
Hershey PA, USA 17033
Tel: 717-533-8845
Fax: 717-533-8661
E-mail: cust@igi-global.com
Web site: http://www.igi-global.com

Library of Congress Cataloging-in-Publication Data

Names: Finch, David J., 1967- editor. | Legg, David, 1968- editor.
Title: Understanding the active economy and emerging research on the value of sports, recreation, and wellness / David J. Finch and David FH Legg, editors.
Description: Hershey PA : Business Science Reference, [2021] | Includes bibliographical references and index. | Summary: "This book investigates how the active economy incorporates all enterprises participating in, or contributing to, improving individual or community prosperity through the development and delivery of active living, sport, active recreation, physical education, physical literacy, indoor and outdoor play, health, wellness, and all other associated sectors"-- Provided by publisher.
Identifiers: LCCN 2021017723 (print) | LCCN 2021017724 (ebook) | ISBN 9781799879398 (Hardcover) | ISBN 9781799879404 (Paperback) | ISBN 9781799879411 (eBook)
Subjects: LCSH: Sports--Economic aspects. | Recreation industry. | Sporting goods industry. | Sports and tourism. | Sports betting. | Health products. | Economics--Sociological aspects. | Stakeholder management.
Classification: LCC GV716 .U53 2021 (print) | LCC GV716 (ebook) | DDC 338.4/77965--dc23
LC record available at https://lccn.loc.gov/2021017723
LC ebook record available at https://lccn.loc.gov/2021017724

This book is published in the IGI Global book series Advances in Finance, Accounting, and Economics (AFAE) (ISSN: 2327-5677; eISSN: 2327-5685)

British Cataloguing in Publication Data
A Cataloguing in Publication record for this book is available from the British Library.

Advances in Finance, Accounting, and Economics (AFAE) Book Series

ISSN:2327-5677
EISSN:2327-5685

Editor-in-Chief: Ahmed Driouchi Al Akhawayn University, Morocco

MISSION

In our changing economic and business environment, it is important to consider the financial changes occurring internationally as well as within individual organizations and business environments. Understanding these changes as well as the factors that influence them is crucial in preparing for our financial future and ensuring economic sustainability and growth.

The **Advances in Finance, Accounting, and Economics (AFAE)** book series aims to publish comprehensive and informative titles in all areas of economics and economic theory, finance, and accounting to assist in advancing the available knowledge and providing for further research development in these dynamic fields.

COVERAGE

- Accounting information systems
- Economics of Risks, Uncertainty, Ambiguity, and Insurance
- Auditing
- Bankruptcy
- Macroeconomics
- Economics of Intellectual Property Rights
- Entrepreneurship in Accounting and Finance
- E-finance
- Labor Economics
- Economics of Innovation and Knowledge

IGI Global is currently accepting manuscripts for publication within this series. To submit a proposal for a volume in this series, please contact our Acquisition Editors at Acquisitions@igi-global.com or visit: http://www.igi-global.com/publish/.

The Advances in Finance, Accounting, and Economics (AFAE) Book Series (ISSN 2327-5677) is published by IGI Global, 701 E. Chocolate Avenue, Hershey, PA 17033-1240, USA, www.igi-global.com. This series is composed of titles available for purchase individually; each title is edited to be contextually exclusive from any other title within the series. For pricing and ordering information please visit http://www.igi-global.com/book-series/advances-finance-accounting-economics/73685. Postmaster: Send all address changes to above address.

Titles in this Series

For a list of additional titles in this series, please visit:
http://www.igi-global.com/book-series/advances-finance-accounting-economics/73685

Handbook of Research on Changing World Economic Order in the Post-Pandemic Period
Vishal Sarin (Lovely Professional University, India) Badri Narayanan Gopalakrishnan (Infinite Sum Modelling, USA) Sushanta Kumar Mahapatra (IBS Hyderabad, The ICFAI Foundation for Higher Education, India) and Tanima Dutta (Lovely Professional University, India)
Business Science Reference • © 2021 • 470pp • H/C (ISBN: 9781799868965) • US $295.00

Financial Management and Risk Analysis Strategies for Business Sustainability
Joaquín Enríquez-Díaz (University of A Coruña, Spain) Laura Castro-Santos (University of A Coruña, Spain) and Félix Puime-Guillén (University of A Coruña, Spain)
Business Science Reference • © 2021 • 320pp • H/C (ISBN: 9781799876342) • US $215.00

Theory of Shocks, COVID-19, and Normative Fundamentals for Policy Responses Emerging Research and Opportunities
Olga Ivanovna Pilipenko (The Russian Presidential Academy of National Economy and Public Administration, Russia) Zoya Andreevna Pilipenko (Bank of Russia, Russia) and Andrey Igorevich Pilipenko (The Russian Presidential Academy of National Economy and Public Administration, Russia)
Business Science Reference • © 2021 • 250pp • H/C (ISBN: 9781799843092) • US $165.00

Handbook of Research on Theory and Practice of Financial Crimes
Abdul Rafay (University of Management and Technology, Pakistan)
Business Science Reference • © 2021 • 650pp • H/C (ISBN: 9781799855675) • US $345.00

Comparative Research on Earnings Management, Corporate Governance, and Economic Value
Elisabete S. Vieira (University of Aveiro, Portugal) Mara Madaleno (University of Aveiro, Portugal) and Graça Azevedo (University of Aveiro, Portugal)
Business Science Reference • © 2021 • 433pp • H/C (ISBN: 9781799875963) • US $215.00

For an entire list of titles in this series, please visit:
http://www.igi-global.com/book-series/advances-finance-accounting-economics/73685

IGI Global
PUBLISHER of TIMELY KNOWLEDGE

701 East Chocolate Avenue, Hershey, PA 17033, USA
Tel: 717-533-8845 x100 • Fax: 717-533-8661
E-Mail: cust@igi-global.com • www.igi-global.com

Table of Contents

Detailed Table of Contents

In the past 20 years, the creative economy has emerged as a framework to explore creativity as an ecosystem with direct and indirect value. The creative economy lens does not view fields such as education, arts, culture, and innovation as isolated. Rather, by adopting an ecosystem view, the creative economy maps the interdependence of these fields as unique drivers of direct and indirect economic outputs. In this book, the authors identify an active ecosystem, incorporating all organizations who participate in, or contribute to, improving individual or community well-being through the development and delivery of sport and active recreational experiences. By viewing them as part of a complex active ecosystem, the authors believe policymakers and practitioners are better positioned to shape ecosystem-level opportunities and maximize its impact on the community.

This chapter will deconstruct the value chain located within the active economy. This value chain includes community input resources (including human, economic, social/structural, built, and natural resources) which generate activities and outputs. The value of the active economy is defined by its impact on a community's economic, human, social, and environmental wellbeing. Herein, the literature associated with the impact of the active economy on the dimensions of community wellbeing is examined.

This chapter builds upon previous discussions conceptualizing the active economy by focusing on one of its key features: the stakeholders. In particular, the authors seek to answer three fundamental questions regarding how to conceptualise active economies including: (1) What stakeholders comprise an active economy? (2) How can we identify stakeholders within an active economy? (3) How do these stakeholders interact in order to produce systems of value? In response to these questions, they provide an overview of the stakeholder saliency literature and discuss how it may be possible to conceptualize stakeholders within the active economy by outlining a topology and a conceptual framework for the identification and classification of stakeholders. Finally, they illustrate how this conceptual framework can be used to identify stakeholders within global, national, and regional active economies and through a case study of Strava Inc.

Organized sport in some form or another has existed since the Ancient Olympic Games. Over time, this sector has evolved to include professional leagues and teams, intercollegiate athletics, and mega events for both men and women. Operating locally, nationally, and internationally, organized sport reaches across boundaries and into communities on various levels. Organized sport will continue its wide-ranging reach into communities as the sport industry and the various constituencies it interacts with evolve into the next century.

Active recreation is defined as activities engaged in for the purpose of relaxation, health and wellbeing, or enjoyment with the primary activity requiring physical exertion. They are often spontaneous in nature and participant-led, with a low level of organization and limited structure. Active recreation has significant links to health and wellbeing and provides its greatest value when it is shared with all citizens.

There are two approaches to health and wellness that are explored throughout this chapter. The first is a socio-ecological response, where the recreation system has been focused on changing individual behaviour at the programmatic level. There is the realization that if programs were the single answer, then all the world's problems would be solved by now. What is needed is a much larger systemic response. The second approach relates to the co-creation of authentic and customized health and wellness solutions. Typically, the notion of health and wellness is viewed through the lens of the "expert" and a prescription model that is grounded in "the expert knows what is best for you." The emerging model is one where the citizen is at the centre of the solution process. People desire the ability to feel more in control and make informed decisions about their health for themselves and their families. In this chapter, the authors explore this topic by reviewing a Canadian health and wellness action study.

According to the World Travel and Tourism Council's (WTTC) most recent reports, one in every ten jobs (an estimated 330 million) is influenced if not directly supported by travel and tourism-related activity, making it one of the world's largest economic sectors. Whilst the boundaries that separate adventure tourism from active/sport tourism are blurred, the subject is certainly not lacking in terms of evidence-based definitions, conceptual frameworks, or typologies. This chapter offers a critical overview of the existing body of knowledge that relates to the emergence of a global active and/or adventure-based tourism economy. The authors complement their review of the literature with a case study looking at the 'home of adventure', Queenstown, New Zealand.

Active technology (i.e. 'wearables' and accompanying health tracking apps) is a multi-billion-dollar industry. Nearly one in every 10 people worldwide generates physiological and biomechanical data from wearable devices every day. This data allows users to evaluate their performance over time, to share with friends, to find like-minded training partners and share this data with their primary healthcare providers. Population-based research related to health, wellness, and physical activity is now feasible as a result of data generated from wearables. This chapter will highlight the major current trends and future applications for wearable devices from a user and research-based perspective across the active economy. The authors aim to highlight the practical and clinical utility of wearables to monitor training, fatigue, and performance on the athletic field, the workplace, and the clinical environments. The goal is to improve health, mobility, and quality of life of the end-user.

This chapter provides a high-level overview of the elements that make up the active economy infrastructure. This includes a focus on urban design, master planning, and a review of facility types. Further discussion involves types of play that occur within various infrastructure, with a particular focus on parks. Finally, the operation of infrastructure is reviewed along with the trends that are impacting the design of active infrastructure.

Historically, sports gaming has existed primarily in brick-and-mortar venues such

Foreword

I have come to realize that there are so many things that shape a man throughout his lifetime. When one deciphers the true meaning of the active economy and all that it entails, I reflect on the many things that set me on my path. My story is not so complicated really, I was built from scratch as an athlete and fully designed to embrace all the things I was steered into. I learned from the young age of five what media was and what it was like to be even somewhat famous on a local level. I learned professionalism from my surroundings. My parents were running their pro wrestling business, and I eventually learned to appreciate the significance of taking a family picture with boxing champion Rocky Marciano.

Over my life I learned of the commitment one needs to strive to the top of any field. The importance of training – getting stronger, fitter, faster, improvising, and improving my skills so that I could climb to the top of the pro wrestling industry. Watching Stampeder games and observing how they marketed and sold their sport instilled in me to train hard, to build myself up, and to be that athlete, that physical machine to reach the top. I learned from TV and newspapers how important it was to have a plan to sell myself if I wanted to be an athlete.

Any illusions I had that my lifetime of amateur wrestling would be similar to pro wrestling was gone by the time I was a teen, but I still benefitted from my lifetime of preparation for the path ahead. Everything is so intricately braided together; the media, the commentator, the cameraman, the writer of the wrestling programs I once sold. The manufacturing or selling of one's industry, the outfits, designs of masks, capes, robes, even the classy detail of the wrestling belt all established a belief in what worked and what didn't. Not to mention the action figures, cards, magazines, posters, DVDs, and everything else marketed today. Whether watching my dad's wrestling or a Calgary Stampeders football game, I had my first initiation into the active economy. I participated all my life competitively reaching for the top. Of what? I wasn't so sure, but I knew I was on my way.

Bret Hart
World Wrestling Entertainment Hall of Fame, Canada

Foreword

I was 4 years old when my mom put me on cross-country skis for the first time in my life. As she tells it, I shuffled around the backyard for a minute or two, then, tearfully threw myself to the ground and demanded to know when we were going in for hot chocolate. My dear Mom propped me back up on my feet, dusted off the snow, and told me to "just keep trying."

Sport was woven into the fabric of our family life and part of my everyday existence. I learned to swim at our local pool and to ski on the local trails with my parents either coaching, volunteering, or cheering from the sidelines. Watching CBC's Sports Saturday together with my Dad was a never-missed weekend ritual and it was there, watching the incredible displays of human spirit as athletes from around the globe competed against each other in stunning displays of passionate, heroic efforts that a vision of myself as an elite athlete; a competitor; an Olympian, began to crystalize.

Like the vast sweeping skies and rolling prairie landscape surrounding my little Canadian town, sport, to me, represented an opportunity that seemed endlessly full of hope. I reveled in the camaraderie created by the spirit of friendly competition, the community of like-minded individuals I discovered, and the passionate pursuit of excellence. I was driven, determined and full of idealistic aspirations. University, financial security and preparation for life-after-sport were put on pause as I kept my sights trained on a singular goal and channeled all that I had, all that I was, toward it. My dream was to stand on the top step of the Olympic podium with a medal around my neck, and flag around my shoulders. The rigors of ruthless training, the fatigue of endless travel, the obstacles and adversity; all of it manageable and worthwhile, as long as I could somehow, "just keep trying."

When I was 27 years old, I won a bronze medal at the 2002 Olympic Games in Salt Lake City. It was the first for Canada in our sport, and a moment of indescribable happiness and pride. Though I was not naive to the risk of doping, I was discomfited to extreme by the sinister possibility lurking in the shadowy corners of my beautiful sport. More than anything I wanted to believe the playing field was level; that the values I had lived, trained and competed with my entire life, were upheld by all.

It was not to be. Days after the race, the gold and silver medalists in my event tested positive for performance-enhancing drugs, and I became an unwitting poster child for fairness and clean sport as the courts twisted in the wind for two years before awarding me Olympic gold. Though I was relieved for it to be finally over, the entire experience was a let-down I could not have imagined. Although I had gained a new medal and title, something much deeper and profoundly more meaningful, had been lost.

I write this today because despite that experience, I still believe in sport and the power it holds to bring out the best in humanity. I have seen first-hand how sport can unite and elevate people across the globe in a way unmatched by almost any other human endeavor. In my work now with Indigenous children and youth, I watch as sport transforms individuals, inspires entire communities, teaches – and perhaps most importantly – heals.

At its core, sport is about connection. Connecting us to broader communities, nature, health, the strength of those around us – and the strength that lies within. It is something around which to gather, and yes, in some cases, fight for. If there is one absolute about sport that I know to be true it is this; uniting around the common goal of supporting, sustaining and elevating sport in our communities is perhaps one of the most important missions we can embark on for ourselves; for others, and for future generations to come.

Beckie Scott
Spirit North, Canada & Olympic Gold Medalist, Canada

Preface

UNDERSTANDING THE ACTIVE ECONOMY

The active economy incorporates all enterprises participating in, or contributing to, improving individual or community prosperity through the development and delivery of active living, sport, active recreation, physical education, physical literacy, indoor and outdoor play, health, wellness, and all other associated sectors. The active economy incorporates eleven interdependent sectors in two macro-level clusters: delivery and enabling. The delivery cluster includes the sectors responsible for the delivery of active experiences, including active living, organized sports, active recreation, active tourism, and sport betting. The enabling cluster includes sectors where the goods and service outputs support the delivery of the active experiences. Examples here are health and wellness, active products and gear, equipment and accessories, design and infrastructure, media and content and professional services.

From an academic and policy perspective, these disciplines are typically viewed as distinct, with only limited spillover and as a consequence, limited research explores the interaction between them. Herein, we view each individual sector as interdependent rather than autonomous. By viewing the various sectors as part of a complex active ecosystem, we contend that policymakers and practitioners are better positioned to shape broad opportunities, while maximizing community value.

This broad ecosystem view of the active economy follows trends found in many other areas of study from management to biology. What makes the ecosystem lens unique is that the interdependency recognizes that the health of the individual components is dependent on the overall health and sustainability of the larger entity. Thus, reliance of the whole depends on the breadth and depth of interconnections between the component parts. Applying this perspective to the active economy then allows for a deeper analysis of the boundaries, networks, and knowledge exchanges across the ecosystem, which is useful in assessing inter-organization collaboration capacity.

ORGANIZATION OF THE BOOK

To provide an overview of the active economy and address its future trends and challenges, the book is organized into twelve chapters. The authors of each chapter include scholars and practitioners from across the globe to provide a holistic perspective of both the theory and practice of the active economy. In each chapter, the respective author explores its diverse themes and intersection with the broader active economy. Below is a summary of each chapter and the questions it considers.

A New Lens: Envisioning an Active Economy

In chapter 1, we provide an overview of the complex and interdependent ecosystem of enterprises and individuals that compose the active economy. In doing so, we look at ecosystems for conceptual guidance on how to map the individual components as part of a larger system. which these interact to create incremental value for all components.

Mapping the Active Economy to Community Value

In this chapter we examine the influence of the active economy as part of a complex value chain composed on community input resources, activities and outputs, and how these together impact dimensions of community wellbeing. The impacts were then divided into economic, human, social and environmental with evidence demonstrating the connections between and among all four.

Stakeholders in the Active Economy

In this chapter we divide active economy stakeholders into three sections focusing on the conceptualization, identification and the dynamic interactions of stakeholders. In doing so we provided an overview of a conceptual framework for evaluating stakeholder saliency and then discussed how it may be possible to conceptualize stakeholders within the active economy by outlining a topology of stakeholders and a conceptual framework for the identification and classification of stakeholders based on their saliency.

Organized Sport in an Active Economy

In this chapter we provide an overview of the organized sport sector and how it interacts with other components of the active economy to generate incremental tangible and intangible value. In doing so, we identify opportunities for managers to not only react to system-level dynamics but also to anticipate and proactively lead these changes.

Active Recreation in an Active Economy

This chapter studies the role of active recreation as part of the larger active economy. Active recreation differs from organized sport in that it is more spontaneous in nature and participant led. Throughout this chapter we highlight where active recreation lives within our lives, its importance and the need for an increased societal value to active recreation investments.

Health and Wellness in an Active Economy

In this chapter we consider the health and wellness sector of the active economy. This includes proposing a model where citizens are incorporated as central to the planning and design of programs and services, built environment and community capacity building.

Active Tourism in an Active Economy

In this chapter we explore active tourism. This includes reviewing the origins and opportunities attached to this expanding international market. To do so, we explore the scope of this sector and examine a case study of Queensland, Australia.

Active Technology and Accessories

In this chapter, we consider active technology, including 'wearables' and accompanying health tracking apps. Today, 1 in 10 people worldwide are generating data for wearable devices. In this chapter, we highlight the major current trends and future applications for wearable devices from a user and research-based perspective across the active economy.

Design and Infrastructure in an Active Economy

This chapter considers one of the most visible and foundational sectors of the active economy, infrastructure. From walking paths to stadiums and ski hills to recreation centres, the enormous variety of venues form a significant part of our investment in the active economy and define the active capacity of a community and region.

Sport Betting and Fantasy Sport in an Active Economy

This first chapter explores the history and growth of eSports. This includes mapping the major components of the business ecosystem. Each following chapter goes into depth on the key themes highlighted in chapter 1.

Media and Content in an Active Economy

Media and content, from traditional to digital communication has emerged as one of the critical sparks that has led to the exponential growth of the global active economy, from professional sports to apparel and footwear. This chapter considers the growth of media and content and its implications today and in the future on the active economy.

Chapter 1
A New Lens: Envisioning an Active Economy

David J. Finch
Mount Royal University, Canada

David Legg
Mount Royal University, Canada

Norm O'Reilly
University of Guelph, Canada

Jason Ribeiro
University of Calgary, Canada

Trevor Tombe
University of Calgary, Canada

ABSTRACT

In the past 20 years, the creative economy has emerged as a framework to explore creativity as an ecosystem with direct and indirect value. The creative economy lens does not view fields such as education, arts, culture, and innovation as isolated. Rather, by adopting an ecosystem view, the creative economy maps the interdependence of these fields as unique drivers of direct and indirect economic outputs. In this book, the authors identify an active ecosystem, incorporating all organizations who participate in, or contribute to, improving individual or community well-being through the development and delivery of sport and active recreational experiences. By viewing them as part of a complex active ecosystem, the authors believe policymakers and practitioners are better positioned to shape ecosystem-level opportunities and maximize its impact on the community.

DOI: 10.4018/978-1-7998-7939-8.ch001

INTRODUCTION: CONCEPTUALIZING AN ACTIVE ECONOMY

The active economy incorporates a number of disciplines that include sport performance, sport business, recreation, tourism, physical activity, urban planning, leisure and health and wellness, among others. From an academic and policy perspective, these disciplines are typically viewed as distinct, with only limited spillover (Gerke, & Pria, 2018; Gerke, Desbordes & Dickson, 2015) and as a consequence, limited research explores the interaction between them. We propose an alternative in this book, building on the narrower but informative work in sport of Gerke and Pria (2018) and Shilbury (2000) and view each individual sector as interdependent rather than autonomous. By viewing the various sectors as part of a complex active ecosystem, we contend that policymakers and practitioners are better positioned to shape broad opportunities, while maximizing community value.

Taking a broad ecosystem view of the active economy follows trends found in many other areas of study. In particular, over the past thirty years, the nature of value creation has evolved dramatically. Competitive advantage has historically been viewed at an organization-level (Porter, 1998), but today value is often addressed at the inter-organization or network-level (Eisingerich, Bell, & Tracey, 2010; Tallman, Jenkins, Henry & Pinch, 2004). Sophisticated forms of inter-organization collaboration range from formal strategic alliances to informal cooperation and provide access to expanded resources and shared capacity to learn, innovate and co-create. To help understand how the creation of value actually takes place, we examine how scholars (e.g., Moore, 1993; Rothschild, 1990) exploit a similarity between biology and forms of inter-organization collaboration, deemed ecosystems. In both of these cases, ecosystems are at risk of collapse if they are unable to adapt to rapid changes. Older ecosystems are replaced by newer ones that possess the capacity to adapt to change. As Rothchild (1990, p. 6) notes, "A capitalist economy can best be comprehended as a living ecosystem. Key phenomena observed in nature – competition, specialization, co-operation, exploitation, learning, growth, and several others – are also central at business life." What makes the ecosystem lens unique is that the interdependency recognizes that the health of the individual components (whether it is a species or organization) is dependent on the overall health and sustainability of the larger one (Moore, 1993). The reliance of the whole thus depends on the breadth and depth of interconnections between the parts. Applying this perspective to the active economy then allows for a deeper analysis of the boundaries, networks, and knowledge exchanges across the ecosystem, which is useful in assessing inter-organization collaboration capacity.

Interconnections and relationships between individual sectors or organizations can take many forms, many of which are measurable. There are physical connections in the form of purchases and sales of goods and services from one organization or sector to another. Examples could be professional services purchased by sport venues such as marketing or ticketing. Others could include equipment manufacturers supplying individuals or teams. There are also flows of workers and investments from one organization or sector to another. This may occur naturally as individuals move from one employer to another, but the same individual may also be simultaneously involved in multiple facets of the active ecosystem. The scale and scope of such flows and their economic footprint can be measured, albeit not easily. The non-physical outputs, such as learning and knowledge flows, while being more difficult to measure, are no less important and form a critical component of an active ecosystem. Capturing such a wide variety of complex interconnections and value creation thus represents a challenge, but not an insurmountable one. It begins with a strong conceptual framework.

Building From the Creative Economy Framework

To help develop an understanding of the active economy, an exploration of how the 'creative economy' emerged is necessary (Florida, 2006; Howkins, 2002). The creative economy is premised on the role of knowledge, creativity, and innovation as drivers of an organization's competitive advantage and growth (Urbancova, 2013). Florida (2002; 2006) proposed that creativity should also be considered at both the societal and community level. His position was that, as a construct, creativity was the output of intentional, sustained, collaborative and social processes with it beginning in childhood and reinforced through social and cultural norms. The result, Florida (2002) argued was that people who were divergent and creative thinkers sought to collaborate with others who shared this mindset. Defined by Florida (2002) as the "creative class," this idea shifted thinking from a traditional sectoral (e.g., film) to mindset lens (e.g., creativity), with the potential of incorporating fields from science and engineering, architecture, design, education, arts, music, and entertainment. The active economy could and should do the same.

The creative economy lens has been influential as it does not view fields such as education, arts, culture, and innovation as isolated. Rather, by adopting an ecosystem view, the creative economy can be used to map the interdependence of these fields as unique drivers of direct and indirect economic outputs. Adopting this lens leads to a fundamental reassessment of the role creativity plays in fields ranging from education to organizational theory (United Nations, 2019; Senge, 2006). One example of where this is operationalized is in the United Kingdom's (UK) Department of Culture, Media, and Sport (DCMS) which defines the creative economy as "those industries which have their origin in individual creativity, skill and talent and which have a potential for wealth and job creation through the generation and exploitation of intellectual property" (1998, p. 3).

As one can well imagine, defining the exact parameters of each field within the sector can be challenging and the boundaries of the creative economy have been highly debated. To help address this challenge, some scholars, and policymakers (e.g., Bakhshi, Freeman, & Higgs, 2012) adopted a sectoral approach, by isolating specific sectors to define and map the creative economy (Refer to Figure 1). Others, meanwhile, such as Florida (2006) and Higgs and Cunningham (2008) adopted a broader societal approach to extend the influence of creativity beyond creative sectors.

Figure 1. The Creative Economy

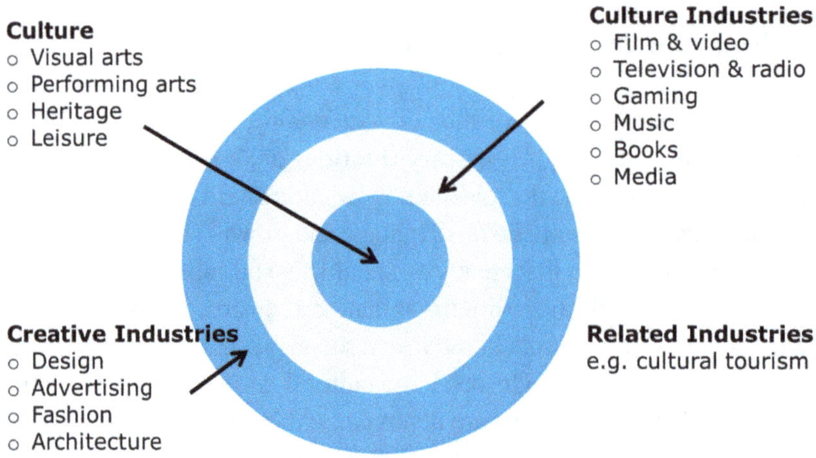

The UK's National Endowment for Science, Technology, and the Arts (NESTA) further refined the DCMS model of creative industries and considered the differences between and within sectors. This model positioned creative industries at the centre of the broader creative economy which was increasingly dependent on the enabling sectors.

Another model proposed by Higgs and Cunningham (2008) adopted both a sectoral and individual level of analysis, exploring creativity as both input and output (not just contained to creative sectors). This model further recognized that a creative mindset thrived in ambiguity and interdisciplinary environments (Higgs, Cunningham, & Bakhshi, 2008). The Conference Board of Canada (2008, p. 3) concurred, stating that "a creative economy extends beyond the culture sector to harness creativity in order to bring about positive social and economic changes across a broad spectrum of industries, sectors and social organizations."

In summary, evidence suggests that the creation of a creative or active economy requires attention to the structure, inter-organizational relationships, and innovation within the ecosystem. Mapping the wide range of interconnections within the active economy is therefore a central contribution of chapter 2 of this book.

REGIONAL ECOSYSTEM CLUSTERS

An extension of the broader ecosystem model is the development of geographically defined regional clusters which include complementary expertise from a range of traditional sectors, who then collaborate to drive competitive advantage at both the regional and organization level (Porter, 2000). The dichotomy, of course, is that while arguing for the recognition of interconnectivity, one must also try to pair this simplifying by limiting the scope to a regional scale.

To do this, the Government of Canada's definition of clusters was adopted as "dense areas of business activity containing a critical mass of large and small companies, post-secondary and other research institutions" (Innovation, Science and Economic Development Canada, 2018). The motivation to collaborate is the recognition that the value of the cluster is more than the sum of its individual components (Porter, 2000). The metaphor here is that a rising tide raises all ships. The relationships between organizations in a regional cluster can then take many forms, including informal cooperation, strategic alliances, and joint ventures. The concept of regional clustering is not new, and in practice, has existed in different forms for centuries (Pitelis, 2012). Examples include London as a financial services hub, the Jingdezhen region of China as a porcelain centre, the Western Cape in South Africa for wine, and Silicon Valley for technology. *Can a jurisdiction become known as the hub for the active economy?*

To help answer that question, Pitelis's (2012) definition of a regional cluster was adopted as "geographical agglomerations of organizations in particular, related, and/or complementary, activities, sharing a common vision, and exhibiting horizontal, vertical intra- and/or inter-sectoral linkages, embedded in a supportive socio-institutional setting, and cooperating and competing in national and international markets" (p. 1361). Similar to the broader ecosystem model, the capacity and adaptability of a regional cluster was rooted in adopting a more holistic and system-level view of competitive advantage, which transcends a traditional single organization or sector (Gerke & Pria, 2018). Theorists further argued that regional clustering provided a variety of advantages including a concentration of knowledge and skills, social embeddedness, economies of scale and diversity and efficiency of information diffusion (Gerke & Pria, 2018; Pitelis, 2012; Porter, 2000; Tallman, Jenkins, Henry & Pinch, 2004; Zeng, 2008). Using the creative economy as an exemplar, Florida (2002) contends that regional creative clusters formed when creative individuals were attracted to locations where there was a critical mass of other creatives. The result was that these clusters then drove information linkages, a concentration of labor and efficiencies that contributed to growth of both creative and non-creative sectors. Cities identified as possessing these characteristics included Montreal, Paris, Shanghai, and Mumbai (United Nations, 2019).

Research undertaken by a number of other authors (e.g., Donahue, Parilla & McDearman, 2018; Gerke & Pria, 2018) further suggested that regional clustering provided the potential for competitive advantage through three mechanisms:

1. The members of the cluster develop and leverage shared resources that may include infrastructure (e.g., office or production collocation, education) or shared supply chains,
2. There is intentionality in developing talent and skill capacity that match the cluster's needs enabling movement and development within the cluster, and
3. Innovation is cultivated through shared learning, rooted in collaboration and experimentation providing accelerated adoption of new knowledge at both an individual and organizational level.

A coordinated and well-functioning cluster can thus provide the foundation for its members to maximize a competitive advantage and create value for both the individual and the whole. For this reason, clustering emerged as a primary strategy to drive regional economic development (Donahue, Parilla & McDearman, 2018; Porter, 2000). The success of this strategy was rooted in an intentional and sustained focus on developing a regional cluster's capabilities from skill development to infrastructure (Zeng, 2008). Some researchers (e.g., Donahue, Parilla & McDearman, 2018; Ketels & Memedovic, 2008) further suggested that the success of regional clusters was driven by maintaining focus on areas of a natural competitive strength, targeting investments, and cultivating structures to facilitate cluster collaboration. The result was increased sustainability and resiliency of the cluster over an extended period of time (Gerke & Pria, 2018).

For example, the emergence of the Nashville Music Cluster (NMC) reflected this intentionality. The music sector in Nashville dates back to the 1860s and the creation of the Grand Ole Opry in the early part of the 20th century. By the 1950s, Nashville had been coined Music City USA (Porter, Bernard, Chaturvedi, Hill, Maddox & Schrimpf, 2012). Today, Nashville is home to over 80 record labels, 100 music publishers, 150 recording studios, dozens of entertainment publications and 17 of the top 25 country music artists in the last quarter century have started their careers there (Raines & Brown 2006). The growth of the NMC is arguably the result of a disciplined strategy developed over decades. To maintain this, the NMC is cultivated and managed by 39 fully integrated collaborative organizations (e.g., Music City Music Council) who align on the shared goal of retaining global leadership. As one example, the Music Council, in coordination with the Mayor's office, Chamber of Commerce and Convention and Visitors Bureau, has collaborated to determine city branding. Moreover, the Country Music Foundation, Visitor's Bureau and city policymakers focused on collaboration with educational institutions to develop talent to grow the music and tourism sectors. For example, country music education is now embedded in primary arts education throughout Nashville. Lastly, the NMC is strategically targeting relocation of music industry operations from both New York and Los Angeles, using its relative cost advantage, combined with NMC capacity (from talent to infrastructure) to ensure a seamless transition (Porter et al., 2012).

In the NMC example, clustering is highly visible and public data is designed to monitor performance relative to goals. Porter (2000) also identified the existence of invisible clusters, which are organic and transcend traditional sectoral boundaries. As a result, data systems. such as industry codes, are dispersed across multiple sectors and sub-groups, rendering them virtually invisible to economists or policymakers (Rosenfeld, 2005). For example, the regional medical devices cluster in Boston, including 400 organizations and 39,000 employees, was practically invisible to policymakers and economists prior to 2000 (Porter, 2000). The reality is that mapping invisible regional clusters is inherently difficult as the data is simply not readily available, hence why they may remain invisible, but it is imperative to note that it does not mean they lack power or influence.

Defining an Active Ecosystem

Similar to the study of the creative ecosystem, an important step in exploring the active ecosystem is defining the scope. The independent disciplines incorporated in the creative ecosystem (e.g., music, visual arts, engineering, and architecture) have been studied extensively by scholars, however, limited research exists that describes the disciplines as part of a broader ecosystem. Similarly, unique fields in the active economy have been studied from a variety of perspectives (Bourdieu, 1978; Foster, O'Reilly, & Dávila, 2016; Sallis, 2009; Silva & Stevens, 2002), yet limited research has explored the interdependencies of them as part of a larger ecosystem (Gerke, & Pria, 2018; Gerke et al., 2015; Shilbury, 2000). In adopting a holistic ecosystem view of these related disciplines, we anticipate larger system-level questions and solutions will emerge.

For this book, the active ecosystem was defined as incorporating all organizations who participate in, or contribute to, improving individual or community wellbeing through the development and delivery of sport and active recreation experiences. In doing so, eleven interdependent sectors were isolated that form the active ecosystem (Gerke & Pria, 2018). This view considers value as being developed by an interdependent value chain composed of sectors, occupations, and individual stakeholders. Viewing the active economy as a complex ecosystem and value chain allows leaders to shape ecosystem-level opportunities to maximize impact on community wellbeing.

In the following section, the active economy is considered from three perspectives:

4. Sector
5. Occupation
6. Stakeholder

THE SECTOR VIEW OF THE ACTIVE ECONOMY

The active economy incorporates eleven interdependent sectors in two macro-level clusters: delivery and enabling clusters (refer to Figure 2).

Delivery Cluster: This includes sectors responsible for the delivery of active experiences, including organized sport, active recreation, active tourism, and sport betting.

Enabling Cluster: This includes sectors where the goods and service outputs support the delivery of the active experiences. Examples are health and wellness, active products and accessories, active technology and equipment, design and infrastructure, media and content and professional services.

Refer to Table 1 for a breakdown of the eleven sectors.

To help understand the size and scope of the active economy the North American Industry Classification System (NAICS) was used.[1] There are three key outputs from this model:

1. Number of establishments
2. Number of paid employees
3. Aggregate number of establishments and paid employees as a proportion of all enterprises and employees

Figure 2. The Eleven Sector Active Economy

NAICS is based on the economic principle that establishments should be grouped together based on their production processes. Economic units that have similar production processes are classified in the same industry, and the lines drawn between industries demarcate, to the extent practical, differences in production processes.

NAICS classifies all economic activities into 20 sectors. For instance, in 2017 there were 20 sectors and 1,057 industries identified. The classification system is done at an establishment-level which is generally a single physical location where business is conducted or where services or industrial operations are performed. An establishment is then classified in an industry when its primary activity meets the definition for that industry. If an establishment is engaged in more than one activity, the industry code is assigned based on the establishment's principal product or group of products or services rendered.

Table 1. The Eleven Sectors of an Active Economy

Delivery Cluster		
Organized Sports	*Organized sports* are activities involving physical exertion and skill as the primary focus of the activity, with elements of competition where rules and patterns of behaviour governing the activity exist formally through social, commercial, or public enterprises. Includes both amateur and professional sports.	Physical sports Motorized sports Coordination sports Animal-supported sports Sport leagues (Amateur and professional) Sport clubs and teams (Amateur and professional) Sport governing bodies Tournaments
Active Recreation	*Active recreation* are activities engaged in for the purpose of relaxation, health and wellbeing or enjoyment with the primary activity requiring physical exertion. They are often spontaneous in nature and participant led, with a low level of organization and limited structure.	Aerobics Jogging/ Running Hiking Recreational hockey Swimming Snowmobiling Horseback riding Tai Chi
Active Life	*Active Life* incorporates embedding unstructured activity as part of daily living. Examples include incorporating active transportation and commuting, gardening, proactive stair use.	Active transportation Cycling Walking Skateboarding Gardening Proactive stair use
Active Tourism	All tourism directly associated with organized sports or active recreation development or delivery.	Tourism authorities Ecotourism Hosting major sporting or active recreation events Wellness tourism Tour companies Accommodation providers Transportation services
Sport Betting	Predicting organized sports results and placing a wager on the outcome.	Lottery and gaming authorities Casinos Fantasy sports Horse racing
Enabling Sectors		
Products & Accessories	Development, manufacturing and sales of products and accessories associated with organized sport or active recreation development or delivery.	Licensed apparel manufacturers Footwear manufacturers Sport and active recreation apparel retailers
Active Technology & Accessories	Development, manufacturing, and sales of technology and accessories associated with organized sport or active recreation development or delivery.	Wearables Bike manufacturers Golf manufacturers Sport and active recreation retailers
Design & Infrastructure	All commercial, social, and public infrastructure required for delivering active transportation, organized sports, and active recreation experiences. Scope includes research, design, planning, construction, maintenance, repair, operation, and the supervision of infrastructure and open spaces.	Includes community-level planning and design enabling active transportation including walking and cycling. Indoor examples include arenas and gymnasiums. Outdoor examples include stadiums, parks, playing fields, play-structures, additional civic infrastructure that supports the delivery of active transportation (e.g., Cycle tracks, sidewalks).
Health & Wellness	Health and wellness products and services supporting the delivery or engagement in organized sport or active recreation.	Traditional & complementary medicine Preventive & personalized medicine and public health Healthy eating, nutrition, and weight loss Fitness and mind-body Workplace wellness Wellness real estate Policymakers associated with health and wellness
Media & Content	Media and content directly associated with organized sport or active recreation development or delivery.	Broadcast rights holders Media enterprises and individuals who specialize in sport or active recreation. Sport and active recreation content developers Sponsors of sport and active recreation
Professional Services	Professional services directly associated with sport or active recreation development or delivery.	Ticketing services Marketing agencies Sport advisory services Sport law

In all, 95 of the 1057 industry codes of NAICS were identified that were fully or partially within the active economy. Each of these were then assigned an intensity factor (Bakhshi, Freeman, & Higgs, 2012) reflecting the proportion of a specific industry linked to the active economy. For example, if an industry had an intensity factor of 100 per cent (e.g., golf courses), all enterprises and employees from it were assigned to the active economy. In contrast, if an industry had an intensity code of 1 per cent (e.g., law offices), only 1 per cent of enterprises and employees from that industry were allocated to the active economy. Table 2 provides a list of the intensity allocations.

Table 2. Intensity Allocation

Intensity	Definition	Sample NAICS
100 per cent	Estimated that 100 per cent of the activity of an enterprise in this category is within the scope of one or more of the eleven sectors of the active economy.	711217 - Sports teams and clubs performing before a paying audience. 711319 - Sports stadiums and other presenters with facilities 712190 - Nature parks and other similar institutions in 451111 - Golf equipment and supplies specialty stores
30 per cent	Estimated that 30 per cent of the activity of an enterprise in this category is within the scope of one or more of the eleven sectors of the active economy.	611110 - Elementary and secondary schools 446191 - Food (health) supplement stores 515110 - Radio broadcasting 515120 - Television broadcasting
10 per cent	Estimated that 10 per cent of the activity of an enterprise in this category is within the scope of one or more of the eleven sectors of the active economy.	414110 - Clothing and Clothing Accessories Wholesaler-Distributors 448210 - Shoe stores 621510 Medical and diagnostic laboratories 621390 Offices of all other health practitioners
1 per cent	Sector provides enabling support services to one or more of the eleven sectors of the active economy. The minimum default is 1 per cent of the activity is allocated to the active economy.	541310 - Architectural services 541320 - Landscape architectural services 541330 - Engineering services

AN OCCUPATION VIEW OF THE ACTIVE ECONOMY

Administrators, enablers, and policymakers are occupations within the active economy. An occupation is a set of jobs that are sufficiently similar in work performed. A job, meanwhile, corresponds to all tasks carried out by a particular worker to complete their duties. An active economy occupation was defined as all paid employment that directly contributes to the delivery of one of the eleven active economy sectors. Following the model of the creative economy, active economy occupations may sit within active economy enterprises (e.g., General Manager of a recreation centre), or outside of typical active economy enterprises (e.g., Wellness Manager for an oil and gas company).

To help with this assessment, the National Occupational Classification (NOC) was used which is a systematic classification of all occupations in Canada. The basic principle of classification here is the kind of work performed is determined by the tasks, duties, and responsibilities of the occupation. Factors such as the materials processed or used, the industrial processes and the equipment used, the degree of responsibility and complexity of work, as well as the products made and services provided, have been considered as indicators of work.

An occupation is then defined as a collection of jobs, sufficiently similar in work performed to be grouped under a common label. A job, in turn, encompasses all the tasks carried out by a particular worker to complete their duties. Using these definitions, the 2016 NOC resulted in approximately 35,000 titles classified into 500-unit groups.

The research team audited all 500-unit groups and 35,000 job titles to identify active economy occupations. In total, 72 of the 500-unit groups (14.2 per cent) include active economy occupations. This translated into thousands of job titles. Refer to Table 3 for a sample of the 72 occupation codes with at least one job title linked to the active economy. In some codes (e.g., athletes) 100 per cent were included in the active economy. In contrast, others (e.g., Retail and wholesale trade managers) had only a fraction of the job titles linked to the active economy.

A challenge of the NOC is that it offers only limited ability to disaggregate the occupation data at the community-level. For privacy reasons, Statistics Canada does not provide NOC data below 1500 counts. As a result, it was impossible to consistently apply NOC data in our study as many of the active economy occupations are below this threshold.

A STAKEHOLDER VIEW OF THE ACTIVE ECONOMY

An important dimension of mapping an active ecosystem is articulating the different roles of each stakeholder. This is essential because communities are composed of diverse stakeholders often with competing and contradictory demands (Harrison & Freeman, 1999). In this book, we define an active ecosystem stakeholder as any individual or organization that has an interest in, or is impacted by, the active ecosystem. This includes all forms of engagement in the active ecosystem which can either be in a professional or a volunteer capacity. Another way of viewing engagement is through specific roles such as participant, administrator, enabler, policymaker, and supporter. Where this becomes complicated is when people hold multiple roles within the same realm. Refer to Table 4 for definitions and examples of each stakeholder in the active ecosystem. These will be explored further in chapter 3.

Table 3. Sample Active Economy by National Occupation Code

Code	Intensity	NOC Category	Sample Active Economy Job title
3142	100 per cent	Physiotherapists	Clinical Physiotherapist, Physical Therapist, Physical Therapy Specialist
5251	100 per cent	Athletes	Athlete, Bowler, Canoeist, Chuckwagon Driver, Diver – Olympic Sport, Gamer – Video Games, Jockey, Professional Sportsman/woman, Table Tennis Player
3144	60 per cent	Other professional occupations in therapy and assessment	Athletic Therapist, Dance Therapist, Exercise Therapist, Kinesiologist, Therapeutic Recreationist
3125	20 per cent	Other professional occupations in health diagnosing and treating	Chiropodist, Doctor of Podiatric Medicine (D.P.M), Podiatrist
714	14 per cent	Facility operation and maintenance managers	Athletic Facility Manager, Fitness Facility Manager, Recreation Facility Manager, Sports Facility Manager, Stadium Manager, Tennis Court Manager
2153	14 per cent	Urban and land use planners	Community Recreation Planner, Municipal Park Planner, Park Planner, Recreation Planner
7445	14 per cent	Other repairers and servicers	Archery Bow Finisher, Archery Bow Repairer, Bicycle Mechanic, Billiard Cue Weigher, Golf Club Head Adjuster, Sporting Goods Repairer
6531	14 per cent	Tour and travel guides	Bicycle Tour Guide, Ski Resort Host/Hostess, Walking Tour Guide
5231	9 per cent	Announcers and other broadcasters	Sports Announcer, Sports Commentator, Sportscaster, Social Media Personality
4165	5 per cent	Health policy researchers, consultants, and program officers	Health Educator, Wellness Program Coordinator

CONCLUSION

In this introductory chapter a brief overview of a new lens on sport and recreation, the active economy has been presented. The active economy is a complex and interdependent ecosystem of enterprises and individuals. Thus, value is generated not only by individual components but also the way in which these interact to create incremental value. To understand the systematic value of the active economy, it must be disaggregated into discrete, but interdependent building blocks. Together, these building blocks form the active economy value chain. Each chapter in this book will then explore these various components of the active economy value chain.

Table 4. Active Economy Stakeholders

Role	Definition	Examples
Participant	One that partakes in an organized sports or active recreation experience.	Participating in a dance class, cycling to work, playing on a recreational soccer team, hiking, and high-performance athletes.
Administrator	One whose role supports the development and/or delivery of organized sports or active recreation experiences. Administrators may be volunteers or professionals.	League coordinator, recreation centre facility manager, recreation program coordinator, promotion or sales coordinator for a local team, role on a sport governing body.
Enabler	One whose role enables others to participate in organized sport or active recreation experiences. Enablers may be volunteers or professionals.	Coach, referee, personal trainer, customer service, physiotherapist, physical education teacher, eco-tourism guide, designer of sport equipment, administrative assistant, lifeguard, urban planner.
Policymaker	One who is a member of a government department, legislature, or other enterprise who is responsible for developing and implementing active economy policy, including in the organized sport, active recreation, and health & wellness sectors.	Minister responsible for sport, physical activity and recreation, Municipal Councillor Director of Parks & Recreation.
Supporter	One who supports or motivates others to participate in organized sport or active recreation experiences.	A parent who registers their child in a program, a spectator who attends a live sporting event, a fan who watches an organized sporting event on television, playing in a fantasy sports league.

REFERENCES

Bakhshi, H., Freeman, A., & Higgs, P. (2012). *A dynamic mapping of the UK's creative industries*. Nesta. https://eprints.qut.edu.au/57251/1/57251.pdf

Bourdieu, P. (1978). *Sport and social class*. International Social Science Council.

Conference Board of Canada. (2008). *Valuing culture: Measuring and understanding Canada's creative economy*. https://www.creativecity.ca/database/files/library/valuingculture.pdf

Department of Digital. Culture, Media & Sport. (1998). *Creative Industries Mapping Documents 1998*. Retrieved from Government of UK website: https://www.gov.uk/government/publications/creative-industries-mapping-documents-1998

Donahue, R., Parilla, J., & McDearman, B. (2018). *Rethinking Clusters Initiatives*. Brookings Institute.

Eisingerich, A., Bell, S., & Tracey, P. (2010). How can clusters sustain performance? The role of network strength, network openness and environmental uncertainty. *Research Policy, 39*(2), 239–253. doi:10.1016/j.respol.2009.12.007

Florida, R. (2002). *The Rise of the Creative Class: And How It's Transforming Work, Leisure, Community, and Everyday Life*. Perseus Books.

Florida, R. (2006). The flight of the creative class: The new global competition for talent. *Liberal Education, 92*(3), 22–29.

Foster, G., O'Reilly, N., & Dávila, A. (2016). *Sports Business Management: Decision Making Around the Globe*. Routledge. doi:10.4324/9781315687827

Gerke, A., Desbordes, M., & Dickson, G. (2015). Towards a sport cluster model: The ocean racing cluster in Brittany. *European Sport Management Quarterly, 15*(3), 343–363. doi:10.1080/16184742.2015.1019535

Gerke, A., & Pria, Y. (2018). Cluster Concept: Lessons for the Sport Sector? Toward a Two-Step Model of Sport Cluster Development Based on Socioeconomic Proximity. *Journal of Sport Management, 32*(3), 211–226. doi:10.1123/jsm.2016-0338

Harrison, J. S., & Freeman, R. E. (1999). Stakeholders, social responsibility, and performance: Empirical evidence and theoretical perspectives. *Academy of Management Journal, 42*(5), 479–485.

Higgs, P., & Cunningham, S. (2008). Creative Industries Mapping: Where have we come from and where are we going? *Creative Industries Journal, 1*(1), 7–30. doi:10.1386/cij.1.1.7_1

Higgs, P., Cunningham, S., & Bakhshi, H. (2008). *Beyond the creative industries: Mapping the creative economy in the United Kingdom*. Retrieved from https://eprints.qut.edu.au/00012166/01/beyond_creative_industries_report_NESTA.pdf

Howkins, J. (2002). The creative economy: How people make money from ideas. Penguin UK.; Urbancova, H. (2013). Competitive advantage achievement through innovation and knowledge. *Journal of Competitiveness, 5*(1).

Innovation, Science and Economic Development Canada. (2018). *Superclusters in Canada*. Retrieved from Government of Canada website: https://www.ic.gc.ca/eic/site/093.nsf/eng/00017.html#:~:text=Clusters%20are%20dense%20area%20of,secondary%20and%20other%20research%20institutions

Ketels, C. H., & Memedovic, O. (2008). From clusters to cluster-based economic development. *International Journal of Technological Learning, Innovation and Development, 1*(3), 375–392.

Moore, J. F. (1993). Predators and prey: A new ecology of competition. *Harvard Business Review*, *71*(3), 75–86. PMID:10126156

Pitelis, C. (2012). Clusters, entrepreneurial ecosystem co-creation, and appropriability: A conceptual framework. *Industrial and Corporate Change*, *21*(6), 1359–1388. doi:10.1093/icc/dts008

Porter, M., Bernard, M., Chaturvedi, R. S., Hill, A., Maddox, C., & Schrimpf, M. (2012). *Tennessee Music Cluster. Microeconomics of Competitiveness*. Harvard Business School.

Porter, M. E. (1998). Clusters and the new economics of competition. *Harvard Business Review*, *76*(6), 77–90. PMID:10187248

Porter, M. E. (2000). Location, competition, and economic development: Local clusters in a global economy. *Economic Development Quarterly*, *14*(1), 15–34. doi:10.1177/089124240001400105

Raines, P., & Brown, L. (2006). *The economic impact of the music industry in the Nashville-Davidson-Murfreesboro MSA*. College of Business Administration, Belmont University and Nashville Area Chamber of Commerce.

Rosenfeld, S. (2005). Industry clusters: Business choice, policy outcome, or branding strategy. *Journal of New Business Ideas and Trends*, *3*(2), 4–13.

Rothschild, M. (1990). *Bionomics: Economy as Ecosystem*. Henry Holt and Company.

Sallis, J. F. (2009). Measuring physical activity environments: A brief history. *American Journal of Preventive Medicine*, *36*(4), S86–S92. doi:10.1016/j.amepre.2009.01.002 PMID:19285214

Senge, P. (2006). *The Fifth Discipline: The Art and Practice of the Learning Organization* (Rev. ed.). Currency Doubleday.

Shilbury, D. (2000). Considering future sport delivery systems. *Sport Management Review*, *3*(2), 199–221. doi:10.1016/S1441-3523(00)70086-6

Silva, J. M., & Stevens, D. E. (2002). *Psychological Foundations of Sport*. Allyn & Bacon.

Tallman, S., Jenkins, M., Henry, N., & Pinch, S. (2004). Knowledge, clusters, and competitive advantage. *Academy of Management Review*, *29*(2), 258–271. doi:10.5465/amr.2004.12736089

United Nations. (2019). *United Nations Development Index*. Retrieved from http://hdr.undp.org/en/content/human-development-index-hdi

Urbancova, H. (2013). Competitive advantage achievement through innovation and knowledge. *Journal of Competitiveness*, *5*(1), 82–96. doi:10.7441/joc.2013.01.06

Zeng, D. (Ed.). (2008). *Knowledge, technology, and cluster-based growth in Africa*. The World Bank. doi:10.1596/978-0-8213-7306-4

ENDNOTE

1 For additional information on the North American Industry Classification System refer to: https://www.statcan.gc.ca/eng/subjects/standard/naics/2017/v3/index

Chapter 2
Mapping the Active Economy to Community Value

David J. Finch
Mount Royal University, Canada

David Legg
Mount Royal University, Canada

Norm O'Reilly
University of Guelph, Canada

Jason Ribeiro
Calgary Economic Development, Canada

Trevor Tombe
University of Calgary, Canada

ABSTRACT

This chapter will deconstruct the value chain located within the active economy. This value chain includes community input resources (including human, economic, social/structural, built, and natural resources) which generate activities and outputs. The value of the active economy is defined by its impact on a community's economic, human, social, and environmental wellbeing. Herein, the literature associated with the impact of the active economy on the dimensions of community wellbeing is examined.

DOI: 10.4018/978-1-7998-7939-8.ch002

DEFINING COMMUNITY WELLBEING

The impact of an active economy can only be measured by the context in which it positively and negatively contributes to community wellbeing. However, the impact of an active economy is far more complicated than mapping the impact of it on traditional economic indicators. This is because in adopting a traditional valuation model, linked exclusively to economic output indicators such as employment or gross domestic product (GDP), the indirect impacts are excluded. Assessing both the tangible and intangible impact of the active economy is therefore challenging and perhaps impossible to do in isolation. Rather, the impact of an active economy is related to the contribution it makes towards the measurable priorities of a community (Kaplan & Norton, 2005). In other words, the active economy is a means to an end, not an end unto itself. Thus, the first step in deconstructing the impact of the active economy is to understand the measurable goals of the community in which it is embedded.

Herein, we adopt individual and community level "wellbeing" as the ultimate goal of a community (King, Huseynli, & MacGibbon, 2018; OECD, 2021). For decades, governments, academics and social enterprises have developed models to measure "wellbeing" and "quality of life". Wellbeing is recognized as a multi-dimensional construct, framed by value judgements (OECD, 2021) with Table 1 providing a variety of models used to measure individual and/or collective wellbeing.

Effective wellbeing indicators serve as both a performance management and communication tool, as they can then align communities on shared purpose and language. For his book, the Organisation for Economic Cooperation and Development's (OECD) *Better Life Index* and the New Zealand Government's *Living Standards Framework* (King, Huseynli, & MacGibbon, 2018) have been used as guides. They both propose a four-dimensional set of wellbeing indicators based on a balanced-scorecard framework that recognize impact as multi-dimensionality, incorporating both tangible and intangible components (Kaplan & Norton, 2005). Moreover, these multi-dimensional instruments were chosen instead of a single measure (e.g., Economist's Global Livability Ranking) because a balanced scorecard acts as a diagnostic tool to transparently evaluate the strengths and weaknesses of an active economy, while minimizing value judgments (e.g., assigning the relative weighting of certain values compared to others). In addition, a balanced scorecard provides the ability to map the systematic factors which contribute to the four dimensions of the community wellbeing.

Table 1. Measuring Community Wellbeing

Source	Factors Measured
Triple Bottom Policy	Economic; Environment; Social
United Nation's Human Development Index	Life Expectancy At Birth Expected Years of Schooling Mean Years Of Schooling Gross National Income Per Capita
New Zealand Living Standard Framework	Social Capital; Human Capital; Natural Capital; Physical/ Financial Capital
Organization for Economic Cooperation and Development Better Life Index	Housing, Income, Jobs, Community, Education, Environment, Civic Engagement, Health, Life Satisfaction, Safety, Work-Life Balance
World Happiness Report	Business & Economic; Citizen Engagement; Communications & Technology; Diversity; Education & Families; Emotions; Environment & Energy; Food & Shelter; Government and Politics; Law & Order; Health; Religion & Ethics; Transportation; Work
UN Human Development Index	Life-expectancy, Education; Standard of Living
Economist Global Liveability Index	Stability; Healthcare, Culture; Environment; Education; Infrastructure
University of Waterloo's Canadian Index of Wellbeing	Community Vitality, Democratic Engagement, Education, Environment, Healthy Populations, Leisure & Culture; Living Standards, Time Use
Government of Canada's Community Wellbeing	Education, Labour Force Activity, Income, Housing

Thus, the community wellbeing indicators in Figure 2.0 incorporates four interdependent perspectives on community impact and value: economic, social, human and environmental. *Economic impact* includes the total level of activity in the defined area and is assessed according to indicators such as economic outputs and employment levels. *Social impact is* a multi-dimensional construct incorporating features of organization that contribute to society by facilitating coordinated actions (1991). Social impact, first and foremost, accrues at a community-level with examples include indicators of trust, safety, social connections, civic engagement and tolerance (Onyx & Bullen, 2000). The existence of these at a community-level, is then what creates impact for individual members. *Human impact* includes an individual's skills, knowledge, mental and physical health (King, Huseynli, & MacGibbon, 2018). Indicators associated with this may include health and wellness, life expectancy, education and competencies. *Natural environment impact* includes indicators associated with the health and sustainability of a community's natural environment and resources. Refer to Table 2, for a review of each perspective, indicators and sources.

Figure 1. Community Wellbeing Indicators

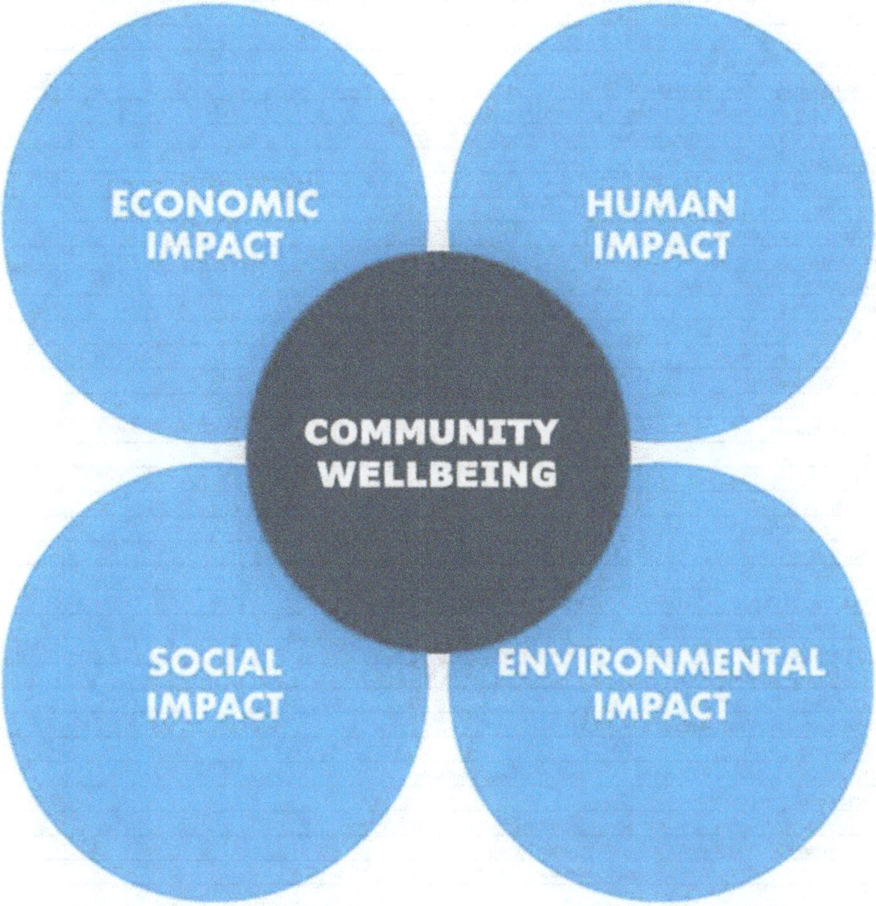

THE ACTIVE ECONOMY VALUE CHAIN

Researchers have long argued that value is generated not by individual components, but rather the systematic interaction of these components (Kaplan & Norton, 2005). As a result, the impact of the active economy is rooted in a complex interdependent value chain. Thus, effective active economy mapping cannot focus solely on individual relationships between components, but rather on identifying the high leverage dimensions that have maximum impact on the overall system (Senge, 2006).

Table 2. Sample Community Wellbeing Indicators

Indicators
Economic Indicators
Living Standards Indicators
1. Percentage of labor force employed
2. After tax median income of economic families
3. Percentage of population that is moderately or severely food insecure
4. Percentage of labor force working less than 30 hours per week, not by choice
5. Percentage of labor force with long-term unemployment
6. After tax median income of economic families
7. Percentage of persons in low income
8. Perceived of standard of living
9. Perceived ability to manage daily stress
10. Perception of economic outlook
Economic Indicators
11. Gross domestic product
12. New businesses formed
13. Building Permits
14. Housing Starts
Human Indicators
Health Indicators
15. Life expectancy
16. Perception of physical health
17. Perception of mental health
18. Perceived sense of purpose
19. Perceived self-efficacy
20. Percentage of Canadians who report 7 to 9 hours of good quality essential sleep
21. Population living near community activity centre
22. Physically active 150 minutes moderate to vigorous weekly
23. Proportion of population obese
24. Proportion of population overweight
25. Proportion of population dealing with mood disorder
26. Suicide rate
27. Percentage of population with an absence of health or activity limitations
Personal Development Indicators
28. Percentage of adults aged 25 or older who participate in education-related activities
29. Percentage of 20 to 24-year olds in population completing high school
30. Percentage of 25 to 64-year olds in population with a postsecondary credentials
31. Level-3 literacy
Social Indicators
Social Vitality
32. Average daily amount of time spent with friends (minutes per day).
33. Percentage of time spent on the previous day in social leisure activities
34. Percentage of time spent on the previous day in arts and culture activities
35. Average number of nights away on vacation trips in the past year to destinations 80 km from home
36. Perception of social isolation
37. Perception [jurisdiction] is a great place for seniors to live
38. Perception [jurisdiction] is a great place to raise children
39. Proportion proud to live in [jurisdiction]
40. Perception of overall quality of life
41. Perception [jurisdiction] is a great place to make a life
42. Perception [jurisdiction] is a great place to make a living
43. Perception [jurisdiction] is moving in the right direction to ensure a high quality of life for future generations
44. The [jurisdiction] practices open and accessible government
Community Engagement
45. Average number of hours in the past year volunteering for culture or recreation organizations
46. Proportion making charitable donations
47. Community association membership

continued on following page

Table 2. Continued

Inclusion
48. Perceived benefits of inclusivity
49. Perceived trust in governments
50. Confidence citizens have opportunity for meaningful input municipal into decision-making.
51. Representative public boards a. Gender diversity b. Ethnic diversity
Safety
52. Proportion feeling safe in neighborhood
53. Proportion having a sense of community belonging
54. Personal crime
55. Property crime
Natural Environmental Indicators
56. Primary access to transit network (within 400M)
57. Frequency of active transportation use
58. Perception of sustainability
59. Proximity to parks and open spaces
60. Reported air quality
61. Litres per capita water consumption
62. Ecological footprint
63. Carbon footprint
64. Per capita waste to landfill
65. Residential energy use per household (terajoules per 1,000 private dwelling)
66. Percentage urban forestry canopy

In the context of the active economy value chain, impact is viewed as a complex system incorporating both tangible and intangible components. Tangible components include objective indicators such as employment, health and wellness (Kaplan & Norton, 2005). In contrast, intangible components involve subjective enabling attributes, including skills, knowledge, relationships and reputation (Bontis & Fitz-Enz, 2002). The challenge with intangible components is that they are rarely of value in isolation; rather, they represent potential value. To unlock this potential, intangibles must be combined with other components in order to be realized (Kaplan & Norton, 2005). Thus, to fully understand the value of the active economy, one must disaggregate and map the active economy to the systematic activity level. As a result, understanding how the active economy impacts a community requires the identification of explanatory relationships among the variables. The impact of one specific component in the value chain is highly influenced by its relationship with others. For example, those engaged in organized sport appear to have higher levels of self-esteem (Fox & Lindwall, 2014). Although this is positive, an individual's self-esteem is of no direct tangible or intangible impact on community wellbeing. Rather, the tangible impact is how it contributes to higher levels of confidence and professional success (e.g., employment, compensation, etc.). Finally, guided by Senge (2006), an ecosystem is interactive and multi-directional, thus a feedback loop is essential to the value chain; Figure 2 provides a conceptual diagram of this.

Figure 2. The Active Economy Value Chain

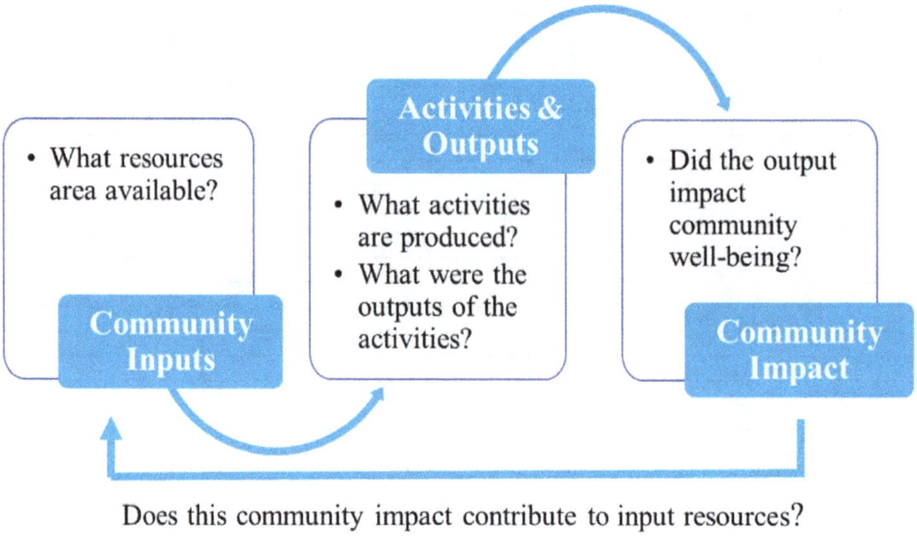

Table 3. Example of Community Input Audit

Resource Categories	Examples
Human Resources	• Socio-demographic factors • Education • Health
Economic Resources	• Economic output • Private sector investments • Public sector investments • Philanthropic investments
Social & Structural Resources	• Sense of belonging. • Volunteering • Intra and inter structural capital
Natural Resources	• Land resources • Water resources • Climate resources
Built Resources	• Indoor facilities • Outdoor facilities • Active transportation facilities

Table 4. Active Economy Activities and Outputs Audit

Activities	Example Metrics
Organized sports	• Total number of enterprises • Total number of employees • Total number of activities • Number of participants • Total hours of engagement • Total number of volunteers • Total hours volunteering
Active recreation	• Total number of enterprises • Total number of activities • Total number of employees • Number of participants • Total hours of engagement • Total number of volunteers • Total hours volunteering
Fan engagement	• Fan attendance • Ticket sales • Broadcast ratings • Social media engagement
Major events	• Total number of major active economy events hosted in jurisdiction. • Total economic impact
Active Products & Accessories	• Total number of enterprises • Total number of employees • Total economic impact
Active Technology & Equipment	• Total number of enterprises • Total number of employees • Total economic impact
Active Design & Infrastructure	• Total number of enterprises • Total number of employees • Total economic impact
Active Media & Content	• Total number of enterprises • Total number of employees • Total economic impact
Active Tourism	• Total number of enterprises • Total number of employees • Total economic impact
Health & Wellness	• Total number of enterprises • Total number of employees • Total economic impact
Professional Services	• Total number of enterprises • Total number of employees • Total economic impact
Sport Betting	• Total number of enterprises • Total number of employees • Total economic impact

ACTIVE ECONOMY VALUE CHAIN: INPUTS

Community input resources are the essential enablers of the active economy. The development of enterprises in the ecosystem and their activities are dependent upon a combination of the five community input resources listed in Table 3

ACTIVE ECONOMY VALUE CHAIN: OUTPUTS

Activities incorporate the enterprises and production processes in a combination of two or more community input resources. For example, it may take human (e.g., skills and experience), economic (e.g., funding) and built resources (e.g., skateboard park) to develop and operate a program that offers free skateboard lessons for youth at risk.

To better understand the value chain, the first step is to audit active economy enterprises. This could use the sector model introduced in the first chapter to analyze the NAICS associated with each of the eleven sectors. The second level of analysis would be to audit the active economy at a structured activity-level. This considers the activities and outputs of the respective organizations. Refer to Table 4 for a sample of activity and output metrics at a sector level.

ACTIVE ECONOMY VALUE CHAIN: IMPACTS

With a complete audit of inputs and outputs, it appears that the active economy value chain impacts one or more of the four dimensions of community wellbeing.

Economic Impact

The economic impact of the active economy incorporates direct employment, reduction of health costs, increased productivity, and contribution to talent acquisition. Examples for this globally would include an Ontario 2016 study that identified a 1.9 per cent reduction in total health care expenditure over the 10-year period. This was based on improved health behaviours such as minimum levels of physical activity (Manuel, 2016). Similarly, a study for the British Columbia Ministry of Health Planning estimated annual cost savings of $49.4 million if they could reduce physical inactivity by 10 per cent (Colman & Walker, 2004). Inactivity imposed economic costs of €80.4 billion per year to the EU-28 through coronary heart disease, type 2 diabetes, colorectal and breast cancer and through the indirect costs of inactivity-related mood and anxiety disorders (International Sport and Culture Association, & Centre for Economics and Business Research, 2015). A Singapore study estimated that the cost of inactivity is $2130 (CDN) annually, per person, including increased healthcare costs and economic impact (Sport Singapore, 2019). The Australian Sport Commission, meanwhile, estimated that for every $1 of investment in physical activity, it translates into $3 of savings in healthcare expenditures (Manatu Hauora Ministry of Health, 2019).

A second area of economic impact was increased productivity. Multiple studies have shown that workplace health and wellness programs demonstrate a minimum of three to one return on investment through lower absentee rates and improved productivity and fewer health-related work limitations (Aldana & Pronk, 2001). One study conducted for the Sport and Recreation Victoria (Australia) estimates that physical activity increases individual productivity between $200 to $1,250 per person (Marsden Jacob Associates, 2018). The Bureau of Transport and Regional Economics, meanwhile, estimated that congestion in Australia's eight capital cities cost nearly US $2.8 billion in lost productivity (Bureau of Transport and Regional Economics, 2007). Another study estimated traffic congestion costs the UK economy approximately £9.5 billion annually (INRIX, 2020).

The active economy also assists with talent acquisition and retention. A jurisdiction's competitive advantage has typically been defined by its proximity to scarce natural resources ranging from lumber to navigable waterways. Over the past four decades, however, the competitive advantage of many cities, driven by economic, social, and cultural factors such as advanced technology and globalization, has transitioned toward their ability to attract and mobilize human capital. Today, a jurisdiction's capacity to develop, acquire and retain high-valued talent thus underpins much of its economic and social wellbeing.[1]

This is now typically seen through place building and the influence of amenities. The principle of place-building is an integral part of the economic development strategy of many cities which is highly contextual and driven by the motivations and opportunities of an individual and their family (Florida, 2002). The factors that seem to influence decision-making amongst highly sought-after talent include proximity to family and friends, economic opportunities and growth, potential income, diversity of population and amenities. From an active economy perspective, it is really the amenities that are controllable.

Economic geographers broadly define amenities to include access to arts, culture, sports, and recreation. More specifically, research focusing on younger workers in the knowledge economy note that they are attracted to communities that are energetic and vibrant, defined by the importance of visual and audio cues such as outdoor dining, active outdoor recreation, a thriving music scene, and an active nightlife. Finally, leisure and recreation opportunities are the leading factors influencing young, single, highly qualified people to live downtown.

The active economy also has an economic impact through active design and transportation. The National Health Service meta-analysis, for instance, identified that increases in walkability and cycling contributed on average a 13 to 1 return on investment (Davis, 2010). A British study also found urban design that an increase in walking and cycling can increase retail sales up to 30 per cent (Lawlor, 2014). A US study found that retail areas with walk scores over 80 had a 29 to 49 per cent increase in property value (Pivo & Fisher, 2011). Similarly, residential property value increased by an estimated 12 per cent in neighborhoods with high walkability scores (Cortright, 2009). A final US study found that there was a property value premium in communities with walkable schools (Kuhlman, 2010). A UK study for the Department of Transport estimated condensed walkable communities reduced municipal infrastructure costs by 33 per cent (Raje & Saffrey, 2016). Specific to cycling, a study conducted for the City of Portland estimated investments in bike facilities (costing from $138 to $605 million) would result in health care cost savings of up to $594 million, fuel savings of up to $218 million over a 25-year period (Gotschi, 2011). Finally, a study in the *Journal of Preventative Medicine* found that capital investment on sidewalk construction and maintenance provides an 18 to 1 return on indicators related to healthcare and air quality (Guo & Gandavarapu, 2009).

A challenge with all of these impacts is that they are typically not coordinated nor aligned to ensure maximum value. Examples include recognition that economic impacts of reduced healthcare costs accrue primarily to the provincial/state government, whereas the investments required to deliver it, are municipal/civic. The economic impact of increased productivity and talent acquisition and retention accrues directly to a specific enterprise yet if coordinated the potential impacts could be exponential. A third example is that the economic impact of active design and transportation is structural and measured in decades, not in election cycles which is sometimes when decisions for these types of investments are made. Finally, active economy expenditures are immediate but fragmented across eleven sectors and their associated supply chains whereas the impacts are more distal, best understood long term and harder to measure for direct impact. Moreover, because they are not tracked as a single industry, the data sources are fragmented and largely unreliable.

Human Impact

The second significant impact from the active economy is human. Research has demonstrated that the active economy directly impacts human impact through a measurable impact on physical and mental health and wellbeing. This includes a reduction of obesity and physical and mental health effects. Studies also confirm that the active economy contributes directly to the measurable development of critical competencies essential for a modern adaptive and resilient labor force (Burnett, 2016).

Specific to physical health Alberta Health reported that obesity is related to 22 major health conditions, including Type 2 diabetes, cardiovascular diseases and 14 types of cancer. Furthermore, it is estimated that 1 in 10 premature deaths among Canadian adults aged 20 to 64 are related to obesity and sedentary lifestyle (Obesity Canada, 2020). A 2016 Statistics Canada report also estimated a sedentary lifestyle reduces life expectancy by 3.8 years (Public Health Agency of Canada, 2016). Consistent with this finding, a 2012 study published in the Lancet, estimated that physical inactivity is responsible for nine per cent of the world's mortality (Lee et al., 2012).

Evidence also illustrates that physical activity can contribute positively to mental health and have a positive effect on anxiety, depression, mood and emotion, self-esteem and psychological dysfunction (Mutrie, 2000). Research by Statistics Canada (2019) identifies that 71 per cent of participants in sports do so for fun and relaxation, compared to 69 per cent for physical fitness. However, there is a poor understanding of the mechanisms that underlie the relationship between physical activity and psychological wellbeing (Scully et al., 1998).

Nevertheless, some research has suggested links including a joint study by the Chief Medical Officers of the UK Home Countries. This suggested that physical activity can reduce the risk of depression and dementia by 20-30 per cent. It also showed that physical activity can enhance psychological wellbeing, by improving self-perception and self-esteem, mood, and sleep quality, and by reducing levels of anxiety and fatigue (Department of Health, Physical Activity, Health Improvement and Protection, 2011). Research has also suggested that membership with a sports club has an equivalent effect on life satisfaction and happiness as moving up approximately one and a half household income categories (approximately $6,100 dollars) (Delaney & Keaney, 2005).

There are of course a multitude of other links to mental health. A Norwegian study, for instance found that body area satisfaction, appearance evaluation and athletic competence moderated a sense of global self-worth among teens, with females having the greatest impact (Haugen, Säfvenbom & Ommundsen, 2011). Other studies addressed impact on ADHD (National Parks and Recreation Association, n.d.), reduced anxiety (Lawlor & Hopker, 2001) and self-esteem (Fox, 2000). Other studies have focused on specific populations, including seniors (Chodzko-Zajko, 1998) and those with physical disabilities (Taub & Greer, 2000). Finally, in a study from Australia, results suggested that up to seven per cent of depression cases and nine per cent of high blood pressure cases could be prevented if all city residents were to visit green spaces at least once a week for an average duration of 30 minutes or more (Shanahan et al., 2016).

One final area of human impact is through personal development. Connections here would include sport increasing enabling skills, including communication, collaboration, and time management (Burnett, 2016). Another example is the development of female leaders with 94 per cent of Canadian women in the C-suite having played sports, 52 per cent at the university level. 74 per cent of executive women in Canada have also reported feeling that sport accelerated their careers. Finally, Canadian executive women are more likely to hire other women who also played (Ernst & Young, & espnW, 2015).

Studies have also demonstrated a relationship between physical activity and cognition and academic performance (Ahn & Fedeawa, 2011). The hypothesized mechanisms underpinning this relationship vary and include a relationship between motor and mental skills and increased self-esteem, increased levels of norepinephrine and endorphins, resulting in a reduction of stress and an improvement of mood (Singh et al., 2012).

In summary, evidence suggests that the active economy has direct and measurable impacts on human impact through enhanced physical and mental health and wellness. What was more difficult to ascertain was the role that the active economy has in developing the critical competencies essential for a modern, adaptive and resilient labor force. Regardless, the evidence shared here provides significant support to the value and importance of the active economy and the human experience. To maximize the impacts, however, increased intentionality and focus on developing these competencies is needed.

Social Impact

The challenge of community cohesion, social inclusion and active citizenship is faced by many societies. When exploring social impact and the active economy, three key themes emerged: social cohesion, volunteering and safety.

Specific examples of the links between the active economy and social cohesion include a Los Angeles based study that found pedestrian-oriented, mixed-use neighborhoods being associated with increased familiarity with neighbors and greater social engagement. Moreover, other research found that walkable, mixed-use neighborhoods had higher levels of social capital, including knowing neighbors, participating politically, trusting others, and being socially engaged (Leyden, 2003). Eight other studies found that community gardens increase community cohesion and reduced graffiti and violence (Maller et al., 2008). Further, community gardens improved the attitudes of residents and resulted in improvements to the maintenance of other properties in the neighborhood, reduced littering and increased pride in the neighborhood (Armstrong, 2000).

Numerous studies have also provided evidence that sport contributes to building local skills, knowledge, and resources, increasing social cohesion, facilitating structures and mechanisms for community dialog, leadership development, and encouraging civic participation (Edwards, 2015). An empirical study of 21 countries demonstrates substantial correlations between indicators of social capital and measures of sporting participation, both at the national and individual level (Delaney & Keaney, 2005). Finally, a three-year ethnographic study of Somali refugees examined the role of sport in bridging and community bonding. The study concluded that sport could play a role in generating social capital within an immigrant community (Spaaij, 2012).

The second primary area of connection between the active economy and social impact was through volunteering, as it supports the development of social networks and cohesion (Bradbury & Kay, 2008). A nine-month UK study of young volunteers (aged 13-16) found an increase in indicators of altruistic attitudes, community-orientation, leadership skills and feeling better about themselves (Eley & Kirk, 2010).

Safety is the third area of connection between the active economy and social health. The causes of youth crime are complex and multi-dimensional; however, evidence suggests that organized sports programs provide young people a positive identity, feelings of empowerment and by helping youth acquire leadership, teamwork, and self-governance skills under adult supervision (Jamieson & Ross, 2007). In Kansas City, for instance, evening and midnight basketball programs reduced the crime rate among African American youth. According to the Kansas City Police, there was a one-third to two-thirds reduction in juvenile crime in areas where there was a midnight basketball program for 10 to 21-year-olds (Hawkins, 1998). In Phoenix, basketball courts and other recreation facilities that were kept open until 2 a.m. led to a reported reduction of juvenile crime drop by up to 55 per cent (Illinois State Library, 1995). Similarly, in Alexandria, Virginia, there was a reduction in crime among young women who participated in a running program sponsored by the Road Runners Club of America (Vibar-Bawzon, 1997).

A multi-agency scheme in a Bristol, UK youth centre which addresses problems of drug-taking and associated levels of criminal activity, claimed a 15 per cent reduction in crime in the local area and a 43 per cent reduction in juvenile crime (Sport England, 1999). In the north-east of England, a program trained 40 young people in youth/sports leadership awards, through supervised activities with recreational activities, organized and facilitated by trained young people. This program claimed a 40 per cent reduction of crime and a £200,000 reduction in vandalism (Institute of Leisure and Amenity Management, 1999).

In summary, evidence has demonstrated that the active economy plays an important role in developing social cohesion and a strong sense of belonging. However, this evidence also suggests that there needs to be increased intentionality and targeted investment in resources to leverage the social impacts within the active economy. This includes a commitment to urban design and planning to promote increased walkability, building and maintaining parks and open spaces, an expansion of community gardens and the leveraging of current infrastructure to promote increased usage by specific demographics.

Environmental Impact

Finally, an active economy has been shown to have links to impacts to the natural environment. This focuses primarily on parks, however there is also value in developing active transit strategies.

A Toronto Dominion study for the City of Toronto suggested that its urban forest provides residents with over $80 million, or about $8 per-tree worth of environmental impacts and cost savings each year. For the average single-family household, this works out to $125 in savings per annum. Thus, for every dollar spent on annual maintenance, Toronto's urban forest returns anywhere from $1.35 – $3.20 worth of impacts and cost savings each year (Alexander & McDonald, 2014).

In a study from Washington State, the non-traditional economic impacts associated with green spaces included the satisfaction and increase in general quality of life in which people get from engaging in outdoor recreation and from the ecosystem services recreational lands provide. The combined benefits were estimated to be between $134 billion and $248 billion annually (Briceno & Schundler, 2015).

An international study looking at 25 urban centres, meanwhile suggested that investing in restoring, protecting and enhancing green infrastructure and ecosystem services in cities was not only ecologically and socially desirable, but also economically viable (Elmqvist et al., 2015). Finally, a study by the Inter-American Development Banks estimates that increasing tree cover by 10 per cent may reduce the total energy needed for heating and cooling by 5 to 10 per cent (Sorensen et al., 1997).

Environmental impacts can also be felt through a reduction of CO2 emissions. A study by the UA Environmental Protection Agency, for instance found that an increase of 13 per cent of walking to school reduces CO2 emissions by 15 per cent (Ewing & Greene, 2003). Another study found that 'Safe Routes to School' programs resulted in a 13 per cent reduction in vehicle drop-offs, and an annual reduction of 1,000 tons of carbon dioxide emissions and 70 tons of other environmental pollutants (Staunton et al., 2003). Through the creation of parks, cities can also address their carbon footprint by sequestering carbon from the air and soil, but also reduce local energy consumption by providing cooler surfaces and additional shade for buildings. Finally, a study in the *Journal of American Planning* suggested that a 5 per cent increase in walkability was linked to a 6.5 per cent decrease in vehicle traffic, equating to a 5.6 per cent decrease in emissions of oxides of nitrogen (Frank et al., 2006).

In summary, evidence has demonstrated that the active economy can have a significant environmental impact by playing an important role in reducing pollution and carbon emissions. This includes commitments to increasing active transportation and urban design and planning that promotes increased walkability and cycling. Outdoor recreation can also have a positive impact on the environment through the increase and/or perseveration of urban forests.

A challenge with many environmental impacts is the temporal distance between the intervention and the benefit. Environmental value and impacts are rarely immediate and must be measured over long periods of time. This makes investments that provide only environmental impact politically challenging although most, if not all, of the activities that trigger environmental impacts, can also provide significant and sometimes short term measurable economic, human, and social impacts.

CONCLUSION

In this chapter, the active economy was examined as a complex value chain composed of community input resources, activities and outputs, and how these can impact dimensions of community wellbeing when combined. The impacts were then divided into economic, human, social and environmental with evidence demonstrating the connections between and among all four. The following chapters will now review the various components of the active economy and how they have specific impacts through their inputs and outputs.

REFERENCES

Ahn, S., & Fedewa, A. L. (2011). A meta-analysis of the relationship between children's physical activity and mental health. *Journal of Pediatric Psychology*, *36*(4), 385–397. doi:10.1093/jpepsy/jsq107 PMID:21227908

Aldana, S., & Pronk, N. (2001). Health promotion programs, modifiable health risks, and employee absenteeism. *Journal of Occupational and Environmental Medicine*, *43*(1), 36–46. doi:10.1097/00043764-200101000-00009 PMID:11201768

Alexander, C., & McDonald, C. (2014, June 9). Urban forests: The value of trees in the City of Toronto. *TD Economics*. https://www.td.com/document/PDF/economics/special/UrbanForests.pdf

Armstrong, D. (2000). A survey of community gardens in upstate New York: Implications for health promotion and community development. *Health & Place*, *6*(4), 319–327. doi:10.1016/S1353-8292(00)00013-7 PMID:11027957

Bontis, N., & Fitz-enz, J. (2002). Intellectual capital ROI: A causal map of human capital antecedents and consequents. *Journal of Intellectual Capital*, *3*(3), 223–247. doi:10.1108/14691930210435589

Bradbury, S., & Kay, T. (2008). Stepping into community? The impact of youth sport volunteering on young people's social capital. In M. Nicholson & R. Hoye (Eds.), Sport and social capital (pp. 285–315). Elsevier Science & Technology.

Briceno, T., & Schundler, G. (2015). Economic analysis of outdoor recreation in Washington State. *Earth Economics*. https://www.tre.wa.gov/wp-content/uploads/Willhite.pdf

Bureau of Transport and Regional Economics. (2007). *Estimating urban traffic and congestion cost trends for Australian cities* [Working Paper 71]. Department of Transport and Regional Services. https://www.bitre.gov.au/publications/2007/files/wp_071.pdf

Burnett, C. (2016). Building social capital through an 'Active Community Club'. *International Review for the Sociology of Sport*, *41*(3-4), 283–294. doi:10.1177/1012690207078381

Chodzko-Zajko, W. J. (1998). Physical activity and aging: implications for health and quality of life in older persons. *President's Council on Physical Fitness and Sports Research Digest*, *3*(4).

Colman, R., & Walker, S. (2004, November). *The cost of physical inactivity in British Columbia*. B.C. Ministry of Health Planning. http://gpiatlantic.org/pdf/health/inactivity-bc.pdf

Cortright, J. (2009, August 1). Walking the walk: How walkability raises home values in U.S. cities. *CEOs for Cities*. https://nacto.org/docs/usdg/walking_the_walk_cortright.pdf

Davis, A. (2010, March). *Value for money: An economic assessment of investment in walking and cycling*. Government Office for the South West. https://bikehub.ca/sites/default/files/valueformoneyaneconomicassessmentofinvestmentinw.pdf

Delaney, L., & Keaney, E. (2005). Sport and social capital in the United Kingdom: Statistical evidence from national and international survey data. *Dublin. Economic and Social Research Institute and Institute for Public Policy Research*, *32*, 1–32.

Department of Health, Physical Activity, Health Improvement and Protection. (2011). *Start active, stay active: A report on physical activity from the four home countries' Chief Medical Officers*. The Department of Health. https://assets.publishing.service.gov.uk/government/uploads/system/uploads/attachment_data/file/830943/withdrawn_dh_128210.pdf

Edwards, M. (2015). The role of sport in community capacity building: An examination of sport for development research and practice. *Sport Management Review*, *18*(1), 6–19. doi:10.1016/j.smr.2013.08.008

Eley, D., & Kirk, D. (2010). Developing citizenship through sport: The impact of a sport-based volunteer programme on young sport leaders. *Sport Education and Society*, *7*(2), 151–166. doi:10.1080/1357332022000018841

Elmqvist, T., Setälä, H., Handel, S. N., Van der Ploeg, S., Aronson, J., Blignaut, J. N., Gómez-Baggethun, E., Nowak, D. J., Kronenberg, J., & De Groot, R. (2015). Benefits of restoring ecosystem services in urban areas. *Current Opinion in Environmental Sustainability*, *14*, 101–108. doi:10.1016/j.cosust.2015.05.001

Ernst & Young, & espnW. (2015). *Where will you find your next leader? EY and espnW explore how sport advances women at every level.* https://wnywomensfoundation.org/app/uploads/2017/11/76.-Where-will-you-find-your-next-leader.pdf

Ewing, R., & Greene, W. (2003). *Travel and environmental implications of school siting*. U.S. Environmental Protection Agency. https://www.epa.gov/sites/production/files/2014-04/documents/school_travel.pdf

Florida, R. (2002). The economic geography of talent. *Annals of the Association of American Geographers*, *92*(4), 743–755. doi:10.1111/1467-8306.00314

Fox, K. R., & Lindwall, M. (2014). Self-Esteem And Self-Perceptions in Sport And Exercise. *Routledge Companion to Sport And Exercise Psychology: Global Perspectives and Fundamental Concepts*, 34-48.

Frank, L. D., Sallis, J. F., Conway, T. L., Chapman, J. E., Saelens, B. E., & Bachman, W. (2006). Many pathways from land use to health: Associations between neighborhood walkability and active transportation, body mass index, and air quality. *Journal of the American Planning Association*, *72*(1), 75–87. doi:10.1080/01944360608976725

Gotschi, T. (2011). Costs and benefits of bicycling investments in Portland, Oregon. *Journal of Physical Activity & Health*, *1*(1), 49–58. doi:10.1123/jpah.8.s1.s49 PMID:21350262

Guo, J. Y., & Gandavarapu, S. (2009). An economic evaluation of health-promotive built environment changes. *Preventive Medicine, 50*, 44–S49. doi:10.1016/j.ypmed.2009.08.019 PMID:19840817

Haugen, T., Säfvenbom, R., & Ommundsen, Y. (2011). Physical activity and global self-worth: The role of physical self-esteem indices and gender. *Mental Health and Physical Activity, 4*(2), 49–56. doi:10.1016/j.mhpa.2011.07.001

Hawkins, B. (1998). Evening basketball leagues: The use of sport to reduce African American youth criminal activity. *International Sports Journal, 2*(2), 68–77.

INRIX. (2020). Traffic congestion cost UK motorists over £37.7 billion in 2017. *INRIX.* https://inrix.com/press-releases/scorecard-2017-uk/

Institute of Leisure and Amenity Management (ILAM). (1999). *The Contribution of the Arts and Sport to Neighbourhood Renewal and Reducing Social Inclusion*. ILAM.

International Sport and Culture Association & Centre for Economics and Business Research. (2015). *The economic cost of physical inactivity in Europe.* International Sport and Culture Association, & Centre for Economics and Business Research.

Jamieson, L. M., & Ross, C. M. (2007). Research update: Using recreation to curb extremism. *Parks & Recreation, 42*(2), 26.

Kaplan, R. S., & Norton, D. P. (2005). The balanced scorecard: Measures that drive performance. *Harvard Business Review, 83*(7), 172. PMID:10119714

King, A., Huseynli, G., & MacGibbon, N. (2018). *Wellbeing frameworks for the Treasury* (No. 18/01). New Zealand Treasury Discussion Paper.

Kuhlman, R. (2010). *Helping Johnny walk to school: Policy recommendations for removing barriers to community-centered schools.* National Trust for Historic Preservation. http://www.bestfacilities.org/best-home/docuploads/pub/214_helping-johnny-walk-to-school.pdf

Lawlor, D. A., & Hopker, S. W. (2001). *The effectiveness of exercise as an intervention in the management of depression: Systematic review and meta-regression analysis of randomised controlled trials.* doi:10.1136/bmj.322.7289.763

Lawlor, E. (2014). The pedestrian pound: The business case for better streets and places. *Living Streets.* https://www.livingstreets.org.uk/media/3890/pedestrian-pound-2018.pdf

Lee, I. M., Shiroma, E. J., Lobelo, F., Puska, P., Blair, S. N., & Katzmarzyk, P. T.Lancet Physical Activity Series Working Group. (2012). Effect of physical inactivity on major non-communicable diseases worldwide: An analysis of burden of disease and life expectancy. *Lancet, 380*(9838), 219–229. doi:10.1016/S0140-6736(12)61031-9 PMID:22818936

Leyden, K. M. (2003). Social capital and the built environment: The importance of walkable neighborhoods. *American Journal of Public Health, 93*(9), 1546–1551. doi:10.2105/AJPH.93.9.1546 PMID:12948978

Maller, C. J., Townsend, M., St. Leger, L., Henderson-Wilson, C., Pryor, A., Prosser, L., & Moore, M. (2008). Healthy parks healthy people: The health benefits of contact with nature in a park context. *Parks Stewardship Forum, 26*(2).

Manuel, D. (2016). *A $4.9 billion decrease in health care expenditure*. Institute for Clinical Evaluative Sciences.

Marsden Jacob Associates. (2018, March 1). Active impacts: The economic impacts of active recreation in Victoria. *Sport and Recreation Victoria*. https://sport.vic.gov.au/__data/assets/pdf_file/ 0026/56537/ the20economic20impacts20of20active20recreation20in20victoria_0.pdf

Ministry of Health. (2019). *Annual Data Explorer 2018/19: New Zealand Health Survey* [Data File]. https://minhealthnz.shinyapps.io/nz-health-survey-2018-19-annual-data-explorer/

Mutrie, N. (2000). The relationship between physical activity and clinically defined depression. In S. J. H. Biddle, K. R. Fox, & S. H. Boutcher (Eds.), *Physical activity and psychological prosperity* (pp. 46–62). Routledge.

National Recreation and Park Association. (n.d.). *Synopsis of 2010 research papers: The key benefits*. https://www.nrpa.org/uploadedFiles/nrpa.org/Publications_and_Research/Research/Papers/Synopsis-of-Research-Papers.pdf

Obesity Canada. (2020). Obesity in Canada. *Obesity Canada.* Retrieved from: https://obesitycanada.ca/obesity-in-canada/#:~:text=As per cent20a per cent20leading per cent20cause per cent20of,is per cent20directly per cent20attributable per cent20to per cent20obesity

Onyx, J., & Bullen, P. (2000). Measuring social capital in five communities. *The Journal of Applied Behavioral Science, 36*(1), 23–42. doi:10.1177/0021886300361002

Organisation for Economic Development and Cooperation. (2021). *Better Life Index*. Retrieved from http://www.oecdbetterlifeindex.org/about/better-life-initiative/

Pivo, G., & Fisher, J. D. (2011). The walkability premium in commercial real estate investments. *Real Estate Economics, 39*(2), 185–219. doi:10.1111/j.1540-6229.2010.00296.x

Public Health Agency of Canada. (2016, December). How healthy are Canadians? A trend analysis of the health of Canadians from a healthy living and chronic disease perspective. *Public Health Agency of Canada.* https://www.canada.ca/content/dam/phac-aspc/documents/services/publications/healthy-living/how-healthy-canadians/pub1-eng.pdf

Rajé, F., & Saffrey, A. (2016). The value of cycling. *Cycling Embassy*. Retrieved from http://www.niagaraknowledgeexchange.com/wp-content/uploads/sites/2/2016/04/value-of-cycling.pdf

Schultz, L. E., Crompton, J. L., & Witt, P. A. (1995). A national profile of the status of public recreation services for at-risk children and youth. *Journal of Park and Recreation Administration, 13*, 1–1.

Scully, D., Kremer, J., Meade, M. M., Graham, R., & Dudgeon, K. (1998). Physical exercise and psychological wellbeing: A critical review. *British Journal of Sports Medicine, 32*(2), 111–120. doi:10.1136/bjsm.32.2.111 PMID:9631216

Senge, P. M. (2006). *The fifth discipline: The Art And Practice of The Learning Organization*. Currency.

Shanahan, D. F., Bush, R., Gaston, K. J., Lin, B. B., Dean, J., Barber, E., & Fuller, R. A. (2016). Health benefits from nature experiences depend on dose. *Scientific Reports, 6*(1), 28551. doi:10.1038rep28551 PMID:27334040

Singh, A., Uijtdewilligen, L., Twisk, J. W. R., Van Mechelen, W., & Chinapaw, M. J. M. (2012). Physical activity and performance at school: A systematic review of the literature including a methodological quality assessment. *Archives of Pediatrics & Adolescent Medicine, 166*(1), 49–55. doi:10.1001/archpediatrics.2011.716 PMID:22213750

Sorensen, M., Smit, J., Barzetti, V., & Williams, J. (1997). *Good practices for urban greening*. Inter-American Development Bank. https://publications.iadb.org/publications/english/document/Good-Practices-for-Urban-Greening.pdf

Spaaij, R. (2012). Beyond the playing field: Experiences of sport, social capital, and integration among Somalis in Australia. *Ethnic and Racial Studies, 35*(9), 1519–1538. doi:10.1080/01419870.2011.592205

Sport England. (1999). *The value of sport*. Sport England.

Sport Singapore. (2019). *Live better through sport: Giving back.* Retrieved from https://issuu.com/sportsingapore/docs/for_ebook_190301_sportsg_live_bookl/2?ff&e=29442121/68402603

Statistics Canada. (2019, May 21). Sports for fun and fitness. *Statistics Canada.* https://www150.statcan.gc.ca/n1/pub/11-627-m/11-627-m2019039-eng.htm

Staunton, C. E., Hubsmith, D., & Kallins, W. (2003). Promoting safe walking and biking to school: The Marin County success story. *American Journal of Public Health, 93*(9), 1431–1434. doi:10.2105/AJPH.93.9.1431 PMID:12948957

Taub, D. E., & Greer, K. R. (2000). Physical activity as a normalizing experience for school-age children with physical disabilities: Implications for legitimation of social identity and enhancement of social ties. *Journal of Sport and Social Issues, 24*(4), 395–414. doi:10.1177/0193723500244007

Vibar-Bawzon, J. (1997, October). Developing sports as a social deterrence to social deviance: The role of sport on women and girl's lives. Presentation at the *Second Scientific International Conference for Women Sport*, Alexandria University, Egypt.

ENDNOTE

1 Herein, we used human capital as a synonym to high-valued talent and defines competencies as capital, similar to other forms of capital (e.g., financial capital, social capital). Human capital can be viewed at the level of an individual, institution (e.g., organization or ecosystem) or city.

Chapter 3
Stakeholders in the Active Economy

Mathew Dowling
Anglia Ruskin University, UK

Becca Leopkey
University of Georgia, USA

Jonathan Robertson
Deakin University, Australia

ABSTRACT

This chapter builds upon previous discussions conceptualizing the active economy by focusing on one of its key features: the stakeholders. In particular, the authors seek to answer three fundamental questions regarding how to conceptualise active economies including: (1) What stakeholders comprise an active economy? (2) How can we identify stakeholders within an active economy? (3) How do these stakeholders interact in order to produce systems of value? In response to these questions, they provide an overview of the stakeholder saliency literature and discuss how it may be possible to conceptualize stakeholders within the active economy by outlining a topology and a conceptual framework for the identification and classification of stakeholders. Finally, they illustrate how this conceptual framework can be used to identify stakeholders within global, national, and regional active economies and through a case study of Strava Inc.

DOI: 10.4018/978-1-7998-7939-8.ch003

STAKEHOLDERS IN THE ACTIVE ECONOMY

This chapter continues to build upon previous discussions conceptualizing the active economy (cf. Finch et al., 2019) by focusing more specifically on one of the key features of the active economy – the stakeholders. In particular, we seek to answer central questions regarding the active economy, namely what stakeholders comprise an active economy? How can we identify stakeholders within an active economy? How do these stakeholders interact in order to produce systems of value? In other words, '*who or what really counts*' as an active economy stakeholder and '*who should we pay attention*?' (Freeman, 1994). To this end, this chapter aims (i) to identify key stakeholders within the active economy, (ii) to discuss the roles and responsibilities of stakeholders within the active economy; and (iii) to explore the relationships and dynamics between stakeholders within the active economy.

These questions at first glance seem simple enough, however, any attempt to delineate what stakeholders comprise an active economy and how they interact is both challenging and problematic for several reasons. First, there are specific conceptual issues regarding the term stakeholder. Not only is the term commonly used, but it is frequently confused, and often conflated. The stakeholder concept emerged in the 1960s at the Stanford Research Institute (SRI), now SRI International Inc. during their corporate planning process (Freeman, 1984). It arose, in part due to a broader recognition that managers needed to move beyond traditional 'shareholder models' (i.e., individuals that have direct ownership) towards a more encompassing understanding of corporate governance (Freeman, 1984).

Since then, a number of definitions have appeared in the general management literature (e.g., Clarkson, 1994, Donaldson & Preston, 1995, Hill & Jones, 1992). The term stakeholder is used to refer to those who have a 'stake' in a particular organization or firm. This most closely aligns with organizational management and business ethics understanding of the term. However, Mitchell et al. (1997) argue that an expansive view of this nature "leaves the notion of stake and the field of possible stakeholders unambiguously open to include virtually anyone" (p. 856).

Second, quite what is meant or understood by stakeholder depends on what unit of analysis - namely the major entity that is being investigated is chosen and it may vary depending on whether you look at international, national, regional or local contexts. If the active economy is multi-disciplinary it is perhaps unsurprising that it likely involves a multiplicity of stakeholders operating within and across multiple levels of jurisdiction. This issue is further complicated by the fact that different active economies operate under different governing arrangements, legal restrictions, and governmental systems or regimens (e.g., federated or non-federated) which will ultimately define the scope and influence stakeholder involvement.

Third, in assuming that the above conceptual issues are resolvable, it is also important to recognize the additional challenges and issues of delineating the stakeholders within an active economy. What constitutes a stakeholder within an active economy is largely dependent upon how you chose to define an active economy and the scope of the boundaries that are placed around it. Our definition of an active economy is consistent Finch et al. (2019) who delineate an active economy as "all organizations who participate in, or contribute to, improving individual or community wellbeing through the development and delivery of sport and active recreation experiences" (Finch et al., 2019, p. 13). Active economies are ecosystems that are constantly evolving and changing. There are always stakeholders entering and exiting the economy and the boundaries of the active economy are blurred and porous. It is for this reason that we view the active economy and the many stakeholders that comprise them as 'open-systems' (Scott & Davies, 2015). More specifically, the complex interrelationships among stakeholders in the active economy are relatively open to the influences of the environment that surrounds them (Chelladurai, 2005). Furthermore, no active economy is the same. We suggest, therefore, that the identification of stakeholders within the active economy is both temporal and context dependent.

Fourth, and in turning to more specific practical and observational issues in identifying stakeholders within the active economy, it is also important to recognize the sheer size and complexity the active economy which can span vast geographical regions and is comprised of hundreds if not thousands of individuals and/or organizations across multiple sectors makes it difficult (if not impossible) to identify, at least with any particular degree of certainty, all the stakeholders.

Fifth, stakeholders do not operate in isolation. They are part of and exist within a complex eco-system involving interaction and interdependencies. Therefore, even if it is possible to identify all stakeholders within an active economy, it is important to understand both structural elements (i.e., what stakeholders exist) and the processual arrangements (i.e., the interaction and dynamics) that exist between them. After all, it is these interactions and relations that ultimately combined to create systems of value.

In short, the above discussion serves to highlight the extent of the challenge faced when attempting to answer the seemingly simple questions. To overcome some of these conceptual and practical issues, this chapter draws upon and is underpinned by elements of stakeholder theory, inter-organizational theory and resource-dependency theory. More specifically, the discussion below primarily draws upon stakeholder theory (Freeman, 1984) as a useful approach to examining groups and individuals (i.e., stakeholders) that affect or can potentially be affected by an organizational entity (Friedman et al., 2004). Friedman, Parent and Mason argue that sport managers are operating within continually changing organizational environments as they work toward short-term and long-term organizational goals. At any given time, decision-makers may have several issues that must be addressed in order to satisfy the demands of their organization's constituents.

These researchers laid the initial groundwork for identifying the potential opportunities of applying stakeholder theory to sport-related issues. Accordingly, aspects of stakeholder theory have been applied to various contexts within the sport management field, sport leadership (i.e., Kihl, Leberman, & Schull, 2010; Parent, Olver, & Séguin, 2009; Peachey, Zhou, Damon & Burton, 2015), sport tourism (i.e., Anderson & Getz, 2008; Kim, Jun, Walker, & Drane, 2015; Ntloko & Swart, 2008) and sport event management (i.e., Kristiansen, Strittmatter & Skirstad, 2016; Leopkey & Parent, 2009a; Parent & Deephouse, 2007; Toohey, 2008).

In particular, Mitchell et al's (1997) *Theory of Stakeholder Salience* is utilized as a conceptual framework to identify and begin to discuss the various stakeholders that collectively constitute an active economy. More specifically, we build upon this framework to propose potential criteria for the evaluation of stakeholders within the active economy based on stakeholder salience attributes of power, urgency and legitimacy.

As will become apparent from our discussion, despite being theoretically informed, our focus and interest with this chapter is pragmatic in that we seek to apply what are often competing and contradictory perspectives to be able to articulate what constitutes an active economy. Furthermore, it is worth explicitly stating from the outset that our intention here is not to empirically identify and classify all possible stakeholders within an active economy – although we believe this may be possible at a later point in time. Nor is it our intention to be overly prescriptive with regards to identifying precisely which stakeholders should or should not comprise an active economy for the reasons cited above. Any attempt to do so, although laudable, we suggest would inevitably be futile. This chapter does, however, seek to provide a conceptual framework by which it might be possible to at least identify the key stakeholders that constitute an active economy regardless of location or context.

The chapter is divided into three sections: The first section discusses how it may be possible to identify and conceptualize stakeholders. Here we outline the stakeholder theory approach in general and the Mitchell et al's (1997) conceptual framework specifically. We then discuss how it may be possible to conceptualize stakeholders within the active economy by outlining a topology of stakeholders and a conceptual framework for the identification and classification of stakeholders. The second section then illustrates how this conceptual framework can be used to identify stakeholders within global, national and regional active economy and discuss their roles and responsibilities within them. In this section we also begin to discuss how stakeholders could be classified based upon their relative saliency (i.e., importance) within the active economy. The third and final section then focuses on the dynamics and interactions between various stakeholders within the active economy in order to understand how these interactions lead to the creation of value.

WHO ARE THE KEY STAKEHOLDERS WITHIN AN ACTIVE ECONOMY?

The neoclassical economist definition of a stakeholder is any entity that has a direct and immediate, often financial, influence over an organization. Adopting this definition for our present purposes would perhaps imply that any organization and entity that generates an economic contribution to the active economy could be labelled a stakeholder. From this perspective, an active economy can therefore be simply understood as a product of the economic sum of its constituent parts. As highlighted in the previous chapter, this is not the case. We suggest this is a narrow view on what constitutes an active economy and its adoption *apriori* would overlook or ignore a number of important stakeholders whose contribution is important to the active economy. Furthermore, we suggest it would also oversimplify the nature and extent of interactions that exists between stakeholders which collectively produce an active economy.

One of the most commonly used definitions of stakeholder is Freeman's (1984) classic definition of any group or individual that "*can affect or is affected by the achievement of an organization's objectives*" (p. 46). Johnson et al.,. (2014) further defines stakeholders as "individuals or groups that depend on the organization to fulfil their own goals and on whom, in turn, the organization depends" (p. 107). Similarly, Thompson et al. (1991) describe a stakeholder as any organization or individual who are "in relationships with an organization" (p. 209). These definitions imply a broader scope with regards to who or what might constitute stakeholders and highlights the bi-directional relationship that exists between them.

As definitions of stakeholders have evolved over time so has the increasing number of organizations and individuals who have been labelled a stakeholder (Sternberg, 1997). The inherent danger here is that everything and everyone can therefore be viewed as a potential stakeholder within an active economy. As such, there is a practical need to provide some sort of scope and boundary on this in order to be able to appropriately delineate the boundaries and scope of an active economy. For example, within the sport event management context Parent (2008) and later Parent and Smith Swann (2013) identified eight primary stakeholders of the focal organization for large-scale sporting events (i.e., the event organizing committee) ranging from sponsors and community members to government and sport organization.

These conceptual issues are reflective of the broader debate within the stakeholder literature about whether to adopt a broad or narrow view of what constitutes a stakeholder (Fassin, 2009). Which side of the debate one sits often depends upon and is reflective of particular research traditions and whether they have adopted a strategic or legal emphasis (Fassin, 2009). The former often requires a broader perspective whereas the latter is often based upon a narrow definition. They are also more generally reflective of those who seek pragmatic and practical solutions to whom or what managers of particular organizations should pay attention (Parent & Deephouse, 2007).

Hence, any attempt to define what constitutes a stakeholder within an active economy finds itself at a *conceptual impasse* and conundrum in deciding whether to adopt a narrow definition of stakeholders that identifies a small-set of organizations "based on the practical reality of limited resources, limited time and attention, and limited patience of managers for dealing with external constraints" on the one hand, versus a broader more encompassing definition formulated "on the empirical reality that companies can indeed be vitally affected by, or they can vitally affect, almost anyone" on the other (Mitchell et al., 1997, p. 857).

CONCEPTUALIZING ACTIVE ECONOMY STAKEHOLDERS

In an attempt to overcome the conceptual issues identified above, we have drawn upon several recent studies which have proposed frameworks for the identification of internal and external stakeholders (Fassin, 2009; Friedman et al., 2004; Xue & Mason, 2011). These previous studies provide a theoretical and empirical basis for developing a conceptual framework for the identification of stakeholders within the active economy. Consistent with these previous studies, we also acknowledge that any attempt to conceptualize stakeholders, is open to empirical and conceptual debate. We have therefore aligned our conception of stakeholders with Fassin (2009) not only because it works with our broad strategic perspective of stakeholders and offers a useful conceptual advancement to Freeman's seminal works, but also like Fassin, we seek a broad and pragmatic solution in order to delineate the boundaries of an active economy. In adopting this view, we define active economy stakeholders as "*any individual or organization that ha[s] an interest in, or [is] impacted by the active economy*" (Finch et al., 2019, p. 21). Not only does this definition enable us to move our understanding of the active economy beyond the neoclassical narrow definitions of stakeholders as direct, immediate and transactional shareholders, but it also recognizes stakeholders from across not-for-profit, private and public sectors (Hoye et al., 2015).

In articulating their conceptual foundation for the active economy, Finch et al. (2020) propose a typology for classifying stakeholders: *Participants, Administrators, Enablers, Policymakers, Supporters*. *Participants* are those stakeholders who take part in organized sport or active recreation. This stakeholder might be described as the 'end user' of the active economy in that they usually purchase and/or consume products or services within them. Examples include participating in yoga class or competing in a recreational basketball league. *Administrators* are those who support the development or delivery of organized sports or active recreation activity. These stakeholders may be voluntary (e.g., club administrator), work in the education sector (e.g., athletic director), or at a professional team (e.g., marketing director). Enablers are those who help others to participate in organized sport or active recreation. Examples of this type of stakeholder include coaches, referees, and personal trainers. *Policymakers* are politicians and decision-makers within governmental departments (or equivalents) that are responsible for developing, implementing, and regulating policy related to the active economy. This includes governmental agencies at all levels (local, regional, national and international) and charitable organizations that have roles and responsibilities within the active economy. *Supporters* are those who support or motivate others to participate in organized sport or active recreation experiences. Examples of this type of stakeholder include parents who register participants and take them to activities and spectators/fans who watch and consume sport and active recreation either live or through a variety of alternative engagement platforms (e.g., social media, fantasy leagues).

Finch's et al's (2020) typology provides a useful conceptual basis for the identification of stakeholders that comprise the active economy. Using this typology, it may be possible to identify key stakeholders by focusing on their role and contributions to an active economy. This approach, we suggest, is consistent and has many parallels with Freeman's original stakeholder model whereby both internal and external stakeholders and how they interact with the firm is reflected.

The principle critique of this simplified approach to identifying stakeholders is it assumes homogeneity between stakeholders and therefore does not consider the variability between stakeholder's influence, their salience and the relationships (Fassin, 2008). We recognize, like Fassin (2009: 119), that "reality is far more complex than the simplified graphical presentation provided by the model", nonetheless it offers a "valuable approximation of reality" (ibid) and therefore it does provide a useful starting point for identifying and discussing the potential stakeholders that make up the active economy. An additional area of concern that has been highlighted in the literature is that differences have also been noted within stakeholder groups which can further complicate the stakeholder network (Parent, 2008; Leopkey & Parent, 2007; Putler & Wolfe, 1999).

One potential avenue for advancing Finch et al's (2020) original typology of stakeholders within the active economy could be to incorporate additional groups (e.g., pressure groups, media) and further classify these stakeholders based upon their importance to an active economy. For example, Clarkson (1995) classifies stakeholders as primary i.e., "one without whose continuing participation the corporation cannot survive as a going concern" (p. 106) and secondary "those who influence or affect, or are influenced or affected by, the firm but they are not engaged in transactions with the firm and are not essential for its survival" (p. 107). In this sense, it could be possible to identify the primary and secondary stakeholders within an active economy by noting those that are essential for an active economy to survive and those that are non-essential. However, some researchers (i.e., Eesley & Lenox, 2006; Mitchell et al., 1997) argued that classifying secondary stakeholders as less salient would devalue the impact these stakeholders had on an organization. There have also been more recent attempts to build upon Friedman's original stakeholder model. Freeman (2004), for example proposes a revised stakeholder framework which broadens potential classifications of stakeholders and more recently Fassin's (2009) *stakeholder model theory of the firm* which augments stakeholder classification even further by identifying stakeholders, stakewatchers, and stakekeepers.

One potential avenue which we think has particular merit and offers a useful alternative approach to enable us to move beyond continued attempts to refine and add additional layers of complexity (or reality) to the original stakeholder model is a shift towards focusing on stakeholder *saliency* i.e., the extent to which stakeholders are vocal, visible and important to an active economy. Mitchell et al., (1997) argued that when identifying stakeholders and their salience, stakeholders "may or may not have legitimate claims, but may be able to affect or are affected by the firm, nonetheless, affect the interests of those who do have legitimate claims" (p. 857). As a result, Mitchell et al. (1997) proposed a normative theory of stakeholder identification and saliency. In drawing upon three social science concepts of power, legitimacy and urgency, the researchers developed an approach based upon salience, i.e., "the degree to which managers give priority to competing stakeholder claims" (p. 854). *Power* is the ability of actors to bring about outcomes they desire based upon coercive, utilitarian, and normative means (Etzioni, 1964). *Legitimacy* is the general assumption that an individual or organization's actions are desirable, proper or appropriate (Suchman, 1995). *Urgency* is the degree to which a stakeholder has time-sensitive or critical claims. Based upon the above three broad attributes (i.e., power, legitimacy, and urgency), Mitchell et al. (1997) developed a typology in order to classify the stakeholder environment into four groups: *Non-Stakeholders* (no attributes), *Latent Stakeholders* (one attribute, low importance), *Expectant Stakeholders* (two or more attributes, medium importance), and *Definitive Stakeholders* (three attributes, high important). From the identification of these groupings Mitchell et al. (1997) propose seven stakeholder types (see Table 1).

Table 1. Mitchell et al., (1997) Typology of stakeholders

Latent Stakeholders
1. *Dormant Stakeholders*: Possess power to impose their will but have little or no interaction /involvement as they lack legitimacy or urgency.
2. *Discretionary Stakeholders*: Possess legitimacy but no power. No pressure on managers to engage with this group.
3. *Demanding Stakeholders*: Those with urgent claims, but no legitimacy or power. Demanding and irritating for management.
Expectant Stakeholders
4. *Dominant Stakeholders*: Viewed by many as the only stakeholders of an organization or project. These stakeholders should matter to management
5. *Dependent Stakeholders*: Stakeholders who are dependent on others to carry out their will because they lack the power to enforce.
6. *Dangerous Stakeholders*: Those with powerful and urgent claims will be coercive and possibly violent.
Definitive Stakeholders
7. *Definitive Stakeholders*: An expectant stakeholder who gains the relevant missing attribute.
Non-Stakeholders
8. Non-stakeholder: Stakeholders with no attributes

Adapted from: Mitchell et al. (1997)

There are many examples of studies that have applied Mitchell et al's (1997) framework to identify the saliency of stakeholders to specific sporting contexts (e.g., Anagnostopoulos, 2011; Friedman et al., 2004; Friedman & Mason, 2004; Parent & Deephouse, 2007; Xue & Mason, 2011). We focus specifically on sport related studies here only because of the authors' own interests in this domain, but there are equally comparable examples that can be drawn from other related disciplines.

Friedman and Mason (2004) utilized Mitchell et al's (1997) framework to explain stakeholder involvement and salience in the decisions surrounding public subsidies and the construction of major sport league franchises. Their analysis reveals how identifying stakeholders early on in the policy-making process will reduce the likelihood of unwanted political outcomes/ decision-making. Similarly, Xue and Mason (2011) applied Mitchell et al's framework to map the saliency of stakeholders surrounding the Formula 1 Shanghai event. Of particular note here were the researchers' attempt to trace stakeholder salience surrounding the event longitudinally through different time periods to a understand changing dynamics and stakeholder interest over time. Parent and Deephouse (2007) examined stakeholder salience through a multi-method, comparative case study within organizing committees of major events. The authors found that most stakeholders were definitive, dominant or dormant and identified power as the most important attribute to stakeholder salience. Furthermore, Parent and Deephouse noted that because only three of the eight stakeholder types were present, their findings indicated that "stakeholder types may be more limited in practice than in theory" (2007, p. 18). Anagnostopoulous (2011) also applied the framework to examine the Greek professional soccer (football) clubs to help managers identify and prioritize stakeholders.

Other scholars have focused on the application and development of the framework on a more conceptual basis. Friedman et al. (2004) argue that stakeholder theory in general and Mitchell et al.,'s (1997) framework in particular have descriptive and prescriptive value for practitioners and academics within sport and sport-related disciplines. They demonstrate how stakeholder theory can be utilized for issues management within sport organizations and suggest that classifying stakeholders on the bases of power, legitimacy and urgency enables sport managers to more effectively allocate resources. More recent research has sought to examine stakeholder perspectives on changes to stakeholder saliency. Huml et al.,. (2018) explored the perceptions of Division II college coaches and their responses to National Collegiate Athletics Association (NCAA) changes. Their study also extends Mitchel et al's framework by proposing the importance of equity in identifying stakeholder salience.

Collectively, these studies demonstrate the general utility of stakeholder theory and Mitchell and colleagues' framework specifically in being able to identify stakeholders across a variety of settings and levels of analysis. Furthermore, although beyond the scope of the present chapter, these studies also identify several methodological approaches that could be used to identify key stakeholders. These studies therefore offer a potential starting point for empirically identifying stakeholders within the active economy.

A Framework for Identifying Stakeholders Within an Active Economy

This next section builds upon Mitchell et al.'s (1997) stakeholder framework identified above to propose potential criteria for the evaluation of stakeholders within the active economy based on stakeholder salience attributes of power, urgency and legitimacy. In doing so, we not only identify some of the key stakeholders that typically operate within global, national and regional the active economy and discuss their roles and responsibilities within them, but we also begin to assess their relative saliency (i.e., their relative importance).

Before we proceed, however, it is necessary to qualify our analysis with two important caveats. First, we acknowledge that determining stakeholder salience is both time and context dependent. It is for this reason that previous research that has applied Mitchell et al.'s (1997) framework have often done so to examine particular issues or events. Like Mitchell et al., (1997) and consistent with viewing the active economy as 'open-systems' (Scott & Davis, 2015), we recognize that the active economy and the stakeholders within them are not static entities but rather are constantly evolving and changing. Therefore, any attempt to identify stakeholders and their relative saliency whilst "heuristically useful if the intent is to raise consciousness about 'Who or What Really Counts'" (Mitchell et al., 1997, p. 879), will depend upon the specific context in question.

Second, we acknowledge that our attempt to classify stakeholder salience within the active economy below is largely based upon our own subjective judgement rather than empirical data. It should therefore be apparent that it is our intention to empirically identify and assess the relative salience of all stakeholders across the active economy. Rather through the application of Mitchell et al., framework, we seek to demonstrate how this might be achieved and to identify specific case study examples of stakeholders drawn from the across the sectors identified by the active economy stakeholder typology discussed previously. We hope that future research might be able to begin to empirically map out the active economy in a more scientific and rigorous manner. As such, we seek to provide a conceptual foundation for future empirical research in order to demonstrate more precisely the contribution of the active economy to society in general and to be able to identify particular contributions of stakeholders more effectively within them.

Identifying Active Economy Stakeholders - Local, Regional and Global

Applying Mitchell et al.'s (1997) stakeholder typology, the salience of stakeholders within the active economy can be categorized into four types: definitive, expectant, latent and non-stakeholders. As noted above, stakeholder salience is subjective and contextual, as well as dependent upon the location of the central organization relative to various stakeholder groups. To illustrate this, this section focuses on one sector within the active economy, the organized sport sector, to demonstrate how salience differs between stakeholder groups.

Due to their position as central funders, regulators and decision makers for the provision of sport globally, international sport federations hold power, legitimacy and urgency within the organized sport sector of the active economy. The possession of each of these attributes gives organizations such as Fédèration Internationale de Football Association (FIFA), *Fédération Internationale de Basketball* (FIBA), and the International Olympic Committee (IOC) as well as large single market leagues such as the National Football League in the United States a high level of salience as definitive stakeholders. Generally, as the keepers of the rules and regulations of given sports these organizations are seen as the legitimate custodians of the sport. Supporting this legitimacy, international federations possess substantive resources to fund and regulate (i.e., power), and the rights to timebound live sport events which give them a continued sense of urgency.

Stakeholders shift from definitive to expectant when any one attribute of power, legitimacy, or urgency is diminished. For example, power is eroded depending on where in the federated system a sport governing body or association operates. Consequently, whilst international federations are definitive stakeholders globally, the power base is slowly eroded for regional, national, state and local sport associations in the organized sport sector. Lacking power, these organizations shift to dependent stakeholders on a global scale, whilst retaining power within their geographies of influence. That is to say, a local football federation remains a definitive stakeholder in the local community, whilst at the same time a dependent stakeholder at the national level. When national sport organizations operate under business as usual (i.e., lack urgency), but simultaneously maintain control over rules, regulations and resourcing for a given sport (i.e., power and legitimacy) they are considered dominant stakeholders. Dominant stakeholders in a given geography include national sport governing bodies, professional leagues, teams, and government funding bodies. The final group of expectant stakeholders are 'dangerous' stakeholders, lacking legitimacy but maintaining power and urgency. We understand the defining aspect of this stakeholder group to be the absence of adherence to rules and norms that are generally considered desirable or proper. Actors who delegitimize sport are generally considered via actions around doping, corruption, violence and cheating. In this sense the delineation between individuals and organizations is difficult to make, however dangerous stakeholders can be seen as ambush marketers; illegal betting organizations; State sponsored team and individual cases of doping; and even some sponsorship categories such as tobacco and gambling, whose saliency as a stakeholder has diminished as social norms toward their products and services have changed.

The final substantive category of stakeholders possesses only one attribute of power, legitimacy or urgency and are considered latent stakeholders. For the organized sport sector, dormant stakeholders can include politicians and key influencers who possess power but are not directly involved within the organized sport system. Arguably politicians are dormant stakeholders outside of their respective election cycles in which they leverage their power to impose their will on the sporting landscape for political purposes. Fans, who lack decision-making power (i.e., not voting members) can be considered discretionary stakeholders. The financial investment of purchasing a membership, coupled with voting rights for key decisions (or decision makers) shifts fans from a discretionary stakeholder group, to members who would be considered a dominant stakeholder group. Demanding stakeholders make up the final stakeholder group and can be broadly considered as shock-jocks, media personalities and public commentators. Generally, this group of individuals are separated from advocates (e.g., environment, equity, pay) as their claims are urgent, but they lack an inherent legitimacy in their messaging. Lastly, it is important to consider that there are a range of organizations and individuals who are non-stakeholders. They do not possess any power, urgency or hold legitimate claims toward the organization and thus form the boundary conditions of whom should be considered by managers.

Within the active economy the salience of stakeholders varies by sector. An international sport federation is a definitive stakeholder in the organized sport sector, whilst only a discretionary stakeholder in the health and wellness sector. Discretionary stakeholders in one sector, may be dominant in another. What is clear, is that managers need to be able to identify and understand how to engage with a wide variety of stakeholders across the active economy.

HOW TO ENGAGE STAKEHOLDERS WITHIN AN ACTIVE ECONOMY?

Up to this point, we have primarily focused our discussion on how to identify active economy stakeholders. In addition to the identification of key stakeholders and the structural boundaries of an active economy i.e., '*who or what really counts*' and '*who should we pay attention*' (Freeman, 1984), it is equally as important to understand the interaction and dynamics (i.e., processes) that exist between the individuals and organizations that have an interest in or are influenced by an active economy. In this sense, we now turn our attention away from the 'stakeholder-manager relationship' (Mitchell et al., 1997) to the 'stakeholder-stakeholder' relationship. As highlighted previously, an active economy can be understood and characterized as a complex *ecosystem* of direct and indirect interactions which collectively contribute to the creation of value. By ecosystem we refer to "the alignment structure of the multilateral set of partners that need to interact in order for a focal value proposition to materialize" (Adner, 2016, p. 42). The remainder of the chapter explores further the alignment and interactions between stakeholders within and across an active economy in order to demonstrate how they produce value.

Interdependencies knit together the vast sectors and stakeholders that make up an active economy. These interdependencies can be thought of as relationships based on a range of variables from pure financial relationships (e.g., direct sponsorship), to sharing of resources (e.g., multi-use facilities) and sharing of knowledge (e.g., industry conferences and committees, best practices). In other words, to achieve any activity of size within the active economy an organization is dependent on a number of relationships with other stakeholder groups. A recreation facility requires ticketing and legal services, an active consumer requires apparel and equipment, media providers require sports broadcasts, who themselves require arenas, and on it goes building into a significant active ecosystem in which each stakeholder is co-dependent both directly and indirectly on a myriad of other stakeholders. After a manager has identified relevant stakeholder groups, the challenge then becomes how to engage and manage relationships with these stakeholders.

To better understand how interorganizational relationships develop, Oliver (1997) outlined six determinants of relationship formation: necessity, asymmetry, reciprocity, efficiency, stability, and legitimacy. *Necessity* occurs when an organization 'establishes linkages or exchanges with other organizations in order to meet necessary legal or regulatory requirements' (Oliver, 1991, p. 243). Implicit within the formation of active recreation facilities a range of organizations will be involved from legal teams, to design and infrastructure specialists, urban planners for active transport and a range of sport and physical activity tenants for the daily operations. *Asymmetry* refers to relationships that are 'prompted by the potential to exercise power or control over another organization or its resources' (Oliver, 1991, p. 243). Relating to the above identification of stakeholders with power, national and international sport governing bodies may choose forms of networked governance and decision making in order to exert influence over the 'rules governing exchange', 'coerce' and narrow the 'decision-making latitude and discretion' within a given federated sport structure. *Reciprocity* refers to relationships that 'emphasize cooperation, collaboration, and coordination among organizations, rather than domination, power, and control' (Oliver, 1991, p. 244). Most professional sport leagues globally rely on a degree of cooperation in order to maintain a competitive balance, reciprocity within these relationships dictates the legitimization of anti-competitive regulatory features such as draft and salary caps concessions. Yet another determinant for an organization to enter into an IOR is *efficiency*, that is, 'to improve its internal input/output ratio [via] increases in return on assets, reductions in unit costs, waste, downtime, or cost per patient or client' (Oliver, 1991, p. 245). It is efficient for an active recreation facility to purchase an off the shelf ticket system and pay the license fees to another organization who can provide ongoing service support, rather than develop such a system internally at a higher cost. *Stability*, or predictability, can prompt the formation of IORs as 'an adaptive response to environmental uncertainty' (Oliver, 1991, p. 246). For example, a number of professional teams are forming IORs with local government and private operators to manage active recreation facilities. Doing so reduces the uncertainty of revenue streams for professional teams whose financial performance is often strongly correlated with on-field performance. Conversely, by selecting a long-term management partner, active recreation facilities utilize their scarce resources effectively. The final prompt that can determine the establishment of an IOR is to increase *legitimacy* which may help an organization 'demonstrate or improve its reputation, image, prestige, or congruence with prevailing norms in its institutional environment' (Oliver, 1991, p. 246). For example, a number of sport organizations are turning to environmental initiatives in order to be seen as good corporate citizens and align with expectations of society (Trendafilova et al., 2013).

Understanding what determines IORs helps managers scope how and why to engage in relationships within the active economy. Critical to the choice of how to engage in partnerships, is the question why are you engaging in such partnerships in the first place. If the determinant of the IOR is efficiency or reciprocity based, then the nature of the relationship is likely to be transactional. One organization can benefit from the product or service offered by another; thus, it is therefore in the mutual interest of these organizations to pursue such a relationship. Conversely, if the nature of the relationship is based on more tacit notions of power (e.g., asymmetry, stability) or legitimacy, then the identification of stakeholders with these attributes (as outlined above) is central to forming and maintaining such relationships.

Once the determinants of an interorganizational relationship have been scoped, the ability for an organization to leverage such relationships becomes paramount. Adopting management parlance, can IORs be utilized to form a competitive advantage, not for the single organizational unit, but rather from the IOR itself – an *interorganizational competitive advantage.* Dyer and Singh (1998) identify that interorganizational competitive advantage (here after competitive advantage) can be formed on the basis of four sources linked to the above determinants:

- Relation-specific assets (i.e., the number and longevity of specialized assets derived from the relationship),
- Knowledge sharing routines (i.e., the level of investment in, and transparency of knowledge sharing between organizations),
- Effective governance (i.e., the ability to develop trust via informal mechanisms and minimize the need for third party enforcement of regulation),
- Complementary resources/capabilities (i.e., the ability to leverage compatible existing resources to generate valuable, rare, and inimitable resources).

Interorganizational competitive advantage is particularly relevant for the active economy given the high density of stakeholders and need to work collaboratively to address substantive problems. Especially, when the organizations must do so with scarce resources and often a non-profit orientation, and the general co-creation bases for much of the active economy's products and services. For example, major events rely on fan atmosphere to boost their product appearance and attendance (e.g., fan noise, atmosphere). Increased fan attendance adds value to the broadcast quality and thus the broadcast rights that national sport organizations are able to accrue. Whilst the attraction of fans to sporting events by tour operators does provide an experience, the specific attraction of parochial fans offers a relation-specific asset that no single organization can provide in isolation (Kennelly & Toohey, 2014). For example, the attraction of the Australian "Fanatics", the English "Barmy Army" or the New Zealand "Beige Brigade" add a level of parochial fan interest, noise and atmosphere that improves the sport product. An interorganizational competitive advantage is formed via the combination of specific assets from organized sport, sport stadia and tour operators.

The Olympic movement has developed interorganizational competitive advantage into an artform. One particular source of competitive advantage is the International Olympic Committee's ability to codify knowledge sharing routines into bid processes, bid books, and major event implementation documentation. Such documentation enables stakeholders from across the expanse of the active economy to coalesce around a single incredibly complex event, with incredible frequencies. The codification of such routines enables the summer, winter, and youth Olympic and Paralympic games to roll on with incredible efficiency and to a level of major event production unapparelled in the active economy. In a similar, albeit less tangible way, sport has been able to develop a distinct form of effective governance via a network of national and international regulative and quasi-legislative bodies such as the Court of Arbitration for Sport, the World Anti-Doping Authority, and various national and regional governance branches to support the strong normative foundations underpinning much of sport and the active economy's legitimacy (Chappelet, 2018). The competitive advantage this offers sport is much more tacit than in pure product and service terminology, but no less important. Legitimacy and the taken-for-granted assumptions that sport has the right to self-govern, via demonstrable 'effective' governance has shielded a subset of activities from typical legislative oversight that applies to non-sport activities (e.g., the acceptance of on-field violence without criminal sanction; the loss of employment or income from taking a substance allowed in everyday life but banned in sport). Such norms are so heavily ingrained in modern society, that when compliance with the laws of the land are enforced (e.g., the Bosman ruling) they have substantive impacts on the sporting landscape.

CASE STUDY

Strava – Forming a Competitive Advantage by Linking Active Economy Stakeholders

Background

Strava was founded by Mark Gainey and Michael Horvath in 2009 and was developed around building a community for technology-oriented and data-centric cyclists. The company's primary service is a digital application that can be downloaded onto a smartphone device. At its core, the Strava application tracks, captures and analyzes GPS data from individuals whilst they exercise. Data is then able to be shared with an online community of individuals in a similar modality to Facebook. Strava leverages the integration of GPS capabilities into mobile phones, watches and trackers and builds on the quantified self-movement in the active economy in which even recreational athletes wish to track their ride or run, relative to other people completing the same circuit or segment. Much in the same way as a sport competition or video game would have a leaderboard, Strava enables a community of otherwise socially disconnected individuals, to develop community around a shared experience of cycling a mountain stage or a particular segment of running track. Within the community this developed a sense of comradery and friendly competition amongst and enabled individuals to tell their story as an athlete, regardless of their level.

Platform Strategy in the Active Economy

Inter-organizational competitive advantages can be formed in a number of ways. Above, we have described inter-organizational relationships as an explicit way to develop our understanding of explicit relationship types such as strategic partnerships or alliances. More recent literature has investigated how the same types of competitive advantages can be formed more organically by adopting a platform strategy (Van Alstyne, Parker, & Choudary, 2016). Platform strategies leverage relation specific capabilities by bringing together producers and consumers on a common, shared platform. Think Uber, Airbnb, or Strava, all these companies created communities of members that utilized their own resources (e.g., their car, house, or running/cycling tracks) to develop a platform that has value to a specific consumer need or needs (e.g., transport, accommodation, fitness). Unlike traditional strategic approaches where the competitive advantage is derived from a physical good (e.g., a pair of sneakers) or service (e.g., watching a game) within a single organization. The value, or inter-organizational competitive advantage is derived from the ecosystem that is created between stakeholders.

Stakeholder Identification

Strava, like many companies born out of Silicon Valley. adopted a consumer centric view to stakeholder identification. Possessing legitimacy, power and urgency, data-centric cyclists were the definitive stakeholder (consumer) group early in the company's development. Avid-cyclists were seen as legitimate as their form of physical activity was appropriate for the application of GPS technology, and data and technology were embedded in the normative foundations of the sport, unlike many team sports. Avid cyclists possessed multiple forms of power. In a utilitarian sense, this community had purchasing power to buy expensive bicycles and technology applications such as early GPS trackers (e.g., Garmin). Coercive power developed from their investment in, and testing of technology solutions to training, their recommendations were seen as legitimate and therefore likely to be taken on board. The cycling community that formed helped develop normative power in that avid-cyclists strong personal identification as 'cyclists' meant that other cyclists associated their actions with underpinning norms and values of what it meant to be a 'serious' cyclist. Like many companies, Strava had found their definitive stakeholder group, or what marketers would often refer to as their 'early-adopters', the recipe that was developed here would later be replicated in other contexts from running to diverse sports as kitesurfing and yoga.

Once Strava had identified its definitive stakeholder group, consumers, it knew who it was 'talking to'. Clarity regarding a target consumer did not however negate the need to conduct a broader stakeholder identification and analysis. Strava's business model essentially relies on collecting and displaying personal GPS data, regulators have powerful and legitimate claims to ensure such data is protected, and whilst not necessarily urgent, require attention and diligence in the design and planning phase to ensure individual data protection. Employees are dependent on the success of the company, yet the ultimate power often lies in the senior management teams. Whilst competitors can be considered as dangerous stakeholders, that compete for access to consumers, such as Nike and Apple, who enter into the market without necessarily the historical legitimacy of a company founded around this service domain.

Developing a Competitive Advantage from Stakeholder Relationships

The platform strategic approach extends beyond the notion of explicit inter-organizational relationships and competitive advantages, by developing the ecosystem infrastructure to support such relationships organically. The value is in the community relations that occur on that platform, rather than in the specific intellectual property developed in a relationship between Company A and Company B. For platform companies such as Strava their 'chief assets are information and interactions, which together are also the source of the value they create and their competitive advantage" (Van Alstyne et al., 2016, p. 56). As the competitive advantage for Strava lies in the interactions of its community, the business model and competitive position can prove enduring. This is because despite the technology, essentially GPS linked to an app, is relatively straightforward to replicate (for example Nike+ and Garmin have existed for longer with arguably more financial and technical resources and expertise than Strava), it is the community interactions and information sharing at scale that is almost impossible to emulate.

As of 2020, Strava has 50 million users globally and is increasing by around one million users per month. The success of the application has meant the wide-ranging adoption of Strava by users throughout the active economy. From casual cyclists, swimmers and joggers, through to world class athletes and a range of physical activities in between. Strava or similar movement trackers are also being installed into stadia around the world for real-time analysis and media capture of professional sport leagues (e.g., pass length, running patterns, sprint speed). Strava also links to a range of nutritional and wellbeing organizations and can interface with a number of applications that directly measure your physical and mental health. Such approaches build on the notion of a 'quantified self' in which Lupton (2016) identifies many individuals becoming forms of 'new hybrid beings' via their adoption of self-tracking technologies. For urban planners, Strava can provide a road map for active transport usage by compiling data on a range of routes and analyzing usage patterns.

What is clear from the diverse usage of a relatively straightforward technology, is that Strava has built a sustainable and envious competitive position within the active economy by developing a community ecosystem amongst stakeholders which is incredibly difficult to emulate. Stretching across the active economy from infrastructure to health and a range of physical activities in between, Strava has demonstrated how identifying and developing relationships between stakeholders can produce substantive systems of value.

CONCLUSION

This chapter was purposely divided into three sections focusing on the conceptualization, identification and the dynamic interactions of stakeholders in the active economy. In doing so we provided an overview of Mitchell et al.'s (1997) conceptual framework on stakeholder saliency and then discussed how it may be possible to conceptualize stakeholders within the active economy by outlining a topology of stakeholders and a conceptual framework for the identification and classification of stakeholders based on their saliency. We then illustrated how this conceptual framework can be used to identify stakeholders within global, national and regional active economy and provided examples of their roles and responsibilities within them. Finally, we turned our focus on the dynamics and interactions between various stakeholders within the active economy in order to understand how these interactions lead to the creation of value.

REFERENCES

Adner, R. (2016). Ecosystem as Structure: An Actionable Construct for Strategy. *Journal of Management*, *43*(1), 39–58. doi:10.1177/0149206316678451

Anagnostopoulos, C. (2011). Stakeholder management in Greek professional football: Identification and salience. *Soccer and Society*, *12*(2), 249–264. doi:10.1080/14660970.2011.548361

Chappelet, J. L. (2018). Beyond governance: The need to improve the regulation of international sport. *Sport in Society*, *21*(5), 724–734. doi:10.1080/17430437.2018.1401355

Clarkson, M. E. (1995). A stakeholder framework for analyzing and evaluating corporate social performance. *Academy of Management Review*, *20*(1), 92–117. doi:10.5465/amr.1995.9503271994

Dyer, J. H., & Singh, H. (1998). The Relational View: Cooperative Strategy and Sources of Interorganizational Competitive Advantage. *Academy of Management Review*, *23*(4), 660–679. doi:10.5465/amr.1998.1255632

Etzioni, A. (1964). *Modern Organizations*. Prentice-Hall.

Fassin, Y. (2009). The stakeholder model refined. *Journal of Business Ethics*, *84*(1), 113–135. doi:10.100710551-008-9677-4

Freeman, E. R. (1984). *Strategic Management: A Stakeholder Approach*. Pitman.

Freeman, E. R. (1994). The Politics of Stakeholder Theory: Some Future Directions. *Business Ethics Quarterly*, *4*(4), 409–421. doi:10.2307/3857340

Freeman, E. R. (2004). The Stakeholder Approach Revisited. *Zeitschrift fur Wirtschafts -und Unternehmensethik*, *5*(3), 220–241.

Friedman, M. T., & Mason, D. S. (2004). A stakeholder approach to understanding economic development decision making: Public subsidies for professional sport facilities. *Economic Development Quarterly*, *18*(3), 236–254. doi:10.1177/0891242404265795

Friedman, M. T., Parent, M. M., & Mason, D. S. (2004). Building a framework for issues management in sport through stakeholder theory. *European Sport Management Quarterly*, *4*(3), 170–190. doi:10.1080/16184740408737475

Hoye, R., Smith, A. C., Nicholson, M., & Stewart, B. (2015). *Sport Management: Principles and Applications*. Routledge. doi:10.4324/9781315733371

Johnson, G., Whittington, R., Scholes, K., Angwin, D., & Regner, P. (2014). *Exploring Strategy*. Pearson Education.

Kennelly, M., & Toohey, K. (2014). Strategic alliances in sport tourism: National sport organizations and sport tour operators. *Sport Management Review*, *17*(4), 407–418. doi:10.1016/j.smr.2014.01.001

Lupton, D. (2016). *The Quantified Self*. Polity Press.

Mitchell, R. K., Agle, B. R., & Wood, D. J. (1997). Toward a Theory of Stakeholder Identification and Salience: Defining the Principle of Who and What Really Counts. *Academy of Management Review*, *22*(4), 853–886. doi:10.5465/amr.1997.9711022105

Oliver, C. (1990). Determinants of Interorganizational Relationships: Integration and Future Directions. *Academy of Management Review*, *15*(2), 241–265. doi:10.5465/amr.1990.4308156

Oliver, C. (1991). Strategic responses to institutional processes. *Academy of Management Review*, *16*(1), 145–179. doi:10.5465/amr.1991.4279002

Parent, M. M., & Deephouse, D. L. (2007). A case study of stakeholder identification and prioritization by managers. *Journal of Business Ethics*, *75*(1), 1–23. doi:10.100710551-007-9533-y

Scott, W. R., & Davis, G. F. (2015). *Organizations and organizing: Rational, natural and open systems perspectives*. Routledge. doi:10.4324/9781315663371

Sternberg, E. (1997). The defects of stakeholder theory. *Corporate Governance*, *5*(1), 3–10. doi:10.1111/1467-8683.00034

Suchman, M. C. (1995). Managing legitimacy: Strategic and institutional approaches. *Academy of Management Review*, *20*(3), 571–610. doi:10.5465/amr.1995.9508080331

Thompson, J., Wartick, S., & Smith, H. (1991). Integrating corporate social performance and stakeholder management: Implications for a research agenda in small business. *Research in Corporate Social Performance and Policy*, *12*(1), 207–230.

Trendafilova, S., Babiak, K., & Heinze, K. (2013). Corporate social responsibility and environmental sustainability: Why professional sport is greening the playing field. *Sport Management Review*, *16*(3), 298–313. doi:10.1016/j.smr.2012.12.006

Van Alstyne, M. W., Parker, G. G., & Choudary, S. P. (2016). Pipelines, Platforms, and the New Rules of Strategy. *Harvard Business Review*, (April), 54–62.

Xue, H., & Mason, D. S. (2011). The changing stakeholder map of formula one grand prix in Shanghai. *European Sport Management Quarterly*, *11*(4), 371–395. doi:10.1080/16184742.2011.599205

Chapter 4
Organized Sport in an Active Economy

Mary A. Hums
University of Louisville, USA

ABSTRACT

Organized sport in some form or another has existed since the Ancient Olympic Games. Over time, this sector has evolved to include professional leagues and teams, intercollegiate athletics, and mega events for both men and women. Operating locally, nationally, and internationally, organized sport reaches across boundaries and into communities on various levels. Organized sport will continue its wide-ranging reach into communities as the sport industry and the various constituencies it interacts with evolve into the next century.

INTRODUCTION

On a Friday night in the United States of America in the summertime, the deafening sound of engines racing around the track fills the air. On a Saturday afternoon in the fall, on many major American college campuses the smell of hamburgers on the grill is back dropped by the sounds of marching bands and excited crowds. On a Sunday afternoon in Europe or Australia, supporters waving home club flags and wearing multi-colored scarves pile out of trams and buses and cram into stadiums to cheer and chant. On the field of play, a tennis player lifts a trophy overhead after a hard-fought international tournament match. On any given evening, sports bars fill with excitement before a playoff game and depending on the outcome, fans head back home with their spirits lifted or crushed. On a workday afternoon, sport managers meet together to decide on stadium policies to implement universal design so as to

DOI: 10.4018/978-1-7998-7939-8.ch004

make the facility accessible for everyone. Finally, when families welcome a new baby, often on their first birthday, the child will receive a pair of "onesies" in their parents' favorite team colors. Sport is part of our daily fabric.

People everywhere are drawn to sport, whether as participants or spectators. As evidenced by the chapters in this book, sport pervades society on many different levels and impacts greater society in many ways, shapes, and forms. To draw a corollary from mathematics, Lorenz came up with the "butterfly effect" back in the 1960s, and posited that "tiny, butterfly-scale changes to the starting point of his computer weather models resulted in anything from sunny skies to violent storms—with no way to predict in advance what the outcome might be" (American Physical Society, 2004, para. 1). So, it is with organized sport. There is no doubt that actions taken by sport managers working in the organized sport sector will have a trickle-down effect across the active economy although those effects may remain, at times, unpredictable at best.

The organized sport sector is quite large and so this chapter will aim to give the reader at least a window into some elements of this segment. The focus and examples will mainly come from professional sport, intercollegiate athletics, and also the Olympic/Paralympic sport milieu. While the sector, of course, includes much more, examples from these areas can serve to illustrate important basics about it.

BACKGROUND

Basic Foundational Information

This particular chapter deals with what we label "organized sport." To begin with, it is necessary to establish a baseline definition of what is included in organized sport. According to Finch, et al., (n.d., p. 23), organized sport includes "activities involving physical exertion, skill as the primary focus of the activity, with elements of competition where rules and patterns of behaviour governing the activity exist formally through organizations." To ensure consistency throughout the chapter, some important words need defining. Two of these are "organization" and "governing."

A formal organization needs to have some standard structure to be more than just a group of people. Chelladurai (2009) points out that organizations must have the following characteristics: (a) identity, (b) program of activity, (c) membership, (d) clear boundaries, (e) permanency, (f) division of labor, (g) hierarchy of authority, and (h) formal rules and procedures.

Next, in order to be a functioning part of the organized sport sector, there must be a governing body that performs the following functions: "the exercise of power and authority in sport organizations, including policy making, to determine the organizational mission, membership, eligibility, and regulatory power, within the organization's appropriate local, national, or international scope" (Hums & MacLean, 2018, p. 5).

Major Sub-Sectors

Just like all the sectors presented in this book, the organized sport sector has a heavy list of constituents. The best way to understand this is to see a few specific examples. A partial list with selected examples is on Table 1.

Table 1. Major Sub-Sectors

Sub-Sectors	Examples
Sport Leagues – Professional	NBA, MLB, EPL, Bundesliga, NPB, KBO, ICL, WNBA
Sport Leagues – Amateur	Great Lakes Lacrosse League, BC Hockey AAA League, Cape Cod Baseball League
Sports Clubs & Teams	Professional Atlanta Braves, Los Angeles Lakers, Louisville Bats, Las Vegas Aces, Bayern Munich, FC Augsburg, Fenerbache, Kolkata Knight Riders
Sports Clubs and Teams - Amateur	Chatham Anglers, Fraser Valley Thunderbirds, KIVA U18 Red Volleyball, Indiana Shock
Sport Governing Bodies	IOC, USOPC, COC, JOC, CPC, NCAA, USports, USA Softball, Hockey Canada, World Athletics, IBSA
Motorized Sports	F1, NASCAR, Motorcycle Grand Prix, American Power Boat Association
Animal Supported Sports	Pro Bull Riders Association, Iditarod, National Thoroughbred Racing Association
Tournaments	Masters, PGA Championships, Solheim Cup, Ryder Cup, Wimbledon, French Open, PBA Players Championship, Little League World Series

Brief History of the Organized Sport Sector

Organized sport goes back as far as the ancient Olympic Games which began in 776 BC. Back then, people and athletes made their way every four years or so to Ancient Olympia for what was a festival of religion, commerce, and also sport. Competitors were limited to free, male, and Greek citizens. Women were not even allowed to be spectators. People arrived from all across the Pan-Hellenic region in order to be a part of the event and lined the hillside of the competition area to cheer and be entertained. Given the constant battling among the Greek city-states, during this time an Olympic Truce was set in place which allowed athletes and event participants to safely navigate areas which may have been in conflict at the time. This formed the basis for the Olympic Truce which is also placed into effect during today's modern Olympic Games. These early Games could clearly be seen as perhaps the earliest version of organized sport. Across the Adriatic Sea, gladiators performed for crowds in places like the Coliseum in Rome and other smaller venues. These became more popular in the first and second centuries AD, and "the sport became professionalized, with managers, a fixed schedule and training centers, where gladiators developed expertise in one of the dozen or so weapon specialties on offer" (Grimes, 2005, para. 5).

During the years following these events, other events took place as well, as indigenous peoples held competitions as did early settlers in various lands. Organized sport began to get more professionalized, however, in the late 1700s. The earliest sports to do so were horse racing and baseball. The founding of the Newmarket Jockey Club in England established parameters for professional horse racing as the club kept track of the thoroughbreds' lineages and their racing records. In the United States, baseball was the first team sport to establish systems for players to be paid and for spectators to purchase tickets to watch games. In 1876, baseball's National League established rules about completing the season schedule, setting ticket prices, setting league membership fees, and most importantly, creating a player reservation system that tied players to their clubs via their playing contracts. These governance steps, along with the founding of the American League, set up the structure for today's Major League Baseball (MLB). As the century turned, the other major professional leagues in North America were established, including the National Basketball Association (NBA), the National Football League (NFL), and the National Hockey League (NHL). Serie A and also La Liga soccer leagues started up in Italy and Spain, respectively. Professional individual sports then began to emerge at this time as well, with the founding of the PGA Tour and the tennis Grand Slam slate (Wimbledon, French Open, Australian Open, and the US Open).

Today's professional sports have exploded. Since the 1950s, the Bundesliga began to play, as did the Premier League (both had differently named and organized predecessors) as well as Major League Soccer (MLS) and the Women's National Basketball Association (WNBA). Motorsports took off as well with Formula One Grand Prix competitions and NASCAR races. Even more recently, professional eSports have become immensely popular worldwide, mainly among a younger demographic, and professional leagues have sprung up for niche sports like softball, indoor lacrosse, and even dodgeball.

Prominent Stakeholders Who Influence This Sector

The active economy consists of a list of stakeholders which includes (a) participants, (b) administrators, (c) enablers, (d) policy makers, and (e) supporters. Some of these stakeholders are similar across the organized sport sector while differences exist as well.

In the organized sport sector, the participants would consist of professional and amateur athletes, including abled-bodied and those living with disabilities among a number of other demographic descriptors. Athletes can be professionals, intercollegiate or interscholastic competitors, as well as elite athletes representing their countries on the highest level in international competitions.

The administrators include people such as general managers and front-office employees in professional sport teams. These people hold positions in departments such as finance, legal, marketing, media relations, community relations, stadium operations, or security.

The enablers for professional sport would include support staff such as head coaches, assistant coaches, athletic trainers, medical staff, strength and conditioning personnel, nutritionists, and mental health support staff. Major intercollegiate athletic programs would mirror pro sport, but in addition, there would be staff associated with the educational experience of the athletes. Corporate sponsors also constitute a whole different type of enablers as well, providing the financial capital to make the games happen and support the athletes in their careers. Organizations which promote sports tourism are also active here when they promote travel to events.

Policy makers in professional sport would include owners and commissioners. Typically, however, the commissioners technically work for the owners and those owners are the people who draw up policies and rules for their respective leagues. Olympic and Paralympic sport, for instance, are governed by boards and also by the annual General Assemblies of International Federations and various IOC and IPC standing committees which deal with areas such as medical, legal, ethics, marketing; and diversity, equity, inclusion.

Finally, there are the supporters and all the different forms they take. Professional sport will have supporters across many levels including stadium luxury suite holders, season ticket holders and single-game attendees. Fans of Olympic and Paralympic sport may range from citizens who simply want to support their country of origin/residence to expats who no longer live in their home country but want to stay connected through sport. Sometimes fans on this level are not just connected by country but by sport. One can watch soccer or basketball any day of the year, but fans cannot say the same for judo, curling or para ice-hockey. These fans will support their teams in various ways: by attending competitions in person or by consuming the product on broadcast media, live-streaming, and on devices ranging from televisions, computers and mobile phones. From there, they may then take to social media to further exhibit their fandom and interact with others who may be supporters or "haters" for that matter!

TRENDS

Size/Scope of This Market Globally Today

The size and scope of the organized sport sector can be measured in different ways, but notably by economic impact. First, let's look at the economic reach of the sector.

The NFL leads the North American leagues in value and has 29 of the world's top 50 valued teams. Within that group, the NFL's Dallas Cowboys are the most valuable pro sports franchise at $5.5 million. The NFL's annual broadcast deals across several networks also average out to approximately $6.5 billion (Badenhausen, 2020). Table 2 provides information on the top ten professional teams with the highest values:

Table 2. World's Most Valuable Clubs

Club	League	Value
Dallas Cowboys	NFL	$5.5B
New York Yankees	MLB	$5.0B
New York Knicks	NBA	$4.6B
LA Lakers	NBA	$4.4B
Golden State Warriors	NBA	$4.3B
Real Madrid	La Liga	$4.2B
New England Patriots	NFL	$4.1B
Barcelona	La Liga	$4.1B
New York Giants	NFL	$3.9B
Manchester United	Premier League	$3.8B

Table 3 lists the professional leagues with the highest values (Randjelovic, 2020, p. 1):

Table 3. World's Most Valuable Leagues

League	Value
National Football League (NFL)	$13B
Major League Baseball (MLB)	$13B
National Basketball Association (NBA)	$7.4B
Indian Premier League (Cricket)	$6.3B
English Premier League	$5.3B
National Hockey League (NHL)	$4.4B
Australian Rules Football	$2.5B
La Liga (Spanish Football League)	$2.2B
Serie A (Italian Football League)	$1.9B
Ligue 1 (France/Monaco Football League)	$1.5B
Nippon Professional Baseball (Japanese Baseball League)	$1.1B

The above table then reflects the valuation of professional sports leagues but doesn't account for numerous leagues that exist on much smaller budgets.

Specific to the United States, intercollegiate athletics also represents a large revenue-generating portion of the organized sport sector, however, the vast majority of intercollegiate athletic programs do not turn a profit. According to the NCAA (2020), at more than 1,100 NCAA schools across all three divisions, more than $18.8 billion was spent on athletics in 2019. Of that figure, $3.6 billion went toward financial aid for student-athletes, and $3.7 billion was spent on coaches' compensation. In total, only 25 athletics departments' generated revenues that exceeded their expenses in 2018.

When it comes to Olympic sport, the IOC itself is a privately funded non-profit, non-governmental organization housed in Lausanne, Switzerland. According to the IOC (2020), the organization generated USD $5.7 billion during the four-year Olympiad spanning 2013-2016.

The percentage breakdown for these revenues is:

- Broadcasting rights 73%
- TOP Program marketing rights 18%
- Other (tickets, merchandise, &c) 5%
- Other rights 4%

Clearly, worldwide broadcasting of the Olympic Games every two years is the IOC's primary source of revenue. For PyeongChang 2018, the Games were broadcasted in 200+ countries (IOC, 2020). To put its value in perspective, the Rio 2016 Summer Games generated $2.68 billion and the 2018 PyeongChang Winter Games generated $1.436 billion (IOC, 2020b).

On the marketing side, the IOC currently has 14 TOP partners who control specific product categories. The TOP Program is the worldwide marketing program managed by the IOC. Initiated in 1984, it was formed "in order to develop a diversified revenue base for the Olympic Games and to establish long-term corporate partnerships that would benefit the Olympic Movement as a whole. The TOP Program operates on a four-year term – the Olympiad" (IOC, 2020, p. 15). During the 2013-2016 Olympiad, the TOP Program generated $1.003 billion in revenues to support the Olympic Movement.

As evidenced by just looking at these two main sources of revenue, it is obvious the Olympic Movement is a worldwide sport industry powerhouse.

Growth Dynamics/Forecasts in the Organized Sport Sector

The world has been completely reshaped by the COVID-19 pandemic. Perhaps "re-growth" would be a better term to use here as it describes not the creation of new jobs but the re-establishment and redefinition of existing jobs. Of course, fans would love to flock to their teams' games again, but for the foreseeable future, sporting environments will look very different. Front office workers' jobs will likely look different as well.

One area that will be reshaped for regrowth will be the sport workforce. Numerous leagues and teams either furloughed or completely dismissed workers. For example, MLS reduced its workforce by 20 per cent even after many employees had already experienced salary reductions (Draper, 2020). A number of college athletic departments had to take similar actions in either furloughing employees or reducing salaries (Christovich, 2020; Minnesota Public Radio, 2020).

As people return to these jobs, will they look the same? While the number of employees will appear to be increasing as people are replaced or return, is this really growth or regrowth? Will the number of people working in a front office or in an athletic department remain the same? With so much work taking place virtually, job responsibilities will likely be redefined, and the number of people needed on staff will be reconsidered.

There is another group of essential sport industry employees who must be included. The individuals who work at stadiums and arenas on game days have been hit particularly hard by the pandemic. This group of employees are typically part-time employees and according to the Washington Center for Equitable Growth (2020, para. 4):

.... Part-time workers are also among the hardest hit by the coronavirus recession. They have accounted for almost one-third of the decline in employment since pre-pandemic February, despite making up less than one-sixth of the U.S. workforce. Between February and May, the unemployment rate of part-time workers surged from 3.7 per cent to 19.7 per cent.

Competitive Dynamics in the Organized Sport Sector

Consumers only have so much discretionary income, which results in competition among the different players in the organized sport sector as they jockey for people's spending priorities. People have had to make choices about how to spend their entertainment money and the organized sport sector has competition within itself as well as with other non-sport entertainment options such as concerts, movies, live theatre, and going to museums. People are having to make choices on when they believe it will be safe for them and their families to venture outside and into public spaces. For example, when it comes to film:

...As movie theatres close their doors and premieres are postponed, all while audience demand is rising, production companies are adjusting their strategy. There is typically a 75-90 day theatrical window before new films are released to VOD (Video on demand) and as a result of COVID-19, studios are accelerating this timeframe. This allows them to shift their distribution costs toward providing at-home access (JP Morgan, 2020, para. 9).

The organized sport sector can likely learn some lessons from the film industry as it reshapes itself while at the same time people are getting accustomed to online at-home access. On a related note, there has been an increase in on-line consumption of sport. According to Alexia Quadrani, JP Morgan's Head of U.S. Media Equity Research:

...With live sports programming on pause for the moment, we are seeing an uptick in video game engagement and believe this can largely be attributed to sports fans, across age ranges, who aren't able to watch their teams...However, sports services are now streaming free as seasons get delayed. The NFL Game Pass, NBA League Pass, and NHL.tv are now free for a limited time period, giving fans complimentary access to replays, archives, and more. We believe this is an effort to maintain continued engagement with fans and live sports are halted across the board (JP Morgan, 2020, paras. 20-21).

In other words, sports fandom and how people choose to consume events in the organized sport sector will have a new look in the post-COVID-19 era.

Trends Influencing the Future of This Sector

Recent events have resulted in changes to everyday life and organized sport in particular. As this chapter is being written, we are in the midst of grappling with three "pandemics" – (a) COVID-19, (b) climate change, and (c) systemic racism. As sport is a mirror of society, these conditions have changed the very landscape of sport from recreational level leagues to the elite organized sport sector.

Sport will be extraordinarily revamped due to the COVID-19 pandemic. Major sporting events have been postponed or cancelled due to restrictions on public gatherings or because of positive tests among players and team staff. League officials are making decisions on how to rebound from these disruptions which has caused the loss of competition (Cobb, et al., 2020), championships, and viewership with a resulting loss of revenue. It must be pointed out that the impact of the COVID-19 pandemic on the sport industry will be far-reaching and it will take many years for the sector to recover. The impact will be felt on the $100 billion US sport industry (ESPN, 2020) and internationally as early estimates placed losses from the postponed 2020 Tokyo Olympic and Paralympic Games close to $2.0 billion (Gillen, 2020). Our sport-related language has even changed as well as we now hear sport show hosts talk about bubbles, testing, positives, unavailable lists, quarantines, and postponements/cancellations.

Some leagues have begun to open up to spectators, but with strict protocols for fans and team members. For example, Mercedes-Benz Stadium in Atlanta is home to the NFL's Atlanta Falcons and has put protocols in place for mask-wearing, social distancing, handwashing, taking fans' temperatures when they enter the stadium, and contactless concessions and merchandise purchasing. In addition, stadium officials are taking the following actions: enhanced cleaning before, during, and after events; selling tickets in "pods" to keep groups of ticket holders separated; designating specific fan ingress/egress plans to reduce congestion; and posting directional signage so fans move through the stadium as socially distanced as possible (Mercedes Benz Stadium, 2020). Given all this, however, the stadium still posts the following COVID-19 warning:

...We have taken enhanced health and safety measures for everyone entering Mercedes-Benz Stadium. All fans must follow all instructions (both from associates and posted throughout the building) while visiting Mercedes-Benz Stadium.

...An inherent risk of exposure to COVID-19 exists in any public place. COVID-19 is an extremely contagious disease that can lead to severe illness and death.

...Under Georgia law, there is no liability for an injury or death of an individual entering these premises if such injury or death results from the inherent risks of contracting COVID-19. You are assuming this risk by entering Mercedes-Benz Stadium (Mercedes Benz Stadium, 2020, p. 1).

This is what attending a sporting event looks like for now. Sport managers will need to decide how many of these types of restrictions will apply, for how long, and which additional rules imposed by local government officials may affect their decisions on safely allowing fans access to venues.

In addition to dealing with the COVD-19 world, sport managers in the organized sport sector are having to confront climate change. For purposes of this chapter, this section will adopt a different approach to the meaning of "climate change" as put forward by Friedman (2017). The first "climate change" to discuss is the one people typically think of first - change in the Earth's actual climate. As scientists have proven, the number of destructive weather events and the degradation of ecosystems are both escalating. These changes have resulted in sporting events being moved to different locations or cancelled altogether. This results in numerous legal issues with game-day contracts and television broadcasts, as well as issues with loss of revenue due to the events not being held (Murfree & Moorman, 2020). Other major multi-sport events have had to make schedule shifts due to weather conditions. For example, the Tokyo 2020 [21] Olympic Games changed the location of the marathon events due to potentially dangerous hot temperatures. Originally scheduled to take place in and around Tokyo, the events were moved north to Sapporo where temperatures can be a number of degrees cooler (BBC, 2019).

The second form of "climate change" according to Friedman (2017) is the change in the "climate" of globalization. The world is moving away from the notion of separation by walls and toward the concept of webs. In this process, citizens of the world are also moving from being simply interconnected to being more truly interdependent. World citizens work together to exchange ideas, trade, innovations, and education. Managers who embrace these concepts will ensure their organizations do not get left behind and can even become leaders in their realms. When the volunteer call for Beijing 2022 came out, it was evident the local organizing committee wanted to diversify their international volunteer base. The call for volunteers stated, "applicants from around the world are welcome to apply and become part of the experience of a lifetime to build dreams together at the Beijing Games" (IOC, 2017, para.). Companies and countries that do not work cooperatively in our global environment will fail. This includes sport organizations.

The third "climate change" is the change in the "climate" of technology and work. Here, Friedman (2017) suggests that the future will be greatly impacted by big data, analytics, and artificial intelligence. Companies now analyze, customize, and digitize information. Jobs, products, and services are becoming increasingly automated. We can look again to Tokyo 2020 [21] and the use of robotics and automated systems. Robots of different forms are slated to make their debut at the Tokyo Olympic and Paralympic Games. These include Field Support Robots which would retrieve shot puts and javelins and also human support robots (HSR). The local organizing committee "hoped to highlight its work with the Paralympic Games by showcasing accessibility technology. The HSR would essentially be an assistant for those seated in the accessible seating area of the different events to help them "to more freely enjoy the competition" (Greenspan, 2020, para. 9).

The third trend sport managers will face going forward is the pandemic of racial injustice and the ways in which people in sport can make a stand for justice. This has most recently been seen in how athletes are using the power of their voices to protest against racial injustice. It is imperative that sport governing bodies stand united with their athletes to support them as they speak out (Hums, et al., 2020). In the US, many athletes in organized sport stood up for causes such as Black Lives Matter and helped mobilize the vote in the 2020 US Presidential election. Numerous sport organizations offered their venues as voting stations where thousands of votes were cast including the Staples Center (home to the NBA's Los Angeles Lakers) or Arrowhead Stadium (home of the NFL's Kansas City Chiefs) (Peter, et al., 2020). While international sport organizations such as the Commonwealth Games Federation are openly supportive of athletes speaking out, others such as the IOC remain somewhat reticent as it grapples with its Rule 50 on athletes making political statements. "The movement is challenging all institutions to really look introspectively at what we can do to be more fair, freer, and have better equality. Sport is no different," former Commonwealth Games Chief Executive, David Grevemberg told reporters (Reuters, 2020, para. 4). The bottom line is that sport managers in the organized sport sector have the ability to use sport as a platform for promoting democracy.

LINKS TO THE ACTIVE ECONOMY

How the Organized Sport Sector Acts as an Enabler/or is Enabled by Other Sectors of the Active Economy

In order to illustrate how the organized sport sector enables other active economy sectors, we will walk through an example using a typical major North American sport franchise – the NBA's Indiana Pacers.

Health and Wellness

One way the Pacers enable health and wellness is through giving fans an attachment point. Associating with the team can improve mental health in that games give fans something to look forward to and identify with. As the COVID-19 pandemic lessens its grip, there will be more options for fans to gather at stadiums, arenas, sports bars, or each other's homes to bond over the team's efforts. Sports fandom is about more than just entertainment. It can boost your self-esteem and make you happier — and you don't have to root for the winning team to reap the benefits. Being a sports fan is a "very psychologically healthy activity," says Daniel Wann, professor at Murray State University whose research program centers on the psychology of sport fandom. Fandom connects us to other like-minded people, which satisfies our human need for belonging (Stieg, 2020, para. 3-4).

In regards to reflecting on this during the COVID-19 pandemic, according to Randle (2020), "one of the things we've misunderstood is the depth of importance that sports, and the accompanying community of fandom, has in so many of our lives." (para. 7).

Sport Betting

In the past, the opportunities to bet on NBA games were quite limited. In the past few years, however, more states within the US now allow betting on NBA games. In Indiana, the home state of the Pacers, full-service betting on NBA games is allowed. In other locations, fans may need to visit a physical sportsbook to place a bet, but now online betting, whether domestic or offshore, is becoming more common. Estimates show that approximately 80 per cent of wagers for the NBA and other sport entities are made online (Legal Sports Report, 2020). There are, of course, both pros and cons to sport betting. On the pro side, people find betting exciting and alluring with the potential to win cash fast. On the other hand, the downsides of gambling addiction and its impact on families is well documented, and organizations exist to help those who may find themselves to be compulsive gamblers (Gamblers Anonymous, n.d.). This is an example of how elements in the active economy can have both downsides and upsides for a community.

Professional Services

As with many entities within the organized sport sector, the Pacers work closely with both national and local sponsors. The local relationships promote both the team as well as the local product. Examples of the marketing and sponsorship opportunities the Pacers make available include building signage (entry pavilion naming rights,

LED signage, arena fascia signage), game day opportunities (scoreboard promotions, radio broadcast spots, social media advertising and promotion, game day program), and logo rights and activation (rights to use Pacers logos in advertising) (NBA Media Ventures, 2020). While it is important to acknowledge that the Pacers connect with the league-wide NBA sponsors, it is worth noting some of the team's local/regional partnerships. These include grocery chains, law firms, and official radio partners (Sports Khabri, 2020).

The team also needs to enlist the support of legal services in order to work, negotiate and enforce the contracts with these sponsors as well as other entities. For example, numerous contracts exist with the city of Indianapolis and the state of Indiana for the Bankers Life Fieldhouse capital improvements agreed upon in 2019. On an everyday basis, the team will negotiate contracts with food vendors, cleaning companies, part-time employment agencies, security firms, and local police departments. All of these organizations play critical roles in game-day operations and their rights and responsibilities must be clearly defined.

Media and Content

While NBA games are broadcasted via their national and regional media partners, the local media benefit as well. For example, the Pacers name 26 television and 20 radio listings (NBA Media Ventures, 2020). This stretches their community reach beyond the Indianapolis area and into the wider state of Indiana. By bringing their games to people on the local level, the Pacers build community outreach as well as extend their fan base.

The information above only refers to traditional media, but this is not the only way people consume information about their favourite teams. The Pacers also have a major presence on social media platforms such as Twitter, Facebook and Instagram. This emergence of social media has enabled the opportunity to examine narratives created by everyday content contributors, rather than just the traditional media (Hums, et al., 2020). A social media presence like this allows fans to frame and broadcast their ideas from the "bottom-up" as opposed to the "top-down" content creation seen on traditional media platforms (Hums, et al., 2020).

Apparel and Accessories

Local sporting goods stores often feature the hometown team's merchandise in their stores. In the city of Indianapolis, sporting goods retailers such as Dick's carry lines of Pacers' jerseys, t-shirts, hats, hoodies, and other team merchandise. While Dick's is a nationally based chain, local stores cater more to the local fans.

In addition to big-box retailers like Dick's, Banker's Life Fieldhouse, the home arena of the Pacers, also features a Pacers Team Store. This is common practice for major teams around the world and in all sports. Fans can visit the Team Store not only on game days, but on other days of the week as well. Team stores such as these cater to a variety of supporters, from people buying a holiday present for a friend or family member, casual fans who may just go to one game in a season, or full season ticket holders who get discounts when they shop at this location.

Equipment

For the purpose of the Indiana Pacers example, basketball equipment would be applicable. Statistics indicate wholesale sales of basketballs equaled $230 million, basketball hoops accounted for $181 million and other basketball accessories equalled $41 million (Statista, 2020). This trickles down to the grassroots level as well; since basketball is such a popular sport in the United States, people old and young like to get together and "shoot some hoops". Basketball hoops are a common addition to driveways and city parks where families, friends, and neighbours can connect, which in turn helps build a sense of community. In many places, including Indianapolis, COIVD-19 took a chunk out of pick-up basketball as Indy Parks closed the playgrounds and basketball courts for all of the 212 it operates, at least temporarily (Klein, 2020).

Tourism

Every year, many people plan trips to Indianapolis to see the Pacers play. In the process, a family may take a weekend to visit other local attractions such as the Children's Museum of Indianapolis, the Indianapolis Motor Speedway, or the NCAA Hall of Champions. If they want to have an outdoor activity, the White River State Park, billed as the United States' only cultural urban state park, offers green space and also cultural attractions (Visit Indy, 2020). In this way, the team promotes not only tourism but also health-related activities.

If people do come in for a weekend, there is then, of course, the need for accommodation and restaurants. All of these add to the value of the team in the community in terms of tourism. According to Indianapolis Mayor Greg Ballard,

...the Indiana Pacers and Indiana Fever [WNBA team] attract hundreds of thousands of people to Indy on an annual basis...Many downtown workers and businesses rely on those fans for their income. Amenities like professional sports, art, and museums make our community a more vibrant and attractive place to live and do business (Flynn, 2014, para. 8).

Design and Infrastructure

The landscape of the city of Indianapolis was enhanced by the presence of what is now called Bankers Life Fieldhouse. The Fieldhouse contributes significantly to the city's development and a major renovation was approved in 2019.

According to a study by the Indiana University Public Policy Institute:

...the economic impact of Pacers Sports & Entertainment, including events at Bankers Life Fieldhouse, totaled $370 million in 2018. Pacers Sports & Entertainment is also responsible for more than 4,000 jobs resulting in $152 million in annual wages. In 2017 Bankers Life Fieldhouse hosted 550-plus sporting and non-sporting events that generated 15 million in annual taxes (Indiana Pacers, 2019).

When the Fieldhouse opened back in 1999 under the name of Canseco Fieldhouse, it was designed as a "throw-back" style arena, which honoured the strong basketball traditions of the Pacers' home state of Indiana. Designed with basketball games as its primary event, the Fieldhouse incorporated historic looks such as those found in old-time high school or college facilities. This was accomplished while infusing all the latest amenities found in the most modern NBA arenas today. This blending of old and new helped connect the team to the local community.

In addition, sustainability is a priority at Bankers Life Fieldhouse. Some of their sustainability initiatives include cardboard recycling, aluminum can recycling, document shredding, and no use of plastic straws. They also established the Threes for Trees Program, which pledged to plant a tree for every three-point basket made during the season (Bankers Life Fieldhouse, 2020).

The Indiana Pacers are active in promoting recreational opportunities for young people in the Indianapolis community. Their Fit Like A Pro program helps children develop knowledge, attitudes and skills to lead a physically active and healthy lifestyle. The Pacers also participate in an annual NBA initiative, NBA Fit Week. With this program, Pacers' personnel join with community members and partners to offer free clinics to highlight the importance of healthy living. These free clinics provide boys and girls from the ages of 8 to 14 with the opportunity to improve their basketball skills and learn life lessons. Finally, the Jr. Pacers program presented by St. Vincent health systems offers basketball instruction for boys and girls taught by Pacers players and alumni (Indiana Pacers, 2020).

How the Organized Sport Sector Generates Tangible and Intangible Community Value

When beginning to examine the value chain of the organized sport sector, it is important to remember what Finch et al., (n.d.) discussed:

...Scholars and policymakers have long argued that community value extends far beyond the narrow scope of economics (King et. al., 2018; OECD, 2019) and this would also appear to apply to the active economy. Rather, the value of the active economy relates to the contribution it makes to the measurable priorities of a community (Kaplan & Norton, 2007). In other words, the active economy is a means to an end, not an end unto itself and thus the first step in deconstructing its value is the deconstruction of measurable community goals.

The active economy takes a multi-dimensional view of community wellbeing. The value added to the community by this sector can be broken down into four categories:

1. Economic
2. Social
3. Human
4. Environmental

This chapter has certainly presented numerous tangible measures of the economic value of the organized sport sector. The sector generates revenues through broadcast media, sponsorships, ticket sales, stadium/arena operations, and employment for people who work sporting events. In addition, the community is strengthened economically by tourism as people will visit a city to watch a sporting event and then spend money in the local economy on food, accommodations, and visiting local attractions. On the intangible side, spending money on facilities creates an image of a city being a "big-time" sports destination, which reflects positively on the community as a whole.

The organized sport sector contributes to social value as well. In a tangible sense, stadiums and arenas in many locations have ties to local government, often through contracts signed with a city or municipality which may deal with venue maintenance or local tax laws. Many more intangible social impacts are created by this sector, however. People identify with a hometown team oftentimes regardless of whether or not the team wins. Additionally, hosting a major event like a World Cup qualifier or the Olympic and Paralympic Games builds a sense of pride and connection. People in the United States are also attached to the university they attended and so will watch their varsity teams in person, via traditional broadcast, or on digital outlets. This sector creates numerous opportunities for social connections.

One measure of human value is mental health. Although for now, gatherings of fans at stadiums or sports bars may not be possible, these events provide opportunities for social interaction and sharing a common bond over a game or match or team. While intangible, sport spectatorship and the identity that accompanies it are good for people's mental health. During the COVID-19 pandemic, pundits have discussed how the lack of being able to socially gather in person (not on Zoom or other digital platforms) can have a deleterious effect on mental health. Once the worst of the COVID-19 pandemic passes, there is little doubt that scholars will begin to undertake studies assessing sports fans' levels of anxiety or depression before, during, and after competition shutdowns in an attempt to connect mental health with the cessation of being able to cheer on one's team. This could hopefully create some tangible data on the subject.

Tangible environmental value is established when sport managers in the organized sport sector take proactive stances in designing environmentally friendly venues and events. Recycling is a bare minimum here, however, it is a strong base from which to start. Designing environmentally sound venues would also include innovative ways to collect rainwater to use in the venue, tree planting initiatives, proper settings for lighting and sound, and even rooftop gardens with beehives. With the world reeling from climate change, taking these steps indicates to the community a commitment that extends beyond just winning games or matches. Knowing a local team is on board with fighting climate change is an intangible benefit to a community.

CONCLUSION

This chapter provided a brief overview of what the organized sport sector in the active economy looks like, how it interacts with other segments in the active economy and also highlighted various future considerations. At face value, it appears much of what this sector contributes relates to financial considerations. Upon further review, however, intangibles are prevalent as well.

It is crucial for participants in this sector to understand the rapid changes that are occurring and the ways in which they can best manage, prepare for and even get ahead of them. This will require a greater level of connection, innovation, and resiliency (Wolff, et al., 2020). Realizing their roles in the active economy will help sport managers to make the right decisions as they move forward as key contributors in the organized sport sector.

REFERENCES

American Physical Society. (2004). Butterflies, tornadoes, and time travel. *APS*. https://www.aps.org/publications/apsnews/200406/butterfly-effect.cfmrlTTJASVimLiZ0o

Badenhausen, K. (2020, July 31). The world's most valuable sports teams 2020. *Forbes*. https://www.forbes.com/sites/kurtbadenhausen/2020/07/31/the-worlds-most-valuable-sports-teams-2020/?sh=29fc03093c74

Bankers Life Fieldhouse. (2020). Sustainability. *Bankers Life Fieldhouse*. https://www.bankerslifefieldhouse.com/sustainability

BBC. (2019, October 16). Tokyo 2020: Olympic marathon and race walks set to move to Sapporo over heat fears. *BBC*. https://www.bbc.com/sport/olympics/50069413

Branhorst, C. (2020, March 20). COVID-19 impact: Sports and entertainment. *University of South Carolina*. https://www.sc.edu/uofsc/posts/2020/03/COVID-19_19_impact_regan_watanabe.php#.X-dPHelKh3k

Chelladurai, P. (2009). *Managing organizations for sport and physical activity: A systems perspective* (3rd ed.). Holcomb Hathaway.

Christovich, A. (2020, September 18). Layoffs sweep college athletic departments nationwide. *Front Office Sports*. https://frontofficesports.com/layoffs-sweep-college-athletic-departments-nationwide/

Cobb, D., Kercheval, B., & Sallee, B. (2020). College football schedule 2020: The 139 games already postponed or canceled due to COVID-19. *CBS Sports*. https://www.cbssports.com/college-football/news/college-football-schedule-2020-the-139-games-already-postponed-or-canceled-due-to-COVID-19

Draper, K. (2020, November 19). M.L.S layoffs cut league staffs by 20 per cent. *New York Times*. https://www.nytimes.com/2020/11/19/sports/soccer/mls-layoffs.html

ESPN. (2020, May 1). Sudden vanishing of sports due to coronavirus will cost at least $12 billion, experts say. *ESPN*. https://www.espn.com/espn/otl/story/_/id/29110487/sudden-vanishing-sports-due-coronavirus-cost-least-12-billion-analysis-says

Finch, D., Legg, D., O'Reilley, N., Ribeiro, J., & Tombe, T. (n.d.). *The active economy: Exploring the systematic value of sports, recreation and health & wellness*. ActiveCITY Collective.

Flynn, J. (2014, April 10). Pacers agree to stay in Indianapolis for $160 million in costs and arena upgrades. *Bleacher Report*. https://bleacherreport.com/articles/2025148-pacers-agree-to-stay-in-indianapolis-for-160m-in-costs-and-arena-upgrades

Friedman, T. (2017, August 2). Climate shifts aren't limited to the weather. *New York Times.* https://www.nytimes.com/2017/08/02/opinion/climate-change-technology-globalization-china.html

Gamblers Anonymous. (n.d.). About us. *Gamblers Anonymous.* http://www.gamblersanonymous.org/ga/content/about-us

Gillen, N. (2020, November 29). Tokyo 2020 estimate puts cost of Games postponement at $1.9 billion. *Inside the Games.* https://www.insidethegames.biz/articles/1101369/tokyo-2020-

Greenspan, R. (2020, January 24.) High-fiving robots are going to be very busy helpers at the 2020 Olympics. Here's everything they can do. *Time.* https://time.com/5763785/robots-2020-olympics/

Grimes, W. (2005, December 14). The gladiators: History's most dangerous sport. *New York Times.* https://www.nytimes.com/2005/12/14/style/the-gladiators-historys-most-dangerous-sport.html

Hums, M. A., Frederick, E., Pegararo, A., Siegfried, N., & Wolff, E. A. (2020a). What's in a name? Examining reactions to Major League Baseball's change from the Disabled List to the Injured List via Twitter. *Baseball Research Journal, 49*(2), 22–32.

Hums, M. A., & MacLean, J. C. (2019). *Governance and policy in sport organizations* (4th ed.). Routledge.

Hums, M. A., Wolff, E. A., & Siegfried, N. (2020, June 23). Making a case for athlete advocacy: Humanitarians, Olympism, and good governance. *Play the Game.* https://www.playthegame.org/news/comments/2020/1006_making-a-case-for-athlete-advocacy-humanitarians-olympism-and-good-governance/

Indiana Pacers. (2019, April 12). CIB approves new 25-year agreement with Pacers Sports Entertainment. *Indiana Pacers.* https://www.nba.com/pacers/news/cib-approves-new-25-year-agreement-pacers-sports-entertainment

Indiana Pacers. (2020). Community relations – Health and wellness. *Indiana Pacers.* https://www.nba.com/pacers/community-relations-health-and-wellness

IOC. (2017). Beijing launches global recruitment programme for volunteers. *IOC.* https://www.olympic.org/news/beijing-2022-launches-global-recruitment-programme-for-games-volunteers

IOC. (2020a). How the IOC funds a better world through sport. *IOC.* https://www.olympic.org/funding

IOC. (2020b). Olympic marketing fact file 2020. *IOC.* https://stillmed.olympic.org/media/Document%20Library/OlympicOrg/Documents/IOC-Marketing-and-Broadcasting-General-Files/Olympic-Marketing-Fact-File.pdf

Kaplan, R. S., & Norton, D. P. (2007). Using the balanced scorecard as a strategic management system. *Harvard Business Review, 85*, 7–8.

King, A., Huseynli, G., & MacGibbon, N. (2018). *Wellbeing frameworks for the Treasury*. New Zealand Treasury.

Klein, D. (2020, March 31). Indy Parks playgrounds, sport courts closed to enforce social distancing. *WISH-TV.* https://www.wishtv.com/news/local-news/indy-parks-playgrounds-sports-courts-closed-to-enforce-social-distancing/

Legal Sports Report. (2020). NBA betting 2020. *Legal Sports Report.* https://www.legalsportsreport.com/sports-betting/nba/

Mercedes Benz Stadium. (2020). Health and safety protocols. *Mercedes Benz Stadium.* https://mercedesbenzstadium.com/health-safety/

Minnesota Public Radio. (2020). College athletic departments cut pay, staff, and teams because of COVID-19. *Minnesota Public Radio.* https://www.marketplace.org/2020/10/19/college-athletics-departments-cut-pay-staff-and-teams-because-of-covid/

Morgan, J. P. (2020, May 1). Media consumption in the age of COVID-19. *JP Morgan*. https://www.jpmorgan.com/insights/research/media-consumption

Murfree, J. R., & Moorman, A. M. (2020, May). *An examination and analysis of Division I football game contracts: Legal implications of game cancellations due to extreme weather events* [Conference session]. North American Society for Sport Management Conference, San Diego, CA.

NBA Media Ventures. (2020). Local TV and radio listings. *National Basketball Association.* https://www.nba.com/pacers/2020-21-local-tv-and-radio-listings

NBA Media Ventures. (2020). Sponsorships. *National Basketball Association.* https://www.nba.com/pacers/team-sponsorships

NCAA. (n.d.). Finances of intercollegiate athletics. *NCAA*. https://www.ncaa.org/about/resources/research/finances-intercollegiate-athletics

OECD. (2019). Better Life Index. *OECD*. http://www.oecdbetterlifeindex.org/#/11111111111

Peter, J., Schad, T., & Zillgit, J. (2020, November 13). How sports arenas ran up score on 2020 election, hosting hundreds of thousands of voters. *USA Today.* https://www.usatoday.com/story/sports/2020/11/13/how-sports-arenas-ran-up-score-election-thousands-voters/6175568002/

Randjelovic, D. (2020, June 3). 11 most profitable sports leagues: Their values will surprise you. *Athletic Panda.* https://apsportseditors.org/others/most-profitable-sports-leagues/

Randle, A. (2020, December 23). The insanity, and social necessity, of sports this year. *New York Times.* https://www.nytimes.com/2020/12/23/opinion/COVID-19-sports-nfl.html

Reuters. (2020, June 12). Commonwealth Games: Athletes to be allowed to take a knee in protest, says Games chief. *Reuters.* https://www.reuters.com/?edition-redirect=br

Sports Khabri. (2020). Sponsorship deals of Indiana Pacers. *Sports Khabri.* https://sportskhabri.com/sponsorship-deals-of-indiana-pacers/

Statista. (2020). Basketball sports equipment wholesale sales in US from 2007-2019 (in millions). *Statista.* https://www.statista.com/statistics/258582/basketball-sports-equipment-wholesale-sales-in-the-us/#:~:text=In%202019%2C%20wholesale%20sales%20of,about%20181.2%20million%20U.S.%20dollars

Stieg, C. (2020, July 23). Sports fans have higher self-esteem and are more satisfied with their lives (whether their teams win or lose). *CNBC.* https://www.cnbc.com/2020/07/23/why-being-a-sports-fan-and-rooting-for-a-team-is-good-for-you.html

Visit Indy. (2020). White River State Park. *Visit Indy.* https://www.visitindy.com/indianapolis-white-river-state-park?utm_source=visitindy

Washington Center for Equitable Growth. (2020). How the coronavirus recession is impacting part-time US workers. *Washington Center for Equitable Growth.* https://equitablegrowth.org/how-the-coronavirus-recession-is-impacting-part-time-u-s-workers/

Wolff, E. A., & Hums, M. A. (2020, May 12). The pillars of connection, innovation, and resiliency in and through sport. *Peace and sport.* https://www.peace-sport.org/opinion/the-pillars-of-connection-innovation-and-resilience-in-and-through-sport/

Chapter 5
Active Recreation in an Active Economy

Brian Torrance
Ever Active Schools, Canada

ABSTRACT

Active recreation is defined as activities engaged in for the purpose of relaxation, health and wellbeing, or enjoyment with the primary activity requiring physical exertion. They are often spontaneous in nature and participant-led, with a low level of organization and limited structure. Active recreation has significant links to health and wellbeing and provides its greatest value when it is shared with all citizens.

ACTIVE RECREATION

Active recreation is defined as activities engaged in for the purpose of relaxation, health and wellbeing or enjoyment with the primary activity requiring physical exertion. It is often spontaneous in nature and participant-led, with a low level of organization and limited structure. For clarity, we have taken a broad view of active recreation and have additionally explored the areas of community sport, physical activity, and recreation activities. Throughout this chapter, we will highlight where active recreation lives within our lives, its importance, and the grand need for an increased societal value of active recreation investments.

DOI: 10.4018/978-1-7998-7939-8.ch005

Active Recreation and Health

Active recreation has traditionally been associated with leisure time. However, as numerous studies have indicated, active recreation is also a driver of good health. Rather than viewing active recreation as something optional or as an extra-curricular activity that people engage in during their free time, active recreation should be understood and re-imagined as an essential driver of health and wellbeing for both the individual and the community.

As an example, there is a direct correlation between increased physical activity and reduced risk for chronic diseases as well as some types of cancer. Physical activity reduces the probability of developing Type 2 Diabetes by 43 per cent, hypertension by 26 per cent, and osteoporosis by 36 per cent (Janssen, 2012). Other benefits include reduced risk for Alzheimers Disease. A 2017 study exploring active commuting also found that cycling to work (compared with commuting by car or public transit) is associated with a 45 per cent lower risk of developing cancer and a 46 per cent lower risk of developing heart disease (Celis-Morales et al, 2017).

Beyond the prevention of chronic disease, active recreation also contributes to building stronger self-efficacy, confidence, quality of life and life satisfaction. Active recreation also ignites positive memories of family outings, community, and social bonds.

It would seem clear then that to support good health, active recreation is essential. People need to move more and reduce sedentary activities such as sitting and working in front of a computer, watching television, or driving or riding in a car. The Canadian Physical Activity Guidelines recommend that adults engage in a minimum of 150 minutes of moderate-to-vigorous physical activity per week and should minimize the amount of sitting time, in order to maximize health benefits. But according to ParticipACTION's Report Card on Physical Activity for Adults, only 16 per cent of adults in Canada are active enough to reap these health benefits (ParticipACTION, 2019).

When people are physically inactive, they are at a greater risk of chronic disease such as many of those discussed earlier. "Physical inactivity is a modifiable risk factor for cardiovascular disease and a widening variety of other chronic diseases, including diabetes mellitus, cancer (colon and breast), obesity, hypertension, bone and joint diseases (osteoporosis and osteoarthritis), and depression." (Warburton, Nicol, Bredin, 2006). A 2016 Statistics Canada report estimates a sedentary lifestyle reduces life expectancy by 3.8 years. (Public Health Agency of Canada, 2016), and it is estimated that one in ten premature deaths among Canadian adults aged 20 to 64 are related to obesity and a sedentary lifestyle (Obesity Canada, 2020).

While there are numerous empirical studies establishing the correlation between increased physical health and participation in physical activity, there is less known about how physical activity contributes to increased mental health. These is evidence, however, to demonstrate that participating in physical activity has positive impacts on anxiety, depression, mood, emotion, self-esteem, and psychological dysfunction (Fox et. al., 1999). According to a joint study by the Chief Medical Officers of the UK Home Countries, physical activity can reduce the risk of depression and dementia by 20-30 per cent. This study also showed that physical activity can increase psychological wellbeing, by increasing self-esteem and self-perception, mood, and sleep quality and by reducing levels of anxiety and fatigue. (Department of Health, Physical Activity, Health Improvement and Protection. (2011). Several studies have also concluded that older senior women have found their overall quality of life has improved with physical activity, and leads to more positive moods, reduced anxiety, improved social functioning and increased life satisfaction (Chodzko-Zajko,, 1998).

Within children and youth, research has also demonstrated those who participate in sport achieve higher academic results and stay in school longer. Participation in sport for instance has contributed to improved peer relationships, increased happiness and self confidence for children diagnosed with ADHD (National Recreation and Park Association, N.D.). There is also a high correlation between regular participation in sport as children and higher lifetime earnings (Ahn & Fedewa, 2011).

These are just some of the benefits that are derived from participating in physical activity and active recreation. With such strong outcomes, it's time to position active recreation as an important and necessary driver of health and wellbeing in education, workplaces, and the community, rather than viewing it a "nice to have," optional, or something only for those living a luxurious lifestyle.

A NEED FOR VALUE

The value from what has already been presented seems obvious but society has not valued or invested in recreation as compared to other services. Public libraries are a good example of a publicly funded service that has none to small financial barriers, is inclusive and accessible to all. Since literacy is valued and considered essential in our society, municipal and provincial governments invest in libraries. Compared to Active Recreation, in Canada, hockey costs an average of $1666 annually per child according to a 2014 report on Canadian Youth Sports (Wong, 2020). With rising costs of equipment, registration, and indoor ice, there is an unfortunate result that the game is no longer financially viable for all. From a February 2020 interview with the New York Times, a long-time NHL player Joe Thornton stated, "The cost is extremely high and it's not really manageable for most working-class families to afford to put their kids in hockey. Never mind if they had two kids or three kids that wanted to play the sport" (Lajoie and Valji, 2020).

Hockey is one example but an important one to cultural and national identity particularly in Canada. Other active recreation activities face similar financial challenges, such as cost-heavy sports including equestrian which has an average of \$1,434 annually and skiing at \$2,028 annually (Wong, 2020).

On the opposite side is the economic benefit of participation. It was estimated that the average Canadian household spends just under \$4000 on sport and leisure. On the savings side, Jansen (2012) found that the estimated direct, indirect, and total health care costs of physical inactivity in Canada in 2009 were \$2.4 billion, \$4.3 billion, and \$6.8 billion, respectively. These values represented 3.8%, 3.6%, and 3.7 per cent of the overall health care costs.

ENHANCING ACCESS FOR ACTIVE RECREATION

Unlike other services which are free and accessible to all, active recreation and sports are usually only available to those who pay and for many people, the cost of participating has become prohibitive. Dr. Nick Holt, a professor in the Faculty of Kinesiology, Sport and Recreation at the University of Alberta has conducted many youth participation studies and suggests that "the majority of youth sport participants in Canada tend to come from middle class, upper-income families… usually Caucasian kids" (Wong, 2020).

While many jurisdictions provide subsidies for recreational programs for low-income people, ongoing participation is not guaranteed. For example, the Canadian Fitness and Lifestyle Research Institute conducted a survey of Canadian municipalities in 2015 which examined their use of financial programs to support families to participate in physical activity and sport when cost was a barrier. Almost two-thirds (63%) of municipal administrators (in communities of at least 1,000 residents) reported their municipality promotes or uses external financial programs in order to assist families to participate in physical activity or sports. The survey also found that 66 per cent of municipalities offered children a subsidy, 60 per cent for seniors, 59 per cent for families, 45 per cent for individuals with lower incomes and 26 per cent for individuals with disabilities.

Often when municipality budgets are facing challenging times, which is certainly happening post pandemic, recreation is an area that is often reduced. (Smith & Doherty, 2019). Children from low-income families are more likely to be physically inactive and engage in sedentary pursuits compared to children from middle and high-income families (Spence et al, 2010). Adults with low incomes also tend to experience more health-related problems than those in higher income brackets. "Low income is associated with a disproportionate number of special problems." (Ross et al., 2000). Social activities that reduce isolation while improving physical activity and community support are all vehicles which support better health. Collective strategies are needed to ensure equitable opportunities and health for all.

These social inequities have also increased over the last 25 years, creating a widening gap between those that can participate and those that cannot. As new sport and recreation plans, and programs are launched post COVID-19, specific attention and strategy should go to addressing these inequities. Cleary, there is a tremendous need for subsidies for recreation programs to ensure that many low-income families, gain access to such programs. Like other vital services, which are universally accessible in many countries, active recreation programs and services should be accessible and available to all.

THE ECOSYSTEM OF ACTIVE RECREATION

Active recreation can potentially play a more significant role in developing a healthier population, while at the same time, reducing healthcare costs, but not without increased policy development and funding from all levels of government.

Active recreation is made up of national organizations, provincial organizations, municipal departments, and non-profit organizations. Having existing and well-established municipal, provincial, and national platforms for organizations, leaders, and non-profits to meet and share practices regularly ca creats a culture of partnership-building and knowledge-sharing. When functioning well, this culture can enable the ecosystem to collaborate and improve the capacity of all partners and lay a foundation for a collective voice, advocacy, and better future opportunities. Partnerships with the health and social sector also help elevate active recreation to a more prominent and important role.

SUCCESS STORIES

Schools are the ideal place to address health priorities, engage youth in healthy behaviors and provide a positive social environment. Schools can play a central role in all communities and are among the most influential in developing long-standing health behaviours, life skills, and self-esteem (International Union for Health Promotion and Education, 2010). Healthy school environments can also give youth a sense of belonging and provide shelter and comfort that may not be available at home. Additionally, school environments can offer a level playing field, regardless of socioeconomic status, culture, ethnicity, and other demographic factors (St Leger, 1999).

Schools that have addressed health and wellness and key priorities such as physical activity successfully have used a comprehensive school health approach (CSH). This is an internationally recognized approach to supporting improvements in students' educational outcomes while addressing school health in a planned, integrated, and holistic way. Schools adopt a CSH approach that addresses priorities of healthy eating, physical activity, and positive mental health. In the classroom, CSH facilitates improved academic achievement and leads to fewer behavioural problems. In the broader school environment, it helps students develop the skills, autonomy, and competencies they need to be mentally and emotionally healthy for life (Pan-Canadian Joint Consortium for School Health).

Highlighting School Based Programs That are Inclusive to all

School Sport and Active Recreation has strength within our school system with numerous benefits including academic, fitness, teamwork, cooperation, social skills and more. However, many students are not able to access positive benefits as they are either "cut" or lose interest in the activity. Specifically, within Middle Schools, the school sport model is not equipped to encourage and foster participation at this incredibly important age of opportunity and development. Schools often lack the best facilities and trained coaches, and sports tend to cater to financially stable families who can afford to put their children in sports outside of the school, and those who can reliably get their kids to and from events. The students who play competitively have more opportunity to develop as athletes in quality facilities with trained coaches, therefore making them better competitors and the ones chosen to play on the school teams. It's a reality that leaves many students behind.

The Power of Active Recreation in Indigenous Communities

Active Recreation and Sport is a powerful mechanism for social impact, community engagement, cultural pride, and self-worth. Participation in school sport and recreation activities has been connected to educational benefits, creating a strong sense of belonging and student attendance and likelihood of attending post-secondary institutions. Within Indigenous communities, active recreation is a way of life and has brought a strong connection to land and culture, including running, cross country skiing, tracking wild game and dancing.

ACTIVE RECREATION THROUGHOUT COVID-19

The longtail or legacy of COVID-19 may be an increased awareness and understanding of the value of active recreation. Municipalities have opened roadways for active travel, people have actively used parks in record numbers and the organized activities that were allowed to proceed went ahead with record participation. COVID-19 has thus changed physical activity levels and also types of recreational activities that people are participating in. Evidence from Garmin suggests that people were altering their typical physical activity with those that can be done at home with minimal equipment. Organized sport and team activities have been replaced with virtual cycling and indoor workouts to maintain and exceed physical activity levels prior to the pandemic (Garmin, 2020). Further, outdoor, and naturally social distanced activities such as golf and cross-country skiing have seen record numbers of participants, and municipalities have scrambled to make them more accessible.

While for some, there has been an increase in some types of physical activity during the pandemic, a recent study has found that children and youth may not be exercising enough. For example, a national sample of Canadian parents (n=1472) of children (5-11 years) or youth (12-17 years) (54 per cent girls) completed an online survey that assessed immediate changes in child movement and play behaviours during the COVID-19 outbreak. The study examined physical activity, sedentary behaviour, and sleep and found that only 4.8 per cent (2.8 per cent girls, 6.5 per cent boys) of children and 0.6 per cent (0.8 per cent girls, 0.5 per cent boys) of youth were meeting combined behaviour guidelines during COVID-19 restrictions. Children and youth also had less outside time and more sleep during the outbreak. Parental encouragement and support, parental engagement in Physical Activity, and family dog ownership were positively associated with healthy movement behaviors. Although families spent less time in PA and more time in SB, several parents further reported adopting new hobbies or accessing new resources (Moore et al., 2020).

According to the Canadian 24-Hour Movement Guidelines for Children and Youth, each child and youth should engage in 60 minutes of moderate to vigorous activity every day, with several hours of structured and unstructured light physical activity. Each child and youth should also sleep uninterrupted for 9 to 11 hours per day, with no more than two hours per day of sedentary behaviour including screen time. Finally, there should be limited sitting for extended periods of time (Canadian Society for Exercise Physiology, n.d.). When compared with other studies conducted before the pandemic, fewer children, and youth (2.6 percent) are now meeting the Canadian 24-Hour Movement Behaviour Guidelines.

CONCLUSION

Active Recreation are activities engaged in for the purpose of relaxation, health and wellbeing or enjoyment with the primary activity requiring physical exertion. They are often spontaneous in nature and participant led, with a low level of organization and limited structure. Active Recreation has significant and important links to health and wellbeing and provides important value, but it is also important to ensure that this is shared with all citizens. Active recreation has traditionally been associated with leisure time, however, as numerous studies have indicated active recreation is also a driver of good health. Rather than viewing active recreation as something optional or an extra-curricular activity that people engage in during free time, it needs to be understood and re-imagined as an essential driver of personal and community health and wellbeing.

REFERENCES

*Active*CITY Collective. (2020). *Playbook 2030: A guide to Building Canada's Most Liveable Region.* Retrieved from: https://www.activecityproject.org/

Ahn, S., & Fedewa, A. L. (2011). A meta-analysis of the relationship between children's physical activity and mental health. *Journal of Pediatric Psychology, 36*(4), 385–397. doi:10.1093/jpepsy/jsq107 PMID:21227908

Canadian Fitness and Lifestyle Research Institute. (2015). *Municipal Opportunities for Physical Activity: 2015 Survey of Physical Activity Opportunities in Canadian Communities.* Retrieved from:https://cflri.ca/sites/default/files/node/1578/files/2015%20Municipalities%20Bulletin%2012%20Financial%20assistance%20to%20support%20physical%20activity.pdf

Canadian Society for Exercise Physiology. (n.d.). *Canadian 24-Hour Movement Guidelines for Children and Youth.* Retrieved from: https://csepguidelines.ca/wp-content/themes/csep2017/pdf/Canadian24HourMovementGuidelines2016_2.pdf

Canadian Society for Exercise Physiology. (n.d.). *Canadian 24-Hour Movement Guidelines for Adults Aged 18-64 Years.* Retrieved from: www.csepguidelines.ca

Celis-Morales, C. A., Lyall, D. M., Welsh, P., Anderson, J., Steell, L., Guo, Y., Maldonado, R., Mackay, D. F., Pell, J. P., Sattar, N., & Gill, J. M. R. (2017). Association between active commuting and incident cardiovascular disease, cancer, and mortality: Prospective cohort study. *BMJ (Clinical Research Ed.), 357*, j1456. doi:10.1136/bmj.j1456 PMID:28424154

Chodzko-Zajko, W. J. (1998). Physical activity and aging: implications for health and quality of life in older persons. *President's Council on Physical Fitness and Sports Research Digest, 3*(4).

Department of Health, Physical Activity, Health Improvement and Protection. (2011, July). *Start active, stay active: A report on physical activity from the four home countries' Chief Medical Officers*. Retrieved from: https://assets.publishing.service.gov.uk/government/uploads/system/uploads/attachment_data/file/830943/withdrawn_dh_128210.pdf

Garmin. (2020). *Are we still moving?* Available at: https://www.garmin.com/en-US/blog/general/the-effect-of-the-global-pandemic-on-active-lifestyles

International Union for Health Promotion and Education. (2010). *Promoting Health in School from Evidence to Action*. Retrieved from: https://www.iuhpe.org/index.php/en/iuhpe-thematic-resources/298-on-school-health

Janssen, I. (2012). Healthcare costs of physical inactivity in Canadian adults. *Applied Physiology, Nutrition, and Metabolism, 37*(4), 803–806. doi:10.1139/h2012-061 PMID:22667697

Moore, S. A., Faulkner, G., Rhodes, R. E., Brussoni, M., Chulak-Bozzer, T., Ferguson, L. J., Mitra, R., O'Reilly, N., Spence, J. C., Vanderloo, L. M., & Tremblay, M. S. (2020). Impact of the COVID-19 virus outbreak on movement and play behaviours of Canadian children and youth: A national survey. *The International Journal of Behavioral Nutrition and Physical Activity, 17*(1), 1–11. doi:10.118612966-020-00987-8 PMID:32631350

National Recreation and Park Association. (n.d.). *Synopsis of 2010 research papers: The key benefits*. Retrieved from: https://www.nrpa.org/uploadedFiles/nrpa.org/Publications_and_Research/Research/Papers/Synopsis-of-Research-Papers.pdf

Obesity Canada. (2020). *Obesity in Canada*. Retrieved from: https://obesitycanada.ca/obesity-in-canada/#:~:text=Asper cent20a per cent20leading per cent20cause per cent20of,is per cent20directly per cent20attributable per cent20to per cent20obesity

ParticipACTION. (2019). *Better with Age: Move More Today for a Healthier Tomorrow, ParticipAction Report Card on Physical Activity for Adults*. Retrieved from: https://www.participaction.com/en-ca/resources/adult-report-card

Public Health Agency of Canada. (2016, December). *How healthy are Canadians? A trend analysis of the health of Canadians from a healthy living and chronic disease perspective*. Retrieved from: https://www.canada.ca/content/dam/phacaspc/documents/services/publications/healthy-living/how-healthy-canadians/pub1-eng.pdf

Ross, P. D. (2000). *The Canadian Fact Book on Poverty*. The Canadian Council on Social Development.

Smith, M., & Doherty, B. (2019). Here's everything you need to know about Calgary's $60 million budget haircut. *Star Calgary*. Retrieved from https://www.thestar.com/calgary/2019/07/24/heres-everything-you-need-to-know-about-calgarys-60-million-budget-haircut.html

Solutions Research Group Consultants Inc. (2014, June 10). *Massive Competition in Pursuit of the $5.7 Billion Canadian Youth Sports Market*. Retrieved from http://www.srgnet.com/2014/06/10/massive-competition-in-pursuit-of-the-5-7-billion-canadian-youth-sports-market/

St Leger, L. H. (1999). The opportunities and effectiveness of the health promoting primary school in improving child health—A review of the claims and evidence. *Health Education Research*, *14*(1), 51–69. doi:10.1093/her/14.1.51 PMID:10537947

Street, G., & Ray, J. (2007). *The Relationship between Organized Recreational Activity and Mental Health*. Centre for Behavioural Research in Cancer Control, Curtin University.

Warburton, D. E. R., Nicol, C. W., & Bredin, S. S. D. (2006). Health benefits of physical activity: The evidence. *Canadian Medical Association Journal*, *174*(6), 801–809. doi:10.1503/cmaj.051351 PMID:16534088

Wong, M. (2020, March 26). *'Out of the question': How the cost of sports excludes low-income kids*. Retrieved from https://theeyeopener.com/2020/03/out-of-the-question-how-the-cost-of-sports-excludes-low-income-kids/

Chapter 6
Health and Wellness in an Active Economy:
An Action Study

Cynthia Watson
VIVO for Healthier Generations, Canada

Tracey Martin
VIVO for Healthier Generations, Canada

ABSTRACT

There are two approaches to health and wellness that are explored throughout this chapter. The first is a socio-ecological response, where the recreation system has been focused on changing individual behaviour at the programmatic level. There is the realization that if programs were the single answer, then all the world's problems would be solved by now. What is needed is a much larger systemic response. The second approach relates to the co-creation of authentic and customized health and wellness solutions. Typically, the notion of health and wellness is viewed through the lens of the "expert" and a prescription model that is grounded in "the expert knows what is best for you." The emerging model is one where the citizen is at the centre of the solution process. People desire the ability to feel more in control and make informed decisions about their health for themselves and their families. In this chapter, the authors explore this topic by reviewing a Canadian health and wellness action study.

DOI: 10.4018/978-1-7998-7939-8.ch006

INTRODUCTION

Health and wellness within the global context of the active economy is significant and has multiple roles. It is defined as the health and wellness products and services supporting the delivery or engagement in organized sport or active recreation. Examples include the government supported health industries or those that are providing medical support and technology from within the private sector. Other examples would include organizations that focus on healthy eating, nutrition, workplace wellness and traditional and complementary medicine. Other examples could include health and wellness products, the fitness industry and wellness real-estate.

In this chapter, the authors, who are leaders for a charitable organization in a diverse sector of Canada's 4th largest city, will interpret how this sector is represented at the micro level. Before doing that, however, it is important as with all stakeholders within the active economy to understand where they fit within larger contexts. As one example, the Canadian Parks and Recreation Association's (CPRA) *Pathways to Well-being* has called for the national recreation sector to shift its focus from facility operations to building individual and community capacity for healthy, active living. According to the report, "our opportunity is to identify concrete ways to work together that enable all people in Canada to enjoy recreation in supportive physical and social environments" (2014).

Canada's public recreation sector is a key driver in developing solutions to the health and wellness challenges the nation faces. In part, this is because of the whole recreation infrastructure that already exists across cities, municipalities, and other political jurisdictions that can address disease-prevention health and well-being systems. Armed with that knowledge, the sport and recreation sector are now challenged to develop practical, evidence-informed solutions to make a positive impact and perhaps merge into the health and well-being sector.

The health and wellness sector as represented by recreation can and must do more to address the needs of communities; there are two approaches that will be explored throughout this chapter:

1. Socio-ecological Response

The recreation system has been focused on changing individual behaviour at the programmatic level. There is the realization that if programs were the single answer, then all the world's problems would be solved by now. We probably do not need more programs; we need a systemic response to focus on health and wellness throughout the recreation sector.

2. Co-Creation of Authentic and Customized Health and Wellness Solutions

Typically, the notion of health and wellness is viewed through the lens of the "expert", a prescription model that is grounded in "we know what is best for you". The emerging model is one where the citizen is at the centre of the solution process and the entire health and wellness system needs to consider this paradigm shift. People desire to be and feel more in control and make informed decisions about their health and wellness for themselves and their families.

The co-creative approach is iterative, ongoing, and based on the individual person; one size does not fit all. People will explore and incorporate different cultural health and wellness practices to customize solutions that suit their lifestyle, values, and beliefs. For example, there is more and more demand for natural, organic, chemical free, ethically sourced materials. As the digital economy expands into the hands of all generations, data and evidence driven decisions will also be more prevalent in helping customize experiences.

BACKGROUND

To help us understand the connection between recreation and the health and wellness industry we use an action study focusing on a charity operating a recreation centre. More specifically, we have provided eight action studies that help to show the connection between recreation and the health and wellness element within the active economy.

Vivo for Healthier Generations is in Calgary, Alberta, Canada and is a charity with a vision for world where individuals and communities ignite change to shape healthier generations. Our Research & Innovation Lab and Centre for Community Well-being, Recreation and Sport are platforms to inspire a healthy life.

The population in the surrounding communities has grown from 79,544 in 2004 to over 132, 204 in 2017 with projections of +190,000 by 2030. 25 per cent of residents are under the age of 19. It is a community composed of many cultures and backgrounds where one in two residents are black, indigenous or a person of color and nearly 40 per cent of residents have immigrated to Canada. The socio-economic and demographic make-up of the community has been said to reflect what Canada is becoming over the next 25 years.

This action study was thought to be appropriate for this chapter as it is a good test bed to prototype the evolution of a disease-prevention, health, and well-being system in other comparable locales. The Research & Innovation Lab at Vivo was launched in 2011 and began asking the community what healthy living meant to them and how all players from across an ecosystem might play a role in raising healthier generations. In retrospect, this may have been a precursor to the notion of an active economy and its role in the social-environment, and human prosperity of a community.

Socio-Ecological Response

The recreation system has been focused on changing individual behaviour at the programmatic level but there is now the realization that if programs were the single answer, then all the world's problems would be solved by now. We probably do not need more programs; we need a systemic response.

In the socio-ecological model, change is looked at more holistically. The socio-ecological model is well referenced in the chronic disease prevention and health promotion methodology. For Vivo, the notion of a socio-ecological model was first presented through a partnership with EverActive Schools and the comprehensive school health model (Figure 1).

The socio-ecological model creates a systemic view of how to create the biggest, sustainable impact for the health and wellness of the community.

The following principles apply in the Vivo socio-ecological approach to population well-being:

Programmatic

Programs help people create change at the individual level.

Social

Behaviour and lifestyle changes are more effective when social networks (friends, families, influences) support the change the individual wants to make.

Built Environment

Supportive environments reinforce health and wellness habits at home, work, school, and play. For example, if a student is learning about good eating habits at the school and then walks across the street to the recreation centre that has vending machines with unhealthy choices, then that negates the learning.

Figure 1. Comprehensive School Health Model

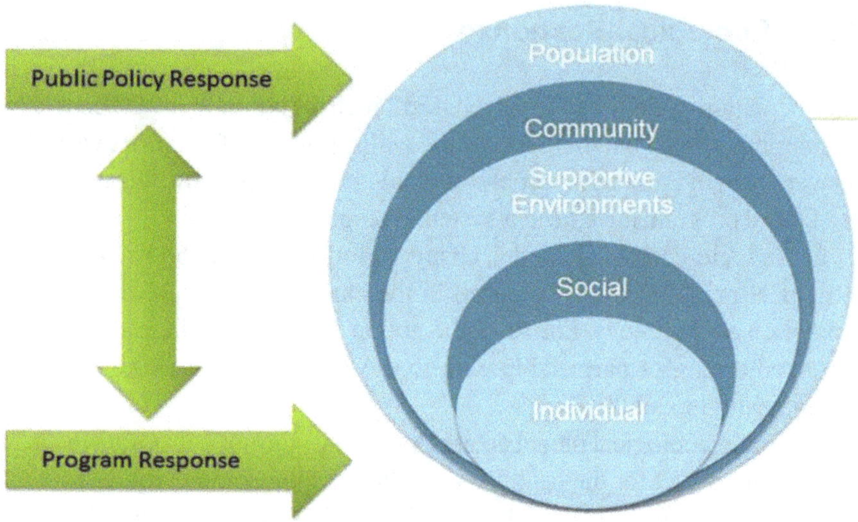

Community

Community-level change for health and wellness then happens when all the environments link together to create stronger, more vibrant communities – the community "wraps around" the individual versus the individual "flexing" to each community environment. For example, when looking at the 24-hour day of the child and all the environments that touch a child's life, instead of the child "role playing" as a brother, a student, a program participant, the environments support the child holistically.

Population

When community change happens, it results in public policy shifts that can help influence healthy living at a population level.

Clearly, no one organization can do this work alone. The key is to work with partners from across the ecosystem to wrap around the needs of the citizen versus the citizen having to work around the silos of organizations.

Knowledge into Action Study 1: *Calgary Adapted Hub – Powered by Jumpstart Project 2019- Ongoing*

During 2020, the Calgary Adapted Hub came together to inspire and empower a city where people living with disabilities belong and have access to diverse sport and recreation activities. The Calgary Adapted Hub is comprised of Calgary based organizations including Mount Royal University, Repsol Sport Centre, WinSport, Vivo, University of Calgary, and Sport Calgary. National partners include Canadian Tire Jumpstart and the Abilities Centre in Whitby, Ontario.

A Leading Equitable and Accessible Delivery (LEAD) baseline was conducted, and through this process the organizations collectively committed to implementing and measuring ten key themes listed in Table 1 around diversity and inclusion that apply to organizational leadership, strategy, systems, practices, and resources.

The project is in its' first year and the ecosystem approach is anticipated to create shifting, advocating, measuring, enhancing, and implementing the knowledge, participation and health of children and youth with disabilities by increasing the level of several key performance metrics that focus on health and wellness. These include:

- Children and youth with disabilities registered in the introduction to typical sport and recreation programs as well as trying more unstructured and community-level programs and initiatives.
- Open spaces accessible to children and youth with disabilities activated for unstructured and structured sport and play experiences.
- Sport programs and initiatives that achieve the quality sport experience standard.
- Children and youth with disabilities that identify an increased comfort level in exploring sport and lifestyle choices.
- Children and youth with disabilities meeting the daily moderate to vigorous activity guidelines because of each program or initiative.
- Children and youth with disabilities who agree they have easy access to places where they can be physically active.

The hope and vision for the Calgary Adapted Hub – Powered by Jumpstart is to ensure that children and youth living with disabilities can lead healthier lifestyles leading to greater overall wellness. The interconnections with the Hub and the health and wellness sector of the active economy are thus of the utmost importance.

Table 1. Action Study 1: Leading Equitable and Accessible Delivery

Key Themes	Improvement Ideas
Programmatic • Anecdotal evidence is mostly being used in organizations with few formal processes in place during the shaping and planning stages. • Surveys have been used to collect feedback retroactively to inform future iterations of programs. • There were few examples of engagement of people with disabilities in the development of an organization's strategy. • Organizations identified equipment purchases, programming, dedicated staff, and facility rentals prioritizing disability groups as ways resources have been allocated specifically to benefit people with disabilities. • Most organizations do not currently have a formal feedback system in place that is specific to people with disabilities.	• Consult with people during the planning phases of new projects like parent panels and focus groups. Undergo client feedback processes specific to components of facilities or programs (e.g., fitness equipment, layout of spaces, door-to-activity pathways/ wayfinding). • Approximately 25 per cent of the population identifies as having one or more disabilities, with an impact of 50 per cent of the population if you then include immediate family. By viewing accessibility and inclusion as a business-driven decision it becomes viewed less as a "nice to do" and more as "it's good business". • Explore ways to measure performance and participant outcomes and increase commitments to inclusion (via staffing, programming time review, actively seeking additional resources to increase the number of programs and their sustainability). • There are many opportunities to use technology to increase accessibility by facilitating discussions with other organizations about ideas or ways they have implemented technology to improve accessibility and offering low-tech alternatives where more accessible. • Carefully document what is happening, what is being learned, how people are learning about programs and whom they are passing the information to for the best communication pathways.
Social • Some organizations had more robust diversity and inclusion staff training and performance management practices than others.	• Review positions and opportunities for ease of accommodation, opportunities for job sharing that might make roles more accessible to people with disabilities. If targeting recruitment towards people with disabilities, ensure roles are meaningful, and equal to similar roles in the organization. • Incorporate disability specific training into general staff onboarding/ongoing training modules or in-service days like interacting with client and job accommodation requests. • Utilize recruiting agencies that can demonstrate they support people with disabilities seeking employment, and work with them to find candidates who fit the actual needs of the role (rather than the job description written for it).
Built Environment • All organizations seemed well positioned in terms of opportunities related to facilities, using space creatively, finding solutions to inaccessibility, and arranging program structures to maximize success. • Most organizations identified digital accessibility as an area for improvement.	• Be creative in terms of how impact is measured – social interaction, behavioural change, follow up with local groups after introduction are all important measures of success. Use testimonials to aid in your case for additional funding, participants, etc. Consider how the climate in Calgary can impact accessibility when making program and facility maintenance plans (as Canadians, snow is often the bane of wheelchair users' existence). • Prioritizing accessible parking spots and clearance to entrances and exits is always noticed. • Ensure you have emergency plans in place that consider people with disabilities. • Adopt accessible communications methods like accessible web space and social media related to enhancing the experience of people using screen reading technology, and availability of multiple versions or presentations of information (using video, PDF, Word, plain language summaries, even translation of videos to ASL in addition to closed captioning).
Community • Organizations identified their board and management as highly supportive of accessibility and inclusion initiatives *when they come up*. Frontline staff were identified as needing more support to feel comfortable accommodating participants with disabilities.	• Embed accessibility, inclusion and diversity in strategic plans and values statements, training, and target/goal setting. • Increase the diversity of voices and contribution are heard at the table – different lived experiences, identities, backgrounds planning and evaluating programs, renovations etc. • When measuring, consider the impact on individuals and at a systemic level, rather than just by counting numbers in terms of mental and physical health, connection to community, feelings of belongingness, and/or changes in competence and confidence.
Population • Most organizations identified a need to be more proactive and target mutual benefit with partners (e.g., a formal process to hold partners accountable to standards of inclusion). • Most organizations use universal targets or goals that are overarching and not specific to disability or population.	• Inventory and formalize memorandums with partners. Consider how partners are determined, whether there are levels or types of partnerships, how and by whom they are managed and what the costs and benefits may be. • Develop a strategy to initiate and influence services for people with disabilities. Formulate an engagement plan for working with diverse organizations and how to measure the impacts. • Formalize your accountability (e.g., targets related to programming, system influence, staff engagement/training, inclusion practices, etc.). • Create a matrix of disability-serving organizations and contacts in the City of Calgary to give a good idea of who might be appropriate future partners, locations for expansion of programming and people or groups who could inform future offerings. • By setting disability-specific or population-specific targets for impact, organizations can hold themselves accountable to being proactive and intentional about including people with disabilities

KNOWLEDGE INTO ACTION STUDY 2: CO-CREATION WITH COMMUNITY LEAD TO VIVO EXPANSION

Typically, the notion of health and wellness is viewed through the lens of the "expert", a prescription model that is grounded in "we know what is best for you". The emerging model now, however, is one where the citizen is at the centre of the solution process. In a practical perspective, Vivo, starting in 2011, has undertaken a longitudinal study of how the community describes what healthy living means to them and to help with expanding their current centre for community well-being, sport, and recreation (The Centre). The study was designed to listen to community members and organizations to understand the diverse needs of its rapidly growing and evolving community over the next 20 years and to ensure the expansion project meets community needs. This multi-level study included pre-design and post-design initiatives with over 150 individuals from small, medium, and large groups participating across all sectors such as community associations; cultural organizations; community services; business; education; innovation; health; design and partners; and sport and recreation (refer to Table 2).

Seven key themes that emerged from listening deeply to the community about their experiences and environments that they felt would help them live a healthier life included the following:

Empower Connections

The community's largest need was to increase social connections across generations and cultures to shift behaviors and attitudes towards healthy living.

Integration of East and West Philosophies

Based on local demographics, the direction was to be more inclusive, both in the built environment and programming to various cultural perspectives.

Spontaneous Active Play

Design spaces that encourage more play that is personally directed, intrinsically motivated, and culturally influenced.

Doing Different

Visibly show pioneering innovative spaces, programs and services that make a purposeful social and sustainable impact.

Table 2. Action Study 2: Study Results

Stakeholder Engagement	Key Messages from Community	Example
Pre-Design 2011-2013	• Help the community get connected: co-create more social vs. sport spaces. • Organizations need space to meet both formally and informally in small and large groups. • New and different types of spaces and experiences that are more than recreation and sport- multi-generational, eastern, and western philosophy based, spontaneous versus structured, community-led vs. facility-led opportunities, mind, body, and soul opportunities. • How can The Centre be more of an innovator and educator to help us create local solutions to issues we are facing in our homes, workplaces, and communities? • More water and fitness for building healthier lifestyles.	"People are looking for a place to create memories with their children, family and neighbors. A place to draw people together and create a sense of community." "The spaces have to be inviting and welcoming, natural feel, for authentic conversations to happen." "Bring in natural elements and the outdoors to create both vibrant and private spaces to explore, connect, play or just unwind both physically and mentally."
Design Phase 2014	• Innovative and exciting. • Bold and inspiring. • Multi-generational and inviting. • All generations benefit. • Social engagement responds to community needs.	"Never seen anything like this. First of its kind locally and nationally." "The indoor park is the most exciting space. It encourages socializing and playing more spontaneously." "Thinking outside the box and creativity… it recognizes the value of those who will be using the facility. It is taking their thoughts and elevating them to a whole new level." "This design really services the broader community needs across all generations." "The opportunity for your children to be connected to children who are not like-minded as far as culture, religious beliefs, family beliefs…it is the opportunity for them to grow and expand." "Responsive, community minded, cultural."

Nature and Outdoors

Build interior and exterior connections to nature.

Educator Role

Demonstrate leadership through coaching, mentoring, and sharing information and experiences.

Beyond the Walls

The vision and goals of The Centre are not limited to the building but extend to the community and beyond.

These themes then outline how a recreation centre can co-create with constituents to develop initiatives that address health and wellness.

The seven healthy living driver findings from the co-creation process then informed the design of Vivo's expansion and renovation efforts whereby the existing facility would increase by approximately 50 per cent and include expanded aquatic and fitness centre facilities, new and renovated change areas, more specialized areas, and highly innovative, research-based spaces to be used as spontaneous, community and programmed space.

Two new community meeting/event spaces were also designed to accommodate between 100-150 people. With spaces to gather, the community could come together to have important conversations about its future. These spaces would allow neighbors from different backgrounds to meet one another and learn about perspectives different from their own.

A six lane-pool, a 300 per cent increase was also proposed from the facility's current two-lanes. This new pool would allow Vivo to dedicate the existing pool to play and eliminate the large (over 1,000 children) waitlists for each session. The sauna and hot tub would create a suburban spa experience and finally the new and renovated aquatic hall has been designed to be more accessible.

Another unique aspect of the expansion was Canada's first indoor park devoted to active living and social connection. The park would be a place for play, relaxation, and events. A literal moving indoors of an outdoor park space, somewhat crucial in Calgary's northern climate. This space will then give seniors a place to walk, a young mom or dad a place to take a break and read a book and the local diverse communities a place for cultural celebrations of all kinds.

Finally, the research and innovation component of the expansion campaign would seek to create new solutions that make confidence and competence an integral part of kids' and families' everyday lives. These learning, meeting and office spaces would then enable Vivo and all partners to work with residents to understand what they hope for their own health and wellness and their community's future and work alongside them to create and evaluate solutions to make it a reality.

KNOWLEDGE INTO ACTION STUDY 3: HAYSBORO COMMUNITY NATURAL PLAY AREA PROJECT

In 2018, Vivo partnered with the Haysboro Community Association and Mount Royal University to conduct a pre and post baseline of a first of its kind Natural Play Area in a Calgary neighborhood park. Evidence was shared with local organizations and the government to enable future park developments to integrate more natural play elements. Table 3 represents the key behaviors and usage changes of the built environment from a typical 'tot lot' using Systematic Observation methodology (Haysboro Community Association et al., 2017).

Table 3. Action Study 3: Usage and Behaviour Changes

Key Indicators	Pre & Post Baseline Results
Sedentary Behavior	Decrease in sedentary activity from 43 per cent to less than 15 per cent.
Moderate to Vigorous Activity Levels (MVPA)	Increase in both walking and vigorous activity from 28 per cent to 45 per cent and 40 per cent, respectively.
Park Usage by Community	83 per cent increase in the number of residents using the 'Natural Play Area' versus previous 'Tot Lot'.

KNOWLEDGE INTO ACTION STUDY 4: HEALTHY LIVING DRIVERS INFORM NEW PRACTICES

The 2018 community focus groups were about engaging those who are not regular frequenters of The Centre and the following insights emerged about generational views of healthy living and wellness.

Healthy living practices had evolved and during the focus groups, participants spoke nostalgically about the days when they were children, when play was non-structured outdoors, neighborhoods felt safe, and the community kept an eye on all children. Food was healthy and often home cooked, with little choice in what you ate. As they grew older, healthy living became harder with time-pressed schedules, juggling careers and home life. Community participants described their own children playing in structured ways with organized sports or lessons comprising schedules. Their children were living in a technology-based world, where they were balancing screen-time temptations with healthy activities. Time was the largest barrier to healthy living, with both parents working and juggling structured activities.

Key Themes

Table 4 reflects the emergent themes: Nostalgia, Social Connections, Nature and the Outdoors, Living Healthy and Beyond the Walls.

Table 4. Action Study 4: Summary Results

Age Group	**Childhood - Past**	**Teenagers**	**Young Adults**	**Parents**
Theme	**Unstructured Play**	**Connectivity**	**Convenience + Choice**	**Role Modelling Dilemma**
Sub themes	**Home cooked meals** with fruit as dessert Less food choice: "feast or famine" **Mother** stays at home and is the primary health decision maker. **Non-structured play** with neighborhood friends: climbing trees, forts, sledding, biking. Some structured play with team sports and community activities • Safe parks and playgrounds play without fear. • Walk or bike throughout the community. • **Communities taking care of one another.** • **Competition** in sports is seen as healthy.	• Follow peers. • Energy drinks and junk foods for diets. Unhealthy behaviours such as **yo-yo dieting** • More **knowledgeable about health** than teens in the past (e.g., many do not smoke) but instead they are **glued to their phones.** • Some turn to new lifestyles, e.g., vegetarian • There is a **drop in team sports** and physical activity.	• Walk less. • **Food becomes easy, convenient, and on-the-go.** • Surrounded with healthy living messages, deciphering what is or is not healthy. Some spend more money on food such as **organic options** and try **new activities or sports.** • Enjoy **craft beer** and fancy **coffee.** • Uptake arts and crafts nights or hobbies such as dance	Less time for play or healthy activity Routine dinners are for family connection. **Scheduled living healthy activities** - team sports for adults and kids. **Worry about health related to technology and screen time for their kids.** **Helicopter parenting,** children struggle to play in an unstructured manner or in their neighborhoods freely. Parents feel they need to entertain kids. **Less competition** among children (competition is taught as negative) One or more parents working, **gender roles shifted** in parenting. • Kids (and the health of kids) are the priority, but **parents are beginning to worry about their own health:** sleep, balance, and positive mental health as well as a slowing down metabolism. • Some **do not know their neighbors**

Nostalgia

The past was nostalgic for many as parents struggled to provide the same standard of health they experienced as children for their own children. As a result, the parents faced a constant dilemma and guilt with conflicting choices and messages. Eastern/western philosophies were also tested in additional exercises and naturally emerged throughout the conversations. The definition of "spontaneous play" was seen by community participants as exploring the world outdoors and indoors — whether by building a snow fort with your children — or finding new activities to try in the city through Groupon deals. Spontaneous play could be both fast-paced activities or slower-paced relaxation. Barriers to spontaneous play could also include time, lack of opportunity (due to cost, weather, or perceived unavailable spaces) and the fear of looking silly.

Community participants wanted to try more spontaneous play in their lives and felt they could do so by scheduling more time such as "a day a week for spontaneity". Play did not have to be structured, but something children and adults could initiate when they wanted to explore and experience the world around them (refer to Table 5).

Table 5. Action Study 4: Summary Results

One way I currently do this is when:	Play with children: outdoors (basketball at the playground, outdoor sledding, or snow fort building), visiting city spots (laser tag, Calaway park), or at home play (creative room with art and dress-up). Find time to oneself: relax outdoors (in a community garden or backyard, splash in a puddle in the rain, explore city trails), find new activities in the city (through Groupon), or play games indoors on a mobile device.
One reason I don't do this is because:	• Time and scheduled demands. • Finances. • Weather (living in a cold climate). • Lack of spaces available for play (e.g., courts). • Feel silly or self-conscious.
A way I would like to try this in the new year is.	• Try something new (ski, snowboard). • Visit a new place (like an indoor beach). • Schedule a designated time one day a week and plan for spontaneity or relaxation. • Activity as a family or individual.

Social Connections

For community participants, another key theme was that social connections could include anything from a phone call, a home cooked meal with friends, team sports with a local club, or volunteering. Meet-up and social media were identified as ways to connect and meet new people while barriers to connecting socially included time, not wanting to travel, feeling shy, or seeking alone time due to a busy schedule. Participants mentioned that they would like to foster social connections by adding it to their routine, joining new groups, planning an activity, or attending new events (refer to Table 6).

Table 6. Active Study 4: Summary Results

One way I currently do this is when:	Have a phone conversation with a friend. Entertain with friends (with food and song) Attend social gatherings. Play team sports or attend scheduled activities (Cross-fit) Meet new friends online - social media platforms or meet-up. Volunteering (community organizations, at children's school) or organizing events (at their work)
One reason I don't do this is because:	Time and business of life Travel to events. Fear and due to shyness. Needing alone time instead of socializing.
A way I would like to try this in the new year is:	Join a new group to meet new people or try new activities. Make it routine, plan to host or attend social gatherings or travel with friends. Allow for spontaneous socialization Attend more local events.

Nature and the Outdoors

Nature and the outdoors could include anything from a structured activity (softball) to an unstructured activity (yard work or a walk-through local parks). The main reason for not spending time outdoors or in nature was weather (smoke in the city from forest fires or cold winter months). Additionally, a few participants did not know of local green spaces and found it time consuming to drive to where they could experience nature. Many were seeking new ways to spend time in the outdoors by planning daily outdoor activities or trying a new outdoor sport or activity such as biking in the summer and snowboarding or cross country-skiing skiing in the winter. They were also looking for ways to explore more local green spaces or adventure to the mountains or outside of the city limits. Refer to Table 7.

Table 7. Action Study 4: Summary Results

One way I currently do this is when:	Outdoor activities: walking (neighborhoods or parks such as Nose Hill), yard work, cross country ski, snowshoe, softball, snowboard, golf, camping, hiking, camping, tobogganing and more!
One reason I don't do this is because:	Weather considerations - smoke or cold Time and other commitments. If doing so in the mountains or outside of the city, may not wish to drive. Lack of green spaces in local areas (e.g. splash parks).
A way I'd like to try this in the new year is:	Register kids in sports (e.g. Snowboard lessons). Play for it (e.g. Suzuki's 20 mins/day challenge). Try new outdoor activities/embrace the weather (e.g. Cross country ski). Introduce new activities as a family (e.g. Biking). Find more activities in local parks and green spaces (e.g. Urban hikes). Activities in alternative areas such as Banff or vacation areas (British Columbia).

Table 8. Action Study 4: Summary Results

One way I currently do this is when:	• Eat healthy, meal preparation (eat at home, bring food to work), growing vegetables. • Personal and family sports: kickboxing, hockey, organized sports for children, biking in the neighborhood, working out, yoga, weightlifting, winter sports activities.
One reason I don't do this is because:	• Lack of information or support systems. • Less time and energy: too busy to work out or go to the grocery store, lack of time to cook. • Cost: Meals and fitness programs seen as expensive; childcare seen as expensive.
A way I'd like to try this in the new year is:	• Establish new routines for food and exercise. • Try new things such as fitness activities. • Meal planning: learn to use a crockpot or prepare meals that can be frozen. • Slow down: Walk outside more, get more sleep, practice yoga (or former activities of interest).

Living Healthy

A fourth theme was that community participants generally engaged in healthy practices and tried to model these behaviours for their families - whether through meal preparation, growing outdoor vegetables, putting their kids in sport activities, or finding time to exercise for themselves (at home exercises or in facilities such as Vivo). The main reason for not doing so was that they may have lacked the skills, found it expensive, or lacked the time or energy.

Table 9. Action Study 4: Summary Results

One way I currently do this is when:	Community activities: community soccer, Stampede Breakfast, and volunteer at child's school. Foster friendships with the parents of their children's friends. Support local businesses or visit the community garden. Watch their community Facebook page, such as Panorama Hills's Facebook page. Walk or explore the neighborhoods on a bicycle.
One reason I don't do this is because:	Difficulty finding commonalities. Prefer alone time or feel shy. Lack of time and energy or cannot always attend activities of interest. Lack of knowledge of local events.
A way I'd like to try this in the new year is:	Volunteering. Attend events or join a group. Plan or attend a neighbourhood block party Schedule local events in my calendar. Support more local business at farmers markets or night markets.

Table 10. Action Study 4: Questions and Responses

Top Questions	Summary of Responses
What were the community's definitions of the healthy living drivers?	1. *Physical Activity and Nutrition*- finding your passion, setting goals, and making it a habit. 2. *Spontaneous Play*- playing your way, anytime & anywhere. 3. *Diversity and Inclusion*- understanding each other's perspectives & caring for relationships in your life. 4. *Balance and Mindfulness*-the space, time, and ability to enjoy life. 5. *Nature and the Outdoors*- learning from and connecting to your surroundings. 6. Community Resilience - helping each other through opportunities and challenges.
Which 3 Healthy Living Drivers matter most to a community?	*1. Social Connections* Participant Quote- 'I want myself and my kids to get to know my neighbours and explore magical spots together, so we feel like we belong to or be part of something greater in the world' *2. Balance and Mindfulness* 'Participant Quote-'Want to be more disciplined at taking time out for me... to learn stuff that I am interested in, to soak in and reflect the surroundings of my life and then translate that into caring with my family, friends, and community. 3. *Physical Activity and Nutrition* 'Participant Quote-'I want to feel strong not just look strong so I can deal with and learn from both the good and bad experiences in my life'
What is the role of places like Vivo with these Healthy Living Drivers?	1. Working with the community as a *facilitator* to bring the community and different kinds of organizations together to figure out solution to complex challenges people are facing in their lives or where they live. 2. *Creating capacity* within the community for social interaction by bringing new and different experiences and collaborations with others- online, outdoors and in people's neighborhood parks to gather, explore, experiment, learn and create meaning together and try new things.

Ideas for living healthy in the next year included learning how to prepare healthy meals, getting back into pre-loved activities such as yoga, or establishing a new nutrition and activity routine. Refer to Table 8.

Beyond the Walls Means Connecting With Community

A final theme was that volunteering was particularly important to community participants and a way in which individuals could speak about connecting with people "beyond the walls". They seek opportunities to attend events and meet new people and items like community Facebook pages helped participants stay involved. They also liked to support local businesses with time and energy being barriers to connecting with the community and a lack of knowledge about opportunities. Many community participants also hoped to volunteer in the next year within their neighborhood or even plan a block party. Finally, they sought a schedule of local events to attend and particularly liked the free night markets, which then allowed them to support local businesses (refer to Table 9).

Table 11. Action Study 5: Shifts in Recreation Program Practices

Traditional Recreation Programming	Vivo 4 in1 New Type of Recreation Curriculum & Practices
Instructor and expert based lesson plans.	Evidence-based and co-created with lesson plans with kids and parents that promote moving and connecting more in daily life.
Alignment with sector trends and organizational outcomes.	Alignment with the Alberta Education curriculum/Sport for Life and SPARK national evidence-based resources.
Skill development and practice across a single built environment at one time.	Skill development and practice across multiple built environments at one-time.
8 -12-week program per season.	Year round, twice a week program and consistent instructor who gets the opportunity to really know each child.
Skill development progress report cards for Swimming and Skating only.	Participants receive personalized progress report cards to track physical activity levels, fundamental movement skills, confidence and competence and connection to their community.
Measure program participation rates, satisfaction levels with program and instructor.	Annual measurements capturing specific built environment insights using Systematic Observation (SOFIT) methodology and tools. Insights captured on moderate to physical activity levels, sedentary behaviors, participant engagement around free play, skills practice, game play, knowledge, and instructor engagement around manage, promotes fitness, managing, praising and role modeling.

Key Healthy Living Insights From The Community

From this process, four key healthy living insights emerged that provided the connection between recreation and health and wellness practices.

1. The main reason for not engaging in healthy living often includes a lack of resources or time.
2. There is an increasing pressure to be healthy. The more conscious we become, the more pressure we put on ourselves to make it happen.
3. Healthy living is no longer spontaneous, the main way participants plan to do more of it in the next year is through changing routines and schedules.
4. For some, being healthy has become perceived as an obligation rather than a way of life.

Table 12. Action Study 6: Spontaneous Play Solutions and Impacts

'Spontaneous Play' Recipe important to Community	'Play Hub' Ingredients designed by Residents	Community Engagement Impacts
Connected- Bring People Together. Outside- embrace the natural world. Open-Ended- Exploring together and playing your own way. Adventurous- Curiosity, Mess, and positive challenges.	A grassy hill is ideal for rolling down in a tube, for building a makeshift foam slide, for sledding in winter or the simple thrill of running down it at full speed. Wooden, metal, and natural structures of different heights and sizes that people can climb, sit on, use as a surface, and that add points of interest to the site. Loose parts like tires, shovels, pool noodles and random other items (including an actual kitchen sink in one!) that can be used to creatively enhance play. Abundance of natural elements: a huge dirt pile, trees, rocks, and logs.	'My children and I LOVE attending the Play Hub. As a stay-at-home mom with two children, sometimes I struggle to plan activities that work into our schedule and are fun for both myself and the children!'- Community Member. 'I think they created the Play Hub so kids like me can play and cause no matter how old people are they can still play too'- 7-year-old Participant. The Vivo Play Project has opened my eyes not only to the importance of active and exploratory play but to intergenerational connection. It is an example of how we desperately as a Canadian Society need to take a break from our fast paced and stressful lives and play more than ever as kids or adults.' – Play Ambassador. 'If our next generations aren't connected or don't understand this incredible place where they live, how can we expect them to care for it.'-Community Leader.

KNOWLEDGE INTO ACTION STUDY 5: 4 IN 1 PHYSICAL LITERACY LONGITUDINAL RESEARCH STUDY (2014-2020)

Traditionally, in a one-hour recreation program, children spend an average of 61 per cent of their time standing, sitting, or lying down. This study attempted to address this concern and had over 30 children participated over an 8-month span, with the goal of developing children's physical activity levels and foundational movement skills. These included coordination, balance, strength and agility, and fine motor skills through four different environments: ice (skating), land (gym-based activities), water (swimming) and air (climbing). Refer to Table 11.

As a result of this study, Vivo has thus tried to flip the 61% statistic by launching the 4 in 1 Physical Literacy Program together with Mount Royal University. The result has been a 60 per cent increase in participant engagement, 18 per cent more movement and an eight per cent increase in motor proficiency compared to conventional recreation programming. More specifically, the 4 in 1 program builds confidence, competence and skills that help children from Kindergarten to Grade 5 and their families, by empowering them to make healthy choices and become active for life.

Table 13. Action Study 7: Baseline of a New Community

Key 'Baseline' Themes from Residents about living in a new Community (Livingston)	Key Actions by Brookfield Residential for Livingston Residents in 2019 and 2020.
23 per cent of Residents chose Livingston because of the Brookfield Residential Experience • Some residents based their buying decision on our positive reputation, considering it a good investment to live in a Brookfield Residential community. Factors like distance from the city and access to main roads, amenities, and the airport also influenced decisions to invest. • 41 per cent of Residents invested in Livingston because green spaces had been planned. Overall satisfaction with the current environmental appeal was low. However, there was a fair degree of trust in the community master plan. Frustrations about the lack of public transport connected a desire for both functionality and beauty. • 22 per cent of Residents feel Neighbours are just acquaintances- Most residents do not know their neighbors. Some believe that they will get to know their neighbors better when winter ends and construction slows. Many did not feel safe letting their children play outside because of traffic and construction. • 45 per cent have encouraged friends and family to buy-Every Livingston family felt at home in their new house, even though they had not been there for long. Most residents have long term plans to stay in Livingston and were striving to develop a sense of belonging in their new community. • 12,224 was the average number of steps families in Livingston take per day. Residents engage in higher levels of moderate to vigorous physical activity compared to the national average of 8950 steps/ day. More natural outdoor spaces are needed and are considered equally as important as manufactured play areas.	**Residents Level-** "Helping people make healthier choices everyday." • Offering a 'Community Hub and staffed with volunteers' to welcome people new to the neighborhood and offered monthly cultural events to encourage early connections with neighbors. • Utilized the resident's insights to adapt the design for the first outdoor park spaces and playgrounds as well the future Homeowners Association's name and amenity features to reflect what the community wanted outdoor adventure play, childcare, community meeting spaces. **Community Level-** 'Reimagining our communities'. • Used left over construction dirt to create a pump track and potential cross-country ski area in the winter. • Working with Vivo to activate a Play Hub with Play Ambassadors to encourage more outdoor play throughout the community's green spaces and streets as well as help families gather and connect more. **Systems Level-** 'Working together for maximum impact.' • Strengthen evidence and bonds with local partnerships with organizations like Vivo and with the government to create a new standard of excellence for community development.

KNOWLEDGE INTO ACTION STUDY 6: VIVO PLAY PROJECT 2018-2022

The fifth action study focuses on a study that utilized systematic observations or parks and play spaces. This study showed that people were only using the parks/ playgrounds 33 per cent of the time and that they rarely had more than 2 people (usually a parent and child) using them at once (North Central Calgary Parks et al., 2015).

Table 14. Action Study 8: Themes and Lessons for Outdoor Parks Design

Six Themes by Community about Neighbourhood Park Development	Community Building 'Secret Sauce' Lessons
Connect individual parks into a network, linking green spaces to each other and to regional park systems. Parks can be connected by physical elements like pathways and bike racks with symbolic elements like signage and road maps. **Enrich** the natural environment of park spaces by including native vegetation and 'wild' spaces. Create habitat for urban wildlife, reduce maintenance and provide beautiful and imaginative play spaces for all four seasons. **Equip** green spaces with fun and popular amenities that invite participation from ALL age groups. **Inspire** adventures, spark imagination, and promote physical and mental health by giving everyone a reason to go to the park. **Activate** park spaces by making them suited to social uses like gathering, relaxing and spending time with friends and families, Consider food, games, and social seating elements in the redesign of spaces. **Re-imagine spaces** and explore beyond the 'tot lot' by introducing social elements like BBQ's, banquet tables and provide new activity uses like a bicycle pump. **Provide seating** to make the park spaces better for families, seniors, and those with reduced mobility. Ensure frequent, well shaded seating along with common pedestrian routes to parks and green spaces.	**Put community at the centre:** Start where people are now. Ask questions that let them tell you what matters to them. Be a great host by including food at events, and never underestimate the value of fun. Go to them to host engagements. **Bring people along on the journey:** Be inclusive; Actively seek ways to broaden the circle of participants and leadership; Communicate to bring people along in the story and Document and share your work- this can be as simple as holding a short Facebook Live session at the end of events or meetings, especially if you ask questions online that participants will want to answer. **Show (and be) trusted faces:** Seeing community leaders and champions builds trust for a project. Know what tasks can be outsourced without changing the face of the project. Develop leaders within the community. Understand how to lead while stepping back to make space for others. **Recognize the value of partners:** You need them. This is not a solo job. Partnerships should be reciprocal, with both sides contributing and benefitting. Look for partners who can connect you with audiences you do not reach and ask for advice on how to engage the audiences they know and have skills you need and may not have. **Be flexible:** Things will change and that needs to be okay. Go where the community's energy is, not where you think it should be (or where your plan said it would be). Be ready for opportunities to present themselves. People may want immediate answers but stay optimistic and flexible and do not over-promise or say "no" too quickly. It is more accurate to say that what the community can get is a matter of the work the community is willing to do.

Vivo's response to this was launching the 'Vivo Play Project', a four-year initiative with the Public Health Agency of Canada and Suncor Energy Foundation to increase knowledge, understanding, value, and participation in outdoor, spontaneous play. Vivo did this by offering free play facilitation and events in the community. Most of this activity happened at a Play Hub with Play Ambassadors – a space that was co-built with individuals specifically trained in facilitating evidence- based play experiences to inspire and empower ten per cent more resilience in children, youth, and adults by moving, connecting, and engaging more in their neighborhood parks.

Vivo also partnered with the University of Calgary through their MakeCalgary initiative to research and evaluate the impact of this initiative by exploring the levels of physical activity and social connection of residents, the effectiveness of Play Hub Experiences and the Play Ambassadors training program and how the lives of families and kids are impacted when they have access to data about how much they move and their chronic disease risk levels (Vivo and Social R & D Practice, 2019). Refer to Table 12.

The success of this project was based on the principle of community engagement and co-creation: the community itself knew what would work and where their comfort level was. Vivo has worked with residents to make each of the Play Hubs unique to their community's needs and desires.

Table 15. Social Justice & Change

One way I currently do this is when:	• Try and meet new people in the community through events and experiences on our street, local parks or at places like Vivo. • Seek out resources or conversations online to learn more about things like racism. • Try new cultural experiences when offered at the local community centre. • Speak up to my teacher if I hear someone bullying my friend.
One reason I don't do this is because:	• Allot places don't address this authentically. • Feel like this is so big I don't know where to start. • Feel like I don't have the knowledge and expertise to say the right thing now. • Lack of time and energy or cannot always attend activities of interest.
A way I'd like to try this in the new year is:	• Reflecting and educating myself about the issues that matter most to me and my family. • Join a group to learn from others about their perspectives on the world and share what I think too. • Plan or attend an event on my street to get to know my neighbors better. • Share what I think needs to change at my workplace in terms of policies and practices.

KNOWLEDGE INTO ACTION STUDY 7: *LIVINGSTON COMMUNITY BASELINE STUDY WITH BROOKFIELD RESIDENTIAL 2019-ONGOING*

A sixth action study comes from 2018, when Vivo partnered with Brookfield Residential and Mount Royal University to focus on understanding and increasing the 'Livability' or essential elements in the design and experiences of new communities that improves resident's overall quality of life including sense of belonging and connection with other neighbors, physical activity levels, outdoor park usage and perceptions about living their first year living in a new community.

KNOWLEDGE INTO ACTION STUDY 8: CREATING COVENTRY PROJECT 2018- ONGOING

A final action study was a study focused on loneliness (social isolation), which is projected to be a global epidemic for individuals of all ages (Government of Canada, 2017). This issue has been further exacerbated by the recent COVID-19 pandemic.

Creating Coventry, was a community-led and driven master planning project created to re-imagine, improve, and connect fifteen neighborhood parks over twenty years. Vivo supported both a local community champion, and the City of Calgary in generating evidence of current usage of the parks, co-creating and prototyping ideas to make the community a healthier, happier, and more connected place. This way achieved this by securing the funding to develop and master plan process and document, as well as advocating to local government to change their decision making and practices around neighborhood park development. Table 14 represents key themes and lessons learned together about what people valued in their neighborhood parks and the community building process.

As of March 2021, four community Parks had been funded and re-developed including a basketball court for youth, an outdoor rink for all ages and a pollination corridor with several plant species to help the local insect population thrive. Creating Coventry was also recognized as an evidence-based, citizen-led planning and development model for other communities to use both locally and nationally.

TRENDS

In the final part of this chapter seven macro-level trends will be focused on that will influence the future of the health and wellness sector within the active economy. There are a number of those touched on this chapter already, however the following three trends will be highlighted: Social Justice, COVID-19 Long Tail and Consumer to Co-Creator.

Social Justice and Change

Diversity and inclusion can include anything from recognizing and appreciating differences across age, gender, race/ethnicity, religion, sexual orientation, socio-economic status. It can also entail seeking, exploring, understanding, and sharing different perspectives on beliefs with others. More authentic conversations in-person and online and advocating for changes in both community and organizational systems, structures, policies, and practices are identified as ways to increase the importance of this driver. Barriers to diversity and inclusion include people becoming too comfortable in only being with their consistent social group. Participants mentioned that they would like to inspire diversity and inclusion by being empathetic and understanding of who people are and where they are at in the moment. Additionally, participants express an urge to increase their own knowledge and exposure to different people and experiences to gain new perspectives from within their community.

COVID-19 Long Tail

The long-term fallout for COVID-19 remains unknown. Therefore, the main implication is for us to track behavioural change and understand how the pandemic has impacted the active economy as a whole. *(ActiveCITY Collective, 2020).*

In Canada, research on Alberta's unique challenges due to the pandemic and the decline of the energy sector has shown important insights regarding citizen behaviours and how they are engaging now and moving forward, and these are likely not unique to this geographic context.

According to a longitudinal study being conducted by Stone-Olafson (2020), Albertans are generally highly active experience consumers, yet the pandemic is creating a market that is frustrated, tired, angry, and worried. 79 per cent of people are no longer comfortable in large crowds. Citizens need to be assured that they (and their cohort) will be safe. Long-term economic considerations carry significant impacts on how people make decisions about spending or investing in experiences. Habits are changing for many, with 39 per cent of people already doing things differently. Citizens are adding to their repertoire of experiences and not just replacing what they used to do. As a result, stakeholders in the active economy must be prepared for changes in not only participant behaviours but also operating environments.

Community as Co-creator for Health and Wellness

In this model, adopted by companies such as Apple, Google, and LEGO, recognizes that when you empower people, you accelerate innovation. In this model, an enterprise transitions from being a linear controller of knowledge to becoming a dynamic broker across the entire ecosystem and supporting interconnected processes. *(ActiveCITY Collective, 2020).*

The active economy needs to learn now to engage consumers throughout the product life cycle. This is of particular importance within the active economy with significant declines being seen in the participation of women, lower household income, persons with a disability and specific ethnic groups.... Similarly, a variety of enabling sectors within the active economy should adopt an open innovation framework as they evolve their products and services. *(ActiveCITY Collective, 2020).*

Vivo's success as it pertains to the health and wellness of its members is based upon the encouragement of citizens to visit the centre. Through this, these citizens become the organizing principle for how resources are allocated and how stakeholders can support their specific needs. To identify both the community's needs, as well as the gaps in service provision, we must continue to directly engage in priority communities. There is currently the anticipation that these needs include reducing isolation and loneliness, accessibility, building community, access to ancillary services, providing safe spaces, opportunities to establish relationships, to name but a few.

CONCLUSION

In this chapter, we use an action study to explore "how to forms" of the health and wellness sector can be more effective in the active economy. These focus on a charity, such as Vivo taking a systemic approach through a socio-ecological model and putting the citizen at the centre of the planning process by engaging them directly in the design of health and wellness programs and services, built environment and community capacity building. As an action study, this two-pronged approach has resulted in a powerful organizational transformation for Vivo including an evolved vision, mission and values, re-designing of systems, processes and practices and seeking new and different collaborations. This was demonstrated through eight Canadian action studies linked in their attempts to connect new kinds of solutions and services to greater health and wellness outcomes.

REFERENCES

ActiveCITY Collective. (2020). *Playbook 2030: A Guide to Building Canada's Most Livable Region* (Rep.). https://www.activecityproject.org/

Canadian Parks and Recreation Association. (2014). *Pathways to Wellbeing: A Framework for Recreation in Canada.* Canadian Parks and Recreation Association. www.cpra.ca

Dooley, J., & Aguirre, C. (2018). Generation H: Healthy Living Drivers [PowerPoint slides]. *Vivo.* https://www.vivo.ca/research-innovation/projects/past-projects/healthy-living-school/

Karen, L. (2020). *Fit Cities: My Quest to Improve the World's Health and Wellness—Including Yours.* Penguin Random House Canada.

Legg, D., Emery, C., Konopaki, J., Black, J., Duggan, J., Booke, J., Martin, T., Watson, C., Le May Doan, C., & Swett, C. (2020). Calgary Adapted Hub Lead Assessment and Recommendations Report. *Vivo.* https://ncsra.sharepoint.com/:w:/s/migration/EY7KLW6oiBhlm7H8oN3vr5QB4RyRhat97dvhvy6z9RYcdQ?e=mP1Btr

Stone-Olafson. (n.d.). The New Experience Economy. *Stone-Olafson.* https://www.stone-olafson.com/thenewexperienceeconomy

Whitehead, M. (2019). *Physical Literacy Across the World.* Routledge. https://play.google.com/store/books/details?id=6qSbDwAAQBAJ&gl=ca&hl=en-CA&source=productsearch&utm_source=HA_Desktop_US&utm_medium=SEM&utm_campaign=PLA&pcampaignid=MKT-FDR-na-us-1000189-Med-pla-bk-Evergreen-Jul1520-PLA-eBooks_Education&gclid=Cj0KCQiApY6BBhCsARIsAOI_GjbCK-rSj6wx_d8KQw1MNMQnTDQzb-FdVtQhuw9mUjWsomoaqu7SX6EaAnsjEALw_wcB&gclsrc=aw.ds

Chapter 7
Active Tourism in the Active Economy

Richard Keith Wright
Auckland University of Technology, New Zealand

Geoff Dickson
https://orcid.org/0000-0002-9913-0125
La Trobe University, Australia

Richard Opara Ajiee
Auckland University of Technology, New Zealand

ABSTRACT

According to the World Travel and Tourism Council's (WTTC) most recent reports, one in every ten jobs (an estimated 330 million) is influenced if not directly supported by travel and tourism-related activity, making it one of the world's largest economic sectors. Whilst the boundaries that separate adventure tourism from active/sport tourism are blurred, the subject is certainly not lacking in terms of evidence-based definitions, conceptual frameworks, or typologies. This chapter offers a critical overview of the existing body of knowledge that relates to the emergence of a global active and/or adventure-based tourism economy. The authors complement their review of the literature with a case study looking at the 'home of adventure', Queenstown, New Zealand.

DOI: 10.4018/978-1-7998-7939-8.ch007

INTRODUCTION

An active tourist tries to educate a good mind in a healthy body.

(Active-Tourism, 2002).

Buckley (2006) distinguishes between adventure tourism and adventure recreation, noting the former requires a commercial transaction between the consumer (client) and the producer (operator) whereas the latter can be experienced with equipment owned and operated solely by the consumer (in his/her leisure time). With the subject of active recreation having been covered within chapter five, the primary focus of this chapter is active tourism, more specifically sport and adventure-based tourism. Active tourism operates at the other end of the spectrum to passive/mass tourism, encapsulating principles and practices from special interest/niche markets such as sport and adventure tourism. The authors have chosen to adopt the active tourism definition presented during the 2019 ActiveCITY Summit. Active tourism is defined as that which is "directly associated with organized sport or active recreation development or delivery" (Finch et al., 2019). The authors have also adopted Finch et al.'s (2019) definition of organized sport and active recreation.

According to Finch et al. (2019), organized sport incorporates "activities involving physical exertion, skill as the primary focus of the activity, with elements of competition where rules and patterns of behaviour governing the activity exist formally through organizations" (p. 15). Active recreation captures "activities engaged in for the purpose of relaxation, health and well-being or enjoyment with the primary activity requiring physical exertion" (2019, p.15). In other words, unlike organized sport, recreational activities are typically unstructured and participant-led with little prior planning. To contextualise the theory and trends presented within the following section, the authors offer a case study of New Zealand's Adventure Capital, Queenstown. The aim is to offer insight into the benefits attached to investing in urban infrastructure, hallmark events, and cultural attractions that appeal to domestic and international active sport tourists.

BACKGROUND

Sport tourism – sometimes referred to as "sports tourism" – refers to travel away from home to play sport, watch sport, or to visit a sports attraction, and includes both competitive and non-competitive activities. It consists of two broad categories of products; sports participation travel (travel for the purpose of participating in sports, recreation, leisure, or fitness activities); and sports spectatorial travel (travel for the purpose of spectating sports, recreation, and leisure or fitness activities or events). (Hudson, 2003).

Weed and Bull (2009) broadly define sports tourism as being a social, economic, and cultural phenomenon that results from the interaction of activities, people, and place. They advocate for the adoption of the term 'sports', as opposed to 'sport', believing that the pluralisation effectively removed the pre-existing parameters placed upon the research by external social constructs attached to our understanding of 'sport' or a particular type of 'sport'.

Despite the connections between sport and tourism being centuries old (Gibson, 1998a), the first academic studies did not appear until the 1980s and 90s (Glyptis, 1982, Hall 1992). De Knop (1990) assessed the historical connections between sport and tourism, whilst Hall (1992) introduced travel to sporting events as a form of special interest tourism. Kurtzman and Zauhar (1997) led the way in terms of creating a conceptual framework for others to apply, dividing the supply-side development of sport tourism into five connected categories: attractions, resorts, cruises, tours, and events. Attractions were said to exist in both natural and manmade environments (e.g., parks, mountains, rivers, museum, stadiums, heritage sites etc.). Resorts were further categorised by their amenities (e.g., accommodation with health and fitness clubs, spas, tennis courts, golf course, water- and snow-sports etc) and their affordability (e.g., luxury retreats, family-friendly, budget, conference venues, school camps). Cruises were essentially seen as mobile resorts on water, offering clients access to sport and recreational activities both on and off the boat (Kurtzman & Zauhar, 1997). The 'Tours' category of Kurtzman and Zauhars' (1997) typology included self-guided or organized trips that ranged in both duration and distance covered. It also included walking and bus tours around urban sport heritage attractions such as museums and stadiums, but also all-inclusive package tours targeting the spectator and participant sports event market. The fifth and final category captures the most visible of all the sport tourism markets; the event attendee.

Like many of the sport event studies published during the 1990s and early 2000s, Kurtzman and Zauhars' (1997) model acknowledged the many different formats and functions of special events, ranging from the high-profile sport fixtures (the Olympics, Super Bowl etc.) to the more niche, cultural, celebrations (Hong Kong Dragon Boat Festival). They acknowledged the large number of local community sports tournaments that require amateur teams to travel away from home for a weekend or week, proposing that individual pilgrimages and organized package tours to participatory and spectator-driven sports events had effectively replaced the more traditional religious pilgrimages of the past and predicted that the market was only going to get bigger (Kurtzman & Zauhar, 1997).

The first critical analysis of sport tourism scholarship was published in 1998 (Gibson, 1998a). Gibson (1998a) identified several opportunities for those looking to build upon the initial foundations created by leisure, sport, and tourism scholars during the 1980s and 1990s. She also noted the lack of a theoretical framework and recommended the adoption of an interdisciplinary approach that embraced established concepts from within the social sciences and humanities (Gibson, 1998a). Gibson also offered a framework built around the existence of three closely related domains. The first domain was referred to as being the active sport tourism market (people who travel to participate). The second was the event sport tourism market (people who travel to watch an event) and the third was the nostalgia sport tourism market (people who travel to a site of historical sporting significance or visit a sport heritage attraction) (Gibson, 1998a).

Standeven and De Knop's (1999) framework model was based on the principles of supply and demand. They argued that the sport tourism market could be divided into 'active' and 'passive' participation, prior to adding a third category for those employed within the sport industry. This third group of sport tourism consumers included professional athletes and administrators as well as those travelling for non-sport related business reasons who, whilst away, might choose (or be invited) to watch a sports fixture. Similarly, Gammon and Robinson (2003) also divided the market into those travelling primarily for sport (the sport tourist) and those who choose to engage in some sport-related activities whilst on holiday (tourism sport). The two segments found within Gammon and Robinson's (2003) framework were further divided into those considered to be "hard" consumers and those deemed to be "soft", with definitions and examples provided for each category (Figure 1).

Figure 1.

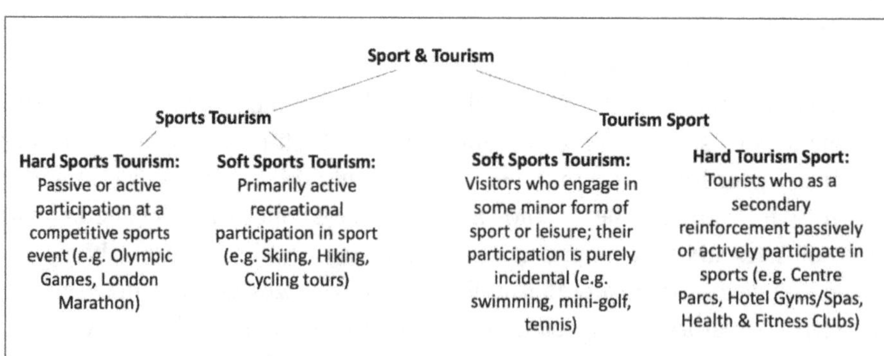

Getz (2003) also identified sports event tourism as being an attractive market for destinations "looking to attract large numbers of high-yield visitors, including spectators, participants, officials, and the media" (p. 84). Getz (2003) further suggested that staging tourism generating sports events had the potential to increase sport participation opportunities and inspire urban renewal, including new and more efficiently operated sport venues and entertainment facilities. Following the growth in sports event research, Kaplanidou and Gibson (2010) proposed the need for active sport tourism scholars to distinguish between 'event active' and 'event passive' sport tourists. Similarly, Hinch and Higham (2011) also differentiated between 'elite' and 'non-elite' sports event tourism, based around the ratio of spectators to participants.

Hinch and Higham (2011) defined 'elite' sports events as those where the number of passive spectators, both live and via mainstream or social media channels, outweigh the number of active, usually professional, participants. 'Non-elite' events are participant dominated and include local recreational fixtures that may take place on a weekly basis. The tourism generated by non-elite events is minimal compared to the larger 'elite' events, which attract a significant, often international, audience. Occasionally, however, the line between these types of events can be blurred, and tourism-generating elite events can co-exist with non-elite events. Lamont and McKay's (2012) ethnographic examination of amateur cyclists attending the Tour de France on package tours, for example, identified that active sport tourists can enact multiple contrasting roles within a single trip, mixing aspects of active, event and nostalgia.

Buning and Gibson's (2015) study of cycle tourists presented a vision of the Active Sport Event Travel Career (ASETC), defined as "a career like pattern of involvement and commitment to event-related travel and participation in physically active sport events, which leads to progression through time in regard to motivations, preferences, and modified behaviour" (p. 556). The ASETC model (Figure 2) was inspired by Getz's suggestion that amateur athletes engaged in serious leisure activities may create a lifelong career of travel to sport events (Getz, 2008; Getz & McConnell, 2011). When applied to cycle tourists, the model identified motivation, temporal, destination criteria, and event types as themes across all stages of the active sport tourism career. The initiation stage corresponds with the theme 'starting out', while the theme 'later in life' corresponds with the withdrawal stage. Reduced involvement/career sabbatical driven by constraints, while preferences for event, destination, and travel style characteristics were based on a participant's orientation towards racing events, travel distance, and the presence of non-cycling travel companions.

Figure 2.

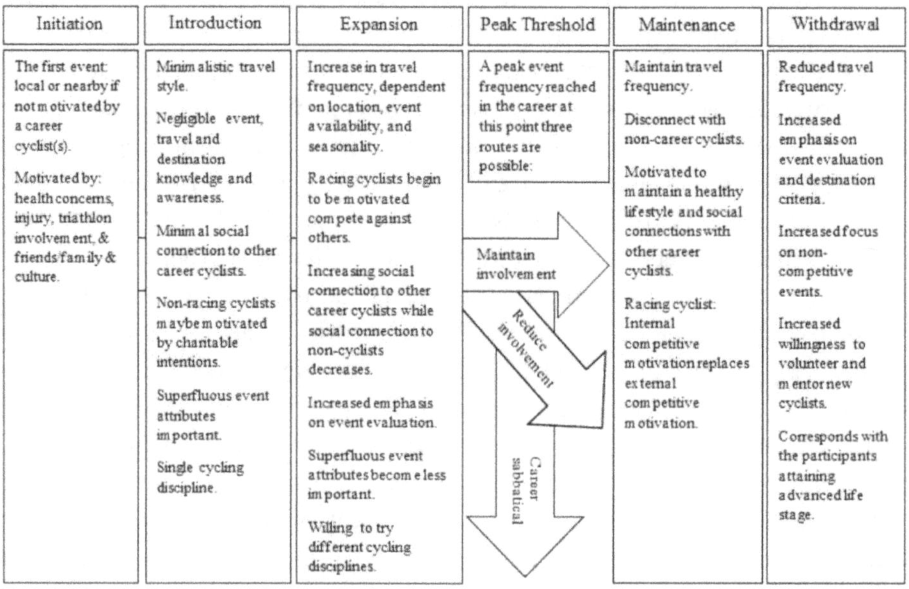

In 2017, as a part of a special edition celebrating the 20th anniversary or the Journal of Sport & Tourism, Gibson was invited to revisit her first critical assessment of the sport tourism research space (Gammon et al., 2017). Having noted the large number of management and marketing-related studies looking at the socio-economic impacts of event sport tourism, Gibson (2017) once again emphasised the importance of studying participatory leisure events and active recreation from a social scientific and humanistic perspective. The subject's emergence out of the shadow of event sport tourism was noted, along with its evolution from an immature emergent area of special interest into an expansive and established international field of academic study (Gibson, 2017). The following year, alongside three others, Gibson guest edited a special edition of Journal of Sport & Tourism dedicated solely to active sport tourism, within which she praised the solid and coherent body of knowledge that had been built over the past decade, including the creation of the ASETC.

ACTIVE SPORTS TOURISM

Active sports tourism is usually defined as tourism driven mainly by active consumption of sports or recreational activities (Gibson, 2004). As noted earlier in the chapter, it differs from events-driven and nostalgia-inspired sport tourism

(Gibson, 1998b). Globally, the most witnessed forms of participatory (active) sports tourism are golf, skiing, and hiking, although there has been a steady increase in those travelling to go sailing, hunting, and fishing or to compete in an organized endurance event such as a marathons or triathlon. Active sports tourism means that tourists take the initiative to directly participate in sports events in the process of sports tourism. According to Gibson et al., (1998), active sports tourism can be divided into two types: leisure/fitness and adventure stimulation. The first category, leisure/fitness sport tourism, occurs when an individual travels to engage in an activity with which they are highly familiar and used to undertaking within their leisure time (i.e., when at home). This form of active sport tourism can be further divided into three sub-groups; leisure sport tourism, vacation sport tourism, and fitness sport tourism (Gibson et al., 1998).

The active leisure sport tourist is likely to travel with their own equipment, rather than relying on hiring them at the destination (e.g., golf clubs, fishing rods, hiking boots, dancing shoes). The activities that they undertake whilst away from home are not new to them. Furthermore, the destination chosen is also likely to be one that they have visited (or will go on to visit) on many occasions. Much of the recent active sport tourism literature has focused upon this type of sport tourist, with many scholars approaching the subject from a serious leisure perspective. The main purpose of active vacation-based sports tourism is to eliminate fatigue, adjust body/mind, and relieve stress (Gibson et al., 1998). Swimming in the resort/hotel's pool and/or at the beach is by far the most witnessed form of vacation-based sports tourism, although there has been a noticeable increase in the number of tourists choosing to make use of the hotel gymnasium and/or signing up for organized fitness/workout sessions (include aquarobics) whilst on holiday (Gibson et al., 1998). Similarly, active fitness sports tourism encapsulates those who seek to exercise their muscles, relax their body/mind through playing some form of social sport that they would not normally play at home (e.g., tennis, table tennis, badminton, squash).

Unlike the leisure sports tourist, those who engage in this type of active sport tourism are more likely to rent/hire the equipment rather than bring their own (some may not own the equipment needed). In sum, the activities are not planned or purchased prior to travelling (Gibson et al., 1998). In contrast, adventure-stimulating active sports tourism differs from the previously mentioned types in that it includes an element of risk and uncertainty (Gibson et al., 1998). The goal is to challenge oneself and embrace the unknown. Adventure-stimulating sports tourism can be divided into extreme and traditional activities. Extreme sports tourism refers to engaging in dangerous activities, such as rock climbing, rafting, adventure, bungee jumping, or hot air balloons. Traditional sports tourism mainly refers to tourism associated with mass sports activities, such as sailing and skiing. The element of risk in these activities is lower but influenced by the tourist's prior experience and ability to learn. The following section looks specifically at the principles and practices of adventure tourism.

ADVENTURE TOURISM

Adventure tourism, also referred to as extreme or outdoor tourism, is big business and a major part of the world's biggest export industry (Adventure Travel Trade Association (ATTA), 2010; Buckley, 2006; Laing & Frost, 2014; Williams & Soutar, 2009). According to Gross and Sand (2019), the "forefather" of modern adventure sport tourism is organized trips to the summits of the European Alps. Similarly, hunting, fishing, skiing, and river canoeing all emerged as a popular domestic tourism activity during the latter half of the 19th Century (Gross & Sands, 2019). "In the 1950s and 1960, adventure tourism was no longer just the pastime for a few madmen but established as an independent form of tourism. It was driven, among other things, by the global coverage of first ascents, such as Mount Everest" (Gross & Sands, 2019, p. 153).

Whilst the boundaries that separate adventure tourism from active sport tourism may be blurred, the subject is certainly not lacking in terms of definitions, conceptual frameworks, or typologies. As with the subject of sport tourism, much of the early foundations were laid around the end of the 20th Century (Rantala & Rokenses, 2018; Taylor et al., 2013). Sung et al. (1997) refers to adventure tourism as "the sum of the phenomena and relationship arising from the interactions of adventure touristic activities with the natural environment away from participant's usual place of residence" (p. 57).

Muller and Cleaver (2000) were amongst the first to study the importance placed upon the provision of high-level sensory stimulation, finding it to be one of the key distinguishing features of adventure tourism. Similarly, Grant (2001) studied the extensive amount of pre-trip planning and preparation involved, claiming it to be another distinguishing factor that separates adventure tourism from other forms of activity-based tourism. Swarbrooke et al. (2003) notes how adventure tourism typically involves leisure activities and experiences that are consumed in the hope that they will produce a range of positive emotions and a heightened sense of excitement. They offer a pluralistic view of adventure tourism that acknowledge the important role played by the marketer of the product or service being packaged and promoted as 'an adventure tourism experience'. According to Swarbrooke et al. (2003), the term 'adventure' is "evocative for many people – images and associations flood into the mind at the mention of the word. Imagination and emotion are very much part and parcel of the adventure experience" (p. 7). They identify and analyze ten core characteristics or qualities of adventure, many of which were found to be interrelated and interdependent (Swarbrooke et al., 2003).

Like sport tourism, the pioneers of this area of activity tourism divided the adventure market into a hard and a soft category (Hudson, 2003). Hard adventure tourism experiences are strenuous physical activities that involve "risk to life and limb" and appeal to the more extreme thrill seekers, adrenaline junkies, and "danger rangers'' (Hudson, 2003, p. 18). Rock climbing, heli-skiing, and white-water kayaking are some of the leisure activities included under this category. Soft adventure tourism operators target more risk averse individuals, families, and groups seeking an outdoor excursion (Hudson, 2003; Schlegelmilch & Ollenburg, 2013). Kane and Tucker's (2004) ethnographical study of adventure tourists on a 14-day white-water kayaking tour of the South Island of New Zealand revealed the importance of creating fun, exciting, and safe experiences that contain an element of risk, danger, and adrenaline related to a potential for injury and loss.

Buckley (2006) considered adventure tourism to be "guided commercial tours where the principal attraction is an outdoor activity that relies on features of the natural terrain, generally requires specialised sporting or similar equipment, and is exciting for the tour clients" (p. 1). He lists many of the same activities previously identified, but also added several other activities where the tour operator or business owner provides all the equipment and the clients need no prior skills, including abseiling, sea-kayaking, skiing, snowboarding, snowmobiling, ballooning, mountain biking, skydiving, parapenting, diving, snorkelling, surfing, sailboarding, hunting, fishing, and off-road or on-track driving (Buckley, 2006).

In 2010, Buckley explored the multiple internal and external motivations identified by experienced adventure tourists and discovered the importance of the psychophysiological adrenaline 'rush' enjoyed by both the operators and the clients (see, also, Schlegelmilch & Ollenburg, 2013). Having provided an overview of the sport and adventure tourism literature, the following section identifies some of the trends observed by those studying these forms of active tourism.

SPORT AND ADVENTURE TOURISM WITHIN AN ACTIVE ECONOMY

Twentieth century globalization and the progressive advancement of travel/transport technology has made it significantly easier for both participants and spectators to experience sporting fixtures of all sizes, regardless of the geographic location or the time of year in which they are held (Hinch & Higham, 2011). Likewise, organized trips into the wilderness or the mountains have never been easier to find or finance (Gross & Sands, 2019). Therefore, sport and adventure-related travel is frequently cited as being among the fastest growing sectors of the global tourism industry (Hinch & Higham, 2018). The niche/special interest market is believed to account for somewhere between 10 per cent and 2 per cent of all international travel and tourism receipts (Parker, 2019). The National Association of Sports Commissions claim that visitor spending associated with sport tourism accounts for 25 per cent of all tourism receipts in the United States (an estimated $8.96 billion). In many other parts of the world, including Australia and New Zealand, the income generated by sports tourism is estimated to be closer to 55 per cent (Parker, 2019).

According to the World Travel and Tourism Council's (WTTC) most recent reports, one in every ten jobs (an estimated 330 million) is influenced, if not directly supported by travel and tourism-related activity, making it one of the world's largest economic sectors (WTTC, 2020). Lock (2020) acknowledges the difficulty attached to defining what is or is not an active component of the tourism industry, noting the many different industries that both affect and are affected by the movement of people from one place to for business or pleasure. He listed the accommodation providers, hospitality businesses, travel agents, transport providers, and visitor attractions, such as theatres, museums, theme parks, water parks, and event venues, as stakeholders that profit from tourism activity (Lock, 2020). Globally, he claims that travel and tourism consumed in 2019 contributed approximately $2.9 trillion U.S. dollars to GDP, $580.7 billion of which was generated by the U.S. market (Lock, 2020).

According to Figueroa (2019), a consumer report compiled by the Adventure Travel Trade Association (ATTA) found that the adventure travel market grew at a rate of 65 per cent annually between 2009 and 2013. The ATTA is a privately held, for-profit industry trade group established in 1990 (ATTA, 2020). It serves members in more than 80 countries worldwide, with the aim of building networking and education opportunities that both professionalise and promote the adventure travel industry (Figueroa, 2019). Their Adventure Tourism Market Study (ATMS) was produced in partnership with the UNWTO, compiling relevant data from North America, South America, and Europe, the three regions that collectively account for approximately 70 per cent of all international outbound travel (Figueroa, 2019).

The findings of the 2014 ATMS revealed that 40 per cent of respondents lists adventure as being the main component of their last trip. In terms of the total value of outbound adventure tourism worldwide, Figueroa (2019) reports that the ATMS study estimated the sector to be worth $263 billion (the 2010 study reported an economic value of $89 million). This total economic impact excluded the additional $82 billion that the respondents spent on equipment and accessories for their travels, including camping gear, walking/climbing shoes, and specialised clothing (Figueroa, 2019). It also excluded the money that these tourists spent on airfares. In total, Adventure travellers were found to have spent an average of $947 per trip (up from $597 per trip in the 2010 report). In terms of demographics, the average

age of the adventure traveller was 36 years (a decrease), whilst 57 per cent were male and 37 per cent had spent at least four years at university. Unsurprisingly, 71 per cent of the respondents had a passport and the average length of soft adventure trips was ten days (an increase). 45 per cent of the ATWS respondents planned to use a tour operator for their next adventure travel trip, compared to 31 per cent of non-adventure travellers. Social media was found to be important to those within the adventure travel community with many conducting online research on Facebook, YouTube, Twitter, and Google+ when planning their travel (Figueroa, 2019).

The ATMS conclusions note the emerging relationship between adventure tourism and responsible tourism. In terms of the future, it predicted further increases in adventure travel from the source markets of North and South America, but a plateau within the European market (ATTA, 2013). China, India, and South Korea are identified as emerging travel markets (Figueroa, 2019). Gross and Sands (2020) predict that adventure tourism operators will witness a noticeable increase in the average age of their clients and an increase in the number of families. This observation was supported by the findings of Pomfret and Bramwell (2014) and Schanzel and Yeoman (2015), both of whom noted a growth in the number of families booking soft and hard adventure tourism experiences.

Another emergent market noted by the ATMS report was that of 'Microadventures', especially those packaged and promoted to professionals as being a means of improving/enhancing mental health and wellbeing (Figueroa, 2019). According to Humphreys (2014), microadventures appeal to young adults living in urban areas who are looking for a break from their everyday routine without having to travel too far from home. Abraham et al. (2009), Clough et al. (2016) and, more recently, Sand and Gross (2019) have all looked at the linkages between outdoor adventure tourism and wellbeing. Finally, Gross and Sand (2020) highlight several new adventure tourism markets expected to emerge over the next ten years, including space tourism, deep sea tourism, and virtual/augmented reality (VR) adventure tourism, the latter of which is already available (Schlegelmilch & Ollenburg, 2013).

Clearly, the forecasts and the facts presented by Figueroa (2019) and Lock (2020) fail to take into consideration the short or long-term impact of the COVID-19 global pandemic that has led to a dramatic and unprecedented, mass closure of international borders and postponement of thousands of sports events (Miles & Shipway, 2020). The following section offers an example of where the elements of active and adventure tourism have combined to grow the local economy of a remote town found on the sparsely populated South Island of New Zealand.

QUEENSTOWN, NEW ZEALAND; 'THE HOME OF ADVENTURE'

Golf, fishing, hunting, hiking (known as tramping), sailing, snow-sports, diving, skydiving, bungee jumping, jet boating, mountain climbing, and mountain biking are but some of the active tourism activities regularly enjoyed by domestic and international tourists in New Zealand (Kane & Tucker, 2004; Jamieson, 2018; Tourism New Zealand, 2020). Queenstown is widely regarded as New Zealand's "Adventure Capital'' and is marketed both domestically and international as the "home of adventure" and an "outdoor sports paradise" (QueenstownNZ, 2020). It is, by any measure, an active tourist resort town. Located in the Otago province in the south-west of New Zealand's South Island, Queenstown was once a gold mining settlement and a summer tourist destination for those living in the City of Dunedin. The heart of the town sits on the shores of the South Island's Lake Wakatipu, set against the dramatic Southern Alps.

The region's remoteness and its natural resources underpin Queenstown's vibrant active tourism economy. The image in Figure 1 was taken from the Summit of Ben Lomond, a six-hour return trek from the top of Queenstown's Skyline Gondola (Figure 4). The town has a permanent urban population of only 15,450 and wider regional population of 44,800 (Informetrics, 2020). These numbers increase during the winter ski-season, from July to October, as migrants on short and long-term visas make their way into town (to work and play). According to Tourism New Zealand, it welcomes approximately 3.2 million visitors every year. In 2019, Queenstown Airport reported 1,178,059 arrivals, 819,863 domestic arrivals and 358,196 international arrivals (Infometrics, 2020). In 2019, domestic visitor spending in Queenstown-Lakes District was estimated at $2.93 billion, just over 10 per cent of the New Zealand tourism economy (Infometrics, 2020). International expenditure in Queenstown was NZ$1.85 billion or approximately 15 per cent of international visitor expenditure in New Zealand (Infometrics, 2020).

Like much of New Zealand, Queenstown's tourism portfolio is heavily geared towards the active tourism market, from backpackers and freedom campers through to the high end/exclusive luxury lodge consumer (QueenstownNZ, 2020; Tourism New Zealand, 2020). Whitewater rafting, jet boating, mountain biking, tramping (i.e., hiking) and fly fishing are popular all year round, but especially during the summer, spring, and autumn seasons. As noted above, however, Queenstown's biggest drawcard are the easily accessible mountain ranges that surround it. While there are ski fields on the North Island and elsewhere in the South Island, Queenstown is the centre for snow sports in New Zealand with domestic and international visitors travelling to ski at the four main mountain ski fields (Cardrona Alpine Resort, Coronet Peak, The Remarkables, and Treble Cone). Cross country skiing, sledding and an eight-lane biathlon range is available at the Cardrona Waiorau Snowfarm (Snowfarmnz, 2020).

Over the past decade, the town's snow sports industry has benefited from being the host of the Winter Games New Zealand, the Southern Hemisphere's biggest snow sports event (Winter Games, 2020). Scheduled during the New Zealand winter (and the northern hemisphere summer), the Winter Games attracts over 800 athletes from over 40 countries, all seeking 'off season' competition (Winter Games, 2020). The economic impact of the 2017 event was measured at $13.5 million (Figure 5). Of note is the significant media attention given to the Winter Games in Asia, the United States, and Europe; areas in which New Zealand seldom gets a mention in a sporting context. When Australian exposure is added, the event reaches a major proportion of New Zealand's key tourism targets (Tourism New Zealand, 2020).

The Queenstown region boasts several golf courses capable of attracting domestic and international golf tourists (Tourism New Zealand, 2020). The golf courses are Queenstown Golf Club, Arrowtown Golf Club, Jack's Point Golf Course, Millbrook Golf Course, and The Hills Golf Course. The New Zealand Open Golf championships has been played at Millbrook (in Arrowtown) since 2014. In 2017, the New Zealand government announced a three-year NZ$2.8 million investment in the event via the Major Events Development Fund (MEDF). The MEDF is designed to invest in major events which are deemed able to generate significant immediate and long-term benefits to New Zealand. The investment sought to pay for broadcasting expenses to showcase New Zealand to a global audience, including (wealthy) golf tourists in the United States, China, and Japan (Tourism New Zealand, 2020).

Several short scenic walks start right from Queenstown's town centre whilst the dramatically beautiful Fiordland and Mount Aspiring national parks are within easy reach for a day trip or the full multi-day hiking expedition. Queenstown is the gateway to three of New Zealand's celebrated Great Walks: the Milford Track, the Kepler Track and the Routeburn. The Kepler Track is a 60 km circular hiking track situated near the town of Te Anau. The track is managed by the Department of Conservation (DOC). Each November, the track hosts the Kepler Challenge where runners from New Zealand and overseas complete the track in as little as 4 and half hours for men and close to five hours for women. The track is normally completed over three days by trampers. Due to environmental and safety considerations, the field is limited to 450 competitors. However, the extreme popularity of the event and the lack of a lottery means the event sells out and fills a waiting list almost immediately.

Fly-fishing opportunities in Queenstown are plentiful, with many fly-fishing tours available throughout the October-March fishing season. Queenstown and the wider Southern Lakes region also have excellent hunting opportunities. Local game includes red stag, fallow deer, chamois, Himalayan tahr, and wild goats. Queenstown has some of New Zealand's most accessible alpine climbing experiences. Abseiling and canyoning are two other popular tourist activities. Kayaking, canoeing, and rafting are also readily available. Queenstown provides a variety of biking tracks and trails for all levels of fitness. Several Queenstown biking tracks start right from the town centre. The 130km Queenstown Trail is a network of off-road trails that cover many of Queenstown's most picturesque locations, including Lake Wakatipu, Lake Hayes, Arrowtown, and Gibbston (QueenstownNZ, 2020).

Like many tourist towns there is concern regarding the impact of tourism on the natural and physical infrastructure. The Queenstown Airport Corporation has proposed new noise boundaries to accommodate the growth and will offer to buy some homes and spend millions of dollars on noise mitigation packages. There is a desperate shortage of affordable housing. Residential housing in the Queenstown area is quite expensive due to factors such as the town being a tourist destination, its lack of land and its desirability to foreigners and investors. Queenstown is rated the least affordable place in New Zealand to buy a property. In December 2016, the average house price in the Queenstown area rose to $1 million NZD (Infometrics, 2020). Roads are clogged at peak times and traffic congestion in Queenstown is one manifestation of an insufficiently rapid response to growth of the local population and visitors. In fact, prior to the COVID-19 crisis, which effectively brought Queenstown's tourism industry to a sudden halt, there was growing unrest amongst locals who were being priced out by the influx of out-of-towners.

CONCLUSION

An active economy includes organizations and individuals who directly or indirectly contribute to the strengthening of physical, mental and/or social health and wellness through the development and delivery of sport and active recreation experiences (Finch et al., 2019). Active tourism is built upon a positive proactive mind-set as much as it is a profitable marketplace. Although the true socio-economic value of the sector is impossible to calculate, its importance to those employed within the billion-dollar tourism industry is both obvious and unquestionable. By sharing the origins and opportunities attached to this expanding international market, the authors have also demonstrated the sector's mass appeal to the paid and paying producers and consumers of a myriad special interest/niche serious leisure pursuits. The aim of this chapter was to offer some insight into the benefits attached to investing in products and services that appeal to those looking to engage in hard or soft natured physical activities during their holidays.

Queenstown exemplifies many aspects of an active tourist town with a significant dimension to its overall tourism portfolio and a large international value chain that impacts many stakeholders both within and beyond New Zealand's active economy.

Examples of active sport events and adventure tourism attractions in New Zealand come in many forms, and tourism is now the largest foreign exchange earning industry for the geographically isolated nation. (Stats New Zealand, 2020). It is also the nation's largest export industry, having overtaken farming/agriculture (meat and dairy), and one of its largest employers, accounting for 21 per cent of foreign exchange earnings and 8.4 per cent of the New Zealand labor market (Stats New Zealand, 2020). In 2017, New Zealand's skiing industry attracted a record 1.6 million international visitors (Jamieson, 2018).

Although the focus of this chapter was Queenstown, the home of adventure, the authors could have easily presented active tourism case studies that focused on the North Island towns of Rotorua, Taupo, New Plymouth, Raglan, Paihia or Waitomo, or the South Island towns of Nelson and Kaikoura, all of which have built an active economy off the back of the active sport and recreation market (surfing, diving, snow-sports, mountain-biking etc). Furthermore, the regional tourism and economic development agencies located in New Zealand's largest urban centres, Auckland, and Christchurch, also invest millions into promoting the many land and water-based active tourism experiences located within their area.

In sum, active tourists participate in organized sport and/or recreational physical activities whilst away from their home environment (Finch et al., 2019). Since the turn of the 21st century, the active/participatory sport and adventure tourism market has profited from globalization, the emergence of the experience economy and the explosion of the health and fitness industry, fully establishing itself across the developed and developing world. It appeals to people of all ages, genders, and cultures, attracting hard and soft consumers with a shared interest and understanding around the benefits of engaging in social and self-indulgent physical activity. Arguably, what separates adventure tourism from other forms of activity-based sports tourism is the inherent element of risk/uncertainty and the extensive amount of pre-trip preparation and specialised equipment required (Grant, 2001). The stakeholder map and value chain attached to active tourism is both large and long, with several industries profiting/profiteering from the noticeable growth in supply and demand interest witnessed over the past twenty years (Lock, 2020). In conclusion, the active tourism market overlaps with many of the other economies presented within this publication, not least those generated by the suppliers of organized sport, active recreation, and a whole host of holistic health/wellbeing-related enterprises. It can no longer be referred to as an emergent or immature market about which little is known or understood. Active tourism is well-established and it will be around for a long time, (and a good time).

REFERENCES

Abraham, A., Sommerhalder, K., & Abel, T. (2009). Landscape and well-being: A scoping study on the health-promoting impact of outdoor environments. *International Journal of Public Health, 55*(1), 59–69. doi:10.100700038-009-0069-z PMID:19768384

Adventure Travel Trade Association (ATTA). (2010). *Adventure tourism market report.* https://www.adventuretravel.biz/research/adventure-tourism-market-report-2010

Buckley, R. (2006). Adventure tourism research: A guide to the literature. *Tourism Recreation Research, 31*(2), 75–83. doi:10.1080/02508281.2006.11081265

Buckley, R. (2010). *Adventure tourism management.* Butterworth-Heinemann.

Buning, R. J., & Gibson, H. J. (2015). The evolution of active-sport-event travel careers. *Journal of Sport Management, 29*(5), 555–569. doi:10.1123/jsm.2014-0215

Clough, P., Houge Mackenzie, S., Mallabon, E., & Brymer, E. (2016). Adventurous physical activity environments: A mainstream intervention for mental health. *Sports Medicine (Auckland, N.Z.), 46*(7), 963–968. doi:10.100740279-016-0503-3 PMID:26895993

De Knop, P. (1990). Sport for all and active tourism. *World Leisure & Recreation, 32*(3), 30–36. doi:10.1080/10261133.1990.10559120

Figueroa, A. (2019, June 26). Adventure tourism is the fastest-growing global niche. *Tripsavvy.* https://www.tripsavvy.com/the-adventure-tourism-boom-3252455

Finch, D. J., Legg, D., O' Reilly, N., Ribeiro, J., & Tombe, T. (2019, September 18). *Calgary's Regional Active Economy: An Exploratory Study of the Role of an Active Ecosystem in Generating Community Value.* ActiveCITY Collective.

Gammon, S., Ramshaw, G., & Wright, R. K. (2017). Theory in Sport Tourism: Some critical reflections. *Journal of Sport & Tourism, 21*(2), 69–74. doi:10.1080/14775085.2017.1319515

Gammon, S., & Robinson, T. (2003). Sport and tourism: A conceptual framework. *Journal of Sport & Tourism, 8*(1), 21–26. doi:10.1080/14775080306236

Getz, D. (2003). Sport event tourism: planning, development, and marketing. In S. Hudson (Ed.), *Sport and Adventure Tourism.* Haworth Hospitality Press.

Getz, D. (2008). Event Tourism: Definition, evolution, and research. *Tourism Management, 29*(3), 403–428. doi:10.1016/j.tourman.2007.07.017

Getz, D., & McConnell, A. (2011). Serious sport tourism and event travel careers. *Journal of Sport Management*, *25*(4), 326–338. doi:10.1123/jsm.25.4.326

Gibson, H. (1996). Thrill seeking vacations: A lifespan perspective. *Loisir et Societe. Society and Leisure*, *19*(2), 439–458. doi:10.1080/07053436.1996.10715527

Gibson, H. (1998a). Sport tourism: A critical analysis of research. *Sport Management Review*, *1*(1), 45–76. doi:10.1016/S1441-3523(98)70099-3

Gibson, H. (1998b). Active sport tourism: Who participates? *Leisure Studies*, *17*(2), 155–170. doi:10.1080/026143698375213

Gibson, H. (2004). Moving beyond the "what is and who" of sport tourism to understanding "why". *Journal of Sport & Tourism*, *9*(3), 247–265. doi:10.1080/1477508042000320232

Gibson, H. (2017). Commentary: Sport tourism and theory and some other developments: Some reflections. *Journal of Sport & Tourism*, *21*(2), 153–158. doi:10.1080/14775085.2017.1319514

Gibson, H., Attle, S., & Yiannakis, A. (1998). Segmenting the active sport tourist market: A life-span perspective. *Journal of Vacation Marketing*, *4*(1), 52–64. doi:10.1177/135676679800400105

Glyptis, S. A. (1982). *Sport and tourism in Western Europe*. British Travel Education Trust.

Grant, D. (2001). Adventure Tourism: A Journey of the Mind. In L. Roberts & D. Hall (Eds.), *Rural Tourism and Recreation: Principles and Practice* (pp. 166–170). CABI Publishing.

Gross, S., & Sand, M. (2019). Adventure tourism: A perspective paper. *Tourism Review*, *75*(1), 153–157. doi:10.1108/TR-06-2019-0211

Hall, C. M. (1992). Adventure, sport, and health tourism. In B. Weiler & C. M. Hall (Eds.), *Special interest tourism* (pp. 141–158). Halsted Press.

Hinch, T., & Higham, J. (2011). *Sport tourism development* (2nd ed.). Channel View Publications.

Hudson, S. (Ed.). (2003). *Sport and adventure tourism*. Haworth Hospitality Press.

Humphreys, A. (2014). *Microadventures. Local discoveries for great escapes*. Harper Collins.

Informetrics. (2020). Queenstown Lake District Economic Profile. *Informetrics.* https://ecoprofile.infometrics.co.nz/queenstown-lakes+district

Kane, M. J., & Tucker, H. (2004). Adventure tourism: The freedom to play with reality. *Tourist Studies*, *4*(3), 217–234. doi:10.1177/1468797604057323

Kaplanidou, K., & Gibson, H. (2010). Predicting behavioral intentions of active event sport tourists: The case of a small-scale recurring sports event. *Journal of Sport & Tourism*, *15*(2), 163–179. doi:10.1080/14775085.2010.498261

Kurtzman, J., & Zauhar, J. (1997). A wave in time – the sports tourism phenomena. *Journal of Sport & Tourism*, *8*(1), 35–47. doi:10.1080/14775080306239

Laing, J., & Frost, W. (2014). *Explorer travellers and adventure tourism.* Channel View Publications. doi:10.21832/9781845414597

Lamont, M., & McKay, J. (2012). Intimations of postmodernity in sports tourism at the Tour de France. *Journal of Sport & Tourism*, *17*(4), 313–331. doi:10.1080/14775085.2012.760935

Lock, S. (2020, March 31). *Tourism worldwide – statistics and facts.* https://www.statista.com/topics/962/global-tourism/

Miles, L., & Shipway, R. (2020). Exploring the COVID-19 Pandemic as a Catalyst for Stimulating Future Research Agendas for Managing Crises and Disasters at International Sport Events. *Event Management*, *24*(4), 537–552. doi:10.3727/152599519X15506259856688

Muller, T., & Cleaver, M. (2000). Targeting the CANZUS baby boomer explorer and adventure segments. *Journal of Vacation Marketing*, *6*(2), 154–169. doi:10.1177/135676670000600206

Parker, R. (2019). The Remarkable Growth of Sport Tourism. *Human Kinetics.* https://humankinetics.me/2019/04/04/the-remarkable-growth-of-sport-tourism/

Pomfret, G., & Bramwell, B. (2014). The characteristics and motivational decisions of outdoor adventure tourists: A review and analysis. *Current Issues in Tourism*, *19*(14), 1447–1478. doi:10.1080/13683500.2014.925430

Queenstown, N. Z. (2020). Queenstown Facts and Statistics. *Queenstown NZ.* https://www.queenstownnz.co.nz/insights-and-stats/

Rantala, O., & Rokenses, A. (2018). Is adventure tourism a coherent concept? A review of research approaches on adventure tourism. *Annals of Leisure Research*, *21*(5), 539–552. doi:10.1080/11745398.2016.1250647

Sand, M., & Gross, S. (2019). Tourism research on adventure tourism – Current themes and developments. *Journal of Outdoor Recreation and Tourism*, *28*, 1–5. doi:10.1016/j.jort.2019.100261

Schanzel, H. A., & Yeoman, I. (2015). Trends in family tourism. *Journal of Tourism Futures*, *1*(2), 141–147. doi:10.1108/JTF-12-2014-0006

Schlegelmilch, F., & Ollenburg, C. (2013). Marketing the adventure: Utilizing the aspects of risk/fear/thrill to target the youth traveller segment. *Tourism Review*, *68*(3), 44–54. doi:10.1108/TR-03-2013-0010

SnowFarm NZ. (2020). About Us. *SnowFarm NZ*. https://snowfarmnz.com/about/

Standeven, J., & De Knop, P. (1999). *Sport tourism*. Human Kinetics.

Sung, H. H., Morrison, A. M., & O'Leary, J. T. (1997). Definition of Adventure Travel: Conceptual Framework for Empirical Application from the Providers' Perspective. *Asia Pacific Journal of Tourism Research*, *1*(2), 47–66. doi:10.1080/10941669708721975

Swarbrooke, J., Beard, C., Leckie, S., & Pomfret, G. (2003). *Adventure tourism – the new frontier*. Elsevier Science.

Taylor, S., Varley, P., & Johnston, T. (2013). *Adventure tourism: Meanings, experience, and learning*. Taylor & Francis. doi:10.4324/9780203120095

Tourism New Zealand. (2020). *Special Interests. Tourism New Zealand*. https://www.tourismnewzealand.com/markets-stats/sectors/special-interest/

Weed, M., & Bull, C. (2009). *Sports tourism: participants, policy, and providers* (2nd ed.). Butterworth-Heinemann.

Williams, P., & Soutar, G. (2009). Value, satisfaction and behavioural intentions in an adventure tourism context. *Annals of Tourism Research*, *36*(3), 413–443. doi:10.1016/j.annals.2009.02.002

Winter Games. (2020). Our Story. *Winter Games NZ*. https://www.wintergamesnz.kiwi/our-story

World Travel & Tourism Council. (2020). *Travel and tourism: Benchmarking trends report 2019*. World Travel & Tourism Council. https://wttc.org/en-gb/Research/Economic-Impact/Benchmarking

Chapter 8
Active Technology and Accessories

Jared R. Fletcher
Mount Royal University, Canada

Christy Tomkins-Lane
Mount Royal University, Canada

ABSTRACT

Active technology (i.e. 'wearables' and accompanying health tracking apps) is a multi-billion-dollar industry. Nearly one in every 10 people worldwide generates physiological and biomechanical data from wearable devices every day. This data allows users to evaluate their performance over time, to share with friends, to find like-minded training partners and share this data with their primary healthcare providers. Population-based research related to health, wellness, and physical activity is now feasible as a result of data generated from wearables. This chapter will highlight the major current trends and future applications for wearable devices from a user and research-based perspective across the active economy. The authors aim to highlight the practical and clinical utility of wearables to monitor training, fatigue, and performance on the athletic field, the workplace, and the clinical environments. The goal is to improve health, mobility, and quality of life of the end-user.

INTRODUCTION

Despite the COVID-19 pandemic, and the impact on the global economy, wearable sales totalled approximately 400 million units in 2020; a near 15 per cent increase from the previous year (International Data Corporation, 2020). The vast majority

DOI: 10.4018/978-1-7998-7939-8.ch008

of these sales in 2020 are hearables: wireless headphones and earphones offering features such as fitness tracking, smart assistants, and language translation. An additional 91 million smart watches and 68 million smart wrist-bands were sold by companies such as Apple, Xiaomi, Huawei, Fitbit, and Garmin topping the sales categories in 2020.

These devices generate an enormous amount of data related to health and fitness. Soon, a tenth of humanity will produce data with wearables. Today, tracking heart rate, speed and distance, or daily step counts from these devices are among the most basic of functions. With such data, a profound research and development potential has been created, both from the user's and the providers' perspectives. From a user's perspective, these wearables offer the opportunity to evaluate their personal data in the sports and fitness area, to analyze data over time, to share data with friends, training partners, and even their primary health-care providers. One may compare themselves with other (even elite) athletes, to find virtual training partners from the surrounding area or across the globe, or to exchange training programs with other athletes and coaches worldwide.

This data is also useful from a research and health-care perspective. It allows coaches, and sports science/medicine practitioners to monitor training intensity and training loads, often in real time, to detect training or lifestyle-related fatigue, and to detect the onset of disease (often before symptom-onset). The latter feature is particularly appealing during and following the global COVID-19 pandemic: wearables will enable telehealth between user and primary health-care provider(s) via remote patient monitoring, making healthcare services more accessible, timely and cost efficient. A key benefit of telehealth is its ability to drive positive patient experience and eliminate access barriers to offer patient-centric and convenient care. Wearables will also play a key role in precision medicine by providing physicians better knowledge of patients' health since patient data are continuously collected and analyzed, throughout the day and night. Integration of sensors such as physiological sensors and biochemical sensors will provide continuous monitoring of a patient's vital signs and timely clinical decisions can be taken such as therapy modifications based on subtle changes observed in health patterns.

Wearables also have the potential to transform the fields of biomechanics and engineering by enabling researchers to measure real-world movement outside of the lab or clinical setting (Chambers et al., 2015; Havens et al., 2018; Hullfish et al., 2019; Peppoloni et al., 2014). This real-world data can be analyzed to quantify sports performance (Camomilla et al., 2018), movement disorders (Johansson et al., 2018), gait analysis (Rebula et al., 2013) and injury risk (Matijevich et al., 2019; Sheerin et al., 2019). Indeed, integration of data from multiple sensors worn by the user at the same time, along with the possibility of machine-learning algorithms to analyze and interpret this data, offers the exciting potential of wearable devices to monitor, assess and intervene in movement analysis across multiple real-world settings (Matijevich et al., 2020).

Here, we aim to describe the use of wearables within the active economy. We will evaluate the historical background of the sector, the function of various wearable devices and evaluate the utility of these devices in the athletic, clinical, rehabilitation and medical communities. Together, we contend that the active technology and accessories sector will impact the lives of the wearer as well as third-party users, such as physicians and researchers who can gain access to enormous amounts of data by millions of users world-wide related to their movement patterns, amount of physical activity and physiological vital signs. Ultimately, this will lead to tangible and intangible economic, societal, and human value.

BACKGROUND

Active technology (i.e. commercial wearables) consists of small, portable, often inexpensive sensors packaged with software algorithms and user interfaces. These wearables often contain various sensors including inertial measurement units (IMUs), consisting of accelerometers, gyroscopes and magnetometers which measure accelerations, position and orientation of individual limbs or the whole-body centre of mass to estimate movement patterns (Mooney et al., 2015). When exercising outdoors, global positioning systems (GPS) can measure speed, distance and topography of the user's movements, and sensors may be imbedded in footwear, to assess the interaction of forces between the user and the ground (Fong et al., 2008; Howell et al., 2013; Hurkmans et al., 2006; Matijevich et al., 2020) or to assess mechanical loads of biological materials to evaluate athletic performance, rehabilitation, recovery, and overuse injury risk (Harper et al., 2020).

What is the History of This Sector?

In the 15th Century, Leonardo da Vinci sketched a wearable device with a pendulum arm that would swing back and forth on every step to track the distance travelled by soldiers. Later, from 1770 to 1777, Abraham-Louis Perrelet, a Swiss watchmaker, invented a self-winding watch that would oscillate with each step of the wearer. This self-winding watch however did not directly calculate step count or distance walked. The first patent for a pedometer was awarded to John Harwood in 1926 (Harwood, 1926), although this was also devised as a "watch with a self-winding movement". The device, which expanded upon Perrelet's watch, wound the main watch spring by an oscillating weight pivoting within the watch as it was worn.

Despite many believing this to be the first pedometer patent, it was not written as such (Harwood, 1926).

The wearable sector became a key contributor to the health & wellness sector of the active economy in the 1960s, when Dr. Yoshiro Hatano, a professor at Kyushu University of Health and Welfare, devised a marketing campaign to signal Japan's commitment to health and wellness prior to the 1964 Tokyo Summer Olympics. Dr. Hatano began selling a compact pedometer, the *Manpo-kei*, in order to promote physical activity as part of a healthy lifestyle. The *Manpo-kei* literally translates to "10000 step meter", an idealized goal for the wearer to achieve 10,000 steps per day according to *Manpo-kei* marketing. This value continues to be a suggested goal for a user's step counts per day by wearable device manufacturers (Tudor-locke et al., 2011).

Wearable devices which track and monitor daily physical activity use IMU-generated data to quantify motion. Each manufacturer uses proprietary algorithms to detect and quantify steps taken from these IMU-generated signals. The common goal of 10,000 steps per day most often incorporated into wearables software remains contentious. There is limited evidence on how many steps per day are needed to improve fitness, reduce the risk of chronic disease and premature death, improve body composition, bone health, cognitive function and maintain or improve one's quality of life. Indeed, it is unclear whether 10,000 steps per day even meet physical activity guidelines of developed countries, including Canada. Furthermore, the measurement of steps per day alone ignores public health recommendations that individuals should aim to achieve at least 150 minutes of moderate to vigorous physical activity per week (Tremblay et al., 2011). It remains unknown or at best, unclear, how these wearable devices' proprietary algorithms decipher whether steps are taken slow or fast, the latter of which would be considered moderate to vigorous physical activity.

HEART RATE MONITORING FROM WEARABLE DEVICES

Heart rate monitoring, which is now commonplace in smart watches, was not introduced as a 'wearable' until 1977 when Seppo Säynäjäkangas, a Finnish professor from the University of Oulu, decided to use fingertip heart rate monitors with the Finnish National Cross Country Ski Team to ensure the athletes were training at the correct exercise intensity he had prescribed (*Wearables – The Big Data Machines.: Hakom*, n.d.). Säynäjäkangas would find Polar Electro and introduced their first consumer product in 1978 – a wearable heart rate monitor. By 1984, The Polar Sport Tester PE3000 allowed athletes to view and analyze their heart rate data following training for the first time.

With the introduction of the Forerunner in 2006, Garmin was able to incorporate Global Position Systems into a wearable watch for consumers to monitor their speed, distance, and elevation gains, along with heart rate measured from a chest strap. In 2009, Apple put an accelerometer in the IPod Nano to monitor step count. In the same year, Fitbit introduced the Classic model, a pedometer worn on the waist. Later, consumers were given fitness bands worn on the wrist, later incorporated into smart watches, to collect and analyze and interpret a host of body signals prior to, during, and following exercise.

Photoplethysmography (PPG) is an optical technique that detects changes in blood volume of the superficial vasculature corresponding to each heartbeat (Bourdillon et al., 2019). Heart rate can be calculated from the interval between pulsatile waveforms (Figure 1 Heart rate and heart rate variability can be quantified reliably using PPG (Lu et al., 2009; Selvaraj et al., 2008).

Current Trends in Fitness: 2007 to 2021

The *American College of Sports Medicine's Health & Fitness Journal* has conducted an annual survey of fitness trends since 2006. The purpose of these annual surveys is to determine current trends within the fitness industry for the forthcoming year. The information regarding potential trends can be used in the commercial (for-profit companies), clinical, community and corporate divisions of industry to provide stakeholders to determine if any of these trends fit their business model and how to best use the information for potential market expansion (Thompson, 2021).

In the first fitness trends survey which forecasted fitness trends for 2007, the top trend was exercise programs for children to fight childhood and adolescent obesity, as childhood obesity was (and continues to be) a growing epidemic in developed countries (Thompson & Ph, 2006). Of the top 20 listed fitness trends of 2007, none were related to active technology or accessories. In contrast, results of the 2021 Fitness Trends survey ranked "wearable technology" as #2 (behind only "online/ virtual training", largely as a result of changes within the fitness industry due to the COVID-19 pandemic). In fact, "wearable technology" has been a regular staple at the top of this survey since first appearing at #1 in 2016 – the first time 'wearable technology' appeared on the list at all (Thompson, 2021). See Figure 2.

Figure 1. The R-to-R interval (RRI) measured from a standard Lead II electrocardiogram relative to the PP interval (PPI) derived from finger-worn transducer. The PPI is derived from variations in infrared reflectance resulting from changes in blood volume within the region of interest. From Selveraj et al., (2008).

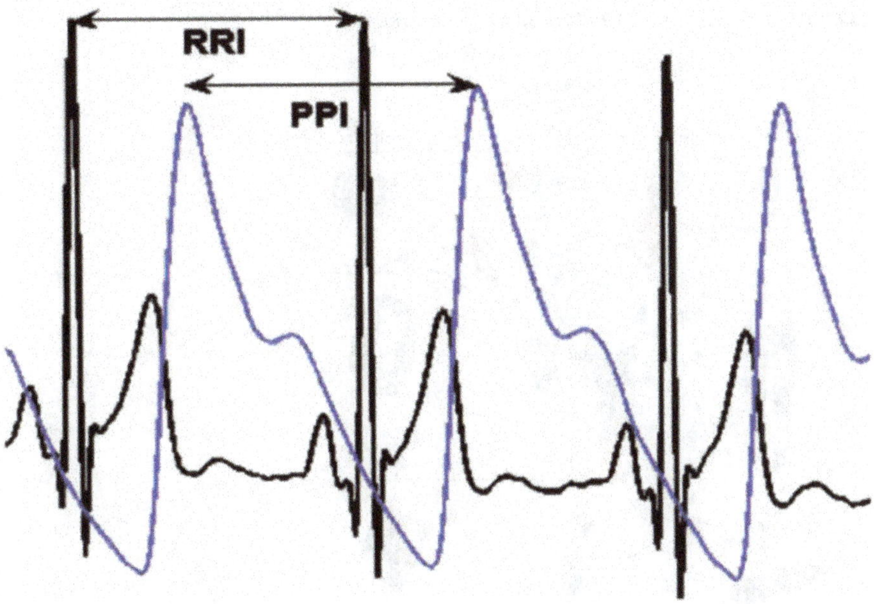

Today, smart watches and bands are used across the active economy to monitor nearly every mechanical and physiological signal one could imagine. Here, we highlight some of the main trends related to the wearables market, summarized in Figure 1. These include using wearable devices to prescribe exercise, to monitor training load, to detect physiological improvements (such as fitness) or impairments (such as fatigue, or disease). We will further describe how wearables are used in some fashion by nearly every professional and collegiate sports franchise to monitor training volume and intensity and to appropriately prescribe exercise. Clinically, we will describe how wearables are being used to improve mobility in patients, to estimate loads on muscles, tendons and bones to detect and avoid potential injury as well as the emerging wearable consumer market related to epidermal electronics: miniature sensors adhering to the skin to monitor biological signals such as: heart rate and muscle activity, sweat composition to monitor hydration, skin temperature to monitor thermal stress, and when the skin is too cold, to incorporate thermal heaters to pre-heat the skin and underlying tissues prior to exercise. While this level of technology development is typically driven by bioengineers, effective validation of this technology, and effective methods for processing this data requires close collaboration across multiple scientific fields (mathematics, computer science, statistics, biomechanics, physiology, medicine etc.).

Figure 2. Summary of current technologies for monitoring health/performance and targeted physical measurements. From Peake et al., (2018)

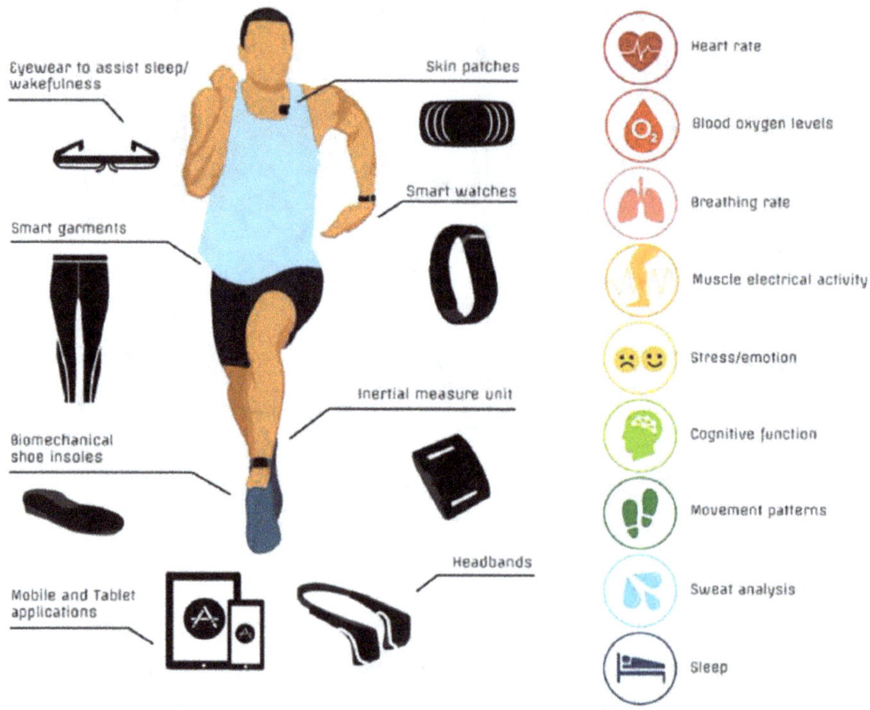

Can Wearables Accurately Quantify Exercise Intensity?

Exercise intensity has historically been prescribed largely by 'feel' and 'intuition' (Bompa & Buzzichelli, 2018). Historically, coaches and practitioners have rarely used objective methods to alternate or plan training intensities. In individual sports like running, cycling, and swimming, coaches typically quantify training volume using distance (for example, miles or kilometers performed per week) or time (e.g. number of minutes per week). Training intensity would be prescribed largely based on some iteration of ratings of perceived exertion scales (Eston et al., 1987). Prior to the 'wearables boom' of the last 10 years and the introduction of GPS technology to objectively quantify speed and distance, aerobic exercise would have to be performed on a running or cycling track, with accurate timing to measure both distance and speed to quantify training volume and intensity.

With the establishment of telemetric heart rate monitors, training intensity could be quantified and prescribed for the first time using an athlete's steady-state heart rate (Figure 3). Wearable devices that included GPS technology could now accurately measure speed and distance of the training session. By periodically evaluating the heart rate vs. speed relationship, this data could also be used by coaches and athletes as a 'field' test as an indirect marker of economy/efficiency and may indirectly serve to indicate states of transient or long-lasting fatigue (Smith et al., 2002). An exemplar field test is shown in Figure 4. Using the linear relationship between heart rate and speed, and knowing or estimating the athlete's maximum heart rate, the speed at maximal oxygen uptake (VO_2max) can be estimated. This speed corresponds to an intensity of exercise that can be sustained for approximately 3-5 minutes (Billat et al., 1996).

While these methods are simple and inexpensive, precisely quantifying training intensity based on heart rate is not straightforward. At the initiation of submaximal, constant-intensity exercise, heart rate will quickly rise until it reaches a steady-state where it remains relatively constant (within a few beats per minute). In the case of steady-state exercise, average heart rate measured after the initial rise accurately reflects the cardiovascular demand of the exercise; training intensity can be quantified and prescribed based solely on the measured heart rate, in absolute units (i.e. in beats per minute) or as a percentage of maximum heart rate.

At intensities of exercise above which all of the energy cannot be met aerobically, termed the anaerobic threshold (Svedahl & MacIntosh, 2003), when submaximal exercise is maintained for long durations, heart rate will continue to rise. In these situations, heart rate will not accurately reflect training intensity since at a constant exercise intensity, heart rate will continue to increase until maximum heart rate. At that point, exercise would soon stop. In other circumstances, such as during short-duration exercise, or high-intensity interval training, the measured heart rate response is too slow to accurately reflect the intensity of exercise. Therefore, quantification of training intensity in strength, speed or power events must necessarily be quantified based on some percentage of maximum speed or power, and not heart rate. Consequently, almost all commercially available wearable devices are equipped with both heart rate and GPS sensors (Peake et al., 2018).

Figure 3. Heart rate measured beat-to-beat during submaximal, steady-state overground running in a 22-year-old, highly trained female distance runner using a Suunto Ambit 3. The vertical dashed line indicates the start of exercise, which was preceded by five minutes of quiet sitting. Her maximum heart rate is 194 b/min and her steady-state heart rate, calculated as the average heart rate in the final 5 minutes was 156 bpm.

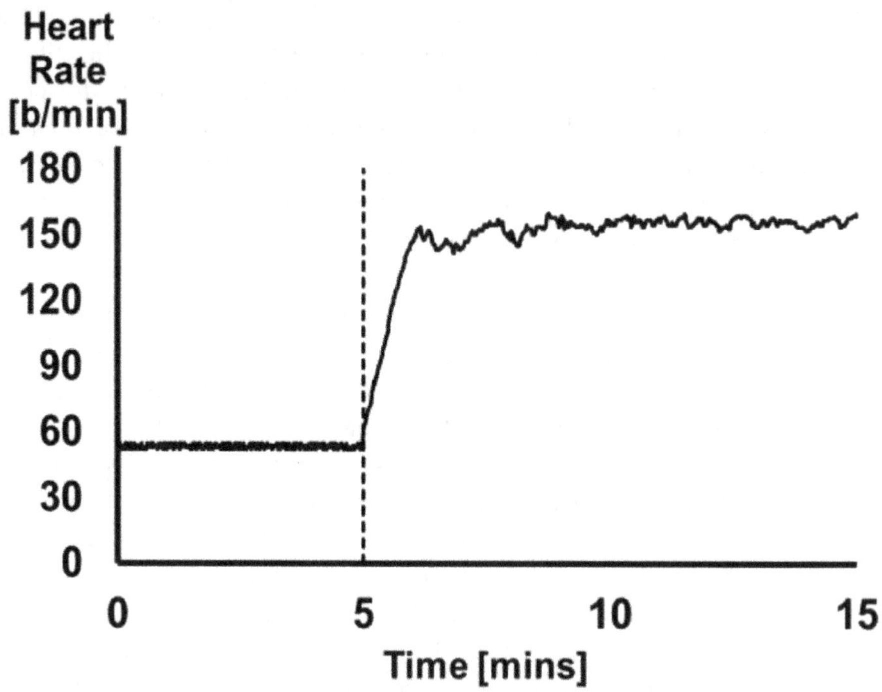

WEARABLES AND HEART RATE VARIABILITY (HRV)

Exercise training results in a transient period of objective and subjectively measured fatigue. This fatigue results in a transient reduction in fitness capacity or performance. With adequate recovery, this short-term fatigue is reduced, and adaptation, above and beyond the initial fitness level occurs. This is often referred to as supercompensation (Issurin, 2010). This is demonstrated in Figure 4. If another training stimulus is applied during the period of super compensation, the transient fatigue and recovery results in a higher level of fitness. Further improvements in aerobic fitness are achieved through purposeful and varied periods of training and recovery. When adequate recovery periods are not permitted, progressive, training-induced fatigue accumulates and can rapidly lead to stagnation or decrease in exercise tolerance or performance, development of burnout, staleness, or chronic fatigue (Kuipers & Keizer, 1988; Lehmann et al., 1993). Thus, consistent monitoring of the fatigue-recovery-super compensation processes in athletes should reduce the incidence of over-reaching and overtraining symptoms. Furthermore, gaining insight into the transient period of fatigue vs. adaptation from a specific exercise stimulus may result in better prescription of frequency, duration, and intensity of training. The ability to adjust a training program will help to avoid maladaptation to training and should lead to improved performances. This may be particularly relevant in recreationally trained athletes, or individuals thinking of engaging in exercise programs, who often do not have access to advanced knowledge of training prescription and periodization. The ability to appropriately prescribe and adjust training programs can be done via artificial intelligence and/or machine learning within wearables' software.

Figure 4. Exemplar steady-state heart rate vs speed relationship of an elite Paralympic swimmer performing a submaximal, incremental field test. Black line shows the linear HR vs speed relationship at some baseline. A higher heart rate at a given speed, illustrated by the red line above the black line, indicates transient or longer-lasting fatigue. The blue line, showing a lower heart rate at a given speed compared to baseline, indicates performance improvement. In all cases, the linear relationship can be extrapolated to maximum heart rate to estimate the speed at VO_2max.

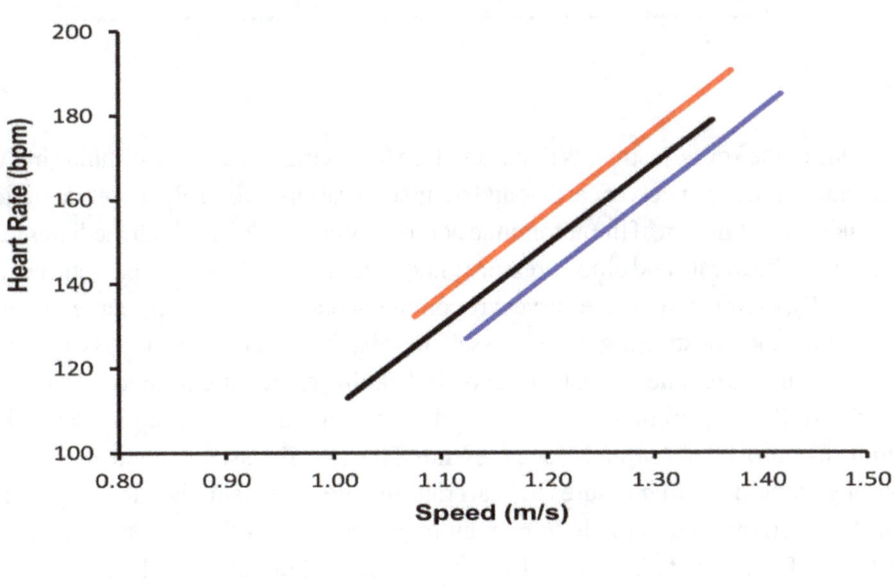

Figure 5. The supercompensation cycle as a result of periodic training. A training load results in a transient phase of fatigue and recovery, followed by a supercompensation of initial fitness. The goal of training periodization is to induce an appropriate training load (volume and intensity) at the appropriate time in order to induce further supercompensation cycles. Note the reduction in fitness ('return to pre-load level') if subsequent training bouts are not initiated. From Issurin (2010).

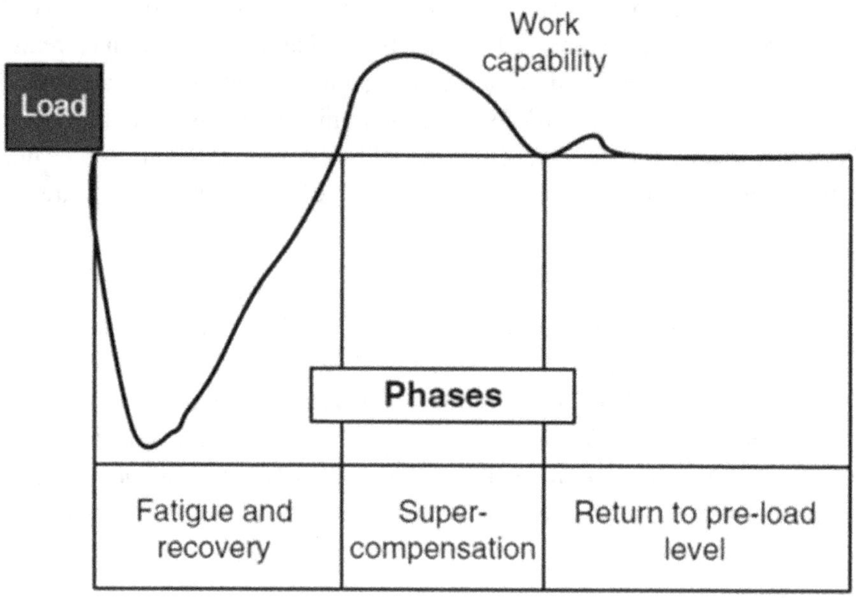

One of the key adjustments that take place following an exercise stimulus include adaptations to all aspects of cardiac and peripheral vascular control. These adaptations include the regulation of the autonomic nervous system (ANS), which mediates rapid changes in heart rate and blood pressure via sympathetic and parasympathetic nerves. Generally, the effects of these nerves are complementary: sympathetic nerves increase heart rate and constricting blood vessels to raise blood pressure. Parasympathetic nerve input causes the opposite effects. In healthy, exercising individuals, the role of the ANS is to optimally control cardiovascular function through beat-to beat adjustments of heart rate and blood pressure. Thus, cardiovascular control, measured through time-domain measures of heart rate and blood pressure is a direct reflection of ANS activity and is likely to play an important role in the training response of athletes (Buchheit et al., 2012; Pichot et al., 2002; Plews et al., 2013).

A non-invasive method to assess ANS function and training adaptation in athletes is by assessing daily, resting heart rate variability (HRV), the regular fluctuation or variability seen in a beat-to-beat heart rate signal, on a daily or weekly basis (Buchheit et al., 2012)

Monitoring changes in HRV is useful because HRV detects non-functional overreaching and negative adaptations to training, increases in fitness (Mourot et al., 2004) and has the potential for improved exercise performance (Atlaoui et al., 2007; Garet et al., 2004a). Specifically, time-domain indices of HRV suggest a low HRV is associated with training maladaptation, and additional stress (sleep disturbances, onset of illness, etc.) whereas high HRV is associated with training adaptation and improved fitness (Baumert et al., 2006; Bosquet et al., 2008; Botek et al., 2014; Koenig et al., 2014; Manzi et al., 2009). Based on these indices of high and low HRV, the timing and specific prescription of intensity and/or duration of exercise may be used across a broad spectrum of athletes and sporting activities. Since HRV is also expected to decrease transiently with the onset of illness (Kuipers & Keizer, 1988), it may be a useful metric already incorporated into many wearable devices to detect maladaptation to training, including the onset of illness. HRV metrics may also be useful to quantify fatigue exposure in the workplace.

WEARABLES AND THE WORKPLACE

By incorporating heart rate monitoring and accelerometry into smart bands or watches, 24-hour movement data can be collected. From this data, metrics of fatigue can be calculated and interpreted. These metrics include 24-hour heart rate variability monitoring to detect and monitor internal stressor. Combined with accelerometry, these wearables can measure the quality and quantity of sleep of the user. Together, fatigue can be quantified. For example, smart bands, such as the Whoop strap or ReadiBand, claim they are able to quantify fatigue in professional athletes, military personnel and industry workers based on proprietary algorithms. Specifically, the ReadiBand, from Fatigue Science calculates an 'alertness score' based on timing, quantify and quality of sleep (Fatigue Science, 2021). Based on this data, the alertness score can be forecasted up to 14-days in advance. Their website claims the following:

With 14-Day Fatigue Forecasting, supervisors and management teams can now view future fatigue hotspots showing the "who, when, and where" of workforce fatigue far enough in advance to take meaningful action to mitigate both routine and mission critical fatigue risks. Authorized supervisors can view scientifically validated "heat maps" of worker fatigue, revealing at-a-glance any workers in their crew who are likely to face significant fatigue on the next two weeks of duty, and on which specific days. Supervisors can then reach out to individuals, sharing data-backed guidance to focus on sleep on certain days and to be particularly cautious at work when those days arrive. Moreover, supervisors can plan critical tasks for the times of least fatigue, choosing the right worker for the right task, at the right time. (Fatigue Science, 2021).

Fatigue-related reductions in worker productivity costs approximately $2000 per employee annually in the United States (Rosekind et al., 2010), and the vast majority of workplace accidents are caused by human error. Many of these human errors were made by personnel who often lacked adequate sleep (Dinges, 1995). Direct costs from these workplace accidents can include workers compensation payouts, significant health care costs and equipment damage, estimated to be approximately $300,000 for fatigue-related accidents (Fatigue Science, 2021). The indirect costs can be many times higher when one considers work stoppages, re-training or replacement of employees, crisis management and workplace safety time and potential legal fees. Together, the projected cost reduction of one fewer fatigue-related accident per 1,000 workers has been estimated to be $1.75 million per 1,000 workers (Fatigue Science, 2021).

These estimates are based solely on accidents made by human error as a result of sleep-related monitoring and improvements. Given the potential for wearables to predict the onset of illness, additional societal and economic benefits may be had when heart rate data from these wearables are further considered.

It is apparent from Figure 3, that small fluctuations are common during overground, steady state running. Some of these fluctuations are due to biological and technical variation; however, some of this fluctuation can be attributed to even slight changes in running speed or grade. In both cases, heart rate is expected to increase linearly with speed and/or grade. Heart rate can also increase as a result of biological variation, psychological and physiological stress, such as stress, sleep and illness, the running surface and weather conditions (Jaén-Carrillo et al., 2020). As such, heart rate itself may not accurately reflect the training intensity. Moreover, heart rate is often used as a surrogate measure of the energy cost of running (typically defined as 'running economy' (Fletcher et al., 2009), which is also influenced by a variety of internal and external factors (Fletcher & MacIntosh, 2017). When training intensity is not accurately quantified, the onset of illness or injury can result (Lehmann et al., 1993; Siegl et al., 2017; Urhausen & Kindermann, 2002).

From a classical mechanics perspective, intensity can be quantified as mechanical power, defined as the product of force and velocity, or the rate of doing mechanical work (Hamill & Knutzen, 2006). In cycling, there is a strong relationship between mechanical power output (i.e. the rate of performing mechanical work, measured in Watts) and metabolic power (i.e. the rate of consuming energy by the body as a result of performing the mechanical work.) In cycling, quantifying mechanical power output is straightforward: the cyclist applies a force about some perpendicular distance to the cycling crank, which can be measured at the pedal, crank, bottom bracket, chair, or rear wheel hub (Passfield et al., 2017). There is a strong relationship between mechanical power output and metabolic power and performance (Faria et al., 2005; Hawley & Noakes, 1992). Consequently, measuring mechanical power output provides a more instantaneous, reliable, and sensitive measure of exercise intensity compared to heart rate or speed (Sanders et al., 2017).

ARE WE READY TO MEASURE RUNNING POWER?

The concept of mechanical power output is not useful in running, since each stride consists of a combination of positive and negative mechanical work: your arms and legs swing forward and back, your tendons stretch, and recoil and muscles lengthen and shorten during the stride cycle. The notion of 'running power meters', from a mechanical and physiological perspective then, is only useful if these devices can successfully estimate metabolic power and/or the force applied to the ground, since metabolic power is determined primarily by the average force to support body weight for the full stride duration (Kram & Taylor, 1990). Within the consumer market, companies such as Stryd aim to validly and reliably estimate metabolic power whereas others, like Garmin's power meter algorithms are designed to estimate the mechanical power (the product of average force and velocity) applied while the foot is on the ground.

Most of the current devices use information from GPS (during outdoor running) and/or inertial measurement units (IMUs) worn by the user to measure accelerations, then estimate forces in three dimensions. Vertical oscillations are measured from the accelerations and metrics such as cadence and ground contact time are estimated. Combined with GPS to track speed and incline, "running power" is calculated and usually displayed either on a smartphone interface or on the device itself (Aubry et al., 2018). Using a Stryd Power Meter, Aubry et al., (2018) assessed the relationship between the calculated 'running power' and metabolic demand (assessed from the measurement of oxygen uptake) in elite and recreational runners. A weak, but statistically significant relationship between "running power" and oxygen uptake was found across all subjects. However, from their Table 8.5, metabolic power (in W/kg) can be calculated from their reported mean oxygen uptake values. Using these values, and the reported mean mechanical power (in W/kg), average gross efficiency of running is 21.3±0.6%; reasonable values from a muscle energetics perspective (Fletcher & MacIntosh, 2017) and in line with gross efficiencies reported during cycling (Ettema & Lorås, 2009; J.R. Fletcher et al., 2019; Passfield & Doust, 2000;

Williams, 1985). Therefore, while mechanical power is not actually quantified with these devices, and less than 5 per cent of these devices have ever been validated (Peake et al., 2018), nor are they incredibly reliable (Cerezuela-Espejo et al., 2020),

Figure 6. Kyrie Irving, then with the Boston Celtics. Credit: Jeremy Brevard-USA TODAY Sports. Copyright: Jeremy Brevard. Inset: Tweet from Boston Celtics twitter account from March 25, 2019 indicating Irving is "OUT", simply stated due to "load management".

this technology appears feasible to advance training prescription and monitoring training load.

Wearables and Load Monitoring / Load Management

Wearable technology is used extensively across professional and amateur sport to improve athlete performance and monitoring. In a 2012 survey of coaches and sport science support staff, Taylor et al., (2012) showed that 91 per cent of respondents used some form of a training monitoring system; 70 per cent of these respondents indicated the focus was on 'load quantification' and the monitoring of fatigue or recovery to "prevent overtraining, reduce injuries, monitor the effectiveness of the training programs and ensure maintenance of performance" (Taylor et al., 2012).

The most common technologies applied to sport include GPS and IMUs. GPS is used in a number of outdoor field sports to track player positions and movements during training and games. GPS requires signals from multiple satellites, and as such, is not useful indoors. Furthermore, GPS may underestimate speed or movement patterns over narrow changes in position. Regardless, monitoring an individual athlete's speed and duration of movement across practice and match scenarios has multiple implications for the active economy. These include training load monitoring for coaches and support staff, prescribing exercise to optimize performance and avoid injury. For example, professional cycling teams are incorporating GPS devices, such as the Garmin Edge to record enormous amounts of data, which can be viewed by the athlete, coach, or support staff, in real time. The kind of data that is collected during these rides include, speed, duration, and altitude from GPS sensors, weather conditions from GPS-driven weather forecasts and temperature/humidity sensors embedded in the device. With additional wearables placed on the athlete and bicycle, cycling cadence, power output and heart rate can be derived. All of this 'big data' is incorporated into a sophisticated athlete management system that integrates the data onto a single platform that can be viewed in real-time on a laptop, tablet, or phone. Data from a single or cumulative training session can be viewed, automated, and interpreted to prescribe future sessions to optimize performance and avoid injury. Indeed, the recent trend in professional sports is to allow athletes complete rest or recovery from games, which is now classified by these teams' injury reports as "load management" (Figure 6).

Not only is this data accessible to athlete and team support staff to prescribe exercise, but it is also accessed by the increasingly growing data analytics department within sports organizations to improve coaching strategy, to evaluate current and future player personnel and to take advantage of trades and free-agent signings. It can also be accessed by media during live broadcasts to improve the production value of the broadcast, or to online bettors to set betting lines based on available big data on players and teams.

When indoors, however, GPS is less useful. While there are make-shift GPS technologies that exist, which use a series of cameras around a court or indoor playing surface, these systems are often expensive. Consequently, inertial measurement units (IMUs) are frequently used when GPS systems are not available, or when costs are prohibitive. IMUs are able to calculate the rate of change in an athlete's position due to changes in acceleration. Typically, these IMUs are worn close to the athlete's centre of mass, near the waist. By integrating the measured acceleration signal, movement velocity can be obtained and using various proprietary algorithms, load variables such as jump count and jump height can be obtained. Indeed, IMUs have been used extensively in sports such as volleyball and basketball, where change in position, as well as jump count and jump height are useful metrics of training load. The quantification of athlete movement from these devices permits sport staff to improve injury prevention, physical preparation, and technical and tactical analysis of their sport (Bourdon et al., 2017; Gabbett et al., 2017). Until recently, however, no IMU device had been validated for the assessment of jump load (Chambers et al., 2015), which would be relevant in court sports such as volleyball, basketball, and handball.

MacDonald et al. (2017) appears to have been the first group to validate a combined accelerometer/gyroscope IMU, a commercially available unit from VERT for total jump count and jump height while performing volleyball-specific movement patterns and volleyball matches. Total jump count was visually inspected by the lead author. Jump height was validated against a 3-D motion capture system while the athlete wore the VERT. As with most commercially available IMUs, the calculation of jump height is contained within a proprietary algorithm analyzing the device's measured accelerometer and gyroscope data but are based on classical mechanics to estimate vertical displacement from forces and/or take-off velocity (Moir, 2008). These devices offer strong sensitivity (96.8%) and perfect (100%) specificity for total jumps and underestimates maximal and submaximal jump height by ~2.5 cm (MacDonald et al., 2017). The same research group later validated the use of VERT IMUs in youth basketball players (Benson et al., 2020). Together, these results demonstrate the utility for field-based measurement of training load.

Expanding on these findings using similar VERT IMUs, Lindsay et al. (2020) quantified for the first-time position-specific jump heights and volumes in a men's collegiate volleyball team during training and competition. This data allowed them to define position-specific training loads for these players based on interquartile ranges of training load throughout the season, shown in Figure 7. This data allows coaches and sport science support staff to better prescribe training volume and intensity based on these interquartile ranges.

WEARABLES TO DETECT AND IMPROVE MOBILITY

Mobility is a broad term describing a person's ability to change positions and move about their home and community (Viceconti et al., 2020). Maintaining mobility, in the face of increased age and/or neurodegenerative diseases is an important consideration for improving or maintaining functional independence and a good quality of life. For example, walking speed is considered a vital sign of health: a predictor of physical capacity, and mortality (Bath & Morgan, 1999; Era & Rantanen, 1997; Sonn, 1996; Woo et al., 1999). Mobility is also a significant burden to patients suffering from (for example): Parkinson's disease, Multiple Sclerosis, Cerebral Palsy, and strokes.

Despite the importance of detecting and improving mobility through rehabilitation programs, mobility assessment is inconsistent, both within and between conditions. Most studies use a form of 'mobility perception' via subjective questionnaires, patient-reported outcomes (Viceconti et al., 2020), or clinical tests, such as the six-minute walk test, timed sit-to-stand test or timed 25-foot walk, aimed at evaluation of functional capacity. IMUs have historically been designed for, and validated on, healthy, fit, physically active adults. These wearable devices have, to a large extent, not been validated in clinical populations with mobility impairments. This has generated intense research activity, which has produced a new role for multisensory IMUs and advanced analytical software that can better detect movement kinematics from the sensor's raw signals, which can be worn continuously to evaluate their mobility on a day-to-day basis. This data may allow clinicians to better prescribe rehabilitation

*Figure 7. (A) Volume of jumps in competition (A) and in practice (B) by each position based on calculated quartiles. Volume of high intensity jumps in competition (C) and practice (D). Significant differences are indicated by the title of position from which they differ ($p < 0.05$). *** = significantly different from all positions. Adapted from Lindsay et al.,. (2020).*

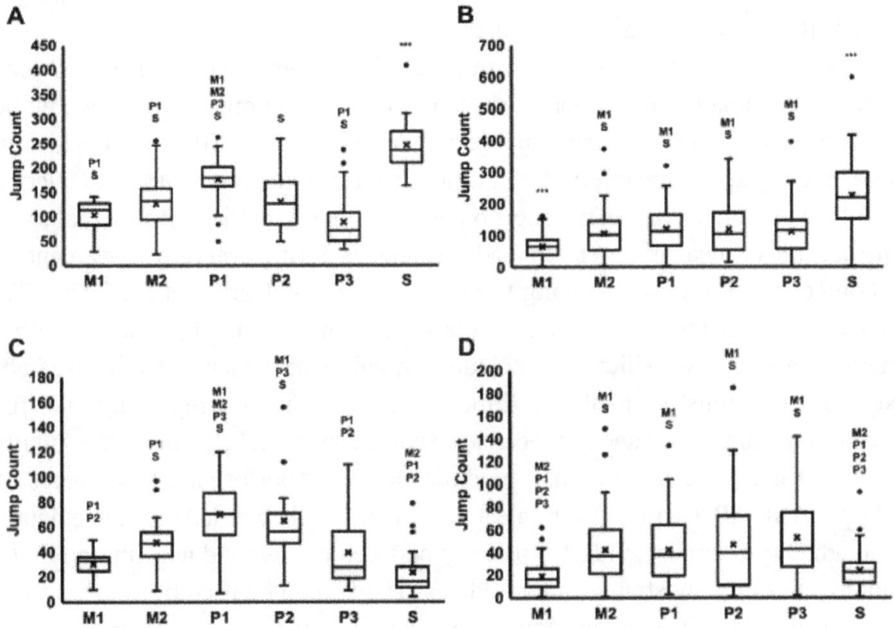

programs, to better evaluate the effectiveness of past and current programs. For example, reliable measurements of joint angles from wearables during rehabilitation exercise will offer a better, more objective understanding of a patient's recovery pathway as a result of the prescribed exercise.

Wearables may also allow clinicians to evaluate the effectiveness of certain medications aimed at improving mobility perceptions and performance (Coates et al., 2020). Parkinson's disease is a degenerative brain disease, characterized by progressive loss of motor function. Digital 'biomarkers', classified from the use of real-world, continuous gait recordings in these patients can be used to detect and evaluate clinical outcomes in these patients. Coates et al. (2020) evaluated gait parameters, assessed from wearable IMUs in old-aged Parkinson's patients over a period of 36 months. Compared to healthy, age-matched controls, wearables from PD patients showed higher variability in gait parameters, suggesting that wearables might classify these patients automatically, as well as daily, longitudinally monitor the disease progression.

These studies emphasize how wearables can be used to assess healthy and pathological gaits through estimates of the user's movement kinematics outside of a sport science laboratory or clinical setting. While informative, kinematics themselves do not confer information regarding joint or tissue loading. For this reason, estimates of forces acting on tissues and/or torques about joints would be valuable to the researcher or clinician to quantify performance, assess injury risk and evaluate rehabilitation procedures.

Wearable sensors themselves can be used to approximate muscle and tendon forces by estimating movement kinematics, and, in combination with whole-body models, estimate ground reaction forces (Karatsidis et al., 2017), from which joint and tissue loads can be inferred. Skin-mounted tensiometers, wearable devices that estimate tendon tension using short bursts of tendon vibration (Bolus et al., 2020), are capable of measuring tendon loading patterns during everyday movement, such as outdoor walking over varying terrain and inclines (Harper et al., 2020). These devices show potential for evaluating tendon loading during natural, uncontrolled movements. Future applications include combining the device with other wearables, such as GPS units to enable real-time feedback to the user regarding their tissue loading and injury risk and to enable new analyzes of muscle loading across multiple sectors of health, rehabilitation, ergonomics, and sport performance. As suggested by Harper et al. (2020), these wearable tensiometers could be used by physiotherapists and athletics therapists to test symmetry between injured and non-injured limbs to guide return to play strategies for athletes. They could be used by coaches to view in real time tendon loading (and subsequent risk of injury) of their athletes, for example in runners prone to achilles tendinopathy, or in professional basketball players prone to tendon pathologies (Amin et al., 2016). These devices could also have workplace-safety implications in that they can be used to estimate soft-tissue loads during repetitive tasks to evaluate muscle fatigue or cumulative tissue damage. Miniaturization, synchronization with other sensors and integration into athletic clothing or footwear also present interesting future applications (Harper et al., 2020).

WEARABLES AND INFECTIOUS DISEASE

When worn on a regular basis, the evidence appears clear that heart rate variability, measured via wearable heart rate sensors, can detect the onset of illness or disease in a variety of populations. Not only is this information to consider when developing an athlete's training plans, but early detection of particularly infectious diseases is important to reduce the spread through social distancing and self-isolation measures. Previously, wearables have been used to detect lyme disease (albeit retrospectively), and viral respiratory infections (Li et al., 2017; Radin et al., 2020; Zhu et al., 2020). The novel coronavirus disease has infected nearly 100 million people to date and resulted in millions of deaths worldwide. Without wide-spread vaccinations, early detection, self-isolation, and contract tracing are currently primary means of reducing the spread of COVID-19. However, most infections only become apparent upon symptom onset, which may be insufficient to stop community-spread of the virus. Moreover, as many as 50 per cent of COVID-19 infected individuals are asymptomatic (He et al., 2020). Since wearable devices collect a multitude of physiological and biomechanical parameters, they may be useful in early detection of respiratory viral infections, including COVID-19. For example, Mishra et al. (2020) retrospectively showed that 63 per cent of their confirmed positive COVID-19 cases could be detected prior to symptoms onset as a result of elevated heart rates relative to baseline.

WHOOP, a wearable smart band launched in 2015 to help athletes track their progress through HRV measurements. They recently completed Series E funding of $100 million, backed by elite athletes Patrick Mahomes, Rory McIllroy, Justin Thomas, Larry Fitzgerald, Eli Manning, and Kevin Durant (Golden, n.d.). WHOOP's business model is based on a subscription service: users sign up for a monthly subscription and are given the wearable strap for free. They are currently valued at $1.2 billion.

Using daily measures of heart rate variability, and the accompanying respiratory sinus arrythmia (Billman, 2011) to estimate respiratory rate from a cohort of 270 WHOOP members, WHOOP developed and trained an algorithm, whose goal it was to identify COVID-19 positive individuals based on changes in respiratory rate during night-time sleep (Miller et al., 2020). The model correctly identified 20 per cent of COVID-19 positive members two days prior to symptom onset and 80 per cent of positive cases by the third day of symptoms.

The model was implemented in June of 2020. Shortly thereafter, and prior to a professional golf tour event, PGA Tour golfer, Nick Watney was alerted by the app of an abnormal night-time sleep respiratory rate. That morning, he was tested, and later confirmed to have COVID-19. Following this diagnosis, the PGA Tour signed a deal with WHOOP to make their product available to all players and caddies on the PGA (and associated Tours who wanted one).

Indeed, person-generated health data, derived from wearables, has the potential for early detection of viral infections, including seasonal flu and COVID-19, or to identify population level 'hot spots' (Shapiro et al., 2020). This information can be critical to countering the spread of COVID-19, future COVID-19 variants, or other infectious diseases by informing health policy and government-imposed restrictions.

WEARABLES AND PERSON-GENERATED HEALTH DATA

Millions of wearable users generate immense amounts of data every minute. This "bid data" has important implications for medical diagnostics and the future of tele-medicine. For perhaps the first time in medical history, a physician can access hundreds of days of physiological, biomechanical and movement data from their patients to establish an appropriate baseline, and to identify departure from this apparent normal baseline. These health data include vital signs such as heart rate or respiratory rate, stress levels (subjective or objectively quantified via HRV), physical activity, weight, diet, and sleep patterns (Wood et al., 2015). This data also has important utility for tele-medicine, when patients are not able to meet with their physician directly, when laboratory tests are not readily available (for example in rural communities), or when specialized medical personnel need to be accessed from across the globe. Apple's smartwatch has the ability to generate electrocardiograms, similar to clinically based 12-lead ECGs. From a population of over 400,000 participants, Apple's smart watch, and accompanying health app were able to correctly identify 84 per cent of all atrial fibrillations that had occurred (Perez et al., 2019). Subsequent iterations are able to directly send these heart rate data to the attending paramedic, nurse, or physician.

LINKS TO THE ACTIVE ECONOMY

Enabling Other Sectors of the Active Economy

Today's wearables allow for the collection, analysis, and interpretation of real-world locomotion data from millions of users on a daily basis. This data allows the footwear industry, and associated research, to examine common biomechanical metrics which previously could only be measured in the lab. Footwear can now be tested on different surfaces (road, track, dirt/gravel, sand, etc) and environmental conditions such as uphill and downhill gradients. Ecotourism and the suggestion for outdoor footwear and/or equipment can be improved using this information derived from wearables.

This data also allows real-world scenarios, such as stepping off or onto raised curbs, navigating obstacles such as puddles or surface irregularities to be analyzed and interpreted. Combining this data derived from IMUs and GPS with tensiometry, muscle and tendon loads during every-day activities can for the first time be quantified. This has important implications to active recreation, health & wellness and apparel & accessories sectors looking to monitor joint loads from their users to avoid injury or mitigate risk, promote workplace safety, and manufacture specialized equipment and apparel. This data permits manufacturers to make athletic and workplace clothing smart, fashionable, functional, and comfortable.

The use of IMUs and/or GPS to monitor player movement during practice and games have important implications to sports betting and organized sport sectors. This data offers additional player information to sports bettors, or fantasy team managers with regards to player talent, strategy, and injury surveillance. The professional services sector of the active economy can further use this information to promote player talent via marketing materials. The organized sport sector can further use this information to refine player contract negotiations, to improve player personnel based on coaching/managerial strategy and to improve resource allocation to players (playing time, health, and fitness recommendations etc.). Further, this data can be consumed by the media & content sector and broadcast rights holders to highlight this data in real time to improve broadcast content and at-home fan experiences. The latter may also partially compensate for loss of live event revenue during the COVID-19 pandemic.

How do Other Sectors of the Active Economy Enable it?

Heart rate and other physiological sensors are well-suited to be incorporated into clothing. For example, 'smart shirts' could include sensors to measure heart rate, respiration rate, sweat rate and composition to assess exercise intensity and suggest post-exercise recovery protocols. Combined with IMU and/or GPS, these apparels would allow researchers and active economy stakeholders to collect and analyze data from multiple days to study work-related fatigue, muscle and tendon loads, training habits and rehabilitations protocols. Human factors, ergonomics and design sectors are integral in this process to ensure users wear it and the data derived from these sensors are reliable and valid.

The economical value of the wearables market has grown exponentially since 2010. Approximately 29 million units were shipped worldwide in 2014, which is expected to grow to over 600 million units by 2024 (Statista, 2019). The global market for medical devices, including fitness monitors, blood glucose monitors and cardiac monitors, is expected to exceed $80 billion by 2025 (Global Market Insights, 2019). The health and wellness impact, among others, is both tangible and intangible in terms of community value: lower health care costs, reduced insurance premiums, increased access to specialized physicians who are increasingly armed with digital health information on their patients, and better quality of life for the wearer. Employment opportunities in data analytics, signal processing, machine learning, and artificial intelligence are required to collect, analyze, and interpret this "big data". Sectors of human factors, ergonomics and design are required in this space to ensure wearables are actually being worn.

Societal benefits include better performance tracking for the user to demonstrate tangible and quantifiable improvements in fitness. The user may achieve their goal of walking 10,000 steps per day or achieving 150 minutes of physical activity per week. The recreational athlete may improve upon their rest and recovery scores indicating better sleep quality and quantity or they may improve upon a set fitness test administered, collected, and interpreted by their wearable device. Wearables also allow amateur athletes and professional sports teams to improve injury surveillance to avoid time lost due to illness or injury. Managerial staff may use this data to develop and exploit key performance indicators for their team (or their opponents) to improve the success of their local team(s).

CONCLUSION

In this chapter, we have provided a brief description of the utility of active technology 'wearables' and accessories' ability to quantify baseline health and physical activity values for the user. Departures from this baseline allows, in many cases, for the device to prescribe appropriate exercise volumes and/or intensities or to prescribe rest and recovery. We have briefly outlined how wearables can quantify and assess fatigue, via heart rate measurements or sleep quality and quantity to improve athletic and workplace performance. Current and future research is dedicated to the reliability and validity of these devices, and the improved signal quality and subsequent interpretation of this data automatically by the device. Recent advances in wearables have further allowed the wearer and the physician access to enormous amounts of daily physiological signals with the goal of improving health, wellness, and quality of life for the wearer.

REFERENCES

Atlaoui, D., Pichot, V., Lacoste, L., Barale, F., Lacour, J. R., & Chatard, J. C. (2007). Heart rate variability, training variation and performance in elite swimmers. *International Journal of Sports Medicine*, *28*(05), 394–400. doi:10.1055-2006-924490 PMID:17111320

Amin, N. H., McCullough, K. C., Mills, G. L., & Jones, H. (2016). The Impact and Functional Outcomes of Achilles Tendon Pathology in National Basketball Association Players. *Clinical Research on Foot & Ankle*, *4*(3), 1–6. doi:10.4172/2329-910X.1000205 PMID:29082269

Aubry, R. L., Power, G. A., & Burr, J. F. (2018). An assessment of running power as a training metric for elite and recreational runners. *Journal of Strength and Conditioning Research*, *32*(8), 2258–2264. doi:10.1519/JSC.0000000000002650 PMID:29912073

Bath, P. A., & Morgan, K. (1999). Differential risk factor profiles for indoor and outdoor falls in older people living at home in Nottingham, UK. *European Journal of Epidemiology*, *15*(1), 65–73. doi:10.1023/A:1007531101765 PMID:10098998

Baumert, M., Brechtel, L., Lock, J., Hermsdorf, M., Wolff, R., Baier, V., & Voss, A. (2006). Heart rate variability, blood pressure variability, and baroreflex sensitivity in overtrained athletes. *Clinical Journal of Sport Medicine*, *16*(5), 412–417. doi:10.1097/01.jsm.0000244610.34594.07 PMID:17016118

Benson, L. C., Tait, T. J., Befus, K., Choi, J., Hillson, C., Stilling, C., Grewal, S., MacDonald, K., Pasanen, K., & Emery, C. A. (2020). Validation of a commercially available inertial measurement unit for recording jump load in youth basketball players. *Journal of Sports Sciences*, *38*(8), 928–936. doi:10.1080/02640414.2020.1737360 PMID:32138609

Billat, V., Faina, M., Sardella, F., Marini, C., Fanton, F., Lupo, S., Faccini, P., de Angelis, M., Koralsztein, J. P., & Dalmonte, A. (1996). A comparison of time to exhaustion at VO2 max in élite cyclists, kayak paddlers, swimmers, and runners. *Ergonomics*, *39*(2), 267–277. doi:10.1080/00140139608964457 PMID:8851531

Billman, G. E. (2011). Heart rate variability - A historical perspective. *Frontiers in Physiology*, *2*(November), 1–13. doi:10.3389/fphys.2011.00086

Bolus, N., Jeong, H.-K., Blaho, B. M., Safaei, M., Young, A., & Inan, O. (2020). Fit to Burst: Toward Noninvasive Estimation of Achilles Tendon Load Using Burst Vibrations. *IEEE Transactions on Biomedical Engineering*, 1. PMID:32746041

Bompa, T. O., & Buzzichelli, C. (2018). *Periodization-: theory and methodology of training*. Human kinetics.

Botek, M., McKune, A. J., Krejci, J., Stejskal, P., & Gaba, A. (2014). Change in performance in response to training load adjustment based on autonomic activity. *International Journal of Sports Medicine*, *35*(06), 482–488. PMID:24129989

Bosquet, L., Merkari, S., & Arvisais, D. (2008). Is heart rate a convenient tool to monitor over-reaching? A systematic review of the literature (vol 42, pg 709, 2008). *British Journal of Sports Medicine*, *42*(12), 1016–1016.

Bourdillon, N., Nilchian, M., & Millet, G. P. (2019). Photoplethysmography Detection of Overreaching. *Medicine and Science in Sports and Exercise*, *51*(4), 701–707. doi:10.1249/MSS.0000000000001836 PMID:30407274

Bourdon, P. C., Cardinale, M., Murray, A., Gastin, P., Kellmann, M., Varley, M. C., Gabbett, T. J., Coutts, A. J., Burgess, D. J., Gregson, W., & Cable, N. T. (2017). Monitoring athlete training loads: Consensus statement. *International Journal of Sports Physiology and Performance*, *12*(s2), 161–170. doi:10.1123/IJSPP.2017-0208 PMID:28463642

Buchheit, M., Buchheit, M., Simpson, M., Simpson, M., Al Haddad, H., Al Haddad, H., Bourdon, P., Bourdon, P., Mendez-Villanueva, A., & Mendez-Villanueva, A. (2012). Monitoring changes in physical performance with heart rate measures in young soccer players. *European Journal of Applied Physiology*, *112*(2), 711–723. doi:10.100700421-011-2014-0 PMID:21656232

Camomilla, V., Bergamini, E., Fantozzi, S., & Vannozzi, G. (2018). Trends supporting the in-field use of wearable inertial sensors for sport performance evaluation: A systematic review. *Sensors (Switzerland)*, *18*(3), 873. Advance online publication. doi:10.339018030873 PMID:29543747

Cerezuela-Espejo, V., Hernández-Belmonte, A., Courel-Ibáñez, J., Conesa-Ros, E., Mora-Rodríguez, R., & Pallarés, J. G. (2020). Are we ready to measure running power? Repeatability and concurrent validity of five commercial technologies. *European Journal of Sport Science*, *0*(0), 1–10. doi:10.1080/17461391.2020.1748117 PMID:32212955

Chambers, R., Gabbett, T. J., Cole, M. H., & Beard, A. (2015). The Use of Wearable Microsensors to Quantify Sport-Specific Movements. *Sports Medicine (Auckland, N.Z.)*, *45*(7), 1065–1081. doi:10.100740279-015-0332-9 PMID:25834998

Coates, L., Shi, J., Rochester, L., Del Din, S., & Pantall, A. (2020). Entropy of real-world gait in parkinson's disease determined from wearable sensors as a digital marker of altered ambulatory behavior. *Sensors (Switzerland)*, *20*(9), 2631. Advance online publication. doi:10.339020092631 PMID:32380692

Dinges, D. F. (1995). An overview of sleepiness and accidents. *Journal of Sleep Research*, *4*(S2), 4–14. doi:10.1111/j.1365-2869.1995.tb00220.x PMID:10607205

Era, P., & Rantanen, T. (1997). Changes in physical capacity and sensory/psychomotor functions from 75 to 80 years of age and from 80 to 85 years of age—a longitudinal study. *Scandinavian Journal of Social Medicine. Supplementum*, *53*, 25–43. PMID:9241699

Eston, R. G., Davies, B. L., & Williams, J. G. (1987). Use of perceived effort ratings to control exercise intensity in young healthy adults. *European Journal of Applied Physiology and Occupational Physiology*, *56*(2), 222–224. doi:10.1007/BF00640648 PMID:3569229

Ettema, G., & Lorås, H. W. (2009). Efficiency in cycling: A review. *European Journal of Applied Physiology*, *106*(1), 1–14. doi:10.100700421-009-1008-7 PMID:19229554

Faria, E. W., Parker, D. L., & Faria, I. E. (2005). The science of cycling: Physiology and training - part 1. *Sports Medicine (Auckland, N.Z.)*, *35*(4), 285–312. doi:10.2165/00007256-200535040-00002 PMID:15831059

Science, F. (2021). Fatigue risk management system. In The return on investment of fatigue risk management. doi:10.1016/B978-0-323-24288-2.00073-8

Fletcher, J. R., Asmussen, M. J., Nigg, S. R., MacIntosh, B. R., & Nigg, B. M. (2019). The effect of torsional shoe sole stiffness on knee moment and gross efficiency in cycling. *Journal of Sports Sciences*, *37*(13), 1457–1463. Advance online publication. doi:10.1080/02640414.2019.1565650 PMID:30657013

Fletcher, J. R., & MacIntosh, B. R. (2017). Running economy from a muscle energetics perspective. *Frontiers in Physiology*, *8*(JUN), 1–15. doi:10.3389/fphys.2017.00433 PMID:28690549

Fletcher, J. R., Esau, S. P., & Macintosh, B. R. (2009). Economy of running: beyond the measurement of oxygen uptake. *Journal of Applied Physiology, 107*(6), 1918–1922.

Fong, D. T.-P., Chan, Y.-Y., Hong, Y., Yung, P. S.-H., Fung, K.-Y., & Chan, K.-M. (2008). Estimating the complete ground reaction forces with pressure insoles in walking. *Journal of Biomechanics*, *41*(11), 2597–2601. doi:10.1016/j.jbiomech.2008.05.007 PMID:18571656

Gabbett, T. J., Nassis, G. P., Oetter, E., Pretorius, J., Johnston, N., Medina, D., Rodas, G., Myslinski, T., Howells, D., Beard, A., & Ryan, A. (2017). The athlete monitoring cycle: A practical guide to interpreting and applying training monitoring data. *British Journal of Sports Medicine, 51*(20), 1451–1452. doi:10.1136/bjsports-2016-097298 PMID:28646100

Garet, M., Tournaire, N., Roche, F., Laurent, R., Lacour, J. R., Barthélémy, J. C., & Pichot, V. (2004). Individual interdependence between nocturnal ANS activity and performance in swimmers. *Medicine and Science in Sports and Exercise, 36*, 2112–2118. doi:10.1249/01.MSS.0000147588.28955.48 PMID:15570148

Global Market Insights. (2019, June 27). *Wearable Medical Devices Market size worth around $87bn by 2025*. https://www.gminsights.com/pressrelease/wearable-medical-devices-market

Golden, J. (n.d.). *Wearable fitness company Whoop raises $100m during pandemic*. CNBC Sports. Retrieved October 28, 2020, from https://www.cnbc.com/2020/10/28/wearable-fitness-company-whoop-raises-100m-during-pandemic-.html

Hakom. (n.d.). Wearables – The Big Data Machines. *Hakom*. Retrieved September 27, 2020, from https://www.hakom.at/en/news-detail/news/wearables-the-big-data-machines/

Hamill, J., & Knutzen, K. M. (2006). *Biomechanical basis of human movement*. Lippincott Williams & Wilkins.

Harper, S. E., Roembke, R. A., Zunker, J. D., Thelen, D. G., & Adamczyk, P. G. (2020). Wearable Tendon Kinetics. *Sensors (Basel), 20*(17), 4805. Advance online publication. doi:10.339020174805 PMID:32858833

Harwood, J. (1926). *Wristwatch and Other watch* (Patent No. 1,576,120).

Havens, K. L., Cohen, S. C., Pratt, K. A., & Sigward, S. M. (2018). Accelerations from wearable accelerometers reflect knee loading during running after anterior cruciate ligament reconstruction. *Clinical Biomechanics (Bristol, Avon), 58*, 57–61. doi:10.1016/j.clinbiomech.2018.07.007 PMID:30029071

Hawley, J. A., & Noakes, T. D. (1992). Peak power output predicts maximal oxygen uptake and performance time in trained cyclists. *European Journal of Applied Physiology and Occupational Physiology, 65*(1), 79–83. doi:10.1007/BF01466278 PMID:1505544

He, X., Lau, E. H. Y., Wu, P., Deng, X., Wang, J., Hao, X., Lau, Y. C., Wong, J. Y., Guan, Y., Tan, X., Mo, X., Chen, Y., Liao, B., Chen, W., Hu, F., Zhang, Q., Zhong, M., Wu, Y., Zhao, L., ... Leung, G. M. (2020). Temporal dynamics in viral shedding and transmissibility of COVID-19. *Nature Medicine*, *26*(5), 672–675. doi:10.103841591-020-0869-5 PMID:32296168

Howell, A. M., Kobayashi, T., Hayes, H. A., Foreman, K. B., & Bamberg, S. J. M. (2013). Kinetic gait analysis using a low-cost insole. *IEEE Transactions on Biomedical Engineering*, *60*(12), 3284–3290. doi:10.1109/TBME.2013.2250972 PMID:23475336

Hullfish, T. J., Qu, F., Stoeckl, B. D., Gebhard, P. M., Mauck, R. L., & Baxter, J. R. (2019). Measuring clinically relevant knee motion with a self-calibrated wearable sensor. *Journal of Biomechanics*, *89*, 105–109. doi:10.1016/j.jbiomech.2019.04.003 PMID:30981425

Hurkmans, H. L. P., Bussmann, J. B. J., Benda, E., Verhaar, J. A. N., & Stam, H. J. (2006). Accuracy and repeatability of the Pedar Mobile system in long-term vertical force measurements. *Gait & Posture*, *23*(1), 118–125. doi:10.1016/j.gaitpost.2005.05.008 PMID:16260142

International Data Corporation. (2020). *Worldwide Quarterly Wearable Device Tracker.* International Data Corporation. https://www.idc.com/tracker/showproductinfo.jsp?prod_id=962

Issurin, V. B. (2010). New horizons for the methodology and physiology of training periodization. *Sports Medicine (Auckland, N.Z.)*, *40*(3), 189–206. doi:10.2165/11319770-000000000-00000 PMID:20199119

Jaén-Carrillo, D., Roche-Seruendo, L. E., Cartón-Llorente, A., Ramírez-Campillo, R., & García-Pinillos, F. (2020). Mechanical power in endurance running: A scoping review on sensors for power output estimation during running. *Sensors (Switzerland)*, *20*(22), 1–20. doi:10.339020226482 PMID:33202809

Johansson, D., Malmgren, K., & Alt Murphy, M. (2018). Wearable sensors for clinical applications in epilepsy, Parkinson's disease, and stroke: A mixed-methods systematic review. *Journal of Neurology*, *265*(8), 1740–1752. doi:10.100700415-018-8786-y PMID:29427026

Karatsidis, A., Bellusci, G., Schepers, H. M., de Zee, M., Andersen, M. S., & Veltink, P. H. (2017). Estimation of ground reaction forces and moments during gait using only inertial motion capture. *Sensors (Switzerland)*, *17*(1), 75. Advance online publication. doi:10.339017010075 PMID:28042857

Koenig, J., Jarczok, M. N., Wasner, M., Hillecke, T. K., & Thayer, J. F. (2014). Heart rate variability and swimming. *Sports Medicine (Auckland, N.Z.)*, *44*(10), 1377–1391. doi:10.100740279-014-0211-9 PMID:24958562

Kram, R., & Taylor, C. R. (1990). Energetics of running: A new perspective. *Nature*, *346*(6281), 265–267. doi:10.1038/346265a0 PMID:2374590

Kuipers, H., & Keizer, H. A. (1988). Overtraining in elite athletes. *Sports Medicine (Auckland, N.Z.)*, *6*(2), 79–92. doi:10.2165/00007256-198806020-00003 PMID:3062735

Lehmann, M., Foster, C., & Keul, J. (1993). Overtraining in endurance athletes: a brief review. Med Sci Sports Exerc., 25(7), 854–862. doi:10.1249/00005768-199307000-00015

Li, X., Dunn, J., Salins, D., Zhou, G., Zhou, W., Schüssler-Fiorenza Rose, S. M., Perelman, D., Colbert, E., Runge, R., Rego, S., Sonecha, R., Datta, S., McLaughlin, T., & Snyder, M. P. (2017). Digital Health: Tracking Physiomes and Activity Using Wearable Biosensors Reveals Useful Health-Related Information. *PLoS Biology*, *15*(1), e2001402. Advance online publication. doi:10.1371/journal.pbio.2001402 PMID:28081144

Lindsay, O. R., & Fletcher, J. R. (2020). Defining low, medium, and high training loads in men's volleyball using a combination of jump count and jump height. *Proceedings of the Canadian Society for Exercise Physiology Annual General Meeting*, S307.

Lu, G., Yang, F., Taylor, J. A., & Stein, J. F. (2009). A comparison of photoplethysmography and ECG recording to analyze heart rate variability in healthy subjects. *Journal of Medical Engineering & Technology*, *33*(8), 634–641. doi:10.3109/03091900903150998 PMID:19848857

MacDonald, K., Bahr, R., Baltich, J., Whittaker, J. L., & Meeuwisse, W. H. (2017). Validation of an inertial measurement unit for the measurement of jump count and height. *Physical Therapy in Sport*, *25*, 15–19. doi:10.1016/j.ptsp.2016.12.001 PMID:28254580

Matijevich, E. S., Branscombe, L. M., Scott, L. R., & Zelik, K. E. (2019). Ground reaction force metrics are not strongly correlated with tibial bone load when running across speeds and slopes: Implications for science, sport, and wearable tech. *PLoS One*, *14*(1), e0210000. Advance online publication. doi:10.1371/journal.pone.0210000 PMID:30653510

Matijevich, E. S., Scott, L. R., Volgyesi, P., Derry, K. H., & Zelik, K. E. (2020). Combining wearable sensor signals, machine learning and biomechanics to estimate tibial bone force and damage during running. *Human Movement Science*, *74*, 102690. Advance online publication. doi:10.1016/j.humov.2020.102690 PMID:33132194

Miller, D., Capodilupo, J., Lastella, M., Sargent, C., Roach, G., Lee, V., & Capodilupo, E. (2020). *Analyzing changes in respiratory rate to predict the risk of COVID-19 infection*. MedRxiv., doi:10.1101/2020.06.18.20131417

Mishra, T., Wang, M., Metwally, A. A., Bogu, G. K., Brooks, A. W., Bahmani, A., Alavi, A., Celli, A., Higgs, E., Dagan-Rosenfeld, O., Fay, B., Kirkpatrick, S., Kellogg, R., Gibson, M., Wang, T., Hunting, E. M., Mamic, P., Ganz, A. B., Rolnik, B., ... Snyder, M. P. (2020). Pre-symptomatic detection of COVID-19 from smartwatch data. *Nature Biomedical Engineering*, *4*(12), 1208–1220. Advance online publication. doi:10.103841551-020-00640-6 PMID:33208926

Moir, G. L. (2008). Three different methods of calculating vertical jump height from force platform data in men and women. *Measurement in Physical Education and Exercise Science*, *12*(4), 207–218. doi:10.1080/10913670802349766

Mooney, R., Corley, G., Godfrey, A., Quinlan, L. R., & ÓLaighin, G. (2015). Inertial sensor technology for elite swimming performance analysis: A systematic review. *Sensors (Basel)*, *16*(1), 18. doi:10.339016010018 PMID:26712760

Mourot, L., Bouhaddi, M., Tordi, N., Rouillon, J. D., & Regnard, J. (2004). Short- and long-term effects of a single bout of exercise on heart rate variability: Comparison between constant and interval training exercises. *European Journal of Applied Physiology*, *92*(4-5), 508–517. doi:10.100700421-004-1119-0 PMID:15461995

Passfield, L., & Doust, J. H. (2000). Changes in cycling efficiency and performance after endurance exercise. *Medicine and Science in Sports and Exercise*, *32*(11), 1935–1941. doi:10.1097/00005768-200011000-00018 PMID:11079525

Passfield, L., Hopker, J. G., Jobson, S., Friel, D., & Zabala, M. (2017). Knowledge is power: Issues of measuring training and performance in cycling. *Journal of Sports Sciences*, *35*(14), 1426–1434. doi:10.1080/02640414.2016.1215504 PMID:27686573

Peake, J. M., Kerr, G., & Sullivan, J. P. (2018). A critical review of consumer wearables, mobile applications, and equipment for providing biofeedback, monitoring stress, and sleep in physically active populations. *Frontiers in Physiology*, *9*(JUN), 1–19. doi:10.3389/fphys.2018.00743 PMID:30002629

Peppoloni, L., Filippeschi, A., Ruffaldi, E., & Avizzano, C. A. (2014). (WMSDs issue) A novel wearable system for the online assessment of risk for biomechanical load in repetitive efforts. *International Journal of Industrial Ergonomics*, *52*, 1–11. doi:10.1016/j.ergon.2015.07.002

Perez, M. V., Mahaffey, K. W., Hedlin, H., Rumsfeld, J. S., Garcia, A., Ferris, T., Balasubramanian, V., Russo, A. M., Rajmane, A., Cheung, L., Hung, G., Lee, J., Kowey, P., Talati, N., Nag, D., Gummidipundi, S. E., Beatty, A., Hills, M. T., Desai, S., ... Turakhia, M. P. (2019). Large-scale assessment of a smartwatch to identify atrial fibrillation. *The New England Journal of Medicine*, *381*(20), 1909–1917. doi:10.1056/NEJMoa1901183 PMID:31722151

Radin, J. M., Wineinger, N. E., Topol, E. J., & Steinhubl, S. R. (2020). Harnessing wearable device data to improve state-level real-time surveillance of influenza-like illness in the USA: A population-based study. *The Lancet. Digital Health*, *2*(2), e85–e93. doi:10.1016/S2589-7500(19)30222-5 PMID:33334565

Rebula, J. R., Ojeda, L. V., Adamczyk, P. G., & Kuo, A. D. (2013). Measurement of foot placement and its variability with inertial sensors. *Gait & Posture*, *38*(4), 974–980. doi:10.1016/j.gaitpost.2013.05.012 PMID:23810335

Rosekind, M. R., Gregory, K. B., Mallis, M. M., Brandt, S. L., Seal, B., & Lerner, D. (2010). The Cost of Poor Sleep: Workplace Productivity Loss and Associated Costs. *Journal of Occupational and Environmental Medicine*, *52*(1), 91–98. doi:10.1097/JOM.0b013e3181c78c30 PMID:20042880

Sanders, D., Myers, T., & Akubat, I. (2017). Training-Intensity distribution in road cyclists: Objective versus subjective measures. *International Journal of Sports Physiology and Performance*, *12*(9), 1232–1237. doi:10.1123/ijspp.2016-0523 PMID:28253026

Selvaraj, N., Jaryal, A., Santhosh, J., Deepak, K. K., & Anand, S. (2008). Assessment of heart rate variability derived from finger-tip photoplethysmography as compared to electrocardiography. *Journal of Medical Engineering & Technology*, *32*(6), 479–484. doi:10.1080/03091900701781317 PMID:18663635

Shapiro, A., Marinsek, N., Clay, I., Bradshaw, B., Ramirez, E., Min, J., Trister, A., Wang, Y., Althoff, T., & Foschini, L. (2020). Characterizing COVID-19 and Influenza Illnesses in the Real World via Person-Generated Health Data. *Patterns*, *2*(1), 100188. doi:10.1016/j.patter.2020.100188 PMID:33506230

Sheerin, K. R., Reid, D., & Besier, T. F. (2019). The measurement of tibial acceleration in runners—A review of the factors that can affect tibial acceleration during running and evidence-based guidelines for its use. *Gait & Posture*, *67*, 12–24. doi:10.1016/j.gaitpost.2018.09.017 PMID:30248663

Siegl, A., Kösel, E. M., Tam, N., Koschnick, S., Langerak, N. G., Skorski, S., Meyer, T., & Lamberts, R. P. (2017). Submaximal Markers of Fatigue and Overreaching; Implications for Monitoring Athletes. *International Journal of Sports Medicine*, *38*(9), 675–682. doi:10.1055-0043-110226 PMID:28704885

Smith, D. J., Norris, S. R., & Hogg, J. M. (2002). Performance Evluation of Swimmers - Scientific Tools. *Sports Medicine (Auckland, N.Z.)*, *32*(9), 539–554. doi:10.2165/00007256-200232090-00001 PMID:12096928

Sonn, U. (1996). Longitudinal studies of dependence in daily life activities among elderly persons. *Scandinavian Journal of Rehabilitation Medicine. Supplement*, *34*, 1–35. PMID:8701230

Statista. (2019). *Wearables shipments worldwide 2014-2024*. https://www.statista.com/statistics/437871/wearables-worldwide-shipments/

Svedahl, K., & MacIntosh, B. R. (2003). Anaerobic threshold: the concept and methods of measurement. *Canadian Journal of Applied Physiology = Revue Canadienne de Physiologie Appliquee, 28*(2), 299–323.

Taylor, K.-L., Chapman, D. W., Cronin, J. B., Newton, M. J., & Gill, N. (2012). Fatigue Monitoring in High Performance Sport: A survey of current trends. *Journal of Australian Strength & Conditioning*, *20*(1), 12–23.

Thompson, W. R. (2021). Worldwide Survey of Fitness Trends for 2020. *ACSM's Health & Fitness Journal*, *25*(1), 10–19. doi:10.1249/FIT.0000000000000631

Thompson, W. R., & Ph, D. (2006). Fitness Trends for 2007. *The Physician and Sportsmedicine*, *10*(6), 7–14. doi:10.3810/psm.2004.01.1627

Tremblay, M. S., Warburton, D. E. R., Janssen, I., Paterson, D. H., Latimer, A. E., Rhodes, R. E., Kho, M. E., Hicks, A., LeBlanc, A. G., Zehr, L., Murumets, K., & Duggan, M. (2011). New Canadian physical activity guidelines. *Applied Physiology, Nutrition, and Metabolism*, *36*(1), 36–46. doi:10.1139/H11-009 PMID:21326376

Tudor-locke, C., Craig, C. L., Brown, W. J., Clemes, S. A., Cocker, K. De, Giles-corti, B., Hatano, Y., Inoue, S., Matsudo, S. M., Mutrie, N., Oppert, J., Rowe, D. A., Schmidt, M. D., Schofield, G. M., Spence, J. C., Teixeira, P. J., Tully, M. A., & Blair, S. N. (2011). How Many Steps / day are Enough? *For Adults*, 1–17.

Urhausen, A., & Kindermann, W. (2002). Diagnosis of overtraining: What tools do we have? *Sports Medicine (Auckland, N.Z.)*, *32*(2), 95–102. doi:10.2165/00007256-200232020-00002 PMID:11817995

Viceconti, M., Hernandez Penna, S., Dartee, W., Mazza, C., Caufield, B., Becker, C., Maetzler, W., Garcia-Aymerich, J., Davico, G., & Rochester, L. (2020). Toward a Regulatory Qualification of Real-World Mobility Performance Biomarkers in Parkinson' s Patients Using Digital Mobility Outcomes. *Sensors (Basel)*, *20*(5920), 1–12. doi:10.339020205920 PMID:33092143

Williams, K. R. (1985). The relationship between mechanical and physiological energy estimates. *Medicine and Science in Sports and Exercise*, *17*(3), 317–325. doi:10.1249/00005768-198506000-00004 PMID:3894868

Woo, J., Ho, S. C., & Yu, A. L. (1999). Walking speed and stride length predicts 36 months dependency, mortality, and institutionalization in Chinese aged 70 and older. *Journal of the American Geriatrics Society*, *47*(10), 1257–1260. doi:10.1111/j.1532-5415.1999.tb05209.x PMID:10522962

Wood, W. A., Bennett, A. V., & Basch, E. (2015). Emerging uses of patient generated health data in clinical research. *Molecular Oncology*, *9*(5), 1018–1024. doi:10.1016/j.molonc.2014.08.006 PMID:25248998

Zhu, G., Li, J., Meng, Z., Yu, Y., Li, Y., Tang, X., Dong, Y., Sun, G., Zhou, R., Wang, H., Wang, K., & Huang, W. (2020). Learning from Large-Scale Wearable Device Data for Predicting Epidemics Trend of COVID-19. *Discrete Dynamics in Nature and Society*, *2020*, 1–8. Advance online publication. doi:10.1155/2020/6152041

ADDITIONAL READING

Camomilla, V., Bergamini, E., Fantozzi, S., & Vannozzi, G. (2018). Trends supporting the in-field use of wearable inertial sensors for sport performance evaluation: A systematic review. *Sensors (Switzerland)*, *18*(3), 873. Advance online publication. doi:10.339018030873 PMID:29543747

Cerezuela-Espejo, V., Hernández-Belmonte, A., Courel-Ibáñez, J., Conesa-Ros, E., Mora-Rodríguez, R., & Pallarés, J. G. (2020). Are we ready to measure running power? Repeatability and concurrent validity of five commercial technologies. *European Journal of Sport Science*, *0*(0), 1–10. doi:10.1080/17461391.2020.1748117 PMID:32212955

Chambers, R., Gabbett, T. J., Cole, M. H., & Beard, A. (2015). The Use of Wearable Microsensors to Quantify Sport-Specific Movements. *Sports Medicine (Auckland, N.Z.)*, *45*(7), 1065–1081. doi:10.100740279-015-0332-9 PMID:25834998

Harper, S. E., Roembke, R. A., Zunker, J. D., Thelen, D. G., & Adamczyk, P. G. (2020). Wearable Tendon Kinetics. *Sensors (Basel)*, *20*(17), 4805. Advance online publication. doi:10.339020174805 PMID:32858833

Johansson, D., Malmgren, K., & Alt Murphy, M. (2018). Wearable sensors for clinical applications in epilepsy, Parkinson's disease, and stroke: A mixed-methods systematic review. *Journal of Neurology*, *265*(8), 1740–1752. doi:10.100700415-018-8786-y PMID:29427026

Karatsidis, A., Bellusci, G., Schepers, H. M., de Zee, M., Andersen, M. S., & Veltink, P. H. (2017). Estimation of ground reaction forces and moments during gait using only inertial motion capture. *Sensors (Switzerland)*, *17*(1), 75. Advance online publication. doi:10.339017010075 PMID:28042857

Li, X., Dunn, J., Salins, D., Zhou, G., Zhou, W., Schüssler-Fiorenza Rose, S. M., Perelman, D., Colbert, E., Runge, R., Rego, S., Sonecha, R., Datta, S., McLaughlin, T., & Snyder, M. P. (2017). Digital Health: Tracking Physiomes and Activity Using Wearable Biosensors Reveals Useful Health-Related Information. *PLoS Biology*, *15*(1), e2001402. Advance online publication. doi:10.1371/journal.pbio.2001402 PMID:28081144

Miller, D., Capodilupo, J., Lastella, M., Sargent, C., Roach, G., Lee, V., & Capodilupo, E. (2020). Analyzing changes in respiratory rate to predict the risk of COVID-19 infection. MedRxiv, 2020.06.18.20131417. doi:10.1101/2020.06.18.20131417

Peake, J. M., Kerr, G., & Sullivan, J. P. (2018). A critical review of consumer wearables, mobile applications, and equipment for providing biofeedback, monitoring stress, and sleep in physically active populations. *Frontiers in Physiology*, *9*(JUN), 1–19. doi:10.3389/fphys.2018.00743 PMID:30002629

Shapiro, A., Marinsek, N., Clay, I., Bradshaw, B., Ramirez, E., Min, J., Trister, A., Wang, Y., Althoff, T., & Foschini, L. (2020). Characterizing COVID-19 and Influenza Illnesses in the Real World via Person-Generated Health Data. *Patterns*, *2*(1), 100188. doi:10.1016/j.patter.2020.100188 PMID:33506230

Chapter 9
Design and Infrastructure in an Active Economy

Chris Dawe
Strategic Healthy Impacts, Canada

Mark Hentze
Independent Researcher, Canada

ABSTRACT

This chapter provides a high-level overview of the elements that make up the active economy infrastructure. This includes a focus on urban design, master planning, and a review of facility types. Further discussion involves types of play that occur within various infrastructure, with a particular focus on parks. Finally, the operation of infrastructure is reviewed along with the trends that are impacting the design of active infrastructure.

INTRODUCTION

As we examine the components of the active economy, one of the most visible and foundational is infrastructure. The built and natural environments which we utilize to be physically active are all around us. They are the foundation and the context in which we all move, and where leaders work to program sport, recreation, and active living. Areas such as walking paths, stadiums, ski hills, recreation centres, all form a significant part of our investment in the active economy. All of these assets were once planned, designed, and outfitted so they could eventually be operated, maintained, programmed in, and renewed on a continual basis. New built environments, and re-imagined uses of the natural environments are being envisioned and are in various

DOI: 10.4018/978-1-7998-7939-8.ch009

stages of planning and development. Each one of these infrastructure projects has people employed, contractors hired, and/or partner organizations producing materials and equipment to bring it all to life. Each element of the built and natural environment significantly impacts the livability of a community; this drives nearly everything else in the economy within that region. In this chapter we will examine each of these elements of the active economy infrastructure, how and why they are designed and utilized the way they are, and some of the factors that influence the places in which the active economy lives.

URBAN DESIGN

Since a significant portion of the world's population lives in urban areas, community design plays an important role in the active economy's infrastructure. Such design influences physical activity and health outcomes in a number of ways due to its influence on the behaviours of those who live, work and play there. Over time, many cities have grown and decentralized with people moving further away from the core. As a result, transportation has become much more about automobile culture. In the past few decades, we have examined the negative health outcomes of those barriers for natural daily physical activity. Communities (even those suburbs that are further out from the core), are increasingly being designed to incorporate more walkability, connectivity and active transportation (Frank et. al, 2003).

Deliberately designing the built environment and incorporating connections to the natural environment is becoming an important intervention to increase physical activity in communities (Omura et. al, 2020). The goal is to remove these barriers and make physical activity more accessible and more a part of everyday life for people in these communities. Improving pedestrian and bicycle transportation systems through street pattern design, connectivity, sidewalks, pathways, and bike lanes all form a part of the community design and active economy infrastructure. Combined with contemporary public transit planning, each of these work to increase active transportation and decrease the need for automobiles (Panter et. al, 2016). Additionally, parks, playgrounds, playing fields and recreation centres are also incorporated into community design. The density of residential housing forms opportunities for additional daily structured and unstructured activities. A UK study for the Department of Transport estimates that condensed walkable communities reduces municipal infrastructure costs by 33 per cent (Raje & Saffrey, 2016).

In examining how developers promote housing sales in a new community, commonly highlighted areas included parks, pathways, natural areas, recreational spaces, and facilities being built for sport, recreation, and active living. These attributes are in high demand and developers understand the ways in which they have drastically increase a community's desirability. These are the communities that grow quickly and become sought after by citizens and businesses that will serve them. Similarly, realtors will promote proximity to these natural and built environments as drivers for property values. A US study found retail areas with walk scores over 80 had a 29 to 49 per cent increase in property value (Cortright, 2009). Similarly, residential property value increased by an estimated 12 per cent in neighborhoods with high walkability scores (Kuhlman, 2010). Finally, a US study found that there was a property value premium in communities with schools that were within a walkable distance (Raje & Saffery, 2016).

City planners are increasingly understanding how these economic impacts are inextricably linked to the health and wellness impacts being sought by those who will become their community members. The National Health Service meta-analysis identifies that increases of walkability yield on average a 13 to 1 return on investment (Lawlor, 2014). A study conducted for the City of Portland estimates investments in bike facilities (costing from $138 to $605 million) will result in healthcare cost savings of up to $594 million and up to $218 million in fuel savings over a 25-year period (Guo & Gandavarapu, 2009). Therefore, policy decisions are being made, and leaders are voting to invest, with multi-pronged return-on-investment (ROI).

There are also goals being set in cities around the world for kilometres of bike paths, percentage of green space, and walkability measures. The Trust for Public Land has a goal that every citizen in American cities lives within a 10-minute walk of a public park and the current national average is 55 per cent (Park Serve, n.d.). They have a city ranking system that measures access, acreage, investment and amenities. Additionally, they are working to share that information, advocate, and build investment in public parks. Around the world there are a growing number of cities, including Paris, who are adopting and activating policies which aim to enable everyone in the city to be within a 15-minute walk or bike to essential urban cities (The 15-Minute City Project, n.d.). These initiatives drive sustainability efforts by getting automobiles off the roads, and the resulting positive impacts of increased physical activity, improved health, and even the economic benefits of pedestrian streets that encourage shopping from local businesses (Euklidiadas, 2020). Indeed, there are direct business economic incentives such as described in the British study that found urban design that increases walking and cycling can increase retail sales up to 30 per cent (Pivo & Fisher, 2011). See Figure 1.

Figure 1. Aggregated Walk and Bike Score of Major Cities

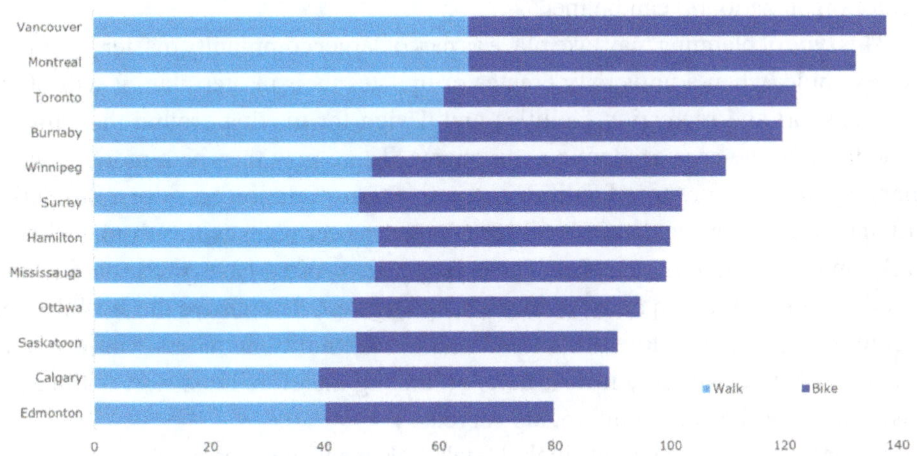

The "health in all policies" approach is increasingly being adopted in major cities around the world (Padron, 2020). It cannot just be a priority for the planning departments or the parks and recreation department; it takes a collaborative approach that cuts across those areas such as health, social services, sustainability, policing, roads, and many more in order for it to be successful and equitable. Urban design then becomes a collective impact imperative.

Evidence demonstrates that the active economy can also have a significant environmental impact by playing an important role in pollution and carbon emissions. This includes commitments to increasing active transportation, urban design and planning that promotes increased walkability and cycling. Therefore, what is needed is greater integration of public transit and micro-mobility options, including innovations in year-round cycling and e-bikes. Moreover, the increasing pressure for densification demands more efficient use of open spaces to support a broad range of sport, recreation, active living, community gardens and more (Keough et al., 2020).

MASTER PLANNING

As we move from the policy level of urban design to determining what to actually build and activate, we are into the topic of master planning. Just like planning process of any business, communities and organizations in the active economy are becoming increasingly more strategic about building, renewing, and expanding their infrastructure needs for sport, recreation, and active living. Building infrastructure is not the primary goal, but it is viewed as the foundation upon which the active economy can be built, and one of the ways that the broader goals of the community and/or organization(s) can be met.

This type of planning may take place as part of larger community master planning. For example, when a university creates or updates their master plan, it will often include sport and recreation facilities and design for moving around the campus in addition to the core academic components. There may then be a more detailed planning exercise for those facilities and active transportation corridors. Similarly, communities, towns, and cities will have larger master plans with sub-plans like a parks and recreation master plan. Those larger plans often have goals that include health, wellbeing, and quality of life. Those larger goals improve the livability of a community and therefore attract and retain community members who drive its economy. Active economy infrastructure planning therefore must start with needs assessment for the community being served.

Components of this planning include stakeholder engagement, needs assessments, feasibility studies and land acquisition.

A great deal of research is also being done about public infrastructure and these will also form a significant foundation for a region's master planning process. For example, in Canada, there is the Canadian Infrastructure Report Card that includes approximately $51 billion in public sport and recreation infrastructure assets across the country (Canadian Infrastructure, 2016). These include such things as 1,800 ice arenas, 950 pools, 500 curling rinks, 17,000 sports fields and many other facilities where the active economy comes to life. A significant portion of those facilities were built between 1950 and 1970, so they are aging and were also designed for needs in a different time and for a different population. In the most recent 2016 report card, nearly half (approximately $23 billion) are in fair to poor condition and declining (Canadian Infrastructure, 2019). In light of the COVID-19 pandemic, it is anticipated that this infrastructure gap will grow as investment is forced to slow. Canada Infrastructure suggests an annual target reinvesting rate of 1.7 per cent to 2.5 per cent for sport and recreation facilities. For example, if we have a facility with a replacement value of $20 million, then we should be reinvesting between $340,000 and $500,000 each year in order to maximize the lifespan and safety of the facility. Many in the field question whether this is occurring because budgets do not allow for such spending. That has the potential consequence of shortening the lifespan even further. These kinds of inventories and lifecycle assessments specific to the community will also form part of the needs assessment. Refer to Figure 2.

Figure 2. Sample Comparative Built Infrastructure per 100,000 Population

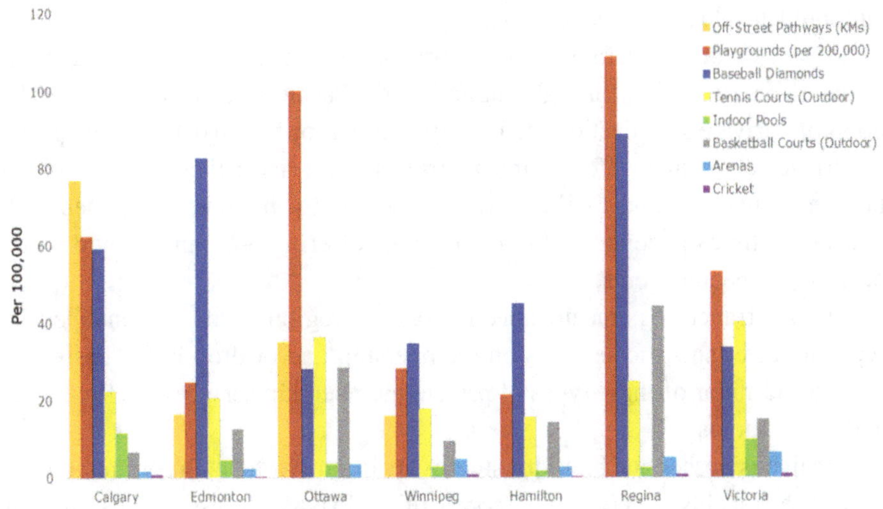

As noted above, significant public engagement is critical to confirm outcomes, identify unmet needs, and set priorities.

FACILITY TYPES

From these master planning exercises, decisions are made regarding building and/ or renewing infrastructure facilities. The ways in which people engage in those facilities for sport, recreation and active living varies from participation in highly organized programs to self-directed activity and occurs in publicly and privately provided facilities. This section provides an overview of some of the participant modes and facility types.

Public vs. Private

Publicly funded sport, recreation, and active living is a common model in many countries. Schools also provide sport and recreation amenities built with public money in the education system. These facilities are typically not open to the public for general use and some school boards have facility agreements with public recreation and private sports associations. Post-secondary institutions also often provide student recreation centres and athletics complexes; primary users are students and faculty, with some facilities accessible to the general public via drop-in fees or memberships. Funding often has a mixture of public dollars, student fees, and debt serviced by entrepreneurial revenue generation.

Private contract operators offer sport, recreation, and active living programs in two primary modes, through Public Private Partnership (P3) and for profit and nonprofit private organizations delivering contracts on behalf of the municipal owner.

Private clubs also offer membership based services; these range from semi-private to private, and facilities vary significantly in their components. These clubs sometimes generate additional revenue offering programs to non-members, or through special events.

Private franchises, meanwhile, operate at regional and national levels and typically offer specific services on membership and/or drop in fee basis. Among the most familiar of these types of private membership services are fitness centres and yoga studios.

Small businesses and boutique studios are often prevalent in communities where corporate franchises may be less competitive. Private fitness studios, martial arts dojos, and fitness trainers are examples. Private sport academies, meanwhile, are a growing infrastructure type in which academies offer lodging, school, and specific sport training to student athletes who aspire to become professional, Olympic and elite athletes.

Recreational vs. Competitive

With the majority of sport and recreation infrastructure being publicly funded, it therefore caters to the entire spectrum of users. Competitive sports are most often accommodated in public facilities through use agreements with the various sport associations. Technical sport facility standards for gymnasiums, lap swimming pools and ice arenas are normally incorporated into the design of public recreation centres to facilitate sport development and provide consistent standards. Private sport facilities provide specific sports training and sometimes include sports academies. While these are not as common as public facilities (for most sports) there has been a growth in private hockey and soccer academies.

Multi-Use vs. Single-Use

In the mid-1980s, the provision of single purpose sport facilities (e.g., the town arena) began to cede to multi-use recreation centres that combined multiple sport, recreation, and active living spaces and program offerings. This model has proven to be more cost effective than single purpose facilities and offers more opportunities for participation. Single purpose public sport facilities, however, are still prevalent.

Community vs. Regional

Facilities vary in age, size, and service area and resulting from factors including costs, demographics, and social trends, are a variety of community, sport, recreation, and active living facility types that serve communities. They include:

Community Halls

These tend to be large rooms with support amenities such as washrooms, change rooms and meeting rooms which host social and recreation activities. It is typical in small and rural locations with lower populations and less financial capacity. Oftentimes, these spaces do not meet specific sport facility standards but suffice for recreational sports and social events.

Outdoor Pools

Outdoor pools often represent legacy projects rooted to infrastructure grants. They typically include a 25 metre or 25 yard pool and change room facility. There is a resurgence in the development of outdoor pools that includes modernized programmatic objectives.

Neighbourhood Recreation Centres

These centres are a common type of sport, recreation, and active living facility that include primary components such as swimming pools, ice arenas and gymnasiums, and are supported by one or more secondary programming spaces. These provide sport, recreation, and active living within a local community (in either a large metro or smaller population) where users access the facility through multi-modal options (pedestrian, cyclist, auto, public transportation).

Community Recreation Centres

These centres are larger versions of neighborhood recreation centres and typically include multiple primary components such as ice arenas, swimming pools and gymnasiums. They support spaces that serve users from a larger catchment area, and typically rely upon personal vehicle transit to the facility.

Destination Recreation Centres

Destination recreation centres are the largest multi-use facilities, include multiple primary and secondary program components and include special features that attract users from an urban catchment and out of town recreational and competitive sport users. Destination centres tend to be in large metropolitan centres, however, smaller communities who promote sport tourism also provide this type of facility.

Indoor Recreation Centre Components

In order to better relate how facility type and size provide services and how it interacts with the active economy as a whole, it is worth acknowledging the multitude of programmatic components that can be included:

Primary Facility Components

- Ice arena(s)
- Aquatics/ swimming pool(s)
- Gymnasium(s)
- Fitness centre
- Spectator arena/ event centre

Secondary Components

- Multi-purpose rooms
- Functional training spaces
- Running track
- Racquet sport courts
- Rock climbing wall
- Leisure skating ice
- Curling ice
- Meeting rooms (various sizes)
- Performance stage
- Music rooms
- Arts studios (wet and dry spaces)
- Daycare (full service)
- Child minding (short term day use)
- Seniors centre (dedicated space or multiple rooms)
- Library
- Food & beverage spaces (concessions to full service restaurants)

Self-Directed Activity | Unstructured Play

The discussion has so far focused on facilities that suit typical organized sport and recreation programs but there is also a significant population seeking less structured options. "Unstructured play" is person-led, open ended and usually does not include predefined learning outcomes. Unstructured play frees people to engage in activities motivated by curiosity and creativity and may include some risk.

There is therefore a demand for less regulated self-directed recreation and active living opportunities. These activities are not necessarily new, yet the increased demand for self-directed recreation is influencing how architects and landscape architects design, how recreation programmers create offerings and how operators manage infrastructure. Example activities include Frisbee golf, pickleball, ultimate frisbee, freestyle and back-country.

Within publicly funded recreation programs also exist a growing range of self-regulated activities influencing services and design. For example, many arenas across Canada offer "shinny" and/ or "stick and puck" sessions that allow a cross section of ages, gender and abilities to play on a drop- in basis.

Designers are thus evolving traditional design standards to accommodate these activities. Architects who specialize in the design of recreation centres are therefore required to be well versed in designing for multi-functionality and flexibility. A relevant example comes from the University of South Denmark's Athletics Exploratorium, which has transformed a traditional 400 metre track and field facility into an undulating track with various features and obstacles that create a wide range of free form recreation and active living opportunities.

Impacting this trend further will be technology and the COVID-19 pandemic. Personal devices, apps, social media provide multiple platforms for people to recreate, and are supported by a growing industry reviewed in an earlier chapter. For example, a hospitality worker finishing work at 3 a.m. can join an online spin class originating anywhere in the world. COVID-19 has also resulted in numerous examples in which online self-directed play, and outdoor unstructured play have thrived while public and private facilities have been in various forms of lockdown. Some popular parks for instance, initiated requirements for free online passes to regulate a surge of outdoor enthusiasts.

Parks

It is also perhaps worth considering the specific role that parks play in relation to unstructured play. While the built environment serves the active economy in many ways, a significant portion of our natural world is available to explore. It is estimated that nearly 15 per cent of the Earth's land surface is now designated as national parks and other protected areas (IUCN, 2017). These include land trusts and private preserves, urban streams, community and regional parks, city parks, playgrounds, trails, ravines, local parks, territorial and provincial parks, marine parks, protected areas, migratory bird sanctuaries, biosphere reserves, Indigenous protected and conserved areas, national parks, and wilderness areas (Parks Canada, 2017). Similarly, there are increasing efforts to protect our lakes, rivers and oceans, while encouraging active pursuits upon them like kayaking, rafting, and fishing.

With this may be natural infrastructure for the active economy, there is a delicate balance. One example is the demand for ski and snowboard facilities, maintained and groomed trails, and camping facilities in national parks. Most people need such support and amenities in order to be enticed to engage with those natural spaces. As seen during the COVID-19 pandemic where people were renewing their connection to getting outdoors, human demand can even drive calls to expand those active opportunities. In order to ensure sustainability, however, there have also been calls to impose restrictions in order to limit the damage that large crowds of careless users can inflict. Continued investments and efforts are thus needed if we want to live in harmony with nature while continuing to benefit from our relationship with the land and generating capital (Parks Canada, 2017). Done well, the active economy can play an important role in environmental sustainability through time spent in nature promoting environmental stewardship among both children and adults. See Figure 3.

A fascinating example of the changing nature for infrastructure usage in our park spaces can be seen in the temporary closure of a highway in a Canadian national park. Among similar examples around the world, highway 1A from Banff to Lake Louise in Alberta, Canada was closed to vehicular traffic during the summer of 2020 (Pike, 2020). This was done to limit crowds and promote physical distancing. It also had the effect of enticing a record number of walkers and cyclists where they could engage in active pursuits without the risks, noise and pollution of sharing the space with automobiles. There have been calls to both maintain and increase these kinds of opportunities, utilizing the built infrastructure in ways to support more active enjoyment of our parks.

Considering more than half of the world's population (over 80 per cent in Canada now, and projected to be over 70 per cent worldwide by 2050) live in cities and urban areas. Getting active and connecting with these remote national parks spaces, however, is not always simple or realistic. Therefore, urban parks are an important part of the active economy infrastructure and we discussed earlier in our urban planning section.

Figure 3. Active Economy and Sustainability

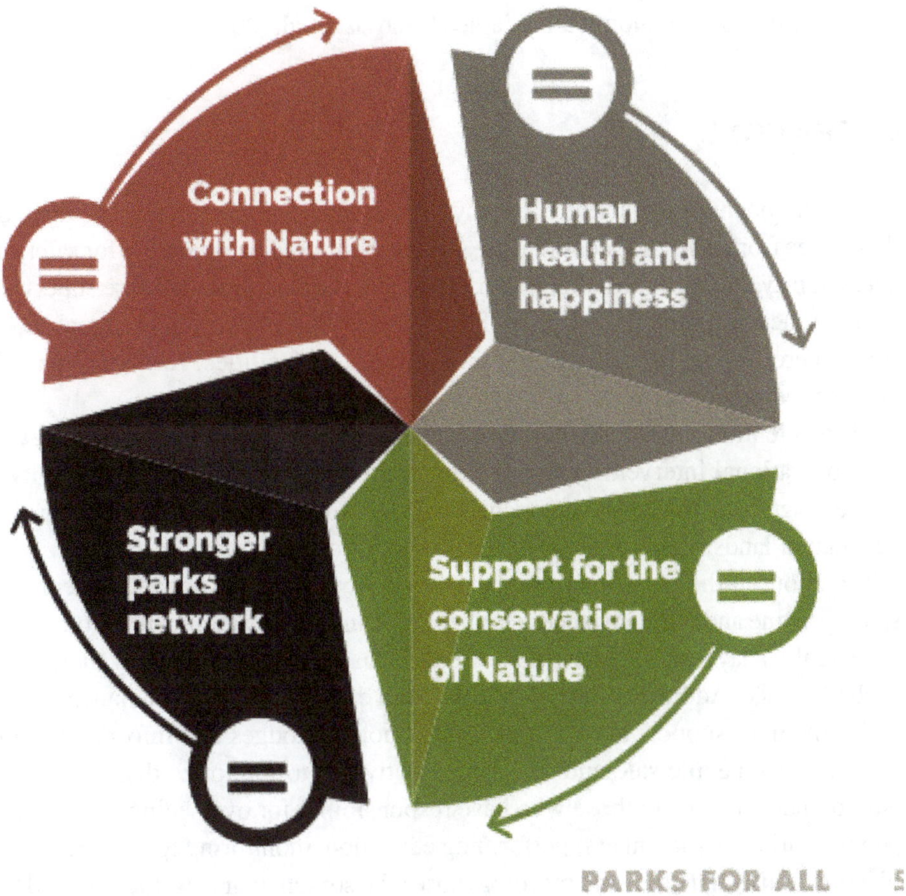

The benefits are both human and economic, as shown in a Toronto Dominion study, which suggested that its urban forest provided residents with over $80 million, or about $8 dollars per-tree worth of environmental impacts and cost savings each year. For the average single-family household, this works out to $125 dollars in savings per annum. For every dollar spent on annual maintenance, Toronto's urban forest returns anywhere from $1.35 – $3.20 worth of impacts and cost savings each year (Alexander & McDonald, 2014). In a study from Washington State, the non-traditional economic impacts associated with green spaces include the increase in general quality of life which people can receive from engaging in outdoor recreation. The combined benefits are estimated to be between $134 billion and $248 billion annually (Briceno & Schundler, 2015). Finally, an international study looking at

25 urban centres which are investing in restoring, protecting, and enhancing green infrastructure and ecosystem services in cities was not only ecologically and socially desirable, but also economically viable (Elmqvist et al., 2015).

OPERATIONS

Each component of the active economy infrastructure requires a level of operation that varies from natural spaces that are simply monitored occasionally for safety and accessibility, to more formalized sport and recreation facilities that are supervised, programmed and maintained daily. There are also a variety of operational models somewhere in between, depending on the types of facilities, resources available and desired outcomes.

The intention of natural environments such as national parks is to have as little operational intervention as possible in order to maintain the opportunity for 'recreating' in a relatively untouched natural world. However, even with these designated lands, there is a fair bit of oversight to keep them in that state. As we talked about in the parks section, there is a delicate balance between keeping the space pristine and allowing access for healthy human interaction with nature. There is generally a layer of governmental oversight that plans for effectively maintaining such a balance. Additionally, there is often trail development, maintenance, signage and sometimes support facilities such as outhouses, lodges and informal camping areas to keep people safe and direct their activities to minimize disruption to the environment. There are those who have responsibility for overseeing the space and people in it (eg: park rangers) performing education, monitoring for natural hazards like fires and avalanches, and rescuing those who stretch their activities beyond their capabilities. Expenses for this level of operation is generally covered through public sources such as government funding and sales of park passes, as well as permit sales for entrepreneurial active tourism activities like guiding, climbing, rafting, heli-skiing, hunting and fishing.

At the next level of formality, there is a range of natural recreational environments with additional support amenities, and therefore, additional operational resources. Ski resorts, campgrounds, paved paths, and groomed cross-country trails are just some of the ways that natural environments get developed for recreational uses. Depending on the land it is on, the operators may be public, private, or some combination of the two. Operations match the type of facilities with ski resorts having significant operational requirements including ski lift maintenance, snow grooming, safety patrol, learn-to ski/snowboard programming, clubs, events (including races up to potential world cup), and potentially even full resort hoteling, food & beverage, etc. The business model includes sales of lift passes, lessons and accommodations, food, and entertainment. These have increasingly become a year-round business venture with mountain biking and support systems for hiking and even golf courses becoming a more regular part of ski resorts. Campground operations may have significant revenue streams for rental bookings that cover the expenses of campsite development and maintenance, pathway paving and snow clearing, firewood, cleaning, etc.

Moving into more urban areas, active infrastructure may take the form of trails and pathways similar to some parks. Again, depending on the model used for that municipality, some or all of these may be paved (requiring upkeep over time) and cleared of snow in the winter to accommodate year-round recreational activities. This applies equally to how well connecting paths and active transportation corridors are maintained year-round and the approach definitely impacts usage. Municipal parks also have a variety of operational models from simple green spaces that are left to grow wild, to manicured spaces for specific recreational activities like softball or cricket. These are mostly all open public spaces with some user fees, but generally supported through the tax base. Therefore, there are significant differences in how various municipalities develop and maintain, based on their budgeted investments.

Of course, there are all kinds of more formal sport and recreation facilities. These tend to have significantly more operational complexities including capital renewal, equipment, repair and maintenance. They are typically programmed in some way for space rental or formal program delivery. Membership sales, program registration fees, facility rentals, and sometimes retail, food and beverage are often a key part of the business model. Depending on whether these facilities are public or private, the fees associated with those generated revenues cover or partially cover all the operational costs. Management, maintenance staff, programmers, human resources and technology support are just some of the many involved in these complex business operations, with all of the resource inputs and corresponding services to their members and customers.

The most complex of infrastructure facilities from both a capital and operational perspective are large performance and event venues. Operating professional sports stadiums (that usually double as entertainment venues), comes with a unique and complex set of challenges. Massive revenue streams primarily from ticket sales and food and beverage are offset with huge expenses for capital costs, utilities, staffing, and resources to convert the facility into its different formats (e.g., from hockey to basketball to a concert to a monster truck event). Media and massive scoreboards are just some of the resource intensive operations that make these venues very different from your average recreation centre.

DESIGNING TO ACTIVATE TRENDS

Recreation professionals are continuously advancing the design of sport, recreation, and active living infrastructure to be responsive to or anticipate societal and environmental change. Climate crisis, inclusion and equity, health and wellness, and reconciliation are at the forefront, and issues that are pertinent to our active economy.

Climate Crisis

Judicious use of non-renewable resources and reduction of carbon footprint is critical when aiming to decrease the impact of humans on the planet. Production of building materials and the construction process account for roughly 30 per cent of greenhouse gas emissions. Those engaged in the building industry share responsibility to reduce greenhouse gases. Within this task, regulatory, optional and innovative solutions have arisen to activate new products, methodologies and participants.

Inclusion & Equity

Recreation infrastructure is also needing to be responsive through design to the principles of inclusion, diversity and belonging. Diversity is defined by multiple sources, however for the purposes of this chapter, it will be summarized as the range of human differences making each unique and/ or possess attributes allowing them to identify with those sharing similar characteristics. These differences can include, but not limited to ethnicity, gender identity, sexual orientation, marital status, age, socio-economic status, physical and/or developmental ability/ disability, religious or ethical values system, national origin and political affiliation.

Inclusion through design gathers diversity in safe and welcoming environments, enriching life experiences intellectually, spiritually, creatively and healthily. It enhances our active economy with new opportunities for participation, employment, volunteerism, product and system development, etc.

In public sport and recreation, programming and design professionals seek strategies to increase inclusivity in response to user needs and characteristics. A majority of users have relatively easy access to sport and recreation facilities, and through their often subsidized registration fees contribute to a robust industry. Noted below are some inclusivity themes that increase the sport, recreation, and active living sector's ability to respond to community diversity.

Figure 4. Universal Design Principles

Universal Design

Accessible design has historically been understood as building features usable for those living with disabilities. Accessibility is an important part of inclusion, however terminology is shifting from accessible design to universal design: "design that's usable by all people, to the greatest extent possible, without the need for adaptation or specialized design" (The Universal Design Project, 2020). While specialized design may be required in some instances, universal design applies design principles that provide physical access, safety and dignified use for all participants (The Universal Design Project, 2020). Refer to figure 4.

Dignity, equity and safety are also terms that are being considered by active economy infrastructure designers. Architects are becoming more sensitive to cultural, socio-economic and environmental factors that contain an opportunity to advance inclusive design. Examples range from providing design sensitivities to address Feng Shui, facilitating smudging ceremonies, incorporating Indigenous art, to functional solutions as mundane as advancing change room design, and room signage. Specific examples include universal change rooms, private change compartments (similar to fitting rooms but with showers), providing functional signage (for example depicting a toilet and sink) and thus replacing gender specific signage in order to identify what is in the room for use, as opposed to who is not allowed. These strategies are still evolving, yet they demonstrate the objective of creating a more welcoming space for a diverse.

Truth & Reconciliation

Overdue, current, evolving and subject to deeper understanding and action in its own right, Truth and Reconciliation for Aboriginal, Indigenous and First Nations people is integral to each topic presented in this chapter. Dialogue and action that includes shared commitment to sport and recreation has the potential to create greater connectivity amongst all people. At a design level, there are numerous strategies that can be applied to be inclusive of Indigenous culture. For example, minor modifications to building mechanical systems can be made to facilitate 'smudging ceremonies'. Facility naming and signage can incorporate names, language and graphics that teach Indigenous knowledge. Public art can celebrate Indigenous artistry and storytelling. Holistic facility planning can also seek indoor and outdoor connectivity that emphasizes the connection to the land. Inclusion of arts and food services, if done in consultation with Indigenous people, can further align cultural strengths that enrich our cultural competency and our shared sport, recreation, and active living facilities and experiences.

CONCLUSION

In this chapter, we have provided a high-level overview of the elements that make up the active economy infrastructure. Some sections have been summarized with some larger topics, perhaps needing whole books in and of themselves. The intention was simply to highlight how so many variables are a part of the consideration in the built and natural environments we utilize to be physically active. After reading this chapter, the reader should not be an expert on any one component, but rather have an overall idea of the key elements in planning, designing, building, operating, programming, and maintaining infrastructure in the active economy.

REFERENCES

Alexander, C., & McDonald, C. (2014, June 9). Urban forests: The value of trees in the City of Toronto. *TD Economics*. https://www.td.com/document/PDF/economics/special/UrbanForests.pdf

Briceno, T., & Schundler, G. (2015). Economic analysis of outdoor recreation in Washington State. *Earth Economics*. https://www.tre.wa.gov/wp-content/uploads/Willhite.pdf

Canadian Infrastructure Report Card. (2016). *Informing the Future* (Rep.). Retrieved from http://canadianinfrastructure.ca/downloads/Canadian_Infrastructure_Report_2016.pdf

Canadian Infrastructure Report Card. (2019). *Monitoring the State of Canada's Core Public Infrastructure* (Rep.). Retrieved from http://canadianinfrastructure.ca/downloads/canadian-infrastructure-report-card-2019.pdf

Cortright, J. (2009). Walking the walk: How walkability raises home values in U.S. cities. *CEOs for Cities*. https://nacto.org/docs/usdg/walking_the_walk_cortright.pdf

Elmqvist, T., Setälä, H., Handel, S. N., Van der Ploeg, S., Aronson, J., Blignaut, J. N., Gómez-Baggethun, E., Nowak, D. J., Kronenberg, J., & De Groot, R. (2015). Benefits of restoring ecosystem services in urban areas. *Current Opinion in Environmental Sustainability*, *14*, 101–108. doi:10.1016/j.cosust.2015.05.001

Euklidiadas, M. (2020, May 18). Paris wants to become a "15-minute city". *Smart City Lab*. Retrieved from https://www.smartcitylab.com/blog/governance-finance/paris-15-minute-city/

Frank, L. D., Engelke, P. O., & Schmid, T. L. (2003). *Health and community design: The impact of the built environment on physical activity*. Washington, DC: Island Press. https://books.google.ca/books?hl=en&lr=&id=fBi8BwAAQBAJ&oi=fnd&pg=PP3&dq=design and infrastructure impact on physical activity&ots=5ik5-AYf5b&sig=1WT10WO-iP-YBMwBh8iEdLdreNs#v=onepage&q=design and infrastructure impact on physical activity&f=false

Guo, J. Y., & Gandavarapu, S. (2009). An economic evaluation of health-promotive built environment changes. *Preventive Medicine*, *50*, S44–S49. doi:10.1016/j.ypmed.2009.08.019 PMID:19840817

IUCN. (2017, March 10). The World Now Protects 15 per cent of Its Land, but Crucial Biodiversity Zones Left Out. *IUCN*. Retrieved from https://www.iucn.org/news/secretariat/201609/world-now-protects-15-its-land-crucial-biodiversity-zones-left-out

Keough, N., Morrison, B., & Lee, C. (2020, May 27). State of our city 2020: An urgent call for a just transition. *Sustainable Calgary*. https://static1.squarespace.com/static/5ab716b9ee1759b04ca2703e/t/5ecd551002f4af1d18d76785/1590514966826/SustainableCalgary_SOOC2020.pdf

Kuhlman, R. (2010). *Helping Johnny walk to school: Policy recommendations for removing barriers to community-centered schools*. National Trust for Historic Preservation. http://www.bestfacilities.org/best-home/docuploads/pub/214_helping-johnnywalk-to-school.pdf

Lawlor, E. (2014). The pedestrian pound: The business case for better streets and places. *Living Streets*. https://www.livingstreets.org.uk/media/3890/pedestrian-pound-2018.pdf

Omura, J. D., Carlson, S. A., Brown, D. R., Hopkins, D. P., Kraus, W. E., Staffileno, B. A., ... Undefined, U. U. (2020). Built Environment Approaches to Increase Physical Activity: A Science Advisory From the American Heart Association. *Circulation*, *142*(11). Advance online publication. doi:10.1161/CIR.0000000000000884 PMID:32787451

Padrón, N. A. (2020). The Role of Physical Infrastructure on Health and Wellbeing. *Creating a Lifestyle Medicine Center*, 47-56. doi:10.1007/978-3-030-48088-2_6

Panter, J., Heinen, E., Mackett, R., & Ogilvie, D. (2016). Impact of New Transport Infrastructure on Walking, Cycling, and Physical Activity. *American Journal of Preventive Medicine*, *50*(2), e45–e53. Advance online publication. doi:10.1016/j.amepre.2015.09.021 PMID:26585051

Parks Canada. (2017). *Parks for All: An Action Plan for Canada's Parks Community* (Rep.). https://static1.squarespace.com/static/57a2167acd0f68183878e305/t/5a79d4b9ec212d1ab6d5ec86/1517933776855/Parks_for_all_Eng_jan31_2018_fnl_web (2).pdf

ParkServe. (n.d.). Retrieved from https://www.tpl.org/parkserve

Pike, H. (2020, July 6). How Parks Canada road closures open opportunities for visitors on two wheels. *CBC*. Retrieved from https://www.cbc.ca/news/canada/calgary/banff-national-park-road-closures-1.5638541

Pivo, G., & Fisher, J. D. (2011). The walkability premium in commercial real estate investments. *Real Estate Economics*, *39*(2), 185–219. doi:10.1111/j.1540-6229.2010.00296.x

Raje, F., & Saffrey, A. (2016). The value of cycling. *Department for Transport.* https://assets.publishing.service.gov.uk/government/uploads/system/uploads/attachment_data/file/509587/value-of-cycling.pdf

The 15-Minute City Project. (n.d.). Retrieved from https://www.15minutecity.com/

The Universal Design Project. (2020). Retrieved from https://universaldesign.org/

Chapter 10
The Sport Gaming Nexus:
A Paradox in the Active Economy

Mark Dottori
McMaster University, Canada

Alex Sévigny
McMaster University, Canada

ABSTRACT

Historically, sports gaming has existed primarily in brick-and-mortar venues such as casinos. This was the case until the internet created the conditions for a dramatic change in the supply of gaming opportunities in live sports. In 2018, a United States Supreme Court ruling legalized sports gaming, which triggered the tabling of similar legislation in Canada. This chapter examines how stakeholders form a network of relationships referred to as the sports gaming nexus. The authors argue that sports gaming presents a paradox – sports gaming will increase revenues and fan engagement for many actors within the sports culture and economy, but will the benefits outweigh potential negative consequences? This question is examined from the active economy, network system perspective. This chapter is informed by current debates in more mature gaming markets such as the United Kingdom and France.

INTRODUCTION

Sports gaming is an understudied area of sport scholarship. Gaming has played a central role in relatively marginal sports such as horse racing (Huggins, 2000), but not in mainstream sports with large markets such American football and basketball (Pradier, 2019). Historically, sports gaming existed primarily in brick-and-mortar

DOI: 10.4018/978-1-7998-7939-8.ch010

venues such as casinos. This was the case until the internet gave sports gaming a global reach. The internet created the conditions for a dramatic change in the supply of gaming opportunities, particularly in live sports. In 2018, a United States Supreme Court ruled for the legalization of sports gaming, triggering a gold rush in North America that has been having an impact on all aspects of the sports economy and sports culture. Indeed, this paper argues that sports gaming presents a paradox – sports gaming will increase revenues for many actors within the sports culture and economy, but will the benefits outweigh potential negative consequences? What do current debates on this question in more mature gaming markets such as the United Kingdom tell us? To explore these questions, this chapter examines sports gaming through an active economy lens.

As described in the first chapter, the active economy incorporates several disciplines that include sport performance, sport business, recreation, tourism, physical activity, urban planning, leisure, health, and wellness, among others. It is generally accepted by scholars that in an active economy analysis, each individual sector should be studied as a network of interdependent areas rather than individual self-contained objects. This viewpoint is founded on the economic concept of the cluster – a spatial metaphor used to characterize a concentration of primarily small- and medium-sized enterprises that exist in both complementary and competitive relationships (Porter, 1998). Other scholars conceptualize the active economy as a social construction (Granovetter, 2002). In the active economy, individual sectors within sport business evolve together through a combination of economic, social, and historical factors that transcend simple spatial proximity. These factors may include, among others: socioeconomic proximity and social interaction (Gerke & Prai, 2017, Gilly & Torre, 2000).

Within the active economy, a nexus is defined as a sub-network of organizations (Parung & Bititci, 2006). Changes in one part of the network may affect other parts. In an active economy systems-based approach, organizations involved in sport are in relationships with one another within the larger network – the sport economic ecosystem. Indeed, they act as interdependent parts of a subsystem – the nexus – within the sport economic network.

In this chapter, we will specifically examine the sports gaming nexus within the larger sport economic network. This subsystem includes five main stakeholders in the sport gambling ecosystem:

1. Gaming operators
2. Governments and regulation
3. The sports property
4. Sport media and sponsors
5. Society

Figure 1 depicts the relationships between these stakeholders, along with the lines of influence they exert on each other within the network. The framework is represented as an open system acknowledging that other externalities may have an impact on the relationships depicted here. Only the most significant connections are represented in the figure below.

Figure 1. Relationship Between Main Stakeholders in the Sport Gaming Active Economy Nexus

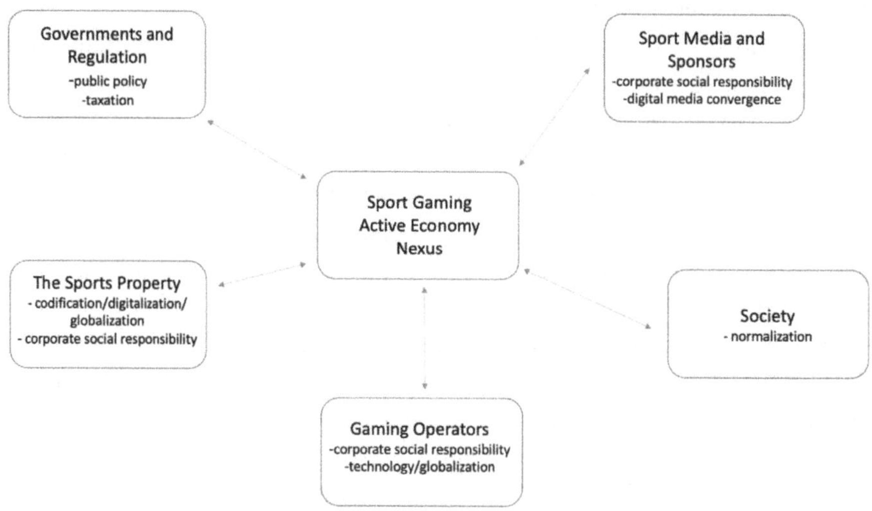

Andreff (2019) suggests that studying sport gaming within an active economy framework requires examining gaming as part of a larger sport ecosystem that moves towards a general and stable equilibrium in which stakeholders engage in non-linear, dynamic interactions. For example, a sports gaming operator will have interactions with government, teams, media, and bettors at the same time, in an asymmetrical, non-linear fashion. Lopez-Gonzalez & Griffiths (2018) suggest studying the sport gaming industry from such a perspective because the industry has undergone fundamental changes in the twenty-first century, led by the emergence of a global market for sport betting based on the speed and ease of internet communication. A similar phenomenon has been seen recently in mainstream financial markets, with the emergence of Reddit; a popular social news sharing platform – as a site for financial and investment communication (Shifflet, Ostroff & Rivas, 2021).

Prior to the internet, few actors had the means to place bets quickly during the live play of a sporting contest. The internet offered 24/7 access to in-play gaming on a wide variety of events world-wide, reducing the attraction of face-to-face gaming activities offered by local bookmakers, including illegal street bookmakers (Forrest, 2018). The move to internet gaming was accelerated by the ongoing convergence of digital media, which allowed greater and quicker connections between sport stakeholders, including, among others, interactions between fans, teams and gaming sites (Dottori et al., 2019; Meikle & Young, 2011). The internet and related technologies have grown the international market for sport gaming actors, which has led to the globalization of sport gaming. This trend toward globalization and the instantaneous access granted by digital technology has transformed the sport gaming's economics (Parke et al., 2014).

Sport gaming was available on the internet as early as 1996 (Pradier, 2019). This led to a proliferation of online sport gaming operators, growing to 8,000 operators in only 10 years (Andreff, 2019). It created a global market for sports gaming, the oldest known form of gaming, with roots that developed in the ancient Olympic Games in Greece and the gladiatorial games of Rome (Ng'etich & Auka, 2019) Sports gaming has grown to an estimated global market size of US$210.8 billion in 2021 according to IBS World (IBS World, 2020).

This growth, and the increasing acceptance of sport gaming by many sports leagues, sports events, governments, and the public of sports fans has had significant consequences. By the early 1900s, British, Italian, and French leagues had little aversion to sports betting, in particular the *pari-mutuel* model[1]. The same cannot be said for American leagues, which displayed a significant peridophobia[2] driven largely by the Major League Baseball's Black Sox scandal of 1919 (Pradier, 2019). Sport gaming is now a revenue-generator for many actors in the sports economy: governments through taxation, sport leagues through sponsorship contracts, media organizations through the generation of novel and engaging content, and data science corporations. It has spawned a rapidly growing online gaming industry with new business lines based on real-time peer-to-peer, or peer-to-organization gaming (Pradier, 2019). In fact, it has been argued that sport has become one of the most prominent arenas through which gambling is being normalized for the general public. This normalization is happening through cultural-cognitive legitimization by professional sport organizations and the media that depend on them for content (Fitzsimmons, 2009; Thomas et al., 2012).

GAMING OPERATORS

Sport betting is one of the oldest forms of gaming. Its origins can be traced back to the classical period (Ng'etich & Auka, 2019). During the medieval period betting was outlawed, but later became popular in England through horse race wagering. The English then helped spread betting around the globe. The influence of gambling played an essential part in the codification and development of rules in sport. Golf and cricket were codified in 1774 as a direct response to the requirements of bookmakers that the sports operate under consistent sets of rules (Forrest & Simmons, 2003). The internationalization of sport codes through the creation of international bodies who organize and regulate each sport, allowed sport events in different locations to produce comparable performances and results. This trend toward international standards allowed for the creation of reliable and globally shared standards of measurement and play. The formalization of sport codes, while aimed at generating an environment of fair play, also meant that fans and bookmakers would have greater confidence in the results of events, resulting in more sports gaming on those events (Lopez-Gonzalez & Griffiths 2018).

Prior to the internet, people were limited in how they could place their sports wagers – a person had to walk into a casino to place a sportsbook wager or they had to visit their local bookie. It is worth noting that in Canada, the United States and most of the West, bookies operated illegally, but were largely left alone by law enforcement (Milton, 2017). This meant that few individuals could place bets in real time while watching live sporting contests unfold. The internet has quickly transformed the sports betting marketplace. Before the internet, sport betting was popular, but much less widespread than it is currently (Milton, 2017). The internet offered, through various means, instantaneous access to information about live events and mechanisms for placing bets in real-time as those live events took place. Indeed, "in-play betting" has become one of the most prevalent forms of sports gambling, accounting for up to 70 per cent of wagers in many markets (Andreff, 2019).

The rise of sports analytics has played a significant role in the evolution of the sports gaming market. The standardization, codification, and quantification of sports through data science has led to the availability of metrics and analytics that were heretofore unimaginable. This quantification has enabled the creation of predictive statistical models that allow for more informed gaming decision-making, as well as gaming on aspects of sport for which it was impossible to previously derive a winner. This began with the Moneyball phenomenon[3], which made it more commonplace for professional sports organizations to use data-driven decision making in the signing and trading of athletes, as well as the optimisation of in-game matchings of player and opponent counterparts. This move toward the quantification of athlete and team performance has meant that data science companies have flourished over the last decade. Data science and sports analytics organizations (such as *Stathletes* in St. Catharines, Ontario) have signed long-term deals with sport organizations worldwide to extract, analyse, and deliver data analytics, some of which becomes media content. Such data are also used by sports gaming operators to produce a rapidly increasing number of elements that gambling operators provide for people to lay wagers on (Lopez-Gonzalez & Griffiths 2018).

Gaming agencies exploded in size and scope when online gaming markets were launched in May 2000. Flutter, a global online gaming provider, was the first to provide matching services for intermediated peer-to-peer gaming (Pradier, 2019). In these gaming exchanges, the operator does not fix the odds, but instead lets individuals place wagers as they wish, facilitating the match with another individual willing to bet on that non-occurrence. In exchange for intermediating the transaction, operators take a fee of typically 3 per cent, leaving a total outlay of up to 97 per cent of the wagered amount to the winner (Andreff, 2019). The key to the business model is that while the margin is slim, the gaming operator of the exchange does not suffer any losses and doesn't seek control of the match between the two gamers. This peer-to-peer model was originally thought to be regulation-proof since "betting amongst friends" was legal in almost every jurisdiction (Pradier, 2019).

Online data-driven technologies have also facilitated the explosion of fantasy sports leagues within the sport betting market. The global fantasy sport market size was valued at USD $18.6 billion in 2019 and is expected to reach USD $48.6 billion by 2027 (Valuates Reports, 2020). In fantasy sports leagues, players compete against others by selecting a team of professional athletes from a particular sports league. Each real-world player is assigned a value, represented by either an assigned salary or a set number of points. Regardless of the valuation system one uses, elite athletes cost more than lesser performing athletes. The selected team must fall under a certain "salary cap" or maximum point budget. The selected team of players then each accumulate points based on how they perform in real sport competitions.

Traditional fantasy sports gaming lasts for the duration of the season or playoffs period (or both) of a league's calendar. In contrast, daily fantasy sports are an accelerated variant of traditional fantasy sports that is conducted over shorter periods of time such as a week or single day of competition. Daily fantasy sports are typically structured as paid competitions often referred to as a "contest"; winners receive a share of a predetermined pot funded by their entry fees. A portion of entry fee payments go to the contest organizer as rake revenue; a scaled commission fee (Kilgore, 2015).

The earliest examples of daily fantasy sports date to 1990, when they were launched in a number of newspapers throughout the United States. These early examples were the first to convert baseball and football statistics into a coherent scoring system. By 2015, the daily fantasy sports industry had experienced major growth and had started to attain mainstream popularity largely due to aggressive advertising, league and team partnerships, the loosening of state restrictions and the growing public acceptance of fantasy sports. The migration of available statistics and the games themselves from newspapers to online and mobile devices was also a major factor in the rapid growth of daily fantasy sports (Fisher, 2015, Harwell, 2015).

There are two main categories of daily fantasy sports competition: cash games and guaranteed prize pools (Kilgore, 2015, Fisher, 2015). In the United States, the daily fantasy sports industry is dominated by two competing services: New York City-based FanDuels, and Boston-based DraftKings (Kilgore, 2015). Both companies were established as venture capital-backed start-ups, receiving funding from investment firms and later sports broadcasters, leagues, and team owners, (Kilgore, 2015, Fisher, 2015). In April 2020, DraftKings was merged with sportsbook technology supplier SBTech by purchaser Diamond Eagle Acquisition Corp, a special-purpose acquisition company (SPAC), in a USD $2.7 billion cash and stock deal. DraftKings has yet to be profitable despite rapidly rising revenues (Waters, 2021).

In September 2015, DraftKings and FanDuel expanded their offerings to include competitive video gaming and esports when FanDuel acquired the esports-focused daily fantasy service AlphaDraft, while DraftKings added contests for the 2015 video game League of Legends World Championship (Grubb, 2015, Wagner, 2015). In its purest formulation, esports involve people playing video games, which are rarely athletic sports simulations. The most popular esport games by betting volume are: League of Legends (38 per cent), Counter Strike: Global Offensive (29 per cent), and Dota 2 (18 per cent), (Legalsportsreport, n.d.). None of these is an athletic sports simulation.

Athletic sports leagues and teams have started to become involved in esports. In 2016, British football club Manchester City announced that an 18-year-old esport FIFA player would be representing the club in international competitions (Wakefield, 2016). This trend to esports by athletic sports leagues and teams accelerated during the COVID-19 pandemic as both bookmakers and bettors looked for new wagering opportunities due to reduced traditional sport schedules as well as the closing of physical casinos and sportsbook destinations. For example, in April 2020, the National Basketball Association organized a tournament with 16 of its most well-known players competing in the basketball simulation game NBA 2K live on ESPN.

Key crossover events between esports and traditional sports, such as the eNASCAR iRacing Pro Invitational Series, are being brought to life with tremendous success and to great fanfare. These types of collaborations, previously a pipedream for esports organizers, are now showcasing the "immense potential of esports," according to Rivalry's Chief Marketing Officer, Kevin Wimer (Luongo, 2020). The fact that more people are opting to watch esports online through digital streaming platforms such as Twitch and YouTube has meant even more live sports/ esports collaborations, as live sports organizations attempt to reach younger and more diverse demographics.

Esports do have live audiences in which people go to arenas to watch competitors play esports games. In South Korea, for example, there is a large market for live, in-person viewing of esports competitions. Using live, in-person events makes esports vulnerable to event cancellation – a similarity to live athletic sports. Despite this vulnerability, however, most esports tournaments and leagues have made a seamless transition to a purely online framework. The cancellation of live athletic sports works in favour of esports gaming as it can more easily shift to all-online platform, given that esports are video games played over a network, regardless of audience. The pandemic-driven cancellation of many live athletic sports events and the resulting shift to esports has result in some spectacular growth for esports betting. For example, when the English Premier League cancelled its season on March 18th, 2020, the esports betting platform Luckbox reported a 54 per cent upswing in new player registrants (Luongo, 2020). The global esports betting market size is expected to grow exponentially and reach USD $18.4 billion by 2026, up from USD $7.7 billion in 2019. North America, Western Europe, and the Asia-Pacific region are expected to be among the top esports markets in 2021 (Sawalka, 2020).

In 2018, the Professional and Amateur Sport Act was declared unconstitutional, lifting the United States federal prohibition on sports betting. This legal change led the two leading fantasy sports operators – DraftKings and FanDuel – to add formal sport betting operations to their portfolio later that year and become full-service sports betting operations (Purdhum & Rovell, 2018, Russ, 2018). In May 2018, FanDuel was acquired by Ireland-based Paddy Power Betfair, one of the largest betting operations in the world, presumably to grow its portfolio of gaming assets in the United States.

The growth of DraftKings and FanDuel and their consolidation into larger gaming organizations are an illustration of the sport gaming active economy. Both DraftKings and FanDuel have significant links to the sport culture audience due to their extensive fantasy sports league operations, which provided a pool of potential bettors, once DraftKings and FanDuel started to offer sports betting post-2018. Also, the sport gaming active economy nexus allowed access to a mature sport culture broadcast space, providing direct media channels with significant reach through which to offer fans gambling content. These channels provide an opportunity for DraftKings and FanDuel's gaming content to be integrated with the entertainment and digital communication media with whom sport organizations have relationships. Digital and social media allow instant gratification and the potential to develop apps to create reward schemes that favour quick, impulsive decision-making in a globalized sports betting market on the internet.

When one combines these factors, it is clear that the active economy construct has explanatory power to demonstrate how, in a globalized and interlinked economy, the move to esports and online sports gaming platforms has the potential to create exponential multiples for successful market entrants (Lopez-Gonzalez & Griffiths 2016). However, the potential for negative psycho-social effects is also multiplied, as will be explored later in the regulatory and governance section of this chapter.

The combination of the United States Supreme Court's lifting of the ban on sports betting in 2018, and the subsequent rapid rise in sophistication and popularity of online sports gaming platforms has led to unprecedented growth in online betting behaviours. For example, William Hill PLC, one of the UK's largest betting operators, saw online betting account for 47 per cent of net revenue and 81 per cent of operating profits in 2019 (William Hill, 2020). Mobile betting – betting transacted through a cell phone, tablet or other mobile-computing device – is further transforming the consumption patterns of sport bettors. Most importantly, it situates live in-play betting at the heart of the betting experience and further facilitates the interactions between mediated sports consumption and wagering. Again, the interconnected nature of the active economy approach suggests that it will be important to also track the negative psycho-social effects of the rise of mobile betting, given the evidence of negative impacts on youth of ubiquitous smart phone use discovered by psychologist Jean Twenge in her landmark 2017 study, refreshed in 2019 (Twenge, 2017; 2019).

The rise of both the burgeoning peer-to-peer betting market, daily fantasy sports, esports, and in-play betting marked the end of the traditionally episodic nature of sport betting. In the traditional market, fans would typically place a bet on a game once a week. In the new digitally facilitated, peer-to-peer market, individuals could place bets from anywhere and at any time. To meet this growing demand for quick and impulsive gambling, betting companies have begun to present a rapidly expanding range of betting offerings from around the globe (Kargün, 2020). These trends have created the conditions for significant revenue growth, possibly accelerated by the COVID-19 pandemic, which threw almost all non-essential workers into working from home through digital means. Working from home, coupled with the stimulus cheques issued by western governments, meant that individuals could increase their savings, pay off debts and have access to greater disposable income (Mitchell, 2021). In the United States, the COVID-19 pandemic resulted in an initial drop in revenues, as sports leagues paused games following the initial outbreak in the country, followed by strongly increasing revenues once live sports seasons resumed, as illustrated in Figure 2.

While the internet and mobile computing devices such as smartphones and tablets allowed access to betting online, bookmakers and gambling agencies also developed software to adjust odds automatically in response to bet-able events in sport competitions, such as the scoring of a goal. Using new technologies such as machine learning and predictive analytics, bookmakers learned how to offer ever-changing odds prior to, and during a match. They did this by developing statistical

Figure 2. Sport Betting Revenues in the United States

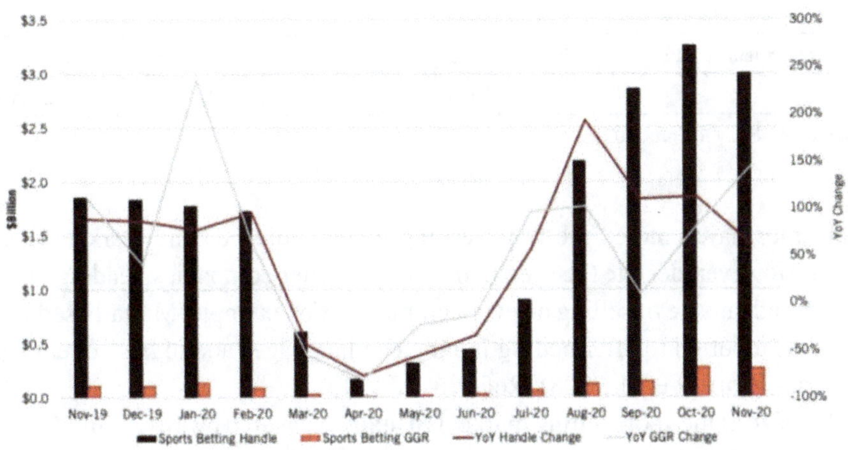

algorithms to automate odds-setting – the algorithm would update the odds with every significant event in the match coupled with the volume of bets placed during the competition (Forrest 2018). Gary Feldman, a professor at the Tulane Law School, said of the 2018 U.S. Supreme Court ruling:

This is a dry constitutional issue about states' rights, but it will likely change how we have viewed sports for the past 100 years. It's called the gamblization of sports. Fans will become much more focused on gambling than following a team. It will make every second of every game of every week interesting to fans as it will give everyone something to root for. (Liptak & Draper, 2018).

The sports gambling market's fluidity and global reach can be illustrated through soccer, where the Asian and European betting markets often adjust to synchronize with another in one minute or less. This has brought increased competition to the betting economy because bettors now have the ability to compare wagering odds across the world using price comparison websites, In the pre-digital, pre-internet past, bettors would have to rely on a local retailer (Andreff, 2019).

It is not only the largest sports betting global operators who have seen skyrocketing growth in both revenues and competition. In fact, thousands of smaller betting

Table 1. 15 Largest Global Betting Operators

The 888 Group	DraftKings	Webis Holdings PLC
Bet365	Fortuna Entertainment Group	WHG International
Churchill Downs Incorporated	Betfred Ltd.	Betsson AB
Flutter Entertainment PLC	Kindred Group PLC	BetAmerica
Entain	Sportech PLC	HKJC Football Betting Limited

Source WiseGuy Reports, 2021

companies have entered the fray, serving niche audiences and markets (Kargün, 2020). However, despite the growth in smaller, better companies, leading operators have the advantage of selling on every continent. For example, Malta-based Expekt.com, has reported to offer betting in nineteen languages and to have clients in 227 countries (Forrest et al. 2008). Refer to Table 1.

The size of the sport betting market is usually measured by gross gaming revenue (GGR) which is the net amount won by betting operators from their clients – this is actually a euphemism for player losses. Some analysts argue that player losses can be used as a proxy for consumer expenditures on betting. However, total expenditures, including all monies staked, are many times higher than GGR, since only a small proportion of stakes are retained by the bookmaker, rather than returned as player winnings (Forrest, 2018). Additionally, many companies are looking to expand their betting reach into emerging global markets. The United States is forecast by many analysts to remain the world's largest and fastest growing market due to deregulation following the United States Supreme Court's 2018 decision legalizing sports betting (Sports Betting Dime, 2020; Flutter, 2020; William Hill, 2020).

GOVERNMENTS AND REGULATION

Governments exert a key influence on the sports gaming market in general through public policy. For example, the issues in which governments choose to act on legislatively, through the passage of regulations or by funding certain priorities, often defines the market (Lamont et al., 2011, Kilpatrick, 2010). Many sports assets such as sports stadiums or arenas, as well as teams themselves, are often heavily publicly funded or only viable when given concessions from city, sub-state or national governments.

When assessing regulatory decisions concerning sports betting, governments have to reconcile inherent tensions between their role as guardians of the public health in regard to gambling addiction, the revenues from taxes on gambling earnings, political pressures from the gambling industry and often negative public perceptions of gambling (Harris, 2005). In 2011, the Canadian municipalities of Toronto and Hamilton faced a serious challenge to their respective plans to build casinos from anti-addiction, anti-exploitation and anti-poverty activists, as well as mental health advocates. Together, these groups successfully made the case that building a casino was a net negative for the cities and the projects were cancelled. Many governments throughout the world have viewed gambling as a relatively easy way to increase revenues, with only minimal attention being paid to the individual and societal costs (Monaghan & Derevensky, 2008). There are some notable exceptions to this utilitarian approach, led by the French government, which acknowledged the negative consequences, such as public harm caused by betting, when passing its 2010 law that made online gambling legal in that country (Vuchot et al., 2020).

Many European countries have sought to tax betting operators by taking a percentage of bets or gambling revenues made within their jurisdictions. While this kind of taxation is easy to administer, it created an incentive for betting operators to relocate to tax havens in a globalized betting market. Long-term, the out-migration of betting operators to tax havens may erode the tax base of the country from which the bets were placed. Approximately 80 per cent of the estimated 10,000 online betting operators are based in what are considered tax haven countries, sub-national areas, or entities within countries in which online gambling is not regulated. Examples of such places are: Alderney (Guernsey), Gibraltar, the Isle of Man, Malta, the Cagayan province in the Philippines, the Kahnawake territory in Quebec (Canada), Antigua and Barbuda, Costa Rica, and Curacao. These areas welcomed betting organizations as sources to attract significant cash flows into the region (Andreff, 2019). This has led to diminishing tax revenue for countries in which gambling was more strictly regulated than in these jurisdictions.

The challenge for governments rests in differences in their various philosophies of taxation. Most European countries use a model that considers the cost of the negative consequences of the practice of gambling such as addiction, increased crime, hospitalization, and family disruption amongst many others. This cost is then placed on the gambling operators, since most European countries tax gambling analogously to lotteries – the winnings have already been taxed, so they cannot be taxed a second time. This can be contrasted to the American model, which taxes both bettors' winnings and operators, at rates that vary from state to state. Some American states also require operators to pay licensing fees (Deloitte, 2021). The benefit of the American model is clear – not exclusively taxing the operators. However, it has a similar weakness to the typical European model – taxing the operators – which encourages operators to relocate to offshore tax havens. The Australian model is similar to the American one, with the difference that operators only pay taxes on bets placed within their state, "not the state the bettor resides in, nor the state where the bet is cashed in." (Deloitte, 2021). The British Gambling Act of 2014 was a first step in discouraging offshore operation, taxing gamblers at point of sale (Pradier, 2019). In the United Kingdom, bettors do not pay taxes on their winnings, rather operators pay a flat 15 percent tax (Deloitte, 2021).

As mentioned earlier, the United States Supreme Court in its decision on Murphy v. National Collegiate Athletic Association, deemed unconstitutional the Professional and Amateur Sports and Protection Act of 1992, otherwise known as PASPA. This was because the Supreme Court deemed that PASPA crossed a line into state jurisdiction. PASPA had previously effectively forbidden states from legalizing and taxing sports gambling within their own borders, with the exception of a few states such as Nevada, Delaware, Oregon, and Montana. The 2018 ruling was a pivotal constitutional decision that went well beyond the remit of sports betting. In the words of Adam Liptak, the Supreme Court reporter for the New York Times:

It's not unusual for a decision to be of interest to me and the Washington bureau, but here we had a Supreme Court case with some real constitutional implications," Mr. Liptak said. The court's opinion sets the precedent for a wellspring of other issues that have to deal with states' rights — including marijuana legalization, guns, and sanctuary cities. "There have only been a couple cases before this where the court said, 'There are things the federal government cannot command the states to do.' (Delkic, 2018)

Congress had originally enacted PASPA "to stop the spread of state sponsored sports gambling." (Rodenburg, 2017) Both states, as well as private individuals, were prohibited under PASPA from authorizing sports gambling operations "in which amateur or professional athletes participate." (Spitz & Terry, 2020). By striking down the law, the power to legalize and regulate sports betting was devolved to states as the federal legislation, the Sports Wagering Market Integrity Act of 2018, continued to stall in Washington (Spitz & Terry, 2020). In the absence of federal regulation, a number of states legalized sports betting soon after the PASPA decision, with many others currently considering legalization (Humphreys, 2021). Each state can now propose and implement legislation for the first time in a generation. Refer to Figure 3.

A substantial result of PASPA's repeal is that casinos and state governments can now attempt to recapture a portion of the surplus betting market that had been held by illegal offshore companies. This newly legal market is expected to contribute an

Figure 3. Legal Sport Betting in the United States

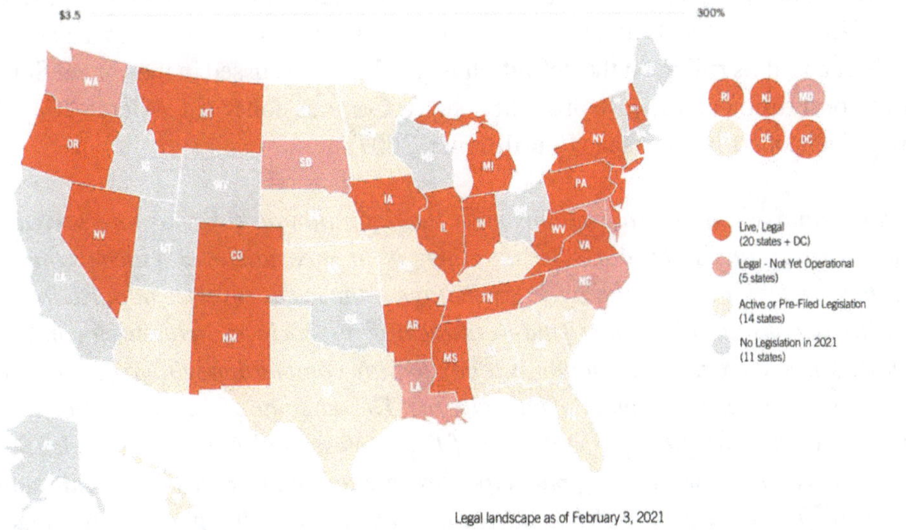

estimated USD $22.4 billion annually to United States GDP (Oxford Economics, 2017), although the costs of the negative consequences of normalized, ubiquitous online sports betting remain to be evaluated. Tax revenues for government could come in several forms: license fees for the operation of sportsbooks, taxes on net revenues earned from bookmaking using such measures such as taxing the sportsbook hold[4], as well as taxes on the winnings of individual bettors.

The repealing of PASPA also laid to rest an ongoing debate in the United States concerning whether daily fantasy sports constituted illegal sports betting – the lack of clarity on this point had previously led to inconsistent laws among states. This gray area in the sport gaming nexus, was a loophole that existed due to a lack of certainty about the relative weight of chance versus skill of the gamer in successful outcomes (Kilgore, 2015). One side of the argument held that the "construction" of teams which play for money under a salary cap constituted a game of skill by the gamer. That is, it was considered that constructing the roster made daily fantasy sports a legitimate game of skill. The counter argument considers daily fantasy leagues are predominantly a game of chance much like sport betting and should therefore be illegal. This argument presumes that the outcome of a given game or player performance cannot be reliably predicted, through knowledge and careful analysis of previous performance, making daily fantasy sports a game of chance (Schrotenboer, 2015). Initially, all American states considered daily fantasy sports a gambling activity, however by the end of 2017, nineteen states had ruled it was a legal game of skill (Gouker, 2017). In 2021 the Internal Revenue Service of the United States published PLR 202042015 (IRS, 2020), a memorandum that ruled that daily fantasy sports did, indeed, constitute a game of chance and not a game of skill. It based its ruling on the definition of gambling discussed in the United States Tax Court ruling on the case of Tschetschot v. Commissioner, T.C. Memo 2007-38 by Judge Robert N. Norman (Courtlistener, 2007):

[Daily fantasy sports] transactions meet the definition of wager as interpreted by the Tax Court and state courts because there is an uncertain event (such as the live performance of individual players), winnings if the event resolves in participant's favor, and consideration is lost if the event does not resolve in participant's favor. Each [daily fantasy sports] transaction is a pay to play competition with predetermined winnings for a certain number of participants. The outcome of the competition turns on the overall statistical performance of live professional players assembled into the fantasy team. The winning participant receives a return of his or her initial bet along with wagering gains, while the losing participant walks away empty handed. This is consistent with the courts' interpretation of the term "wager."

This ruling followed an IRS memo of July 23, 2020, which ruled that the usual excise taxes[5] levied on wagering would subsequently apply to daily fantasy sports (Internal Revenue Service, 2020). These IRS memos have clarified the tax status of daily fantasy sports to the advantage of bettors, but to the great disadvantage of daily fantasy sports operators such as DraftKings, which discussed earlier in this chapter.

In Canada, the legalization of sports betting has had a tortuous journey. In 2016, Brian Masse, the New Democratic Party Member of Parliament for Windsor-West introduced private member's bill C-221, *Safe and Regulated Sports Betting Act.* His motive in proposing this legislation was to support the casino industry in his Windsor, Ontario constituency. C-221 was not supported by the Liberal government and was defeated at second reading (Parliament of Canada, 2016).

The political context of sports betting in Canada changed after the legalization of sports gambling in the United States in 2018. On November 26, 2020, the Government of Canada introduced Bill C-13, *An Act to amend the Criminal Code (single-event sport betting),* that proposed to decriminalize single-event sport betting (Parliament of Canada, 2021c). However, on February 25, 2020, Kevin Waugh, Conservative Member of Parliament for Saskatoon-Grasswood, had already introduced Bill C-218 (Parliament of Canada, 2020d) that resurrected Masse's private member's bill C-221 *Safe and Regulated Sports Betting Act,* which was defeated in 2016 (Parliament of Canada, 2020a). C-218 was supported by the commissioners of the six professional sports leagues operating in Canada in a joint statement (Silver et al., 2020) issued on

June 8, 2020, which was signed by Adam Silver (National Basketball Association), Gary Bettman (National Hockey League), Rob Manfred (Major League Baseball), Don Garber (Major League Soccer) and Randy Ambrosie (Canadian Football League):

The National Basketball Association, the National Hockey League, Major League Baseball, Major League Soccer, and the Canadian Football League support an amendment to Canada's federal laws that would authorize provinces to offer betting on single sporting events. Sports betting gives fans another exciting way to engage with the sports they love. Because a legal and regulated sports betting market in Canada would be beneficial to sports and their fans, we urge prompt action to make this a reality. Sports betting already happens illegally in Canada; creating a legal framework would shift consumers from illicit, unregulated markets to a legal and safe marketplace. Regulating single-game betting would allow for strong consumer protections as well as safeguards to further protect the integrity of sports.

Not all sport actors have been supportive. Tony Clark, then executive director of the Major League Baseball Players Association said:

The court's decision is monumental, with far-reaching implications for baseball players and the game we love. From complex intellectual property questions to the most basic issues of player safety, the realities of widespread sports betting must be addressed urgently and thoughtfully to avoid putting our sport's integrity at risk as states proceed with legalization (Liptak & Draper, 2018).

Waugh and Unifor Local 444 both put forward the argument that legalizing sports betting would support employment in both the casino and professional sports sectors, particularly during a pandemic, when people cannot attend live games. Member of Parliament Brian Masse added that event sports betting would reduce revenues to offshore and organized crime operations (Waddell, 2020). On February 18, 2021, the Honourable Anthony Rota, Speaker of the House of Commons ruled that: "Consequently, as long as C-218 follows its course through the legislative process during this session, Bill C-13 may not be proceeded with." (House of Commons, 2021). The differences between C-13 and C-218 are small, pertaining mostly to horse racing. Bill C-218 would:

...make it lawful for the government of a province, or a person or entity licensed by the Lieutenant Governor in Council of that province, to conduct and manage a lottery scheme in the province that involves betting on a race or fight or on a single sport event or athletic contest (Parliament of Canada, 2019).

Currently, Canadians are only allowed to engage in parlay[6]. According to the Government of Canada, sports betters across the country spend approximately CAD $500 million dollars a year on parlay bets through government sanctioned betting games like Pro-Line (Deloitte, 2021). A small number when compared to the CAD $14 billion the Canadian Gaming Association estimates is spent annually through black market bookies (CAD $10 billion), and offshore online outlets (CAD $4 billion) who allow single game betting (Tasker, 2020). An analysis by Deloitte (2021) suggests that "within five years of legalization, sports betting could grow from CAD $500 million to nearly CAD $28 billion in legal-market wagering." The same report goes on to say that the CAD $15 billion that Canadians bet on sports in 2020 was:

... roughly 3.75 times the size of the country pre-COVID-19 spectator sports market, which comprises all professional, semi-professional, and amateur sports clubs that perform for an audience. However just 3 percent – of CAD$450 million—of that $15 billion in bets was done legally (Deloitte, 2021).

Up to now, the Government of Canada has not taxed winnings from gambling activities, using the same theory of avoidance of double taxation as that of the United Kingdom and other European countries.

While the legalization of sports betting may seem to be a bonanza of potential tax revenues, these must be weighed against the costs of negative consequences caused by the legalization – therefore normalization – of sports gambling. Indeed, unhealthy outcomes may well result from sport gambling (Lamont et al., 2011). In Australia, a report commissioned by the Australian Federal Government in 2009 titled *The Future of Sport in Australia* (Independent Sport Panel, 2009) expressed community concerns about the legalization of gambling sponsorship of sport. Specifically, the report asked whether such activities undermine the promotion of a healthy lifestyle and activity created by sport (Lamont et al., 2011). In the United Kingdom, British legislation has prohibited gambling advertisements during timeslots commonly watched by youth (Gambling Act, 2005) although, as noted by Monaghan and Derevensky (2008), this does not include the promotion of gambling organizations during the sporting events themselves.

In England, half of the Premier League clubs had gambling sponsors on their shirts for the 2019-20 season, accounting for $349.1 million British pounds sterling in revenue, a rise of more than 10 per cent over the 2018-19 season (Davies, 2019). The Premier League does not currently have a gambling partner, so sponsorship deals are left to the individual clubs. In the top two tiers of English football, nearly 60 per cent of clubs, have signed sponsorship agreements with gambling operators in the 2019-20 season (Grant, 2020).

There has recently been serious concern expressed in the United Kingdom about the tightening relationship between European football and gambling. Former FA Chief Executive, Mark Palios, who currently chairs Tranmere Rovers FC, stated "football has to wean itself off the position it is in at the moment - and that's the best verb I can use. It's certainly gone too far." (Grant, 2020). This concern about the psycho-social effects of sports betting on young fans was validated by University of Bath researcher Darragh McGee (2020). McGee's study, conducted with 32 adult men aged 18-35 years found that "gambling has become a normalised aspect of sport fandom for male youth demographics as vital to their enjoyment of sport." McGee also found that 'perceived 'facelessness' of sports gambling platforms via mobile app technologies was reported to increase inclination to engage in sports betting." His two other main findings were that 'free bet' incentives and in-play promotions lead to more sport gambling, and that online sports gambling had a potential role "as a gateway to gambling-related harms, including financial precarity, indebtedness, mortgage defaults, family breakdown, loss of employment and mental health struggles" (McGee, 2020). McGee's findings, coupled with findings from researchers at Goldsmiths University who "found gambling logos or branding were on screen for between 71 per cent and 89 per cent of Match of the Day programmes, even though the BBC does not carry actual advertising," suggest that potential negative impact of the normalization of sports betting is a concern (Conn, 2019).

Growing public concern about the link between sports betting and young fandom led Britain's sports minister, Nigel Adams, to say that he would be reviewing the Gambling Act 2005, which permitted gambling organizations to advertise on television and radio (Magowan, 2020). It also led the British Labour Party's deputy leader, Tom Watson, to state the Party would ban gambling company logos from football shirts and ban gambling-related television advertisements should Labour form a government (Davies 2019). These proposals would go much further than the "whistle-to-whistle" television advertising ban as well as increasing funding for addiction treatment that Britain's biggest gambling companies voluntarily agreed to in 2018. The 2018 voluntary bans did not include on-shirt advertising and were deemed insufficient by critics. Indeed, Watson commented that:

... less than a year ago, we were told by the gambling industry that they are committed to reducing the amount of advertising in football. We were told that we are facing a 'watershed moment' in which they would strive to provide an ever-safer gambling environment. But it is impossible to take these words in good faith when we are actually seeing an increase in gambling advertising around matches. (Davies, 2019)

The Betting and Gaming Council, which represents most bookmakers in the United Kingdom, has said it was "considering" a voluntary ban on football shirt sponsorship and pitch-side advertising. However, no action has been taken other than that of Ladbrokes and Paddy Power Betfair who broke ranks with their industry peers, calling for shirt and pitch-side advertising bans (Davies 2019b; Scott, 2020).

THE SPORT PROPERTY

The sport property is a key stakeholder in the sport gaming active economy nexus. Sport and gambling organizations enter into potentially co-dependent commercial relationships with sport properties by signing partnership and sponsorship deals at different levels: competition (leagues), organization (teams) and individual (athletes). On the one hand, there is a strong argument that sports properties benefit from additional revenues through team sponsorships and advertising and in-kind resources such as earned or co-developed media. On the other hand, as suggested by McGee's preliminary research, it can be argued that sports betting has the potential to create an unhealthy and ultimately counterproductive relationship between sport fandom and betting.

Initially much like governments, sport properties grappled with how to handle sports betting. As noted earlier, many new online betting operators skirted sub-national and national regulations by locating to "offshore" in tax havens of various sorts where betting is legal and largely unregulated. Often, such tax havens have lax anti-money laundering standards (Pradier, 2019). This has led to accusations of match-fixing in soccer leagues such as the Chinese Super League in 2004 (AFP, 2020) and later in Germany's Bundeliga in 2005 (Landler, 2005). Such actions were not limited to soccer. In 1919, players on the Major League Baseball's Chicago White Sox were accused of losing the World Series against the Cincinnati Reds in exchange for money. This led to the appointment of baseball's first commissioner, Judge Kenesaw Mountain Landis, to help restore the sports' integrity and led to a strong anti-gambling sentiment in North American sports leagues that persisted until very recently (Thorn, 2019).

More recently, National Basketball Association (NBA) referee Tim Donaghy pleaded guilty in 2007 to conspiracy charges for communicating inside information to bookies as well as betting on games himself. Over two seasons, Donaghy's actions led to possible gains of hundreds of millions of dollars for gamblers (Eden, 2020). This case prompted David Stern, the NBA commissioner at the time to state, "this is the most serious situation and worst situation that I have even experienced either as a fan of the NBA, a lawyer for the NBA, or a commissioner of the NBA" (ESPN, 2007). Stern perceived the situation to be a betrayal to the sport and a challenge to the NBA's image and integrity (Lockwood, 2008).

Despite such concerns, major sports have embraced fantasy sport and daily fantasy sport games, an aforementioned gray area in the sport gaming nexus. In April 2013, Major League Baseball (MLB) invested an undisclosed amount in DraftKings, becoming the first American professional sport organization to invest in daily fantasy sports. Shortly thereafter, the NBA invested in FanDuel, which is DraftKings' biggest competitor (Kilgore, 2015; Fisher, 2015). Some franchises, such as Kraft Group, which owns the New England Patriots, have also invested in daily fantasy sports. In addition, media companies, such as the Walt Disney Corporation and Fox Sports signed agreements with DraftKings, some of which included an equity stake (Spangler, 2015; Woodward, 2015).

While sport organizations embraced daily fantasy sport for years, the fight over nationwide sports gambling was simple: casinos wanted it and major league sports did not. However, as mentioned earlier, the sport betting landscape changed in North America when the Professional and Amateur Sports Protection Act was struck down by the Supreme Court of the United States in 2018. As a result, the NBA, which under Stern's leadership was one of the leagues that had the strongest anti-gambling positions, now embraced legalized sports betting more openly and vigorously than other American professional sports. In fact, shortly after taking over as NBA commissioner in 2014, Silver penned an op-ed in *The New York Times* advocating for sport betting legalization, saying "I believe that sports betting should be brought out of the underground and into the sunlight where it can be appropriately monitored and regulated" (Silver, 2014).

After the 2018 United States Supreme Court decision, both the NBA and MLB asked legislatures to require casinos to pay leagues one percent of all wagers placed on their sports, what the two leagues called an integrity fee. NBA commissioner Adam Silver arrived at the one per cent number by looking at overseas jurisdictions like France and Australia, where leagues are given a cut of wagers placed on their games. The leagues justified the fee as a royalty, one owed to leagues for the rights of betting operators to profit off their games. The leagues also suggested it was a type of insurance policy that would offset the risk of corruption to the leagues – indeed they suggested that the royalty revenues would be used to ensure competition integrity. "Sports betting is built on our games," Dan Spillane, NBA General Counsel, told a hearing of Connecticut legislators in March 2018 "if something goes wrong, if there's a scandal, something that tarnishes the image of the game, that's going to be a cost borne by the sports leagues, and less of a cost borne by the operators that offer sports bets" (Novy-Williams, 2018b).

It is not surprising that casinos and sportsbook operators were vehemently opposed to such a royalty. In fact, some threatened to shut down their sportsbooks. The royalty would generate significant revenues for all leagues. Research firm Eilers & Krejcik estimated that the legal American sports betting market could grow to USD $245 billion a year by 2023, which, under the one per cent regime, would translate to a potential annual royalty of USD $2.5 billion for the leagues. In addition, leagues also asked that bookmakers agree to: (i) use official league data with compensation to the leagues for providing the data; (ii) share consumer information; and (iii) allow the league's final approval of what types of wagers would be allowed (Novy-Williams, 2018b).

The NBA and MLB were the public face of the sport betting legalization lobby effort, working on behalf of major league sports. Major League Soccer (MLS) supported the fee, but did not campaign actively, while National Hockey League (NHL) deputy commissioner Bill Daly said his league had no current position. A National Football League (NFL) spokesperson declined to comment, and the National Collegiate Athletic Association (NCAA) remained staunchly opposed to any sort of legalized sports betting (Novy-Williams, 2018b).

A path forward to resolving the royalty fee sticking point was found when, in July of 2018, Silver announced a multi-year deal making MGM Resorts the "official gambling partner of the NBA" (Eden, 2020). The deal between MGM Resorts and the NBA marked the first partnership of its kind (Draper, 2018, Novy-Williams, 2018). In the absence of a law that included royalty and data sharing, making a deal with MGM Resorts offered a way for the NBA to achieve some of their goals using a strategy of signing partnerships operator-by-operator. In Silver's words: "we thought we could accomplish commercially a lot of what we were trying to achieve with the state legislatures" (Novy-Williams, 2018).

The MGM Resorts – NBA partnership was a major step toward sports betting becoming an accepted part of sports culture. The deal allowed MGM Resorts to use the NBA, WNBA, and all team logos and trademarks. In addition, MGM Resorts was allowed to use official NBA data on its betting platforms in exchange for working with the league to detect and prevent fraud and game fixing. This solidified the interdependence of the two partners. MGM Resorts also agreed to work on a coordinated marketing plan for their gambling services with the NBA (Draper, 2018). When he announced the partnership, Silver said the collaboration "will result in the best possible gaming and entertainment experience for consumers through the use of accurate, real-time NBA and WNBA data, and our collective efforts to maintain and enhance the integrity of our games" (NBA, 2018).

Silver also noted that it was important that the NBA establish a commercial relationship which would compensate them for the intellectual property and official data provided (Novy-Williams, 2018). MGM Resorts' chief executive, Jim Murren, commented that "integrating the NBA's assets and having official NBA data showcased across the MGM Resorts platforms will provide us with a distinct advantage and instill more confidence in knowing that our data is directly from the NBA" (Draper, 2018). Financial details were not disclosed, but it is believed the deal is worth USD

$25 million over three years. In addition, while the "official gaming partner of the NBA" tag is exclusive, the underlying business arrangements are not. Thus, the NBA could sign similar deals with other betting operators, as they did with Groupe FDJ (France's national lottery operator) and later the FanDuel Group. NBA teams were also free to sign their own deals with betting operators, resulting in the Philadelphia 76ers signing a deal with Caesars Entertainment (Philadelphia 76ers, 2018).

Other leagues and teams soon followed; the NHL signed a similar deal to the NBA with MGM Resorts, while NHL teams such as the Las Vegas Golden Knights and New Jersey Devils struck deals that included themed lounges and sports betting advertising within the stadiums, as well as engagement on media, advertising, and promotional platforms. The NHL also became the first of the North American professional sport leagues to install sportbooks in their arenas, with companies like FanDuel and William Hill advertising throughout the game (Brennan, 2018). The NHL philosophy was that sports betting would make hockey more accessible for non-fans and increase television ratings with its American media partner NBC (Spitz & Terry, 2020). The NHL specifically sees sports betting as a way to grow its fan base and make the in-game experience more engaging.

The NHL's approach to sport gambling has already produced results. Specifically, it sees predictive gambling as a way to grow its fan base and enhance the in-game experience. The 2019 Stanley Cup champion St. Louis Blues became the first NHL team to offer a free, real-time gaming platform during the playoffs called "Enter the Zone" (St. Louis Blues, 2019). "Enter the Zone" gave fans the opportunity to make wagers based on in-game statistics, such as the number of saves made by a team's goalie, or the number of shots on net. Fans who made winning predictions earned points that could be exchanged for prizes such as signed merchandise and tickets. The results were remarkable: 70 per cent of users played multiple times and 30 per cent of users used the app in at least 12 of 13 playoff games after the platform was launched (Spitz & Terry, 2020).

The fact that the NFL already boasts high fan engagement led Christopher Halpin, the league's executive in charge of strategy to remark that "we don't need to integrate sports betting directly" (Draper, 2019). The Dallas Cowboys were the first NFL team to seek a betting sponsorship, making a deal with WinStar Casino in Oklahoma that allowed WinStar to use team logos and trademarks as part of their promotions (Legal Sports Report, n.d.). Legalized sports betting is expected to benefit the NFL more than any other North American professional sports league, adding up to USD $2.3 billion in annual revenue. This projected increase is based on assumptions of projected growth in sponsorship rights, media rights, merchandise sales, and ticket sales. The American Gaming Association (2018) projects that television advertising from gambling services and money flowing directly from betting operators to the league are expected to account for USD $1.4 billion of these additional revenues. The latest NFL collective bargaining agreement allows sport gambling in its stadiums, with revenues to be shared with players (Purdum, 2020).

The 2019-20 NFL season was the first in which legal wagering was permitted. FanDuels reported a 1,200 per cent increase in NFL spending on its online platform, while rival DraftKings reported a 200 per cent increase in bets from a year earlier, with site traffic increasing 65 per cent (Kerber, 2019). These results are not surprising considering that the American Gaming Association had already estimated that 19 per cent of NFL fans already gambled on games using either illegal bets with bookies or illegal offshore accounts. Prior to the 2019-20 season, the American Gaming Association also found that 31 per cent of football fans expected they would bet on games once sports betting became legal – a 60 per cent increase (Isadore, 2018). Betting lounges are expected to appear in NFL stadiums in the near future (Silverstein, 2020).

Like the NHL, MLB views gambling as a "great source of fan engagement" (Ryan, 2019). Like the NBA, MLB originally advocated for a uniform federal framework, but eventually adopted a state-by-state strategy after PASPA was struck down in 2018 (Berra, 2019). Again, following the NBA's lead, MLB entered into partnerships with MGM Resorts and DraftKings to ensure its readiness for proposition bets (Associated Press, 2018; Reuters, 2019). The American Gaming Association estimates MLB revenues will increase by USD $952 million from legalized gambling, of which USD $154 million will directly come from betting operators and data providers (AGA, 2018).

The Washington Nationals and Chicago Cubs were the first MLB teams to enter into agreements with sport betting operators. The Nationals entered into a multi-year, exclusive partnership with the digital gaming company BetMGM prior to the 2021 season. The BetMGM-Nationals deal included the opening of a sportsbook adjacent to Nationals Park, the team's home stadium. This followed a similar deal by the Chicago Cubs with DraftKings in September 2020 (Red, 2021). Both teams presented their sports betting deal as providing necessary additional revenue sources during the difficult COVID-19 pandemic time. Other MLB teams are considering pursuing comparable agreements. For example, at the time of this writing, the Mets and Yankees were awaiting the ratification of sport betting laws in New York (Red, 2021).

In March 2019, Major League Soccer (MLS) signed a multi-year agreement with MGM Resorts, its first gaming partner. The MGM Resorts – MLS deal included funding to create enhanced MLS game data for fans and sports betting customers. The agreement also included television-visible signage for MGM Resorts' sports betting operations and collaborations to bring world-class soccer events to the city

Table 2. List of North American Sport Leagues and Teams and Betting Partnerships (as of October 2020)

League/Team	Casino/Sports Betting Partner
Leagues	
MLB	MGM Resorts, FanDuel, DraftKings, Fox Bet
NBA	MGM Resorts, Fox Bet, FanDuel, William Hill, Française des Jeux
WNBA	MGM Resorts
NHL	MGM Resorts, FanDuel, William Hill
NFL	Caesars
MLS	MGM Resorts
UFC	Fox Bet
Teams	**Casino/Sports Betting Partner**
New York Jets (NFL)	MGM Resorts, 888 Casino
Dallas Cowboys (NFL)	WinStar Casino
Baltimore Ravens (NFL)	Caesars
New York Giants (NFL)	DraftKings
Philadelphia Eagles (NFL)	DraftKings, Fox Bet
Indianapolis Colts (NFL)	PointsBet
Chicago Bears (NFL)	PointsBet
Tennessee Titans (NFL)	MGM Resorts
Denver Broncos (NFL)	FanDuel, MGM Resorts, Betfred USA
Las Vegas Raiders (NFL)	MGM Resorts
Detroit Lions (NFL)	MGM Resorts
Indiana Pacers (NBA)	PointsBet, DraftKings
Philadelphia 76ers (NBA)	Caesars, Fox Bet, DraftKings
Vegas Golden Knights (NHL)	William Hill
New Jersey Devils (NHL)	William Hill, Caesars, FanDuel
Pittsburgh Penguins (NHL)	BetRivers
Colorado Avalanche (NHL)	PointsBet
Philadelphia Flyers (NHL)	BetRivers
Colorado Rockies (MLB)	DraftKings
Chicago Cubs (MLB)	DraftKings
Detroit Tigers (MLB)	PointsBet
Washington Nationals (MLB)	MGM Resorts

Source: Red, 2021; MLS, 2019a; Legal Sports Report https://www.legalsportsreport.com/sports-betting-deals/

Bonus.com https://www.bonus.com/sports-teams-betting-partnerships-us/

of Las Vegas. The partnership will also develop an exclusive "free to play" app for fans (MLS, 2019a). Later, in June of 2019, MLS allowed companies in the sports betting and spirits categories to advertise their brands on team jerseys, stadium signage, stadium naming rights, field-board advertising, and custom programming. Sports gaming companies can also set up a presence in private lounges at MLS stadiums, or on property adjacent to the stadium (MLS, 2019b). Refer to Table 2.

Overall, the major American professional sports leagues are expected to realize enormous revenue increases due to partnerships with sport betting operators. Sara Slane, senior vice president of public affairs for the American Gaming Association puts it this way:

...the four major sports leagues will earn a collective USD $4.2 billion from widely available legal sports betting, further proving that working together with the gaming industry will pay dividends for all sports stakeholders. Legal sports betting will also create substantial opportunities for state and local economies, generating tax revenue, jobs and supporting small businesses across the country. (AGA, 2018)

This rosy outlook requires nuance as it does not appear to account for the negative consequences that have been experienced in more mature sports betting jurisdictions such as the United Kingdom.

Of the major North American spectacle sports, the National Collegiate Athletic Association (NCAA) remains the sole organization against any form of sports gambling. The NCAA's rules prohibit participation in sports wagering activities. The NCAA believes that sports wagering has the potential to undermine the integrity of sports contests and jeopardizes the well-being of student-athletes and the intercollegiate athletics community (NCAA, n.d.). Spitz and Terry (2020) suggest that the NCAA's position has more to do with control of revenue flows than it is to do with integrity, claiming that the NCAA holds a near-monopoly over the revenue generated from its game.

In addition to revenues, sport gambling is expected to contribute other intangible benefits to sport properties. Economist Andrew Zimbalist, a Smith College professor and Forbes contributor notes that with increased betting will come increased viewership, which may raise media revenues:

...if more people are betting, more people are watching, and that raises TV revenue. It would also enable teams to raise ticket prices, depending of course, upon when fans are allowed back into stadiums. There is greater fan avidity. One of the things sport leagues are contending with is the proliferation of the internet and all different types of entertainment sources. There is more competition than ever before. If you're going to build a fan base, sports betting is going to do that (Red, 2021).

While the relationship between gambling operators and the sports industry appears beneficial to both stakeholders, the issues experienced by a mature gambling market – such as in the United Kingdom – illustrates the need to balance profit and social responsibility in regard to gambling addictions and other negative psycho-social effects of sports betting. Sports organizations are expected to represent the values of the communities in which they play and as sport organizations become increasingly transparent, external perceptions of their core values become more important to their success (Alonso & O'Shea, 2012). This includes demonstrations of social responsibility (Hopwood et al., 2010; Stoldt et al., 2012).

SPORT AND MEDIA SPONSORS

While both traditional, online, and social media can be effective platforms for disseminating responsible gambling services and attempts to enable genuine informed choice surrounding gambling for fans (Parke, et al., 2014), there has been widespread acknowledgement that these channels have often been used to normalize sport betting and present it as a form of entertainment (Lopez-Gonzalez, et al., 2017). One of the first examples of the sport gaming active economy nexus can be seen in the Boston Gazette of 1733, which included racing fixture tables so readers could bet money on horses (Boyle, 2006).

Sports content delivered through media technologies has two main implications for the development of gambling. First, that the media validate and reinforce the relationship between betting bookmakers and bettors. Second, that the media has allowed fans to become more familiar with sport, and sport betting, as fans are exposed to more such messages than ever before (Lopez-Gonzalez et al., 2017). As a result of deregulation, gambling has become more readily available in the sport media environment and more prominent in sport media content. Sports events are no longer relegated to a few hours on a Saturday or Sunday afternoon. Rather, an increasing number of broadcast sport events from around the world now provide 24/7 content.

Sponsorship of professional sports teams by the gambling industry and the resulting increase in fan-exposure to pro-betting messages are creating a shift in public perception of gambling from a vice to a socially acceptable leisure activity (Claussen & Miller, 2001). This was one of the biggest effects of the United Kingdom's 2005 Gambling Act (Johnson et al., 2006). Such a change in perception has not just occurred in the United Kingdom. In North America and Australia, the blurring of the line between gambling and sport has allowed betting organizations to engage in a process of legitimising gambling as culturally acceptable (Johnson et al., 2006). Indeed, research indicates that gambling advertisements present the activity as a fun and entertaining leisure pursuit (McMullan & Miller, 2008; 2010) as a harmless activity, or as an intrinsic feature of professional sport and an inherent part of the fan experience (Harris et al., 2014; Monaghan & Derevensky, 2008).

Spending on advertising and marketing to promote sports betting has increased exponentially in Europe and North America (Van Rompuy and Asser Institute, 2015, Lopez-Gonzalez & Griffiths, 2018). This trend has led to a corresponding greater exposure of sports fans to betting messages. Live matches now often include advertisements from different betting companies, in-arena advertising and signage that is visible on the telecast. As well, sports betting operators have signed deals for stadium naming rights and shirt and jersey sponsorships (Lopez-Gonzalez, Guerroro-Sole, & Griffiths, 2017). Telecasts and pregame shows may now also include frequent verbal updates or narrative by commentators about odds of victory. In fact, it is becoming increasingly common to hear commentators inform and discuss gambling lines in sport news broadcasts. Some journalists have even transitioned from being sport experts to becoming betting experts or have accepted sponsorships from sports betting operators (Fitzsimmons, 2009; Lopez-Gonzalez & Griffiths, 2018).

Organizations offering daily fantasy sports have had a particularly close relationship with media organizations. NBC Sports Ventures and Comcast Ventures have invested in FanDuel (Chernova, 2014). NBC Sports Ventures also entered into a content sharing partnership agreement with fantasy sports news and analysis website rotoworld.com, which included an equity stake (SVG, 2014). The partnership between NBC Sports Ventures and FanDuel is an example of how the content delivered by sport data companies is associated with both leagues and betting companies. Such content identifies patterns in past matches between two teams and makes projections that build hype for the next game by creating narratives around probable betting outcomes without explicitly encouraging viewers to bet on the game (Lopez-Gonzalez & Griffiths, 2018). In 2015, Fox Sports president Erik Shanks noted that he felt that daily fantasy sports help improve television viewership (Harwell, 2015). This integration of sports leagues/teams, sports media and sports betting operators has been called the "gamblification of sports" and the "sportification" of gambling. Researchers have characterized this integration as an attempt to build credibility and legitimacy for the act of betting by associating it with sport, while also framing gambling as a form of sport or an expression of sport (McMullan, & Miller, 2008; Thomas et al., 2012).

In the United States, at the time that sport betting was legalized, it was expected to generate an incremental increase in advertising spending by betting operators of USD $7 billion in 2019 alone, with half of that money spent on digital advertising. In 2018, some analysts estimated in 2019 that this spending will account for as much as four per cent of Google's ad revenue and seven per cent of Facebook's (Roettgers, 2018). Such spending has also resulted in the growth of online media websites such as The Action Network, which has hired broadcast sport commentators to present betting data and analysis, as well as to track betting odds. Some of these sport websites even have affiliate agreements with sports betting operators. Such agreements allow for a revenue generating strategy for sports media websites that work like this: readers who click on a digital banner on a sports media website are redirected to a sports betting site. Should the reader place a bet using the sports betting site, then the sports site receives a portion of the net gaming revenue generated by the betting activity (Lopez-Gonzalez & Griffiths, 2018).

In Canada, the sports cable channel TSN launched TSN Edge in September 2020, a microsite within the larger TSN website that provides information and analysis relating to sports betting. In addition, they host fantasy leagues and offer columns and videos to assist with fantasy league activities (TSN, 2020). Other media organizations such as ESPN, CBS Sports, and even the sport leagues themselves, offer similar services with many media content providers crossing over to provide betting and fantasy gaming advice on broadcasts. In Europe, broadcaster Sky Sports, offers its own betting app, Sky Bet, for viewers to place bets anytime from anywhere (Sky Sports, n.d.). Fox Sports has a similar arrangement in the United States called Fox Bet (Fox Sports, n.d.).

In a case study assessing the frequency and content of both broadcast and terrestrial advertising strategies for a single professional sport, Thomas et al. (2012) noted a saturation of sport betting advertisements at both the sporting venue and during the broadcast at Australian Football League matches. They observed that the marketing strategies represented gambling as an intrinsic feature of the sport and an inherent part of the fan experience with no attempt to balance the positive messages and framing of gambling with its potential addictive consequences. Researchers have estimated that viewers of the Australian Football League and the National Rugby League – the two most followed sports in Australia – are exposed to 10 to 15 minutes of gambling advertisements per game (Gordon and Chapman, 2014). Attributes such as loyalty to the team, and being brave enough to prove your sporting knowledge, are implicit in some sports betting messages, including stereotyped gender depictions and sexualized imagery (Thomas et al., 2012, 2015). In the United States, a study by Salaga and Tainsky (2015) found that audience ratings spiked when the scoring in games moved closer to the scoring margin of the closing point spread, even if the outcome of games was certain. In the past, certainty of game outcome led to declining viewership (Paul & Weinbach, 2007).

The interdependent relationship between sport, media, and betting economies can be illustrated through a hypothetical scenario. A sporting event is happening in a country that has legalized gambling and allows sport sports betting organizations to advertise. This permits a betting organization to buy advertising in a national newspaper, on the sports broadcast, or on a social media platform. The online edition of that paper and the social media platform will have an active link that will allow a user direct access to the betting website. The newspaper or social media platform will receive an advertising fee, either a set fee or click-through rate. In a country such as Spain, the newspaper may even receive a percentage of the wager of lost bets of net gaming revenue (Lopez-Gonzalez, Estevez, & Griffiths, 2017). To boost click-through rates and advertising effectiveness, the ad is placed with related content about that sporting event and may even mention the head-to-head records of the two teams and the scoring differential of the games. The content may also remark that a starting player has their highest career scoring average against their upcoming opponent, or that that one of teams is suffering from a rash of injuries that may affect their play. That story is then tweeted by the journalist who may also appear on sport broadcast, or a sport broadcaster may read the story and note these statistics on the broadcast. The journalist might even mention the betting odds.

This broadcast may be watched by a fan at home, or that tweet read, either at home or in the stadium. A stadium that may have in-stadium Wi-Fi sponsored by a sport betting company, done in part to help facilitate sport bets (Butler, 2020). At the stadium, that bet would be preferably made in the proprietary app of the team or league playing, or in the growing number of in stadium sportsbooks. So, while sitting in the stands, a ticket holder could order food to their seat, check the game's statistics, and then decide to place an in-game bet.

Those watching the game at home will be exposed to a litany of statistics and also potentially shown gambling odds and insights provided by the media network through the commentary of broadcasters, or as part of the content available on the sports media website. For example, many online sports media websites such as The Athletic, TSN, and CBS Sports may have stories focused on fantasy picks and betting odds around sport events. These media outlets use the same data that the league provides to the sport gambling organization. This data is also used to inform daily fantasy sports leagues hosted by the professional sports league or betting company.

After the game, fans may be solicited in advertisements for other gambling activities such as poker or fantasy sports, endorsed by their favorite sport star such as soccer star Cristiano Ronaldo (PokerStars), MMA fighter Connor McGregor (Parimatch), or golfer Bryson DeChambeau (DraftKings). The intertwined relationship between league data, sports media, sports betting operators means that for the sports fan, appreciation and consumption of sport will become associated with sports betting (Hing et al., 2015; Lamont et al., 2016; Lopez-Gonzalez & Griffiths, 2016; Lopez-Gonzalez & Tulloch, 2015; Milner et al., 2013).

SOCIETY

In the scenario above, in addition to the sports fan, there might be other members of the family watching the game at home. This can potentially include those who may suffer from or be predisposed to gambling addiction, or minors who cannot legally gamble for money, for whom the availability of social gaming alternatives such as non-monetary fantasy leagues, can serve as gateways toward gambling using real currency in the future (Cassidy, 2013).

To date, there has only been fragmented empirical evidence concerning the impact of sports-related gambling messages to problem gambling behaviours. However, concerns have been raised by psychologists, politicians and mental health specialists about how online social gaming promoted by leagues to encourage fan engagement could become a gateway to gambling with real money. Social gaming may teach the players about the rules, and expose them to the atmospheres, adrenaline rush, strategic thinking, and group excitement of gambling products, without having to experience the inconvenience and financial dangers of real money gambling. The internalization of these gambling-like experiences might predispose a minority of individuals to develop a gambling problem later in their lives (Griffiths, 2014). A study in British Columbia found that 23.6 per cent of at-risk or problem gamblers had gambled on sports either offline or online (Malatests & Associates Ltd, 2014). A smaller proportion (16.2 per cent) was found in the Spanish population in a national gambling survey. However, this population was entirely composed of online bettors (DGOJ, 2016).

From a public health perspective, gambling advertising could be seen to be a societal risk factor encouraging gambling participation (Shaffer et al., 2004), where greater levels of exposure to gambling messages may put more of the population at risk of engaging in problem gambling (Shaffer et al., 2004). Grant and Kim (2001) for example, reported that 46 per cent of a sample of treatment-seeking problem gamblers self-reported television, radio, and billboard advertisements as triggering an urge to gamble.

In contrast, Binde (2007) suggests that the impact of mass gambling advertising in a mature gambling market such as the United Kingdom is more likely to create sport betting normalization as opposed to an overall increase in participation. Such a normalizing effect may be distinct from the impact of mass advertising of sports betting in an immature market where sports fans had been exposed to fewer gambling opportunities and enticements.

While there has been a lack of consensus evidence for the causal relationship between positive attitudes toward gambling and intention to gamble, there remains a concern that the content of sports betting advertisements may create a distorted perception of the realities of gambling (Friend & Ladd, 2009). This has been borne out in more recent studies which noted that gambling on live games has taken on a significant social aspect for fans when they discuss sport or watch games with friends. The study also noted that fans do not experience gambling losses "as real" due to how easy it is to bet electronically on phones, rather than having to travel to a bookmaker to gamble using physical currency.

Such concerns about the tightening relationship between European football, the media, and gaming companies have been recently voiced in the United Kingdom's more mature gambling market. Some have said that it has gone too far. They have expressed the concern that the current generation of young fans strongly associate their support for the game with gambling, with research showing that many young fans would not watch football matches without multiple bets on the game, and other studies have discovered links between gambling and suicide (McGee, 2020).

As previously mentioned, such sentiment has led the United Kingdom's sports minister, Nigel Adams, to say that he would review the Gambling Act of 2005 that permitted gambling organizations to advertise on television and radio (Magowan, 2020). It also has led Labour's deputy leader Tom Watson, to state that the party would ban gambling companies from football shirts if the party won power in the next election (Davies, 2019).

In North America, the active economy of the sport gambling nexus continues to expand and the more mature gambling industry within the United Kingdom provides context that there is a need for a balanced and deliberate approach regarding the representation of gambling within sport and media. A deliberate approach which requires an understanding of the interconnectedness of the sport nexus. For example, such an approach could include regulatory or voluntary inclusion of responsible gambling awareness messages within the marketing strategies used by betting operators. However, the problem may not necessarily be the absence of public health messages, but that public health messages are disproportionately outnumbered by messages promoting a positive image of gambling as a pleasurable entertainment activity (Friend & Ladd, 2009; Lee et al., 2008).

Social media has been suggested to increase the public's awareness of the causes and effects of sport gambling (Kurian et al., 2019). Social media has been shown to be an effective platform for promoting awareness of responsible gambling for selected populations such as adolescents, that trust social media messaging and information (Foux, 2006). Indeed, social media has proven effective as a form of word-of-mouth advocacy, particularly when the social media marketing strategy includes peer messaging (Luo et al., 2011), since social media audiences have been measurably prone to trust "someone like me" (Edelman, 2005). It has also been suggested that betting operators should include more responsible gambling messages since it is widely accepted that corporate social responsibility acts as a tool for brand differentiation in saturated markets (Kesavan et al., 2013).

Gambling operators may wish to better utilize social media as an effective platform for disseminating responsible gambling strategies and to enable genuinely informed choice surrounding gambling for their customers. However, there is little evidence to suggest that gambling awareness campaigns are effective as a harm minimization strategy. Furthermore, in a review of mass media responsible gambling awareness campaigns, Williams et al. (2012) identified that such an approach would be relatively ineffective as a primary strategy to reduce problem gambling as research indicates that gamblers who do not experience gambling problems tend not to pay attention and retain information presented to them in responsible gambling campaigns, because the campaigns are not salient to them.

The impact of sport gaming advertising will vary between mature and immature gambling markets. Advertising will lead to greater awareness and normalization of sports gambling, which will result in greater uptake of sports gambling. It is important to note that neither the situational or structural characteristics, nor the cross-marketing convergence in the sport gaming nexus act as singular factors when determining online betting behaviours. Rather, it is the convergence and interdependence of the various elements of the sports gaming nexus of the active economy that may facilitate and propagate sport gambling behaviours.

CONCLUSION

The convergence of digital technologies, the increasing number of broadcasted sporting events, the softening government regulations and societal attitudes and the growth in betting operators has led to exponential growth of gambling in the active economy of sport. The interconnections between the elements in the sport gaming active economy have multiplied the possible combinations of sports betting products available. Many products that originated in one area evolved into a different object in the increasingly global sport ecosystem. For instance, fantasy leagues and video games (esports) existed in the pre-internet era, but it was not until the arrival of the internet that their convergence with gambling materialized and contributed to the easing of global gambling restrictions by governments. Historically, the codification of sport allowed for the subsequent measurement of sporting activities which also further enhanced the ability to digitize sport. In the past, this has supported the integration of sports-themed gambling products, or the gamblification of sport. Current advances in sports data science and the dissemination of these advances across the sport gaming nexus have taken the gamblification of sport to an entirely new level. The sport gaming nexus has become increasingly efficient and more prevalent by building, increasing, and accelerating network ties between stakeholders in the sport active economy. The lines have become blurred between formerly distinct gambling, sport, and media markets.

The integration of betting with fans' experience of sports competitions, whether offline or online, has magnified the scope of gambling stimuli to which sports fans are regularly exposed. This increased integration – facilitated by the internet and free apps – allows for instant gratification and a reward scheme that favours quick and impulsive decision making when gambling on sport. Sports gaming is being normalized and embedded in everyday routines and objects associated with sport. This has led to an explosion in the size and scope of the global sport gambling economy. In turn, this explosion in size has led to greater acceptance of the sport and gaming nexus across many societies whose sports gambling markets are at different levels of maturity. This broadening acceptance has had ramifications for governments attempting to regulate sport betting and the subsequent need for societal support for vulnerable populations who suffer negative consequences as a result of the sports gaming nexus.

Considering the speed of technological change affecting sport, media and betting operators, the convergence and integration processes described in this chapter are likely to continue to evolve rapidly. These integration processes can be interpreted as growth opportunities from the point of view of the sport teams and leagues, sports media, and the gaming industries. Conversely, if they are not effectively regulated, these same processes of integration may well bring about negative social consequences that will demand a significant investment of public resources to remedy.

In North America, there is a strong trend towards deregulation and an increasing *laissez-faire* attitude towards sport gaming. This is contrasted by a growing movement in the United Kingdom, a more mature gambling market, to rethink and potentially develop greater social guardrails to protect vulnerable populations and ultimately to protect sport culture. This trend should serve as a signal to leagues, teams, and sport media who have embraced sport gambling as a way to increase fan engagement and revenues – proceed deliberately with a full understanding of the interdependence of stakeholders involved.

REFERENCES

AFP. (2020). When China faced down rampant soccer corruption. *Taipei Times*. Retrieved from https://www.taipeitimes.com/News/sport/archives/2020/05/28/2003737179

AGA. (2018). NBA & MLB could see combined $1.7 billion from legalized sports betting. *American Gaming Association*. Retrieved from https://www.americangaming.org/new/nba-mlb-could-see-combined-1-7-billion-from-legalized-sports-betting/

Alonso, A. D., & O'Shea, M. (2012). You only get back what you put in. Perceptions of professional sport organizations as community anchors. *Community Development (Columbus, Ohio)*, *43*(5), 656–676. doi:10.1080/15575330.2011.645048

Andreff, W. (2019). Global criminal networking in sport: Online betting-related match fixing. In An Economic Roadmap to the Dark Side of Sport (pp. 1-18). Palgrave Pivots, Macmillan. doi:10.1007/978-3-030-28615-6_1

Associated Press. (2018). MLB strikes deal with MGM as legal gambling expands in US. *USA Today*. Retrieved from https://www.usatoday.com/story/sports/mlb/2018/11/27/mgm-resorts-is-mlbs-official-gaming-partner-after-nba-nhl/38627859/

Berra, L. (2019). A major gamble: MLB embraces sports betting. *Baseball America*. Retrieved from https://www.baseballamerica.com/stories/a-major-gamble-mlb-hopes-legalized-sports-betting-will-engage-new-fans/

Binde, P. (2007). Selling dreams – or causing nightmares? On gambling advertising and problem gambling. *Journal of Gambling Issues*, *20*(20), 167–191. doi:10.4309/jgi.2007.20.5

Boyle, R. (2006). Sports journalism: Context and Issues. *Sage (Atlanta, Ga.)*.

Brennan, J. (2018). NHL Commissioner Bettman completes 180-degree turn on sports betting. *NJ Online Gambling*. Retrieved from https://www.njonlinegambling.com/nhl-bettman-embraces-sports-betting/

Butler, R. (2020). In-stadium wagering could spark retail and mobile sports betting growth. *Action Network*. Retrieved from https://www.actionnetwork.com/general/sports-betting-news-stadium-wagering-capitol-one-arena-wrigley-field

Cassidy, R. (2013). Partial convergence. Social gaming and real money gambling. In R. Cassidy, A. Pisac, & C. Loussouarn (Eds.), *Qualitative research on gambling. Exploring the production and consumption of risk* (pp. 74–91). Routledge.

Chernova, Y. (2014). FanDuel raises $70 million as daily fantasy sports battle heats up. *Wall Street Journal*. Retrieved from https://www.wsj.com/articles/BL-VCDB-15379

Claussen, C. L., & Miller, L. K. (2001). The gambling industry and sports gambling: A stake in the game? *Journal of Sport Management*, *15*(4), 350–363. doi:10.1123/jsm.15.4.350

Conn, D. (2019). Revealed: the 'dire consequences' of football's relationship with gambling. *The Guardian*. Retrieved from https://www.theguardian.com/football/2019/jan/10/football-gambling-dire-consequences-young-men-bet-new-study

Court Listener, D. (2007). Tschetschot v. Comm'r, 2007 T.C. Memo. 38. *Courtlistener.* Retrieved from https://www.courtlistener.com/opinion/4559086/tschetschot-v-commr/

Cunningham, G., & Rosenberg, C. (1997). Excise tax and occupational tax on wagering. *Internal Revenue Service*. Retrieved from https://www.irs.gov/pub/irs-tege/eotopice97.pdf

Davies, R. (2019). Half of Premier League clubs to have gambling sponsors for 2019-20 season. *The Guardian*. Retrieved from https://www.theguardian.com/football/2019/jul/19/half-of-premier-league-clubs-to-have-gambling-sponsors-for-201920

Davies, R. (2019b). Government under fire for failing to back mandatory betting levy. *The Guardian*. Retrieved from https://www.theguardian.com/business/2019/apr/25/ladbrokes-owner-proposes-ban-on-gambling-ads-linked-to-sport-gvc

Delkic, M. (2018). A supreme court decision that was a wild card. *The New York Times*. Retrieved from https://www.nytimes.com/2018/05/22/insider/supreme-court-sports-betting.html

Deloitte. (2021). New stakes in the game. Bill C-13 and unlocking opportunities through sports betting reform in Canada. *Deloitte*. Retrieved from https://www2.deloitte.com/content/dam/Deloitte/ca/Documents/consumer-business/ca-sports-betting-pov-en-aoda.pdf

DGOJ. (2016). Study on the prevalence, behavior and characteristics of gambling users in Spain. *Ministry of Finance and Public Administrations*. Retrieved from: https://www.ordenacionjuego.es/cmis/browser?id=workspace://SpacesStore/131754ec-1411-4fa5-b6dd-b85364aea75c

Dottori, M., Séguin, B., & O'Reilly, N. (2018). Public relations in strategic management: Strategizing in the communicative organization. *Journal of Professional Communication*, *5*(2), 59–98. doi:10.15173/jpc.v5i2.3749

Draper, K. (2018). NBA makes MGM Resorts International its first gambling partner. *The New York Times*. Retrieved from https://www.nytimes.com/2018/07/31/sports/nba-betting-mgm.html

Edelman. (2005) Edelman Trust Barometer 2005. *Edelman*. Retrieved from https://www.edelman.com/sites/g/files/aatuss191/files/2018-10/2005-Edelman-Trust-Barometer-Executive-Summary.pdf

Eden, S. (2020). From the archives: How former ref Tim Donaghy conspired to fix NBA games. *ESPN*. Retrieved from https://www.espn.com/nba/story/_/id/25980368/how-former-ref-tim-donaghy-conspired-fix-nba-games

ESPN. (2007). David Stern's Donaghy news conference transcript. *ESPN*. Retrieved from https://www.espn.com/nba/news/story?id=2947534

Fisher, E. (2015). Daily fantasy pushes to continue growth streak. *Sports Business Journal*. Retrieved from https://www.sportsbusinessjournal.com/Journal/Issues/2015/03/16/Marketing-and-Sponsorship/Daily-fantasy.aspx

Fitzsimmons, P. (2009, September 19). I bet this is an issue. *The Sydney Morning Herald*, p. 14.

Flutter. (2020). Flutter annual report and accounts 2019. *Flutter*. Retrieved from https://www.flutter.com/sites/paddy-power-betfair/files/Annual %20reports/2019-annual-report-28-02-20.pdf

Forrest, D. (2018). Match-Fixing. In M. Breuer & D. Forrest (Eds.), *The palgrave handbook on the economics of manipulation in sport*. Palgrave Macmillan. doi:10.1007/978-3-319-77389-6_6

Forrest, D., McHale, I., & McAuley, K. (2008). Risks to sport from the betting sector. In P. Rodriguez, S. Késenne, & J. Garcia (Eds.), *Threats to sports and sports participation* (pp. 139–160). Ediciones de la Universidad de Oviedo.

Forrest, D., & Simmons, R. (2003). Sport and gambling. *Oxford Review of Economic Policy*, *19*(4), 598–611. doi:10.1093/oxrep/19.4.598

Foux, G. (2006). Consumer-generated media: Get your customers involved. *Brand Strategy*, 38-39.

Fox Sports. (n.d.). *Fox Bet*. Retrieved from https://www.foxbet.com

Friend, K., & Ladd, G. (2009). Youth gambling advertising: A review of some of the lessons learned from tobacco control. *Drugs Education Prevention & Policy*, *16*(4), 283–297. doi:10.1080/09687630701838026

Gainsbury, S., & Derevensky, J. (2008). An appraisal of the impact of the depiction of gambling in society on youth. *International Journal of Mental Health and Addiction*, *6*(4), 537–550. doi:10.100711469-008-9155-3

Gerke, A., & Dalla Pria, Y. (2018). Cluster concept: Lessons for the sport sector? Toward a two-step model of sport cluster development Based on socioeconomic proximity. *Journal of Sport Management*, *32*(3), 211–226. doi:10.1123/jsm.2016-0338

Gilly, J. P., & Torre, A. (2000). *Dynamiques de proximité*. L'Harmattan.

Gordon, R., & Chapman, M. (2014). *Brand community and sports betting in Australia*. Victorian Responsible Gambling Foundation.

Gouker, D. 2017. Daily fantasy sports - bill tracker. *Legal Sports Report*. Available at http://www.legalsportsreport.com/dfs-bill-tracker/

Granovetter, M. (2002). A theoretical agenda for economic sociology. Academic Press.

Grant, J., & Kim, S. (2001). Demographic and Clinical Features of 131 Adult Pathological Gamblers. *The Journal of Clinical Psychiatry*, *62*(12), 957–962. doi:10.4088/JCP.v62n1207 PMID:11780876

Grant, P. (2020). Football gambling links 'gone too far', ex-FA boss says. *BBC*. Retrieved from https://www.bbc.com/news/uk-51536687

Griffiths, M. (2014). Child and adolescent social gaming: What are the issues of concern? *Education for Health*, *32*, 9–12.

Grubb, J. (2015). DraftKings brings its daily-fantasy sports empire to esports. *Venture Beat*. Retrieved from https://venturebeat.com/2015/09/23/draftkings-brings-its-daily-fantasy-sports-empire-to-esports/

Harris, R. (2005). When giving means taking: Public relations, sponsorship, and morally marginal donors. *Public Relations Review*, *31*(4), 486–491. doi:10.1016/j.pubrev.2005.08.006

Harwell, D. (2015). The rise of daily fantasy sports, online betting's newest empire. *Washington Post*. Retrieved from https://www.washingtonpost.com/news/wonk/wp/2015/07/28/how-daily-fantasy-sites-became-pro-sports-newest-addiction-machine/

Hing, N., Lamont, M., Vitartas, P., & Fink, E. (2015). Sports-embedded gambling promotions: A study of exposure, sports betting intention and problem gambling amongst adults. *International Journal of Mental Health and Addiction*, *13*(1), 115–135. doi:10.100711469-014-9519-9

Hopwood, M., Skinner, J., & Kitchin, P. (2010). *Sport public relations and communication*. Routledge.

House of Commons. (2021). *Bill C-13*. Retrieved from https://openparliament.ca/bills/43-2/C-13/

Huggins, M. (2000). *Flat Racing and British Society 1790-1914: A social and economic history*. Frank Cass.

Humphreys, B. R. (2021). Legalized sports betting, VLT gambling, and state gambling revenues: Evidence from West Virginia. *Eastern Economic Journal*, *47*(1), 1–20. doi:10.105741302-020-00178-0 PMID:33424046

Independent Sport Panel. (2009). The future of sport in Australia. *Independent Sport Panel*. http://www.health.gov.au/internet/main/publishing.nsf/Content/1DDA76A44E5F4DD4CA257671000E4C45/$File/Crawford_Report.pdf

Internal Revenue Service. (2020). Memorandum no. AM 202042015. *Internal Revenue Service*. Retrieved from https://www.irs.gov/pub/irs-wd/202042015.pdf

Isadore, C. (2018). NFL could pocket billions from coming boom in sports gambling. *CNN*. Retrieved from https://money.cnn.com/2018/09/05/news/companies/nfl-sports-gambling-revenue/index.html

Johnson, C., Dowd, T. J., & Ridgeway, C. L. (2006). Legitimacy as a social process. *Annual Review of Sociology*, *32*(1), 53–79. doi:10.1146/annurev.soc.32.061604.123101

Kargün, M., Ağaoğlu, Y. S., & Kaya, M. (2020). The economics of sports betting. *European Journal of Physical Education and Sport Science*. doi:10.5281/zenodo.3829624

Kerber, R. (2019). Online sports betting sites score as NFL season gets underway. *Reuters*. Retrieved from https://www.reuters.com/article/us-usa-gambling-nfl/online-sports-betting-sites-score-as-nfl-season-gets-under-way-idUSKCN1VU2AZ

Kesavan, R., Bernacchi, M. D., & Mascarenhas, O. A. J. (2013). Word of mouse: CSR communication and the social media. *International Management Review*, *9*(1), 58–66.

Kilgore, A. (2015). Daily fantasy sports web sites find riches in internet gaming law loophole. *Washington Post*. Retrieved from https://www.washingtonpost.com/sports/daily-fantasy-sports-web-sites-find-riches-in-internet-gaming-law-loophole/2015/03/27/92988444-d172-11e4-a62f-ee745911a4ff_story.html

Kilpatrick, D. (2010). *Definitions of public policy and law*. Retrieved from https://www.musc.edu/vawprevention/policy/definition.shtml

Kurian, S., Sinha, S., & Nanda, N. (2019). Sports and betting: A media intervention. *Journal of Critical Reviews*, *6*(6), 84–88. doi:10.22159/jcr.06.06.12

Lamont, M., Hing, N., & Gainsbury, S. (2011). Gambling on sport sponsorship: A conceptual framework for research and regulatory review. *Sport Management Review*, *14*(3), 246–257. doi:10.1016/j.smr.2011.04.004

Landler, M. (2005). Germany still consumed by a scandal. *New York Times*. Retrieved from https://www.nytimes.com/2005/03/23/sports/soccer/germany-still-consumed-by-a-scandal.html

Lee, H., Lemanski, J., & Jun, J. (2008). Role of gambling media exposure in influencing trajectories among college students. *Journal of Gambling Studies*, *1*(1), 25–37. doi:10.100710899-007-9078-0 PMID:17901930

Legalsportsreport (n.d.a). Esports betting – overview of the esports gambling vertical. *Legalsportsreport*. Retrieved from https://www.legalsportsreport.com/esports-betting/#:~:text=Esports%20gambling%3A%20Popular%20games%20 1%20Sports%20betting.%20Sports,3%20Jackpot%20games.%20...%204%20Casino-style%20games.%20

Legalsportsreport. (n.d.b). US sportsbook and casino team sponsorship tracker. *Legalsportsreport*. Retrieved from https://www.legalsportsreport.com/sports-betting-deals/

Liptak, A., & Draper, K. (2018). Supreme Court Ruling Favors Sports betting. *The New York Times*. Retrieved from https://www.nytimes.com/2018/05/14/us/politics/supreme-court-sports-betting-new-jersey.html

Lockwood, R. I. (2008). The best interests of the league: Referee betting scandal brings commissioner authority and collective bargaining back to the frontcourt in the NBA. *Sports Law eJournal*, *15*, 137.

Lopez-Gonzalez, H., & Griffiths, M. D. (2016). Is European online gambling regulation adequately addressing in-play betting advertising? *Gaming Law Review and Economics*, *20*(6), 495–503. doi:10.1089/glre.2016.2064

Lopez-Gonzalez, H., & Griffiths, M. D. (2018). Understanding the convergence of markets in online sports betting. *International Review for the Sociology of Sport*, *53*(7), 807–823. doi:10.1177/1012690216680602

Lopez-Gonzalez, H., Guerrero-Sole, F., & Griffiths, M. D. (2017). A content analysis of how 'normal' sports betting behaviour is represented in gambling advertising. *Addiction Research and Theory*. Advance online publication. doi:10.1080/16066359.2017.1353082

Lopez-Gonzalez, H., & Tulloch, C. D. (2015). Enhancing media sport consumption: Online gambling in European football. *Media International Australia, 155*(1), 130–139. doi:10.1177/1329878X1515500115

Luo, M. M., Chen, J., Ching, R. K. H., & Liu, C. (2011). An examination of the effects of virtual experiential marketing on online customer intentions and loyalty. *Service Industries Journal, 31*(13), 2163–2191. doi:10.1080/02642069.2010.503885

Luongo, C. (2020). ESI gambling report: Esports betting, a global lifeline for operators. *Esports Insider*. Retrieved from https://esportsinsider.com/2020/04/esi-gambling-report-esports-betting/

Magowan, A. (2020). Gambling in football: Call on Prime Minister to ban betting sponsorship. *BBC*. Retrieved from https://www.bbc.com/sport/football/51638731

Malatests & Associates Ltd. (2014). *2014 British Columbia Problem Gambling Prevalence Study*. Victoria, Canada: Gaming policy and enforcement branch, Ministry of Finance. Retrieved from https://www2.gov.bc.ca/assets/gov/sports-recreation-arts-and-culture/gambling/gambling-in-bc/reports/rpt-rg-prevalence-study-2014.pdf

McGee, D. (2020). On the normalisation of online sports gambling among young adult men in the UK: A public health perspective. *Public Health, 184*, 89–94. Advance online publication. doi:10.1016/j.puhe.2020.04.018 PMID:32546295

McMullan, J. L., & Miller, D. (2008). All in! The commercial advertising of offshore gambling on television. *Journal of Gambling Issues*, (22), 230–251. doi:10.4309/jgi.2008.22.6

McMullan, J. L., & Miller, D. (2010). Advertising the "new fun-tier": Selling casinos to consumers. *International Journal of Mental Health and Addiction, 8*(1), 35–50. doi:10.100711469-009-9201-9

Meikle, G., & Young, S. (2011). *Media convergence: Networked digital media in everyday life*. Red Globe Press.

Milner, L., Hing, N., Vitartas, P., & Lamont, M. (2013). Embedded gambling promotion in Australian football broadcasts: An exploratory study. *Communication. Política y Cultura, 46*(2), 177–198.

Milton, J. (2017). History of sport betting. *BigonSports*. Retrieved from https://www.bigonsports.com/history-of-sports-betting/

Mitchel, J. (2021). U.S. household income, savings rose at end of last year. *Wall Street Journal*. Retrieved from https://www.wsj.com/articles/consumer-spending-personal-income-coronavirus-december-2020-11611873351

MLS. (2019a). MLS announces multi-year gaming partnership with MGM Resorts International. *Major League Soccer*. Retrieved from https://www.mlssoccer.com/post/2019/03/19/mls-announces-multi-year-gaming-partnership-mgm-resorts-international

MLS. (2019b). MLS opens up commercial sponsorships to sports betting, spirits categories. *Major League Soccer*. Retrieved from https://www.mlssoccer.com/post/2019/06/26/mls-opens-commercial-sponsorships-sports-betting-spirits-categories

Monaghan, S., & Derevensky, J. (2008). An appraisal of the impact of the depiction of gambling in society on youth. *International Journal of Mental Health and Addiction*, *6*(4), 537–550. doi:10.100711469-008-9155-3

National Basketball Association. (2018). MGM Resorts International becomes official gaming partner of NBA. *National Basketball Association*. Retrieved from https://www.nba.com/news/mgm-resorts-international-becomes-official-gaming-partner-nba-official-release?collection=news

NCAA. (n.d.). Sports Wagering. *NCAA*. Retrieved from https://www.ncaa.org/enforcement/sports-wagering

Ng'etich, E. K., & Auka, D. O. (2019). Influence of advertising on consumer purchase decision of sport betting: A case study of students in Nakuru Town university campuses, Kenya. *International Journal of Business Management and Finance*, *3*(2).

Novy-Williams, E. (2018). NBA makes deal with MGM for betting, first for a U.S. league. *Bloomberg*. Retrieved from https://www.bloomberg.com/news/articles/2018-07-31/nba-partners-with-mgm-for-betting-a-first-for-a-u-s-pro-league?sref=2WOTxT1z

Novy-Williams, E. (2018b). If sports betting's going to be legal, major leagues want a cut. *Bloomberg*. Retrieved from https://www.bloomberg.com/news/articles/2018-03-19/if-sports-betting-s-going-to-be-legal-major-leagues-want-a-cut?sref=2WOTxT1z

Oxford Economics. (2017). Economic impact of legalized sports betting. *Oxford Economics*. Retrieved from https://www.americangaming.org/wp-content/uploads/2018/12/AGA-Oxford-Sports-Betting-Economic-Impact-Report1-1.pdf

Parke, A., Harris, A., Parke, J., Rigbye, J., & Blaszczynski, A. (2014). Facilitating awareness and informed choice in gambling. *The Journal of Gambling Business and Economics*, *8*(3), 6–20. doi:10.5750/jgbe.v8i3.971

Parliament of Canada. (2020c). *House Government Bill C-13 An Act to amend the Criminal Code (single-event sport betting)*. Parliament of Canada. Retrieved from https://www.parl.ca/LegisInfo/BillDetails.aspx?Language=E&billId=10983057

Parliament of Canada. (2021a). Private Member's Bill C-221. *LEGISinfo*. Retrieved from https://parl.ca/LegisInfo/BillDetails.aspx?Language=E&billId=8092059

Parliament of Canada. (2021b). Hansard – 61. *Ourcommons.ca*. Retrieved from https://www.ourcommons.ca/DocumentViewer/en/43-2/house/sitting-61/hansard#11138272

Parliament of Canada. (2021d). *Private Member's Bill C-218 Safe and Regulated Sports Betting Act*. Parliament of Canada. Retrieved from https://www.parl.ca/LegisInfo/BillDetails.aspx?Language=E&billId=10639805

Parung, J., & Bititci, U. S. (2006). A conceptual metric for managing collaborative networks. *Journal of Modelling in Management*, *1*(2), 116–136. Advance online publication. doi:10.1108/17465660610703468

Paul, R. J., & Weinbach, A. P. (2007). The uncertainty of outcome and scoring effects on Nielsen ratings for Monday Night Football. *Journal of Economics and Business*, *59*(3), 199–211. doi:10.1016/j.jeconbus.2006.05.001

Philadelphia 76ers. (2018). Caesars Entertainment signs deal with HBSE. *Philadelphia 76ers*. Retrieved from https://www.nba.com/sixers/caesars-entertainment-signs-deal-hbse

Porter, M. E. (1998). Clusters and the new economics of competition. *Harvard Business Review*, *76*(6), 77–90. PMID:10187248

Pradier, P. (2019). Betting on sport: history, regulation, measurement. In J. K. Wilson & R. Pomfret (Eds.), *Historical perspectives on sports economics*. Elgar Publishing., doi:10.4337/9781788977845.00018

Purdhum, D., & Rovell, D. (2018). NBA signs deal with MGM to be gaming partner. *ESPN*. Retrieved from https://www.espn.com/chalk/story/_/id/24245142/nba-first-league-betting-sponsor-deal-mgm

Purdum, D. (2020). New CBA allows owners, players to cash in on stadium sportsbooks. *ESPN*. Retrieved from https://www.espn.com/chalk/story/_/id/28930507/new-cba-allows-owners-players-cash-stadium-sportsbooks

Red, C. (2021). Sports gambling partnerships offer MLB new revenue streams, but there are still hurdles to consider. *Forbes*. Retrieved from https://www.forbes.com/sites/christianred/2021/01/12/major-league-baseball-teams-and-a-new-revenue-stream-online-gaming-business-partners/?sh=2a2ce285ef95

Reuters. (2019). Major League Baseball and FanDuel strike sports betting deal. *CNBC*. Retrieved from https://www.cnbc.com/2019/08/15/major-league-baseball-and-fanduel-strike-sports-betting-deal.html

Rodenberg, R. (2017). Sports betting has an equal sovereignty problem. *Duke Law Journal*, *67*(6). https://dlj.law.duke.edu/2017/06/sports-betting-has-an-equal-sovereignty-problem/

Roettgers, J. (2018). The big gamble: Is sports betting really a $7 billion media windfall? *Variety*. Retrieved from https://variety.com/2018/biz/news/sports-betting-media-revenue-forecasts-1202818070/

Russ, H. (2018). DraftKings launches mobile sports betting in New Jersey. *Reuters*. Retrieved from https://www.reuters.com/article/us-usa-betting-draftkings-new-jersey-idUSKBN1KM60H

Ryan, G. (2019). I'm a realist: MLB boss Manfred on sports gambling, Disney and Trump. *Boston Business Journal*. Retrieved from https://www.bizjournals.com/boston/news/2019/03/06/mlb-s-boss-on-sports-gambling-disney-and-trump.html

Salaga, S., & Tainsky, S. (2015). Betting lines and college football television ratings. *Economics Letters*, *132*, 112–116. doi:10.1016/j.econlet.2015.04.032

Sawalka, V. (2020). 4 stocks to buy on COVID-led e-sports uptick in 2021. *Zacks*. Retrieved from https://www.zacks.com/stock/news/1142863/4-stocks-to-buy-on-covid-led-e-sports-uptick-in-2021#:~:text=The%20global%20e-sports%20betting%20market%20size%20is%20projected,the%20huge%20video-game%20industry%2C%20it%20is%20growing%20exponentially

Schrotenboer, B. (2015). Fantasy sports debate: Gambling or not gambling? *USA Today*. Retrieved from https://www.usatoday.com/story/sports/fantasy/2015/01/11/fantasy-sports-gambling-debate-fan-duel/21612771/

Scott, L. (2020). Gambling in football: Bookmakers considering ban of shirt and pitchside advertising. *BBC*. Retrieved from https://www.bbc.com/sport/football/51377202

Shaffer, H. J., LaBrie, R. A., & LaPlante, D. (2004). Laying the foundation for quantifying regional exposure to social phenomena: Considering the case of legalized gambling as public health toxin. *Psychology of Addictive Behaviors*, *18*(1), 40–48. doi:10.1037/0893-164X.18.1.40 PMID:15008684

Shifflet, S., Ostroff, C., & Rivas, A. (2021). How redditors find the next GameStop stock. *Wall Street Journal*. Retrieved from https://www.wsj.com/articles/how-redditors-find-the-next-gamestop-stock-11613644201

Silver, A. (2014). Legalize and Regulate Sports Betting. *The New York Times*. Retrieved from https://www.nytimes.com/2014/11/14/opinion/nba-commissioner-adam-silver-legalize-sports-betting.html

Silver, A., Bettman, G., Manfred, R., Garber, D., & Ambrosie, R. (2020). Joint statement from the commissioners of the National Basketball Association, National Hockey League, Major League Baseball, Major League Soccer and Canadian Football League. *Canadiangaming.ca*. Retrieved from http://canadiangaming.ca/wp-content/uploads/Leagues-Joint-Statement.pdf

Silverstein, E. (2020). NFL inches toward stadium sports betting as sportsbook sponsors permitted. *Casino.org*. Retrieved from https://www.casino.org/news/nfl-inches-toward-stadium-sports-betting-as-sportsbook-sponsors-permitted/

Sky Sports. (n.d.). *Skybet*. Retrieved from https://m.skybet.com

Spangler, T. (2015). ESPN teams with DrafKings as exclusive daily fantasy-sports partner. *Variety*. Retrieved from https://variety.com/2015/digital/news/espn-draftkings-daily-fantasy-sports-1201527028/

Spitz, D. J., & Terry, R. P. (2020). We can handle it: Advocating in support of state legislation of legal sports gambling post-Murphy v. NCAA. *Legal Aspects Sport*, *30*(2), 153–169. doi:10.18060/24366

Sports Betting Dime. (2020). The size and increase of the global sports betting market. *Sports Betting Dime*. Retrieved from https://www.sportsbettingdime.com/guides/finance/global-sports-betting-market/

St. Louis Blues. (2019). Introducing enter the zone – the real-time prediction game. *St. Louis Blues*. Retrieved from https://www.nhl.com/blues/news/introducing-enter-the-zone---the-real-time-prediction-game/c-307326448

Stoldt, G. C., Dittmore, S. W., & Branvold, S. E. (2012). *Sport public relations: Managing stakeholder communication*. Human Kinetics.

SVG. (2014). NBC's Rotoworld, RotoGrinders ink fantasy sports partnership. *Sports Video Group*. Retrieved from https://www.sportsvideo.org/2014/10/14/nbcs-rotoworld-rotogrinders-ink-fantasy-sports-partnership/

Tasker, J. (2020). Federal government to table bill to legalize single-evet sports betting. *CBC*. Retrieved from https://www.cbc.ca/news/politics/legalize-single-event-sports-betting-1.5816059

Thomas, S., Lewis, S., Duong, J., & McLeod, C. (2012). Sports betting marketing during sporting events: A stadium and broadcast census of Australian Football League matches. *Australian and New Zealand Journal of Public Health, 36*(2), 145–152. doi:10.1111/j.1753-6405.2012.00856.x PMID:22487349

Thorn, J. (2019). Forget what you know about the Black Sox scandal. *New York Times*. Retrieved from https://www.nytimes.com/2019/10/09/opinion/black-sox-scandal-1919.html

TSN. (2020, September). *Morning Coffee: Welcome to The TSN Edge*. Retrieved from https://www.tsn.ca/morning-coffee-welcome-to-the-tsn-edge-1.1522030

Twenge, J. M. (2017). *iGen: Why Today's Super-Connected Kids Are Growing Up Less Rebellious, More Tolerant, Less Happy and Completely Unprepared for Adulthood*. Atria.

Twenge, J. M. (2019). More Time on Technology, Less Happiness? Associations Between Digital-Media Use and Psychological Well-Being. *Current Directions in Psychological Science, 28*(4), 372–379. doi:10.1177/0963721419838244

United Kingdom. (2005). Gambling Act. *Government of the United Kingdom*. Retrieved from https://www.legislation.gov.uk/ukpga/2005/19/contents

Valuates Reports. (2020). Fantasy sports market by sports yype (football, baseball, basketball, hockey, cricket, and others), platform (website, and mobile application), and Demographics (under 25 years, 25 to 40 years and above 40 years): Global opportunity analysis and industry forecast, 2021–2027. *Valuate Reports*. Retrieved from https://reports.valuates.com/market-reports/ALLI-Manu-1E22/fantasy-sports

Van Rompuy, B. & Asser Institute (2015). *The odds of match fixing facts & figures on the integrity risk of certain sports bets*. Brussels: Asser International Sport Law Centre.

Vuchot, A., Joly, C., & Kawkabani, R. (2020). The Gambling Law Review: France. *The Law Reviews.* Retrieved from https://thelawreviews.co.uk/title/the-gambling-law-review/france

Waddell, D. (2020). Professional sports leagues' commissioner urge federal government to allow single-game betting. *Windsor Star.* Retrieved from https://windsorstar.com/news/professional-sports-leagues-commissioners-urge-federal-government-to-allow-single-game-betting

Wagner, K. (2015). FanDuel acquired esports company AlphDraft, also jumps into competitive video gaming. *Vox.* Retrieved from https://www.vox.com/2015/9/24/11618896/fanduel-acquires-esports-company-alphadraft-also-jumps-into

Wakefield, J. (2016). Manchester City sign first e-sports player. *BBC.* Retrieved from https://www.bbc.com/news/technology-36734518

Waters, M. (2021). DraftKings goes public after shareholder approval, business combination. *Legal Sports Report.* Retrieved from https://www.legalsportsreport.com/40250/draftkings-vote-going-public/

William Hill. (2020). William Hill annual report and accounts 2019. *William Hill.* Retrieved from https://www.williamhillplc.com/media/13522/ara19_v2.pdf

Woodward, C. (2015). DraftKings raises $300m in frenzied fantasy sports land-grab. *Boston.com.* Retrieved from http://www.betaboston.com/news/2015/07/26/draftkings-raises-300m-in-frenzied-fantasy-sports-land-grab/

World, I. B. S. (2020). Global sports betting & lotteries - Market size 2005-2026. *IBS World.* Retrieved from https://www.ibisworld.com/global/market-size/global-sports-betting-lotteries/

ENDNOTES

1. Created by Joseph Oller, *pari-mutuel* is a pool-based better model, where no bookkeeper is required, because no odds are calculated. The winner simply takes all of the money put into the pool by the participants. Unfortunately for him, Oller was jailed in France in 1874, well before *pari-mutuel* was legalized in France in 1887.
2. Peridophobia is fear of betting.
3. Moneyball was a 2011 film starring Brad Pitt that followed the adventures of Billy Beane, general manager of the Oakland A's as he used quantification

and computer models to inform his trades for new players. Since then, "to moneyball something" has become a verb.

4 The "sportsbook hold" is the percentage of money the bookmaker or house holds onto after all bets have been settled. (Humphreys, 2021).

5 The United States Internal Revenue Service applies excise taxes of .25% on legal wagering and 2% on any wager not authorized by state law (Cunningham & Rosenberg, 1997).

6 The United States Internal Revenue Service applies excise taxes of .25% on legal wagering and 2% on any wager not authorized by state law (Cunningham & Rosenberg, 1997).

Chapter 11
Media and Content in an Active Economy

Cheri L. Bradish
Ryerson University, Canada

Nick Burton
Brock University, Canada

ABSTRACT

A vibrant active economy is dependent upon many factors to thrive and be successful. At the very core of this, is centralized communication—and links to myriad communication networks and tools—to keep the community engaged. Media and content, from traditional to digital communication, and its content through other outlets are key when engaging individual citizens and key stakeholders to share vital information as well as provide a means of storytelling. And, as media has been democratized by a variety of social platforms (such as Facebook, Twitter, etc.), the distinction and diversity of voices active via media and content in an active economy is significant. This chapter reviews the concepts of media and content for an active economy including an historical overview of media, digital transformation, related trends, and includes relevant case studies for discussion and critical analysis.

INTRODUCTION

A vibrant active economy is dependent upon many factors to thrive and be successful. Paramount to this is centralized communication - and links to a myriad of communication networks and tools - to keep the community engaged. Media and content, from traditional to digital communication and its content through other

DOI: 10.4018/978-1-7998-7939-8.ch011

outlets, is key to engaging individual citizens and key stakeholders, to share vital information as well as provide a means of storytelling. And, as media has been democratized by a variety of social platforms (such as Facebook, Twitter, etc.) the distinction and diversity of voices active via media and content in an active economy is significant. This chapter will then review many of the common principles and strategies for a media and content understanding for an active economy.

BACKGROUND

Sport media is the core discipline of 'media & content' as we will refer to it and as relevant for the discussion related to the active economy. This is a critically important area of investigation within sport and recreation study, and as such, a key vertical of the active economy. Sport media emerged through traditional sport publications, namely print newspaper, primarily in the mid-1800s, to television broadcasting through to the 1980s and 1990s, when it accelerated and proliferated through a number of innovations, along with the emergence of the internet and an array of digital media communication (Nachman & Bennett, 2011).

Further, to level-set, it is important to note that 'sport media' has been defined in sport management and marketing study, and has emerged as a tool and consideration, via 'public relations' which includes 'media relations' and 'community relations.' This is important as this reflects the power of the medium of media for the active economy: a) as a public relations tool, it is understood as communication that can foster a positive image for related activities, b) as a media relations function, it can help harness and shape favorable public opinion, and as related to core values, c) as a community relations based initiative, it can help build goodwill for a sport organization (Mullin et al., 2014).

Historical Overview of Media Related to the Active Economy

The history of newspaper sports journalism in the United States and across North America dates back two hundred years and is linked by both the growth of sport as a core cultural offering, and the development of journalism, print newspapers, and the expectation of community commentary; both becoming professional and commercial pursuits.

Sport Journalism

Sport journalism throughout North America began in the 1820s and 1830s, via specialized sport magazines, focusing on sport and often related to the 'gaming' of the times, including horse racing and boxing. Interestingly, sport media profiles tended to focus more on the social element of the events, rather than the athletic pursuits themselves or the box score presentation of the events. As sport grew and became a greater means and mechanism for the pursuit of leisurely activity, the news via print newspapers had become the accepted and popular means of profiling sport throughout North America (Betts, 1953; Raney & Bryant, 2006).

Into the 1800s, two major developments in the evolution of North American newspaper journalism occurred. One, the 'Penny Press' emerged in the 1830s and 1840s, when newspapers expanded their circulation by dropping the price of an issue in an attempt to appeal to a new demographic of middle-class, urban readers, and when newspapers began to support their ventures via advertising, rather than paid circulation, for revenues (Raney & Bryant, 2006). The second was the Industrial Revolution in the mid-1800s, with urbanization, which had a great impact on the growth of professional sport as well; individuals flocking to cities had increased leisure time to spend engaged in sporting pursuits, in particular as spectators – which resulted in many positive effects for communities and metropolitan areas. This included the linking of local team engagement driving immense civic pride, especially for new citizens – further supporting the growth of regional newspaper sport coverage, and the growth of regional sport. In 1895, the first stand-alone sport section was offered for community fan consumption, by the New York Journal (Moritz, 2017).

Sport Broadcasting

Sport journalism transitioned from print to include radio in the early 1920s and evolved to a point where every major metropolitan area, and team, had their own in-house productions and live broadcasts, where sport activities and related commentary were broadcast over the radio. This created an accessibility to the growing commercial sport landscape, which continued with the major transformation of television and access to live audio of sport telecasts around the 1950s (Barnfield, 2013) radically igniting the professional nature of sport, via the growth and expansion of sport properties, partners and related stakeholders, intensifying the fan experience and access, while at the same time enhancing revenue opportunities.

Sport Media Ownership

As media prominence rose, and peaked into the 1980s, a new trend in the relationship between media and sport and leisure emerged: moving from a key stakeholder, to owner, with a number of leading sport media properties purchasing in whole or in part professional sport and recreation ventures. As this dynamic in the industry changed, the role of content development changed as well, and became fluid between property and end-user.

CASE STUDY:

Sport Media Ownership: The Ownership of Maple Leaf Sports and Entertainment (MLSE) and Bell and Rogers

In December of 2011, it was announced that Rogers and Bell, Canada's two largest media and telecommunications companies, would become part owners and shareholders in MLSE, estimated to be over a $1 billion-dollar deal, giving each company approximately 37.5 per cent stake in the company, along with owner and Board Chair Larry Tanenbaum (Canadian Press, 2011). Within its portfolio, MLSE owns the Leafs of the NHL, the NBA's Toronto Raptors, Major League Soccer's Toronto FC, the Toronto Marlies of the AHL and the Air Canada Centre (now, Scotiabank Arena). This was a landmark deal across the global sport business industry, and unprecedented in Canada. The strategic benefit of this deal for both Bell and Rogers was that it effectively created a wealth of opportunity for, and access to, sport content among the MLSE properties. This case is important to the conversation about media and content and active economies for a number of reasons, including its support for the importance of rich content and the access to it, and the strong and valuable role media can play in the sport and leisure arena.

In short, the development and commercialization of sport media in North America is important and relevant to the topic of the active economy, providing important commentary about the key linkages and opportunities between media, media distribution and community citizen engagement within the sport, activity, and leisure spaces.

Digitizing Media and Content for the Active Economy

Just like the evolution of sport media outlets, the rise and support of digital technologies are unlocking new and unprecedented opportunities for growth in the sport and leisure industry, offering the potential to draw citizens engaged in the active economy closer to the field of activity through a myriad of innovative and customized experiences (Ballouli, 2012). To capitalize on this opportunity, however, digital will need to be embedded in every aspect of the community association and business, connected to and via all people, processes, and technologies. Benefits of a digital transformation includes expanding content reach, enhancing the sport consumer experience, enriching the relationship with partners and stakeholders, and driving new and alternative revenue. This digital revolution can occur for key consumers and markets, to reposition how citizens communicate and work, prioritize management processes around digitization, and support for new and emerging technologies (Deloitte, 2018).

Embarking on the digital transformation journey requires a deep understanding of current capabilities, as well a vision for the future that will determine how capabilities, processes, organizational structure, and technology will need to change. As sports organizations become comfortable with life as digital enterprises, they will not only develop affinity with their fans, but may also find it more meaningful means and mediums to create innovative and customized experiences that will both broaden and strengthen their current and future consumers (Hutchins & Rowe, 2012).

New and Emerging Technologies: Redefining the Active Experience

Sport and recreation spectators and participants throughout modern times have embraced leisure activities via a variety of media and content, to the landscape today, which provides an overwhelming number of digital technologies to experience the active economy, enhancing online consumption and increasing shared communication for the industry, which has been discussed and researched broadly, noting the following benefits for the overall consumer experience (Capgemini, 2021):

- Consumers are savvy, smart and engaged in new technology offerings, and members of the active economy would be well-positioned to understand their expectation of advanced digital communication to succeed.
- Brand engagement and loyalty, and in turn, revenue generation, is linked to the digital transformation for key participants of the active economy.
- Firms in the active economy should prioritize the need to build trust through their digital transformation strategies and utilizing the related rich data capture capabilities to focus on the future needs of the active economy consumer.

In short, emerging technologies offer a multitude of opportunities to rethink and reposition traditional media communication and content for the active economy, targeting new and meaningful ways to respective stakeholders and consumers.

Gender Equity, Diversity and Inclusion

One of the most important themes of media and content in the past decade related to the active economy is the importance of fair and adequate representation of key members and stakeholders from a variety of diverse groups, and portraying gender equity, among other concerns. Research and evidence strongly point to the importance of 'representation matters' in the physical and activity space (Jones, 2006), and the need for far greater integration and inclusion of individuals and engaged citizens across the active economy to be considered and addressed in all mediums and media communication.

LINKS TO THE ACTIVE ECONOMY

Much of what has been discussed in this chapter is a review of how central media and content creation, from historical to current times, is critical understanding and strategy for the entire spectrum of the active economy. This section will review the links between media and content and the active economy, as well as highlight the opportunities and challenges they present for the active economy. In the case below, we outline how media and content, when amplified correctly, can play a powerful role in significantly lifting and assisting a particular issue of cause, applicable to our review of the topic.

CASE STUDY:

Hayley Wickenheiser, Ryan Reynolds Helping 'Conquer COVID-19'

Related to sport and leisure, there are many examples of how the exploding power of new and emerging mediums have transformed economies and industry segments, in particular over the past twenty years. These examples include the opportunity that is created for the active property, consumer and citizen, engaged stakeholder, and greater good of the community at large. For instance, a recent example of how the power of media and content via storytelling is in the good work and social media messaging of Canadian heroes Hayley Wickenheiser and Ryan Reynolds, who actively teamed up to support 'Conquer COVID-19' early on in Canada's challenges with the pandemic. Their campaign and fundraising efforts raised millions of dollars for the Conquer COVID-19 charity, which supported frontline workers and delivered essential health equipment including personal protective equipment (PPE) to medial support staff (Chidley-Hill, 2020). What is remarkable, and important here, with regard to this case, is the role of the media and related content in propelling this initiative onto a national and North American agenda. The combined efforts of these two celebrities were significantly amplified via new technologies and storytelling, providing a powerful example of how media and content can be used to benefit active, engaged, and social communities.

Thus, as noted throughout this chapter, much good work and goodwill can be accomplished via an understanding and integration of media communications for the active economy. On the other hand, it is important to be aware that media, as much as it has democratized many forms of communication, has been professionalized and globalized, influencing business models. In many cases, it has created a divide between a variety of segments, and provided challenges for related leisure and active industries (Thibault, 2009). For example, with regard to professional sport, increased media profiling and profits has created skyrocketing rights fees for professional sport leagues, resulting in increased revenues and player salaries. This has resulted in creating significant opportunity for primarily men's leagues, athletes, and related events – leaving a wide commercial gap with women's professional sports and enhancing gender equity challenges (Gibson, 2020). In turn, these realities convert to related media metrics, and have affected other diverse sport and fitness community divides, such as that between the Olympic and Paralympic Games. Commercial and media support favours the Olympic Games offerings, including athlete profiles and support, leaving the Paralympic Games, and athletes under-resourced and under-profiled (Wolbring, 2012).

CONCLUSION

Media and content, from traditional to digital communication and its content through other outlets, is a key engaging individual citizens and key stakeholders, to share vital information as well as provide a means of storytelling. And, as the media has been democratized by a variety of social platforms (such as Facebook, Twitter, etc.) the distinction and diversity of voices active via media and content in an active economy is significant. This chapter has reviewed many of the common tools and strategies for a media and content plan for an active economy.

REFERENCES

Ballouli, K. (2012). It's a whole new ballgame: How social media is changing sports. *Sport Management Review*, *15*(3), 381–382. doi:10.1016/j.smr.2012.02.008

Barnfield, A. (2013). Soccer, broadcasting, and narrative: On televising a live soccer match. *Communication & Sport Journal*, *1*(14), 326–341. doi:10.1177/2167479513479107

Betts, J. R. (1953). Sporting journalism in nineteenth-century American. *American Quarterly*, *5*(1), 39–56. doi:10.2307/3031289

Capgemini. (2021). *Emerging technologies in sports*. Capgemini Research.

Chidley-Hill, J. (2020). Hayley Wickenheiser begins personal protective equipment drive in Toronto. *CBC Sports*. https://www.cbc.ca/sports/hayley-wickenheiser-personal-protection-drive-toronto-1.5529933

Deloitte. (2018). *A whole new ball game: Navigating digital change in the sports industry*. Deloitte Development LLC.

Gibson, C. (2020). Report finds strides made in women's sports in past few years, but inequality remains. *ESPN*. https://www.espn.com/espn/story/_/id/28489077/report-finds-strides-made-women-sports-years-inequality-remains

Hutchins, B., & Rowe, D. (2012). *Sport beyond television: The internet, digital media and the rise of networked media sport*. Routledge. doi:10.4324/9780203120415

Jones, D. (2006). The representation of female athletes in online images of successive Olympic Games. *Pacific Journalism Review*, *12*(1), 108–129. doi:10.24135/pjr.v12i1.848

Moritz, B. P. (2017). The history of sports journalism (Part 1). *Sports Media Guy*. https://www.sportsmediaguy.com/blog/2017/5/9/the-history-of-sports-journalism-part-1-of-3

Mullin, B., Hardy, S., & Sutton, W. (2014). *Sport marketing* (4th ed.). Human Kinetics.

Nachman, C., & Bennett, D. (2011). 14 innovations that changed sports broadcasting forever. *Business Insider*. https://www.businessinsider.com/evolution-how-we-watch-sports-2011-4

Raney, A., & Bryant, J. (2006). *Handbook of sports and media* (1st ed.). Routledge.

The Canadian Press. (2011). Rogers, Bell buy control of MLSE. *CBC Sports*. https://www.cbc.ca/sports/hockey/nhl/rogers-bell-buy-control-of-mlse-1.997655

Thibault, L. (2009). Globalization of sport: An inconvenient truth. *Journal of Sport Management*, *23*(1), 1–20. doi:10.1123/jsm.23.1.1

Wolbring, G. (2012). Paralympics vs Olympics coverage: Uneven at best. *The Conversation*. https://theconversation.com/paralympics-vs-olympics-coverage-uneven-at-best-9429

Conclusion

JUST THE START

This book proposes a new conceptual lens through which researchers and practitioners can better appreciate how community value is generated through the active economy. Herein, we propose that the traditional isolated sectorial lens of sport and recreation (and associated sectors) may be masking a highly interdependent active economy.

Predicting the future with precision is an impossible task, however, for any movement, macro-level trends and the resulting implications must be considered. When becoming aware of the context and the global environment, thoughtful planning is necessary to indicate what is reasonably possible. The author team identified seven macro-level trends influencing the future of the active economy. Each trend is analyzed and factored into our strategic recommendations.

Trend 1: Social Justice and Change
Trend 2: The COVID-19 Longtail
Trend 3: Sustainability at The Centre
Trend 4: The War for Talent
Trend 5: Accelerating Technological Disruption
Trend 6: From Consumer to Co-Creator
Trend 7: Changing Media Consumption

It is important to remember that these trends are highly dynamic, and the descriptions provided are only a starting point for ongoing research and intelligence gathering to support evidence-based decisions at both the enterprise and system level. An accelerating reality, and an anchor principle within the active economy, is that the world is a complex system and therefore, it is essential to think bigger. The challenge is that humans are inclined to break big problems down into small pieces. Such simplification leads us to believe that a single cause has single corresponding effect; which is very rarely the case. Therefore, planners must consider the entire system and recognize the first challenge is not problem solving, but rather, it is problem identification. Once great planners discover the real problem, their focus can be shifted towards exploring the solutions.

Trend 1: The COVID-19 Longtail

In March 2020, the spread of COVID-19 resulted in the closing of all non-essential organizations around the world. Some active economy enterprises were able to pivot their business models fully or partially, while most suspended operations, hoping to reopen once there was a return to 'normalcy'. Those who adapted their programming varied from altering their distribution to reassessing the sustainability of their entire business model. Many enterprises, including organized sports, active recreation, active tourism, health and wellness, and retail, however, were forced to close.

The unprecedented COVID-19 conditions forced many enterprises within the active economy to evaluate their 'offer and deliver' value to customers in new and innovative ways, including virtual live experiences sometimes referred to as the 'no touch' active economy. As the economy reopens, many of the government-directed guidelines and policies alongside public health authorities include the implementation of physical distancing guidelines. For the active economy, these changes are increasing operating costs, reducing traditional revenue opportunities, and fundamentally altering the customer experience.

The long-term fallout the COVID-19 pandemic remains unknown. Therefore, the first main implication is for us to track behavioural change and understand how the pandemic has impacted the active economy as a whole. We anticipate that the implications on the active economy, however, will be far reaching.

Operational Implications

This includes operational implications in regard to sanitization and hygiene and financial impact through reduced access to private or public funding. Moreover, there will be additional organizational implications as a result of COVID-19, many of which will be tied to risk management systems and insurance. In some cases, the market dynamics may lead some of these enterprises to fully exit a business model that requires physical interactions. In other cases, enterprises may see a path forward which blends both touch and no touch offerings into a unique and compelling value proposition. Finally, the path forward for some active economy sectors may be identical to the path that got them here. What is needed is patience, financial prudence, planning, and a focus on short and long-term sustainability.

Facility Design

Facility infrastructure will need to be far more flexible than it is today. This will include smaller spaces for smaller group activities and designing egress to provide the required physical distancing. An outstanding question remains, however, regarding the large sport venues and the impact of COVID-19 on longer-term demand.

Employment Mobility

In some sectors, the COVID-19 pandemic demonstrates that physical co-location is not essential for certain roles. This impacts the assumption that an enterprise's workforce must be physically in the same geographic area. The result will be skilled workers having greater flexibility in choosing a place to reside. For example, a software designer who is an avid skier may choose to live in a mountain town, while working for a company based in a major urban centre. In some sectors and professions, this level of flexibility has existed for years, but the acceleration and expansion triggered by COVID-19 is changing the calculations for many enterprises and employees. As a result, some areas may become more or less appealing to different people depending on their values. An opportunity exists in some areas to position the regional active economy as a competitive advantage for the attraction and retention of talent.

Trend 2: Social Justice and Change

Many of the other trends resulting from COVID-19, such as technology, demographics, and media consumptions, are redefining the relationship between people and institutions. Over the past decade, there has been a significant decline in the trust of institutions such as government, media, corporations, and social enterprises. Amplified through mediums like social media, people's values are framed by the echo chamber of others who may share similar values and views. This creates an increased animosity or fear of others that may not look or think like you. Brexit, the 2016 American presidential election and the Black Lives Matter movement are partial reflections of this fundamental breakdown in institutional trust.

This data demonstrates a broad discontent in much of the world and an increasing demand for change. As a result, there are enormous movements occurring which aim towards confronting some of the core injustices in society. These range from systematic inequality to the consistently growing wealth gap. It must be recognized that in order for the active economy to be successful, it must be for all people. Data shows the active economy in many parts of the world is not inclusive and explicitly or implicitly discriminates based on ethnicity, age, gender, sexual orientation and physical ability.

Over the next decade there will be an increasing pressure and responsibility to deal with these core societal issues. This will accelerate a new approach in solving community problems through increasing harmonization of the commercial, social, and public sectors that will spawn social innovations. The result blurs the line between the role of commercial, social, and public sectors as innovation trumps traditional institutional silos.

The active economy transcends the commercial, social and public sector; however, these sectors have historically had limited levels of collaboration or harmonized system-level planning. To move forward, these sectors must work together to maximize the value of scarce resources to deliver an inclusive active economy. This includes rethinking how the ecosystem builds and designs active infrastructure. It also leads to a significantly increased demand for investment in the structural and social capital required to ensure the diverse stakeholders in and outside of the active economy are better coordinated. Part of this reframing is a focus on aligning investments towards defined metrics. Active economy enterprises must demonstrate how an investment in their enterprise creates not only value for the enterprise, but more so to the community. The ability to develop evidence-based quantitative and qualitative models, evidence and narratives that can link investments to outcomes is a minimum requirement regardless of the source of funding.

Consistent with this, it will also contribute to the expansion of Corporate Social Responsibility (CSR) and Corporate Social Innovation (CSI) initiatives. Strategic assets here may offer a sustainable competitive advantage on the same level of other assets such as intellectual property (e.g., patents) and brands. CSI is about ground-breaking ideas that take social, economic, and environmental sustainability to the next level. Continued pressure may result in a shift to a CSR and CSI strategy that combines corporate assets in collaboration with other sectors and firms to co-create solutions for complex social, economic, and environmental issues.

In the active economy, this will lead to a need for new and innovative built infrastructure and programming. This includes balancing a need to build infrastructure that is in close proximity to unique communities, while simultaneously facilitating bridges between diverse ones. Evidence demonstrates that a well-designed active economy can facilitate community integration and social bonding. Practical examples could include flexible multi-use facilities (both indoor and outdoor) to meet the diversity of active living, organized sports, or active recreation demands.

Trend 3: Sustainability at the Centre

The environment and our efforts in sustaining it are not new trends. However, driven by the effects of climate change such increasing forest fires and flooding, sustainability is a priority at the federal, provincial, and municipal levels.

Broadly speaking, sustainability is defined as meeting the needs of the present without compromising the ability of future generations to meet their own needs. This definition recognizes that development is essential to satisfying human needs and improving quality of life, but that it must be based on the efficient and responsible use of natural, human, and economic resources.

The combined sustainability and associated economic pressures have numerous direct and indirect impact on the regional active economy. A changing climate may impact the ability to reliably deliver certain active experiences. The impacts could extend across different snow or water-based sports. Similarly, the sustainability of certain active infrastructure may be challenged. This may include artificial snow-making and indoor pools. Another potential impact is the use of land for recreation purposes. Will areas be built purposefully for specific activities or persons from specific demographics and or socio-economic groups or will land be more multi-purposed in nature and inclusive in those that can use it?

This will also accelerate the adoption of the 15-minute principle for city planners. The adoption of a 15-minute city will have seismic implications for many cities and regions. What is needed then is a greater integration of public transit and micro-mobility options, including innovations in year-round cycling and e-bikes. Moreover, the increasing pressure for densification demands more efficient use of open spaces to support a broad range of activities from sports, active recreation, and community gardens. This already appears to be occurring.

Trend 4: The War for Talent

For most of human history, a city's competitive advantage was defined by its proximity to scarce natural resources such as lumber or access to navigable waterways. For the past two hundred years, these natural advantages have contributed to the growth of cities through commodity extraction or manufacturing centres. Over the past four decades, the competitive advantage of many cities, driven by economic, social, and cultural factors, such as advanced technology and globalization, has transitioned from proximity to natural resources, to the ability to attract and mobilize human capital. Human capital views competencies as capital, similar to other forms of capital (e.g., financial capital, social capital). Human capital can be viewed at the level of an individual, institution (e.g., enterprise or ecosystem) or city. Thus, today, a city's capacity to develop, acquire and retain high-valued talent underpins much of its economic and social prosperity (World Economic Forum, 2020). This is defined as the war for talent.

How will talent be defined in the future? The exponential pace of change in many sectors of the economy has transitioned the war for talent from one of domain-specific skills. Domain specific competencies incorporate the knowledge, skills, attitudes, values, and behaviours required to complete specific tasks associated with a role (e.g., coding, welding, engineering) and/or a sector (e.g., energy, sport). However, today, employers are searching for people who can adapt and pivot in a constantly dynamic environment. For example, the World Economic Forum forecasts that by 2022, 75 million jobs will be displaced across the leading 20 economies, while 133 million new jobs will be created in nascent sectors. It is estimated that between 2018 and 2022, 50 per cent of employees globally will need to be reskilled or upskilled (World Economic Forum, 2018)

Adaptive capacity is the ability for an individual to anticipate systematic changes and proactively develop new or refine existing competencies that are valued as demand changes. Adaptive capacity is rooted in possessing enabling competencies. Enabling competencies (also referred to as meta-skills, human-skills, soft-skills, and transferable-skills) is the ability to incorporate knowledge, skills, attitudes, values, and behaviours required to deliver analytical thinking, interpersonal communication, foundational literacies, and professional competencies across a range of contexts.

Related to this has been the increase of what is referred to as the "gig economy". For example, almost 40 per cent of the U.S. workforce is made up of freelancers who work for themselves (Lindzon, 2016). That is more than 4 million people and growing by ten per cent each year. (Krashinsky, 2016). This freelance economy has become mainstream as companies and talent alike recognize the benefits of employment on-demand (Dishman, 2017). It is too early to tell how the COVID-19 pandemic may impact the gig economy, but it is a trend that will continue to evolve over the next decade for both enterprises and individuals.

This war for talent has two direct implications on the active economy. Firstly, there is a demand to evolve the current labour force to meet emerging needs. The development of high-valued talent incorporates both enabling competencies and domain specific competencies.

The development of these competencies has traditionally been developed through two mediums: (1) Formal education, encompassing accredited and non-accredited training that contribute to the development of an individual's cognitive and personality resources; and (2) through lived experience, including, professional (e.g., paid), volunteer (e.g., not compensated work) and contextual (e.g., personal experiences, such as travel). The development and refinement of these competencies is also an iterative and nonlinear process, incorporating feedback loops through education and experience. This then provides jurisdictions an opportunity to leverage its active economy as a strategic asset to develop demanded competencies that contribute to a region's economic growth and prosperity.

Evidence shows that engagement in both organized sports and recreation directly contributes to the development of valued competencies ranging from interpersonal to leadership skills. However, the relationship between developing high-demand competencies and an individual's participation in sport and recreation is largely informal. This then provides communities an opportunity to leverage its active economy as a strategic asset to develop demanded competencies that contribute to a city's economic growth and prosperity.

The second implication is the ability to leverage the active economy for talent acquisition. Many people are attracted to (or have remained in) a region due to the robust active economy. This includes natural assets such as rivers, mountains and built assets, such as extensive pathway systems. In some cities, such as Melbourne, Austin, Vancouver, or Copenhagen, the active economy has been used as an asset for talent acquisition essential for economic prosperity.

Trend 5: Accelerating Technological Disruption

In the past two decades, technological innovation has disrupted society. The internet, social media, mobile devices, and big data analytics are only the tip of the digital iceberg. In the future, wireless connections will be built specifically to keep up with the "internet of things." The internet and other innovations such as social media, mobile devices and big data have redefined the way society produces and consumes media. Currently, there are close to 30 million smartphone users in Canada, increasing to 33 million by 2024 (Statista Digital Market Outlook, 2018) A study of US children and teenagers ages eight to 18 years, found tweens spend five hours a day on screens and teenagers 7.5 hours per day (Rideout & Robb, 2019).

In 2025, with the rapid advancement of the "internet of things," it is estimated that more than 50 billion devices—from your car to your refrigerator—will be connected. Ericsson is predicting 90 per cent of all devices will have mobile broadband capability by 2022 (Erriccson, 2016).

Advancements related to artificial intelligence, machine learning, and cognitive computing are also going to change lives and careers. But how? Over a decade ago when the first Nintendo Wii was introduced, the world had a glimpse of the potential of immersive computing. Computing is no longer a passive activity, rather it is evolving with the potential to be active. The next decade may see an explosive growth in immersive visual computing, such as virtual and augmented reality (AR/VR), which may be a technological game changer for the active economy. Today, 70 per cent of the top VR apps use video. Sports such as boxing and mixed martial arts are anticipated to be the most appealing in the near-term for VR.

Over the next decade, audiences' expectations of content will continue to be redefined. For example, new 360-degree cameras enable the production of three-dimensional virtual reality video with surround sound to allow a viewer to move within a video wearing a headset (Hanlon, 2016). There will also be significant technological advancements in neuro-coaching and machine medicine. This could include non-invasive brain stimulation to accelerate muscle memory and precision, brain scanning technology to manage cognition and emotion, supplements to accelerate reaction time, immersive visual computing training, RFID tags to track performance, and implantable sensors to monitor blood and technology to help people sleep better.

Driven by these technological advancements in addition to increased social networking and video streaming, the global gaming market exceeds two billion participants or 30 per cent of the world's total population (Merwin et al., 2018). In competitive esports, there were an estimated 110 million competitors in 2018 (Newzoo, 2019). For perspective, a video game released in 2019, *Red Dead Redemption 2* generated $725 million in sales in its first three days. If *Red Dead Redemption 2* were a movie, it would rank as the third largest box office opening in history; larger than any *Star Wars* or *Harry Potter* movie (Box Office Mojo, 2019). In fact, three of the top five "opening weekends'' in history are held by games, not movies. The growth of esports is also represented by the size of the prize pools, which now rival prize pools from the largest professional sports in the world from Wimbledon to The Masters.

Another technological disruption is the advancements in battery technology. This contributes to continued advancement in e-transportation, including electric bikes and vehicles. Finally, most analysts believe autonomous transportation contributes to the redefining of transportation. The positive from this is increased efficiency and reduction of traffic accidents; the negative is the loss of millions of jobs for trucking, taxi and public transportation sectors. Autonomous vehicles, combined with active transportation, could then redefine transportation networks and patterns of movement which could then have a significant impact on broader planning.

The variety of technological advancements discussed here creates both opportunities and threats to the active economy. For example, the explosion of smartphones and other devices has led to the exponential increase in "screen time" and concurrent decrease in participation in organized sports and active recreation. Today, studies suggest that over 80 per cent of parents believe that screens are negatively impacting their children from engaging in other activities (The Kids & Family Reading Report, 2017) Technology has led to children growing up in an environment where inactivity has become the norm. For example, it is estimated that children spend 50 per cent less time outside playing compared to their parents. Children must be engaged much earlier on the importance of active living in schools and at home. Creating an active living culture is imperative to overcome the rise of technology.

In addition, each device generates data that is used to predict behaviour and reveal preferences. In other words, every credit card transaction, click on Google, Instagram post and GPS ping from your smartphone generates data that is collected and used by enterprises to increase efficiencies, lower costs, accelerate decision-making, and increase customer satisfaction. The use of this 'big data' will continue to grow over the next decade as the volume, velocity and variety of data grows in influencing critical decision-making in the active economy. However, one implication on society as a whole, and the active economy specifically, is the increased risk to privacy and its implications. In the active economy, this may range from financial transactions to personal information and health records that are shared and at risk of being used by others. The ability for enterprises in the active economy to protect and secure this data is therefore of increasing importance.

Other impacts of technology on the active economy can include micro examples such as the continued advancements in e-bikes. There is the potential for these to enable seniors to cycle and remain active for an extended period, offering both health and environmental impacts.

- Implications of wearable technology - Body suits/wearables – see the change in HR or cadence; greater understanding about what is actually occurring in the game.
- Greater data on one's performance as a runner, athlete.
- Technology has moved people to think differently and disrupt sport; offers a fresh perspective.
- To thrive, we will need to embrace the change and disruption and resist the urge to stay static.
- Esport is global and possesses the ability to connect and engage fans easily. It is social, interactive, and accessible – a real threat to traditional sports.
- Implications for online learning and online delivery of services via digital buying.

Trend 6: From Consumer to Co-Creator

Traditional innovation processes focus on controlling innovation which allows a company to retain ownership of and control over knowledge and intellectual property. In other words, this is the exploration of new knowledge and exploitation of existing knowledge in a closed loop and limited to employees within an enterprise. Traditional innovation, however, has limited access to knowledge from external sources and therefore an enterprise is challenged to effectively tackle the most complex problems. In contrast, open innovation encourages the development of partnerships and the leveraging of complementary knowledge for innovation from individuals and enterprises across ecosystems. This model, adopted by companies such as Apple, Google and LEGO, recognizes that when you empower people, you accelerate innovation. In this model, an enterprise transitions from being a linear controller of knowledge to becoming a dynamic broker across the entire ecosystem and supporting interconnected processes. Over the next decade, the role of the active economy consumers and other stakeholders will expand dramatically as the system transitions to the open innovation model just described.

Other changes that will impact the active economy include the democratization of participation. Linked to the shift below, the definition of an athlete is evolving (e.g. eSport), as is the understanding of who a 'reporter' is, with many having access to a phone camera and social media. The changing world of communication, connectivity, and collaboration allows one to connect with anyone on the planet, anywhere, at any time. One implication for the active economy is that people are now looking for immediate access to highlights, and post-game press conferences and not just the game.

The active economy needs to learn how to engage consumers throughout the product life cycle. This is of particular importance within the active economy due to the significant declines being seen in the participation of women, lower household income, persons with a disability and specific ethnic groups. As noted earlier, seniors are also a critical part of the active economy and it is therefore essential to meet their diverse and emerging needs. Similarly, a variety of enabling sectors within the active economy should adopt an open innovation framework as they evolve their products and services.

Enterprises and ecosystems that have successfully developed open innovation systems have done so systematically. This includes the tangible and intangible processes and structures that facilitate effective collaboration and harmonization of individuals and institutions. At this stage, with no shared vision or purpose, the active economy lacks the core structural capital that underpins the capacity to aggregate individuals and enterprises into one system. Instead, most mechanisms remain limited internally to enterprises, with only limited examples of aggregation at the ecosystem level. The result is risk of system-level duplication and inefficiencies. The foundation of a shared vision for an active economy, instead should be the commitment to develop the required structural capital for regional active economy to work as a harmonized system. The anchor should include establishing mechanisms for system-wide knowledge mobilization, harmonized experiments, and shared open resources.

Trend 7: Changing Media Consumption

Between 2009 and 2019, media advertising revenues nearly doubled in size globally from $1.2 to $2.1 trillion. Ironically, the fragmentation of media has led to a concentration of advertising revenues as both Google and Facebook control one-fifth of all advertising revenue globally (Kollewe, 2017). This disruption of the media's financial model also extends into the active economy, where broadcasters are struggling to monetize sports content to balance the extreme rights fees. Sport continues to be one of the dominant forms of media content in Canada, with 24 per cent reporting they watch live sports daily. 42 per cent consume sports through television. However, one-third of Canadians consume sports content online (through a variety of media such as online clips, articles, and live-streamed broadcasts), but only three per cent subscribe to a dedicated sports streaming service (Rody, 2018).

Concurrent with this financial disruption, technology has transformed how society consumes media, forms opinions, and makes decisions. For example, active economy media consumers are no longer at the mercy of broadcast schedules. They can increasingly watch and listen to the programming they want when they want. The result is that people digest bite-sized stories through Tik Tok or YouTube, often consuming multiple screens simultaneously.

Studies suggest that how society processes information is changing as we gradually adapt from text to video or other forms of content. Some consumers want to dig deeper than those few seconds; but many may not. For example, some may simply read a headline, whereas others watch embedded video and follow links to related stories. Today, more so than ever, the medium really is the message.

An additional implication of this changing media landscape is developing shorter-length versions of traditional sports such as Rugby Sevens, 20/20 cricket matches, three on three basketball and 12-hole golf courses.

Moreover, user-generated content such as social media posts or online reviews becomes increasingly valuable as trust in brands and large institutions (including governments) is displaced by trust in people. This dynamic has massive implications on how people are influenced and behave. Our reliance on recommendations from trusted friends and family is growing with a study by the Pew Research Centre showing that 40 per cent of American adults define Facebook as a primary news source. In fact, according to BuzzFeed, the top 20 best-performing fake news stories of the 2016 U.S. election shared on Facebook had higher readership than the top performing election stories in the *New York Times*, the *Washington Post*, *Huffington Post* and *NBC News*. In Canada, 60 per cent of the population use Facebook daily and 21 per cent define it as their first source of information. Interestingly, this transcends age groups with 49 per cent individuals 60 years and older reporting a daily use of Facebook (Delacourt, 2017).

Twitch has also emerged as a potentially game (no pun intended) changing media platform that may provide a guide to the future of the active economy media. Twitch, owned by Amazon, is a platform that allows you to watch others play video games (Wulf et al., 2017). The scope of Twitch is difficult to comprehend. Twitch averages 2.2 million daily broadcasters or streamers and 15 million daily viewers; 41,000 concurrent broadcasters/streamers and 1.1 million concurrent viewers (CCV) (Iqbal, 2019). At peak hours, its CCV numbers outpace some of the top-rated US cable channels, such as CNN and MSNBC (Taylor, 2018). In Alexa's ranking of global websites, Twitch is just behind Netflix and LinkedIn at number 26.

As a platform, Twitch streamers have launched their own channels, and with a webcam and headset microphone, livestream themselves playing games and offering commentary for audiences. Twitch then uses algorithms to make content suggestions to users, facilitating navigation. Twitch is also interactive, allowing viewers to comment or ask questions in a chat sidebar, and streamers in turn can react to the posts. Furthermore, Twitch has built features into the program to monetize viewer interests. This includes traditional advertising and sponsorship, but also opportunities for viewers to make donations to the streamers they follow. As part of the interaction that occurs, streamers offer to complete certain tasks or play certain games in exchange for contributions. Streamers can also draw revenue through a base subscription to their channel for a fee that then allows subscribers to comment in the channel's chat.

The changing media landscape is having a similarly significant impact on the active economy as television did in the 1950s. Short-form and user-generated media, such as Twitch or Tik Tok, does not spell the end of long-form storytelling in sport, but it will continue to redefine it over the next decade. Advancements in technology have also triggered a hyper-social generation with unique values and demands. Many younger fans follow the star player, and not necessarily a team, and these younger fans feel connected to the players. This connection may be through social media, fantasy sports or real-time content off the field. Most fans do not want to sit for three hours to watch a game but, instead, prefer bite-sized content which they can control on their own terms.

Therefore, story forms, promotional or otherwise, will continue to adapt and evolve from single form to transmedia storytelling where the consumer is able to seamlessly shift from text, video, audio, and images and potentially simultaneously with multiple-screen consumption. Future media will involve telling multiple stories, with each one working as a standalone or with associated pieces. For example, through television, radio and the internet, the NHL uses hockey players to tell continuous stories. Some are short term such as single games, a fight, comebacks, or trade speculation. Others are drawn out over a longer period, such as a player's career, the Stanley Cup playoff run, or a team's rebuilding efforts. All of these narratives are built and shared using transmedia storytelling which enables the media producer to customize the message or story elements for the channel and the audience who consume it.

For the active economy, the expansion of transmedia storytelling, offers a new and innovative platform for both enterprises and the ecosystem. The organic and user-generated model can be leveraged to tell more compelling students, educators, and athletes.

THE NEXT STEP

Herein, we argue that the active economy lens must become the foundation for future collaborative and systematic empirical research. This includes focusing on further deconstructing and empirical testing of the systematic dynamics of the active economy down to an activity, stakeholder, and community level through a regional active economy case study. If adopted, like the creative economy scholarship from over two decades ago, the active economy lens may be able to provide the potential for scholars, practitioners, and policymakers to access to new forms of rich data to better understand the complex and dynamic nature of the active economy and its impacts on community value.

Future active economy research can build upon a rich, discipline-specific scholarship in sport performance, sport business, active recreation, active tourism, health and wellness, urban planning, and economics. Moreover, further mapping of the active economy could leverage the rich literature and the more than two decades of empirical research which continues to examine the complex role of business ecosystems, regional clusters, and the creative economy. Research questions that could be considered include:

1. How can researchers and policymakers define sub-sectors as a proportion of activity associated with the active economy, enabling the isolation of factors such as employment and economic output directly associated with the active economy?
2. How can researchers and policymakers articulate the active economy and map how it and its' individual components measurably contribute to community well-being?
3. How can researchers and policymakers learn from benchmarks, such as the Nashville Music Cluster, to harness the scope and depth of the current active economy to maximize community value?

Moreover, it is essential that this area of research engage a broader range of researchers from a multitude of disciplines and contexts. Since there are many scholars, practitioners, policymakers, and community leaders who share a common passion about the positive role that the active economy has on society.

For the practitioner, the active economy provides an opportunity to better understand how and where independent clusters and specific organizations can create value by partnering and ensuring that a "rising tide raises all ships". The success of one sector can lead to the success of another, and entrepreneurs and policy makers can plan and work together to better design the success of the whole, leading to greater community value.

From an academic and policy perspective, disciplines such as sport performance, sport business, active recreation, active tourism, health and wellness, economic development and urban planning should now be seen as interrelated within a larger active economy. The active economy can then be viewed as creating value through the inter-relationships of 11 individual and interdependent (not autonomous) sectors, from organized sports to health and wellness. Understanding this can then allow policymakers and practitioners to be better positioned to shape ecosystem-level opportunities and maximize community impact.

REFERENCES

Box Office Mojo. (2019). All time box office: Worldwide openings. *Box Office Mojo.* Retrieved April 19, from https://www.boxofficemojo.com/alltime/world/worldwideopenings.htm

Delacourt, S. (2017, February 7). Facebook nation: Social media titan now dominates Canadian news. *iPolitics.* http://ipolitics.ca/2017/02/07/facebook-nation-social-media-titan-now-dominates-canadian-news/

Dishman, L. (2017, January 5). How the gig economy will change in 2017. *Fast Company.* https://www.fastcompany.com/3066905/how-the-gig-economy-will-change-in-2017

Ericsson. (2016, November 16). *5G subscriptions to reach half a billion in 2022.* Ericsson Mobility report [Press release]. http://mb.cision.com/Main/15448/2243795/660363.pdf

Hanlon, P. (2016, November 1). 'The New York Times' launches daily 360 VR news. *Forbes.* https://www.forbes.com/sites/patrickhanlon/2016/11/01/the-new-york-times-launches-daily-360-vr-news/#242e8f36226d

Iqbal, M. (2019). Twitch revenue and usage statistics. *Business of Apps*. Retrieved from https://www.businessofapps.com/data/twitch-statistics/

Kollewe, J. (2017, May 2). Google and Facebook bring in one-fifth of global ad revenue. *The Guardian*. https://www.theguardian.com/media/2017/may/02/google-and-facebook-bring-in-one-fifth-of-global-ad-revenue

Krashinsky, S. (2016, September 9). Specialized freelancers shaking up the traditional advertising business model. *The Globe and Mail*. https://www.theglobeandmail.com/report-on-business/industry-news/marketing/specialized-freelancers-shaking-up-the-traditional-advertising-business-model/article31777643/

Lindzon, J. (2016, August 23). Freelance work expanding to more sectors, report finds. *The Globe and Mail*. https://www.theglobeandmail.com/report-on-business/careers/career-advice/life-at-work/freelance-work-expanding-to-more-sectors-report-finds/article31519391/

Merwin, C. D., Sugiyama, M., Mubayi, P., Hari, T., Terry, H. P., & Duval, A. (2018, October 12). The world of games eSports: From wild west to mainstream. *Goldman Sachs*. https://www.goldmansachs.com/insights/pages/infographics/e-sports/report.pdf

Newzoo. (2019). *Global eSport Market Report*. Retrieved from https://newzoo.com/insights/trend-reports/newzoo-global-esports-market-report-2019-light-version/

Rideout, V. J., & Robb, M. B. (2019). *The commonsense census: Media use by tweens and teens*. Common Sense Media. https://www.commonsensemedia.org/sites/default/files/uploads/research/2019-census-8-to-18-full-report-updated.pdf

Rody, B. (2018). Big sports fans are big TV consumers: study. *Media in Canada*. https://mediaincanada.com/2018/10/12/big-sports-fans-are-big-tv-consumers-study/

Statista Digital Market Outlook (Canada). (2018). Individuals of any age who own at least one smartphone and use the smartphone(s) at least once per month. *Statista Digital Market*. https://www.statista.com/outlook/200/108/digital-media/canada#market-revenue

Taylor, H. (2018, February 14). Twitch surpasses CNN and MSNBC with record-breaking viewership. *Games Industry Biz*. Retrieved from https://www.gamesindustry.biz/articles/2018-02-14-twitch-surpasses-cnn-and-msnbc-with-record-breaking-viewership

The Kids & Family Reading Report, Canadian Edition. (2017). *The Kids & Family Reading Report*. www.scholastic.ca/readingreport/about.php

World Economic Forum. (2018). *Future of jobs report*. Retrieved from https://www.weforum.org/reports/the-future-of-jobs-report-2018

Wulf, T., Schneider, F. M., & Beckert, S. (2018). Watching players: An exploration of media enjoyment on Twitch. *Games and Culture*, *15*(3). doi:10.1177/1555412018788161

Compilation of References

Abraham, A., Sommerhalder, K., & Abel, T. (2009). Landscape and well-being: A scoping study on the health-promoting impact of outdoor environments. *International Journal of Public Health*, *55*(1), 59–69. doi:10.100700038-009-0069-z PMID:19768384

*Active*CITY Collective. (2020). *Playbook 2030: A guide to Building Canada's Most Liveable Region.* Retrieved from: https://www.activecityproject.org/

ActiveCITY Collective. (2020). *Playbook 2030: A Guide to Building Canada's Most Livable Region* (Rep.). https://www.activecityproject.org/

Adner, R. (2016). Ecosystem as Structure: An Actionable Construct for Strategy. *Journal of Management*, *43*(1), 39–58. doi:10.1177/0149206316678451

Adventure Travel Trade Association (ATTA). (2010). *Adventure tourism market report.* https://www.adventuretravel.biz/research/adventure-tourism-market-report-2010

AFP. (2020). When China faced down rampant soccer corruption. *Taipei Times*. Retrieved from https://www.taipeitimes.com/News/sport/archives/2020/05/28/2003737179

AGA. (2018). NBA & MLB could see combined $1.7 billion from legalized sports betting. *American Gaming Association*. Retrieved from https://www.americangaming.org/new/nba-mlb-could-see-combined-1-7-billion-from-legalized-sports-betting/

Ahn, S., & Fedewa, A. L. (2011). A meta-analysis of the relationship between children's physical activity and mental health. *Journal of Pediatric Psychology*, *36*(4), 385–397. doi:10.1093/jpepsy/jsq107 PMID:21227908

Aldana, S., & Pronk, N. (2001). Health promotion programs, modifiable health risks, and employee absenteeism. *Journal of Occupational and Environmental Medicine*, *43*(1), 36–46. doi:10.1097/00043764-200101000-00009 PMID:11201768

Alexander, C., & McDonald, C. (2014, June 9). Urban forests: The value of trees in the City of Toronto. *TD Economics*. https://www.td.com/document/PDF/economics/special/UrbanForests.pdf

Alonso, A. D., & O'Shea, M. (2012). You only get back what you put in. Perceptions of professional sport organizations as community anchors. *Community Development (Columbus, Ohio)*, *43*(5), 656–676. doi:10.1080/15575330.2011.645048

American Physical Society. (2004). Butterflies, tornadoes, and time travel. *APS*. https://www.aps.org/publications/apsnews/200406/butterfly-effect.cfmrlTTJASVimLiZ0o

Amin, N. H., McCullough, K. C., Mills, G. L., & Jones, H. (2016). The Impact and Functional Outcomes of Achilles Tendon Pathology in National Basketball Association Players. *Clinical Research on Foot & Ankle*, *4*(3), 1–6. doi:10.4172/2329-910X.1000205 PMID:29082269

Anagnostopoulos, C. (2011). Stakeholder management in Greek professional football: Identification and salience. *Soccer and Society*, *12*(2), 249–264. doi:10.1080/14660970.2011.548361

Andreff, W. (2019). Global criminal networking in sport: Online betting-related match fixing. In An Economic Roadmap to the Dark Side of Sport (pp. 1-18). Palgrave Pivots, Macmillan. doi:10.1007/978-3-030-28615-6_1

Armstrong, D. (2000). A survey of community gardens in upstate New York: Implications for health promotion and community development. *Health & Place*, *6*(4), 319–327. doi:10.1016/S1353-8292(00)00013-7 PMID:11027957

Associated Press. (2018). MLB strikes deal with MGM as legal gambling expands in US. *USA Today*. Retrieved from https://www.usatoday.com/story/sports/mlb/2018/11/27/mgm-resorts-is-mlbs-official-gaming-partner-after-nba-nhl/38627859/

Atlaoui, D., Pichot, V., Lacoste, L., Barale, F., Lacour, J. R., & Chatard, J. C. (2007). Heart rate variability, training variation and performance in elite swimmers. *International Journal of Sports Medicine*, *28*(05), 394–400. doi:10.1055-2006-924490 PMID:17111320

Aubry, R. L., Power, G. A., & Burr, J. F. (2018). An assessment of running power as a training metric for elite and recreational runners. *Journal of Strength and Conditioning Research*, *32*(8), 2258–2264. doi:10.1519/JSC.0000000000002650 PMID:29912073

Badenhausen, K. (2020, July 31). The world's most valuable sports teams 2020. *Forbes*. https://www.forbes.com/sites/kurtbadenhausen/2020/07/31/the-worlds-most-valuable-sports-teams-2020/?sh=29fc03093c74

Bakhshi, H., Freeman, A., & Higgs, P. (2012). *A dynamic mapping of the UK's creative industries*. Nesta. https://eprints.qut.edu.au/57251/1/57251.pdf

Ballouli, K. (2012). It's a whole new ballgame: How social media is changing sports. *Sport Management Review*, *15*(3), 381–382. doi:10.1016/j.smr.2012.02.008

Bankers Life Fieldhouse. (2020). Sustainability. *Bankers Life Fieldhouse*. https://www.bankerslifefieldhouse.com/sustainability

Barnfield, A. (2013). Soccer, broadcasting, and narrative: On televising a live soccer match. *Communication & Sport Journal*, *1*(14), 326–341. doi:10.1177/2167479513479107

Bath, P. A., & Morgan, K. (1999). Differential risk factor profiles for indoor and outdoor falls in older people living at home in Nottingham, UK. *European Journal of Epidemiology*, *15*(1), 65–73. doi:10.1023/A:1007531101765 PMID:10098998

Baumert, M., Brechtel, L., Lock, J., Hermsdorf, M., Wolff, R., Baier, V., & Voss, A. (2006). Heart rate variability, blood pressure variability, and baroreflex sensitivity in overtrained athletes. *Clinical Journal of Sport Medicine*, *16*(5), 412–417. doi:10.1097/01.jsm.0000244610.34594.07 PMID:17016118

BBC. (2019, October 16). Tokyo 2020: Olympic marathon and race walks set to move to Sapporo over heat fears. *BBC*. https://www.bbc.com/sport/olympics/50069413

Benson, L. C., Tait, T. J., Befus, K., Choi, J., Hillson, C., Stilling, C., Grewal, S., MacDonald, K., Pasanen, K., & Emery, C. A. (2020). Validation of a commercially available inertial measurement unit for recording jump load in youth basketball players. *Journal of Sports Sciences*, *38*(8), 928–936. doi:10.1080/02640414.2020.1737360 PMID:32138609

Berra, L. (2019). A major gamble: MLB embraces sports betting. *Baseball America*. Retrieved from https://www.baseballamerica.com/stories/a-major-gamble-mlb-hopes-legalized-sports-betting-will-engage-new-fans/

Betts, J. R. (1953). Sporting journalism in nineteenth-century American. *American Quarterly*, *5*(1), 39–56. doi:10.2307/3031289

Billat, V., Faina, M., Sardella, F., Marini, C., Fanton, F., Lupo, S., Faccini, P., de Angelis, M., Koralsztein, J. P., & Dalmonte, A. (1996). A comparison of time to exhaustion at VO2 max in élite cyclists, kayak paddlers, swimmers, and runners. *Ergonomics*, *39*(2), 267–277. doi:10.1080/00140139608964457 PMID:8851531

Billman, G. E. (2011). Heart rate variability - A historical perspective. *Frontiers in Physiology*, *2*(November), 1–13. doi:10.3389/fphys.2011.00086

Binde, P. (2007). Selling dreams – or causing nightmares? On gambling advertising and problem gambling. *Journal of Gambling Issues*, *20*(20), 167–191. doi:10.4309/jgi.2007.20.5

Bolus, N., Jeong, H.-K., Blaho, B. M., Safaei, M., Young, A., & Inan, O. (2020). Fit to Burst: Toward Noninvasive Estimation of Achilles Tendon Load Using Burst Vibrations. *IEEE Transactions on Biomedical Engineering*, 1. PMID:32746041

Bompa, T. O., & Buzzichelli, C. (2018). *Periodization-: theory and methodology of training*. Human kinetics.

Bontis, N., & Fitz-enz, J. (2002). Intellectual capital ROI: A causal map of human capital antecedents and consequents. *Journal of Intellectual Capital*, *3*(3), 223–247. doi:10.1108/14691930210435589

Bosquet, L., Merkari, S., & Arvisais, D. (2008). Is heart rate a convenient tool to monitor over-reaching? A systematic review of the literature (vol 42, pg 709, 2008). *British Journal of Sports Medicine*, *42*(12), 1016–1016.

Botek, M., McKune, A. J., Krejci, J., Stejskal, P., & Gaba, A. (2014). Change in performance in response to training load adjustment based on autonomic activity. *International Journal of Sports Medicine*, *35*(06), 482–488. PMID:24129989

Bourdieu, P. (1978). *Sport and social class.* International Social Science Council.

Bourdillon, N., Nilchian, M., & Millet, G. P. (2019). Photoplethysmography Detection of Overreaching. *Medicine and Science in Sports and Exercise, 51*(4), 701–707. doi:10.1249/MSS.0000000000001836 PMID:30407274

Bourdon, P. C., Cardinale, M., Murray, A., Gastin, P., Kellmann, M., Varley, M. C., Gabbett, T. J., Coutts, A. J., Burgess, D. J., Gregson, W., & Cable, N. T. (2017). Monitoring athlete training loads: Consensus statement. *International Journal of Sports Physiology and Performance, 12*(s2), 161–170. doi:10.1123/IJSPP.2017-0208 PMID:28463642

Boyle, R. (2006). Sports journalism: Context and Issues. *Sage (Atlanta, Ga.).*

Bradbury, S., & Kay, T. (2008). Stepping into community? The impact of youth sport volunteering on young people's social capital. In M. Nicholson & R. Hoye (Eds.), Sport and social capital (pp. 285–315). Elsevier Science & Technology.

Branhorst, C. (2020, March 20). COVID-19 impact: Sports and entertainment. *University of South Carolina.* https://www.sc.edu/uofsc/posts/2020/03/COVID-19_19_impact_regan_watanabe.php#.X-dPHelKh3k

Brennan, J. (2018). NHL Commissioner Bettman completes 180-degree turn on sports betting. *NJ Online Gambling.* Retrieved from https://www.njonlinegambling.com/nhl-bettman-embraces-sports-betting/

Briceno, T., & Schundler, G. (2015). Economic analysis of outdoor recreation in Washington State. *Earth Economics.* https://www.tre.wa.gov/wp-content/uploads/Willhite.pdf

Buchheit, M., Buchheit, M., Simpson, M., Simpson, M., Al Haddad, H., Al Haddad, H., Bourdon, P., Bourdon, P., Mendez-Villanueva, A., & Mendez-Villanueva, A. (2012). Monitoring changes in physical performance with heart rate measures in young soccer players. *European Journal of Applied Physiology, 112*(2), 711–723. doi:10.100700421-011-2014-0 PMID:21656232

Buckley, R. (2006). Adventure tourism research: A guide to the literature. *Tourism Recreation Research, 31*(2), 75–83. doi:10.1080/02508281.2006.11081265

Buckley, R. (2010). *Adventure tourism management.* Butterworth-Heinemann.

Buning, R. J., & Gibson, H. J. (2015). The evolution of active-sport-event travel careers. *Journal of Sport Management, 29*(5), 555–569. doi:10.1123/jsm.2014-0215

Bureau of Transport and Regional Economics. (2007). *Estimating urban traffic and congestion cost trends for Australian cities* [Working Paper 71]. Department of Transport and Regional Services. https://www.bitre.gov.au/publications/2007/files/wp_071.pdf

Burnett, C. (2016). Building social capital through an 'Active Community Club'. *International Review for the Sociology of Sport, 41*(3-4), 283–294. doi:10.1177/1012690207078381

Butler, R. (2020). In-stadium wagering could spark retail and mobile sports betting growth. *Action Network*. Retrieved from https://www.actionnetwork.com/general/sports-betting-news-stadium-wagering-capitol-one-arena-wrigley-field

Camomilla, V., Bergamini, E., Fantozzi, S., & Vannozzi, G. (2018). Trends supporting the in-field use of wearable inertial sensors for sport performance evaluation: A systematic review. *Sensors (Switzerland), 18*(3), 873. Advance online publication. doi:10.339018030873 PMID:29543747

Canadian Fitness and Lifestyle Research Institute. (2015). *Municipal Opportunities for Physical Activity: 2015 Survey of Physical Activity Opportunities in Canadian Communities*. Retrieved from:https://cflri.ca/sites/default/files/node/1578/files/2015%20Municipalities%20Bulletin%2012%20Financial%20assistance%20to%20support%20physical%20activity.pdf

Canadian Infrastructure Report Card. (2016). *Informing the Future* (Rep.). Retrieved from http://canadianinfrastructure.ca/downloads/Canadian_Infrastructure_Report_2016.pdf

Canadian Infrastructure Report Card. (2019). *Monitoring the State of Canada's Core Public Infrastructure* (Rep.). Retrieved from http://canadianinfrastructure.ca/downloads/canadian-infrastructure-report-card-2019.pdf

Canadian Parks and Recreation Association. (2014). *Pathways to Wellbeing: A Framework for Recreation in Canada*. Canadian Parks and Recreation Association. www.cpra.ca

Canadian Society for Exercise Physiology. (n.d.). *Canadian 24-Hour Movement Guidelines for Adults Aged 18-64 Years*. Retrieved from: www.csepguidelines.ca

Canadian Society for Exercise Physiology. (n.d.). *Canadian 24-Hour Movement Guidelines for Children and Youth*. Retrieved from: https://csepguidelines.ca/wp-content/themes/csep2017/pdf/Canadian24HourMovementGuidelines2016_2.pdf

Capgemini. (2021). *Emerging technologies in sports*. Capgemini Research.

Cassidy, R. (2013). Partial convergence. Social gaming and real money gambling. In R. Cassidy, A. Pisac, & C. Loussouarn (Eds.), *Qualitative research on gambling. Exploring the production and consumption of risk* (pp. 74–91). Routledge.

Celis-Morales, C. A., Lyall, D. M., Welsh, P., Anderson, J., Steell, L., Guo, Y., Maldonado, R., Mackay, D. F., Pell, J. P., Sattar, N., & Gill, J. M. R. (2017). Association between active commuting and incident cardiovascular disease, cancer, and mortality: Prospective cohort study. *BMJ (Clinical Research Ed.), 357*, j1456. doi:10.1136/bmj.j1456 PMID:28424154

Cerezuela-Espejo, V., Hernández-Belmonte, A., Courel-Ibáñez, J., Conesa-Ros, E., Mora-Rodríguez, R., & Pallarés, J. G. (2020). Are we ready to measure running power? Repeatability and concurrent validity of five commercial technologies. *European Journal of Sport Science, 0*(0), 1–10. doi:10.1080/17461391.2020.1748117 PMID:32212955

Chambers, R., Gabbett, T. J., Cole, M. H., & Beard, A. (2015). The Use of Wearable Microsensors to Quantify Sport-Specific Movements. *Sports Medicine (Auckland, N.Z.), 45*(7), 1065–1081. doi:10.100740279-015-0332-9 PMID:25834998

Chappelet, J. L. (2018). Beyond governance: The need to improve the regulation of international sport. *Sport in Society*, *21*(5), 724–734. doi:10.1080/17430437.2018.1401355

Chelladurai, P. (2009). *Managing organizations for sport and physical activity: A systems perspective* (3rd ed.). Holcomb Hathaway.

Chernova, Y. (2014). FanDuel raises $70 million as daily fantasy sports battle heats up. *Wall Street Journal*. Retrieved from https://www.wsj.com/articles/BL-VCDB-15379

Chidley-Hill, J. (2020). Hayley Wickenheiser begins personal protective equipment drive in Toronto. *CBC Sports*. https://www.cbc.ca/sports/hayley-wickenheiser-personal-protection-drive-toronto-1.5529933

Chodzko-Zajko, W. J. (1998). Physical activity and aging: implications for health and quality of life in older persons. *President's Council on Physical Fitness and Sports Research Digest*, *3*(4).

Christovich, A. (2020, September 18). Layoffs sweep college athletic departments nationwide. *Front Office Sports*. https://frontofficesports.com/layoffs-sweep-college-athletic-departments-nationwide/

Clarkson, M. E. (1995). A stakeholder framework for analyzing and evaluating corporate social performance. *Academy of Management Review*, *20*(1), 92–117. doi:10.5465/amr.1995.9503271994

Claussen, C. L., & Miller, L. K. (2001). The gambling industry and sports gambling: A stake in the game? *Journal of Sport Management*, *15*(4), 350–363. doi:10.1123/jsm.15.4.350

Clough, P., Houge Mackenzie, S., Mallabon, E., & Brymer, E. (2016). Adventurous physical activity environments: A mainstream intervention for mental health. *Sports Medicine (Auckland, N.Z.)*, *46*(7), 963–968. doi:10.100740279-016-0503-3 PMID:26895993

Coates, L., Shi, J., Rochester, L., Del Din, S., & Pantall, A. (2020). Entropy of real-world gait in parkinson's disease determined from wearable sensors as a digital marker of altered ambulatory behavior. *Sensors (Switzerland)*, *20*(9), 2631. Advance online publication. doi:10.339020092631 PMID:32380692

Cobb, D., Kercheval, B., & Sallee, B. (2020). College football schedule 2020: The 139 games already postponed or canceled due to COVID-19. *CBS Sports*. https://www.cbssports.com/college-football/news/college-football-schedule-2020-the-139-games-already-postponed-or-canceled-due-to-COVID-19

Colman, R., & Walker, S. (2004, November). *The cost of physical inactivity in British Columbia*. B.C. Ministry of Health Planning. http://gpiatlantic.org/pdf/health/inactivity-bc.pdf

Conference Board of Canada. (2008). *Valuing culture: Measuring and understanding Canada's creative economy*. https://www.creativecity.ca/database/files/library/valuingculture.pdf

Conn, D. (2019). Revealed: the 'dire consequences' of football's relationship with gambling. *The Guardian*. Retrieved from https://www.theguardian.com/football/2019/jan/10/football-gambling-dire-consequences-young-men-bet-new-study

Cortright, J. (2009). Walking the walk: How walkability raises home values in U.S. cities. *CEOs for Cities*. https://nacto.org/docs/usdg/walking_the_walk_cortright.pdf

Cortright, J. (2009, August 1). Walking the walk: How walkability raises home values in U.S. cities. *CEOs for Cities*. https://nacto.org/docs/usdg/walking_the_walk_cortright.pdf

Court Listener, D. (2007). Tschetschot v. Comm'r, 2007 T.C. Memo. 38. *Courtlistener.* Retrieved from https://www.courtlistener.com/opinion/4559086/tschetschot-v-commr/

Cunningham, G., & Rosenberg, C. (1997). Excise tax and occupational tax on wagering. *Internal Revenue Service*. Retrieved from https://www.irs.gov/pub/irs-tege/eotopice97.pdf

Davies, R. (2019). Half of Premier League clubs to have gambling sponsors for 2019-20 season. *The Guardian*. Retrieved from https://www.theguardian.com/football/2019/jul/19/half-of-premier-league-clubs-to-have-gambling-sponsors-for-201920

Davies, R. (2019b). Government under fire for failing to back mandatory betting levy. *The Guardian*. Retrieved from https://www.theguardian.com/business/2019/apr/25/ladbrokes-owner-proposes-ban-on-gambling-ads-linked-to-sport-gvc

Davis, A. (2010, March). *Value for money: An economic assessment of investment in walking and cycling*. Government Office for the South West. https://bikehub.ca/sites/default/files/valueformoneyaneconomicassessmentofinvestmentinw.pdf

De Knop, P. (1990). Sport for all and active tourism. *World Leisure & Recreation*, *32*(3), 30–36. doi:10.1080/10261133.1990.10559120

Delaney, L., & Keaney, E. (2005). Sport and social capital in the United Kingdom: Statistical evidence from national and international survey data. *Dublin. Economic and Social Research Institute and Institute for Public Policy Research*, *32*, 1–32.

Delkic, M. (2018). A supreme court decision that was a wild card. *The New York Times*. Retrieved from https://www.nytimes.com/2018/05/22/insider/supreme-court-sports-betting.html

Deloitte. (2018). *A whole new ball game: Navigating digital change in the sports industry*. Deloitte Development LLC.

Deloitte. (2021). New stakes in the game. Bill C-13 and unlocking opportunities through sports betting reform in Canada. *Deloitte*. Retrieved from https://www2.deloitte.com/content/dam/Deloitte/ca/Documents/consumer-business/ca-sports-betting-pov-en-aoda.pdf

Department of Digital. Culture, Media & Sport. (1998). *Creative Industries Mapping Documents 1998*. Retrieved from Government of UK website: https://www.gov.uk/government/publications/creative-industries-mapping-documents-1998

Department of Health, Physical Activity, Health Improvement and Protection. (2011). *Start active, stay active: A report on physical activity from the four home countries' Chief Medical Officers*. The Department of Health. https://assets.publishing.service.gov.uk/government/uploads/system/uploads/attachment_data/ file/830943/withdrawn_dh_128210.pdf

Department of Health, Physical Activity, Health Improvement and Protection. (2011, July). *Start active, stay active: A report on physical activity from the four home countries' Chief Medical Officers*. Retrieved from: https://assets.publishing.service.gov.uk/government/uploads/system/uploads/attachment_data/file/830943/withdrawn_dh_128210.pdf

DGOJ. (2016). Study on the prevalence, behavior and characteristics of gambling users in Spain. *Ministry of Finance and Public Administrations.* Retrieved from: https://www.ordenacionjuego.es/cmis/browser?id=workspace://SpacesStore/131754ec-1411-4fa5-b6dd-b85364aea75c

Dinges, D. F. (1995). An overview of sleepiness and accidents. *Journal of Sleep Research*, *4*(S2), 4–14. doi:10.1111/j.1365-2869.1995.tb00220.x PMID:10607205

Donahue, R., Parilla, J., & McDearman, B. (2018). *Rethinking Clusters Initiatives*. Brookings Institute.

Dooley, J., & Aguirre, C. (2018). Generation H: Healthy Living Drivers [PowerPoint slides]. *Vivo.* https://www.vivo.ca/research-innovation/projects/past-projects/healthy-living-school/

Dottori, M., Séguin, B., & O'Reilly, N. (2018). Public relations in strategic management: Strategizing in the communicative organization. *Journal of Professional Communication*, *5*(2), 59–98. doi:10.15173/jpc.v5i2.3749

Draper, K. (2018). NBA makes MGM Resorts International its first gambling partner. *The New York Times*. Retrieved from https://www.nytimes.com/2018/07/31/sports/nba-betting-mgm.html

Draper, K. (2020, November 19). M.L.S layoffs cut league staffs by 20 per cent. *New York Times*. https://www.nytimes.com/2020/11/19/sports/soccer/mls-layoffs.html

Dyer, J. H., & Singh, H. (1998). The Relational View: Cooperative Strategy and Sources of Interorganizational Competitive Advantage. *Academy of Management Review*, *23*(4), 660–679. doi:10.5465/amr.1998.1255632

Edelman. (2005) Edelman Trust Barometer 2005. *Edelman*. Retrieved from https://www.edelman.com/sites/g/files/aatuss191/files/2018-10/2005-Edelman-Trust-Barometer-Executive-Summary.pdf

Eden, S. (2020). From the archives: How former ref Tim Donaghy conspired to fix NBA games. *ESPN*. Retrieved from https://www.espn.com/nba/story/_/id/25980368/how-former-ref-tim-donaghy-conspired-fix-nba-games

Edwards, M. (2015). The role of sport in community capacity building: An examination of sport for development research and practice. *Sport Management Review*, *18*(1), 6–19. doi:10.1016/j.smr.2013.08.008

Eisingerich, A., Bell, S., & Tracey, P. (2010). How can clusters sustain performance? The role of network strength, network openness and environmental uncertainty. *Research Policy*, *39*(2), 239–253. doi:10.1016/j.respol.2009.12.007

Eley, D., & Kirk, D. (2010). Developing citizenship through sport: The impact of a sport-based volunteer programme on young sport leaders. *Sport Education and Society*, *7*(2), 151–166. doi:10.1080/1357332022000018841

Elmqvist, T., Setälä, H., Handel, S. N., Van der Ploeg, S., Aronson, J., Blignaut, J. N., Gómez-Baggethun, E., Nowak, D. J., Kronenberg, J., & De Groot, R. (2015). Benefits of restoring ecosystem services in urban areas. *Current Opinion in Environmental Sustainability*, *14*, 101–108. doi:10.1016/j.cosust.2015.05.001

Era, P., & Rantanen, T. (1997). Changes in physical capacity and sensory/psychomotor functions from 75 to 80 years of age and from 80 to 85 years of age—a longitudinal study. *Scandinavian Journal of Social Medicine. Supplementum*, *53*, 25–43. PMID:9241699

Ernst & Young, & espnW. (2015). *Where will you find your next leader? EY and espnW explore how sport advances women at every level.* https://wnywomensfoundation.org/app/uploads/2017/11/76.-Where-will-you-find-your-next-leader.pdf

ESPN. (2007). David Stern's Donaghy news conference transcript. *ESPN*. Retrieved from https://www.espn.com/nba/news/story?id=2947534

ESPN. (2020, May 1). Sudden vanishing of sports due to coronavirus will cost at least $12 billion, experts say. *ESPN*. https://www.espn.com/espn/otl/story/_/id/29110487/sudden-vanishing-sports-due-coronavirus-cost-least-12-billion-analysis-says

Eston, R. G., Davies, B. L., & Williams, J. G. (1987). Use of perceived effort ratings to control exercise intensity in young healthy adults. *European Journal of Applied Physiology and Occupational Physiology*, *56*(2), 222–224. doi:10.1007/BF00640648 PMID:3569229

Ettema, G., & Lorås, H. W. (2009). Efficiency in cycling: A review. *European Journal of Applied Physiology*, *106*(1), 1–14. doi:10.100700421-009-1008-7 PMID:19229554

Etzioni, A. (1964). *Modern Organizations*. Prentice-Hall.

Euklidiadas, M. (2020, May 18). Paris wants to become a "15-minute city". *Smart City Lab*. Retrieved from https://www.smartcitylab.com/blog/governance-finance/paris-15-minute-city/

Ewing, R., & Greene, W. (2003). *Travel and environmental implications of school siting*. U.S. Environmental Protection Agency. https://www.epa.gov/sites/production/files/2014-04/documents/school_travel.pdf

Faria, E. W., Parker, D. L., & Faria, I. E. (2005). The science of cycling: Physiology and training - part 1. *Sports Medicine (Auckland, N.Z.)*, *35*(4), 285–312. doi:10.2165/00007256-200535040-00002 PMID:15831059

Fassin, Y. (2009). The stakeholder model refined. *Journal of Business Ethics*, *84*(1), 113–135. doi:10.100710551-008-9677-4

Figueroa, A. (2019, June 26). Adventure tourism is the fastest-growing global niche. *Tripsavvy*. https://www.tripsavvy.com/the-adventure-tourism-boom-3252455

Finch, D. J., Legg, D., O' Reilly, N., Ribeiro, J., & Tombe, T. (2019, September 18). *Calgary's Regional Active Economy: An Exploratory Study of the Role of an Active Ecosystem in Generating Community Value.* ActiveCITY Collective.

Finch, D., Legg, D., O'Reilley, N., Ribeiro, J., & Tombe, T. (n.d.). *The active economy: Exploring the systematic value of sports, recreation and health & wellness.* ActiveCITY Collective.

Fisher, E. (2015). Daily fantasy pushes to continue growth streak. *Sports Business Journal.* Retrieved from https://www.sportsbusinessjournal.com/Journal/Issues/2015/03/16/Marketing-and-Sponsorship/Daily-fantasy.aspx

Fitzsimmons, P. (2009, September 19). I bet this is an issue. *The Sydney Morning Herald*, p. 14.

Fletcher, J. R., Esau, S. P., & Macintosh, B. R. (2009). Economy of running: beyond the measurement of oxygen uptake. *Journal of Applied Physiology, 107*(6), 1918–1922.

Fletcher, J. R., Asmussen, M. J., Nigg, S. R., MacIntosh, B. R., & Nigg, B. M. (2019). The effect of torsional shoe sole stiffness on knee moment and gross efficiency in cycling. *Journal of Sports Sciences, 37*(13), 1457–1463. Advance online publication. doi:10.1080/02640414.2019.1565650 PMID:30657013

Fletcher, J. R., & MacIntosh, B. R. (2017). Running economy from a muscle energetics perspective. *Frontiers in Physiology, 8*(JUN), 1–15. doi:10.3389/fphys.2017.00433 PMID:28690549

Florida, R. (2002). The economic geography of talent. *Annals of the Association of American Geographers, 92*(4), 743–755. doi:10.1111/1467-8306.00314

Florida, R. (2002). *The Rise of the Creative Class: And How It's Transforming Work, Leisure, Community, and Everyday Life*. Perseus Books.

Florida, R. (2006). The flight of the creative class: The new global competition for talent. *Liberal Education, 92*(3), 22–29.

Flutter. (2020). Flutter annual report and accounts 2019. *Flutter.* Retrieved from https://www.flutter.com/sites/paddy-power-betfair/files/Annual%20reports/2019-annual-report-28-02-20.pdf

Flynn, J. (2014, April 10). Pacers agree to stay in Indianapolis for $160 million in costs and arena upgrades. *Bleacher Report.* https://bleacherreport.com/articles/2025148-pacers-agree-to-stay-in-indianapolis-for-160m-in-costs-and-arena-upgrades

Fong, D. T.-P., Chan, Y.-Y., Hong, Y., Yung, P. S.-H., Fung, K.-Y., & Chan, K.-M. (2008). Estimating the complete ground reaction forces with pressure insoles in walking. *Journal of Biomechanics, 41*(11), 2597–2601. doi:10.1016/j.jbiomech.2008.05.007 PMID:18571656

Forrest, D. (2018). Match-Fixing. In M. Breuer & D. Forrest (Eds.), *The palgrave handbook on the economics of manipulation in sport.* Palgrave Macmillan. doi:10.1007/978-3-319-77389-6_6

Forrest, D., McHale, I., & McAuley, K. (2008). Risks to sport from the betting sector. In P. Rodriguez, S. Késenne, & J. Garcia (Eds.), *Threats to sports and sports participation* (pp. 139–160). Ediciones de la Universidad de Oviedo.

Forrest, D., & Simmons, R. (2003). Sport and gambling. *Oxford Review of Economic Policy, 19*(4), 598–611. doi:10.1093/oxrep/19.4.598

Foster, G., O'Reilly, N., & Dávila, A. (2016). *Sports Business Management: Decision Making Around the Globe*. Routledge. doi:10.4324/9781315687827

Foux, G. (2006). Consumer-generated media: Get your customers involved. *Brand Strategy,* 38-39.

Fox Sports. (n.d.). *Fox Bet.* Retrieved from https://www.foxbet.com

Fox, K. R., & Lindwall, M. (2014). Self-Esteem And Self-Perceptions in Sport And Exercise. *Routledge Companion to Sport And Exercise Psychology: Global Perspectives and Fundamental Concepts*, 34-48.

Frank, L. D., Engelke, P. O., & Schmid, T. L. (2003). *Health and community design: The impact of the built environment on physical activity*. Washington, DC: Island Press. https://books.google.ca/books?hl=en&lr=&id=fBi8BwAAQBAJ&oi=fnd&pg=PP3&dq=design and infrastructure impact on physical activity&ots=5ik5-AYf5b&sig=1WT10WO-iP-YBMwBh8iEdLdreNs#v=onepage&q=design and infrastructure impact on physical activity&f=false

Frank, L. D., Sallis, J. F., Conway, T. L., Chapman, J. E., Saelens, B. E., & Bachman, W. (2006). Many pathways from land use to health: Associations between neighborhood walkability and active transportation, body mass index, and air quality. *Journal of the American Planning Association, 72*(1), 75–87. doi:10.1080/01944360608976725

Freeman, E. R. (2004). The Stakeholder Approach Revisited. *Zeitschrift fur Wirtschafts -und Unternehmensethik, 5*(3), 220–241.

Freeman, E. R. (1984). *Strategic Management: A Stakeholder Approach*. Pitman.

Freeman, E. R. (1994). The Politics of Stakeholder Theory: Some Future Directions. *Business Ethics Quarterly*, *4*(4), 409–421. doi:10.2307/3857340

Friedman, T. (2017, August 2). Climate shifts aren't limited to the weather. *New York Times.* https://www.nytimes.com/2017/08/02/opinion/climate-change-technology-globalization-china.html

Friedman, M. T., & Mason, D. S. (2004). A stakeholder approach to understanding economic development decision making: Public subsidies for professional sport facilities. *Economic Development Quarterly, 18*(3), 236–254. doi:10.1177/0891242404265795

Friedman, M. T., Parent, M. M., & Mason, D. S. (2004). Building a framework for issues management in sport through stakeholder theory. *European Sport Management Quarterly*, *4*(3), 170–190. doi:10.1080/16184740408737475

Friend, K., & Ladd, G. (2009). Youth gambling advertising: A review of some of the lessons learned from tobacco control. *Drugs Education Prevention & Policy*, *16*(4), 283–297. doi:10.1080/09687630701838026

Gabbett, T. J., Nassis, G. P., Oetter, E., Pretorius, J., Johnston, N., Medina, D., Rodas, G., Myslinski, T., Howells, D., Beard, A., & Ryan, A. (2017). The athlete monitoring cycle: A practical guide to interpreting and applying training monitoring data. *British Journal of Sports Medicine*, *51*(20), 1451–1452. doi:10.1136/bjsports-2016-097298 PMID:28646100

Gainsbury, S., & Derevensky, J. (2008). An appraisal of the impact of the depiction of gambling in society on youth. *International Journal of Mental Health and Addiction*, *6*(4), 537–550. doi:10.100711469-008-9155-3

Gamblers Anonymous. (n.d.). About us. *Gamblers Anonymous*. http://www.gamblersanonymous.org/ga/content/about-us

Gammon, S., Ramshaw, G., & Wright, R. K. (2017). Theory in Sport Tourism: Some critical reflections. *Journal of Sport & Tourism*, *21*(2), 69–74. doi:10.1080/14775085.2017.1319515

Gammon, S., & Robinson, T. (2003). Sport and tourism: A conceptual framework. *Journal of Sport & Tourism*, *8*(1), 21–26. doi:10.1080/14775080306236

Garet, M., Tournaire, N., Roche, F., Laurent, R., Lacour, J. R., Barthélémy, J. C., & Pichot, V. (2004). Individual interdependence between nocturnal ANS activity and performance in swimmers. *Medicine and Science in Sports and Exercise*, *36*, 2112–2118. doi:10.1249/01.MSS.0000147588.28955.48 PMID:15570148

Garmin. (2020). *Are we still moving?* Available at: https://www.garmin.com/en-US/blog/general/the-effect-of-the-global-pandemic-on-active-lifestyles

Gerke, A., Desbordes, M., & Dickson, G. (2015). Towards a sport cluster model: The ocean racing cluster in Brittany. *European Sport Management Quarterly*, *15*(3), 343–363. doi:10.1080/16184742.2015.1019535

Gerke, A., & Pria, Y. (2018). Cluster Concept: Lessons for the Sport Sector? Toward a Two-Step Model of Sport Cluster Development Based on Socioeconomic Proximity. *Journal of Sport Management*, *32*(3), 211–226. doi:10.1123/jsm.2016-0338

Getz, D. (2003). Sport event tourism: planning, development, and marketing. In S. Hudson (Ed.), *Sport and Adventure Tourism*. Haworth Hospitality Press.

Getz, D. (2008). Event Tourism: Definition, evolution, and research. *Tourism Management*, *29*(3), 403–428. doi:10.1016/j.tourman.2007.07.017

Getz, D., & McConnell, A. (2011). Serious sport tourism and event travel careers. *Journal of Sport Management*, *25*(4), 326–338. doi:10.1123/jsm.25.4.326

Gibson, C. (2020). Report finds strides made in women's sports in past few years, but inequality remains. *ESPN*. https://www.espn.com/espn/story/_/id/28489077/report-finds-strides-made-women-sports-years-inequality-remains

Gibson, H. (1996). Thrill seeking vacations: A lifespan perspective. *Loisir et Societe. Society and Leisure*, *19*(2), 439–458. doi:10.1080/07053436.1996.10715527

Gibson, H. (1998a). Sport tourism: A critical analysis of research. *Sport Management Review*, *1*(1), 45–76. doi:10.1016/S1441-3523(98)70099-3

Gibson, H. (1998b). Active sport tourism: Who participates? *Leisure Studies*, *17*(2), 155–170. doi:10.1080/026143698375213

Gibson, H. (2004). Moving beyond the "what is and who" of sport tourism to understanding "why". *Journal of Sport & Tourism*, *9*(3), 247–265. doi:10.1080/1477508042000320232

Gibson, H. (2017). Commentary: Sport tourism and theory and some other developments: Some reflections. *Journal of Sport & Tourism*, *21*(2), 153–158. doi:10.1080/14775085.2017.1319514

Gibson, H., Attle, S., & Yiannakis, A. (1998). Segmenting the active sport tourist market: A life-span perspective. *Journal of Vacation Marketing*, *4*(1), 52–64. doi:10.1177/135676679800400105

Gillen, N. (2020, November 29). Tokyo 2020 estimate puts cost of Games postponement at $1.9 billion. *Inside the Games*. https://www.insidethegames.biz/articles/1101369/tokyo-2020-

Gilly, J. P., & Torre, A. (2000). *Dynamiques de proximité*. L'Harmattan.

Global Market Insights. (2019, June 27). *Wearable Medical Devices Market size worth around $87bn by 2025*. https://www.gminsights.com/pressrelease/wearable-medical-devices-market

Glyptis, S. A. (1982). *Sport and tourism in Western Europe*. British Travel Education Trust.

Golden, J. (n.d.). *Wearable fitness company Whoop raises $100m during pandemic*. CNBC Sports. Retrieved October 28, 2020, from https://www.cnbc.com/2020/10/28/wearable-fitness-company-whoop-raises-100m-during-pandemic-.html

Gordon, R., & Chapman, M. (2014). *Brand community and sports betting in Australia*. Victorian Responsible Gambling Foundation.

Gotschi, T. (2011). Costs and benefits of bicycling investments in Portland, Oregon. *Journal of Physical Activity & Health*, *1*(1), 49–58. doi:10.1123/jpah.8.s1.s49 PMID:21350262

Gouker, D. 2017. Daily fantasy sports - bill tracker. *Legal Sports Report*. Available at http://www.legalsportsreport.com/dfs-bill-tracker/

Granovetter, M. (2002). A theoretical agenda for economic sociology. Academic Press.

Grant, P. (2020). Football gambling links 'gone too far', ex-FA boss says. *BBC*. Retrieved from https://www.bbc.com/news/uk-51536687

Grant, D. (2001). Adventure Tourism: A Journey of the Mind. In L. Roberts & D. Hall (Eds.), *Rural Tourism and Recreation: Principles and Practice* (pp. 166–170). CABI Publishing.

Grant, J., & Kim, S. (2001). Demographic and Clinical Features of 131 Adult Pathological Gamblers. *The Journal of Clinical Psychiatry*, *62*(12), 957–962. doi:10.4088/JCP.v62n1207 PMID:11780876

Greenspan, R. (2020, January 24.) High-fiving robots are going to be very busy helpers at the 2020 Olympics. Here's everything they can do. *Time*. https://time.com/5763785/robots-2020-olympics/

Griffiths, M. (2014). Child and adolescent social gaming: What are the issues of concern? *Education for Health*, *32*, 9–12.

Grimes, W. (2005, December 14). The gladiators: History's most dangerous sport. *New York Times*. https://www.nytimes.com/2005/12/14/style/the-gladiators-historys-most-dangerous-sport.html

Gross, S., & Sand, M. (2019). Adventure tourism: A perspective paper. *Tourism Review*, *75*(1), 153–157. doi:10.1108/TR-06-2019-0211

Grubb, J. (2015). DraftKings brings its daily-fantasy sports empire to esports. *Venture Beat*. Retrieved from https://venturebeat.com/2015/09/23/draftkings-brings-its-daily-fantasy-sports-empire-to-esports/

Guo, J. Y., & Gandavarapu, S. (2009). An economic evaluation of health-promotive built environment changes. *Preventive Medicine*, *50*, 44–S49. doi:10.1016/j.ypmed.2009.08.019 PMID:19840817

Hakom. (n.d.). Wearables – The Big Data Machines. *Hakom*. Retrieved September 27, 2020, from https://www.hakom.at/en/news-detail/news/wearables-the-big-data-machines/

Hall, C. M. (1992). Adventure, sport, and health tourism. In B. Weiler & C. M. Hall (Eds.), *Special interest tourism* (pp. 141–158). Halsted Press.

Hamill, J., & Knutzen, K. M. (2006). *Biomechanical basis of human movement*. Lippincott Williams & Wilkins.

Harper, S. E., Roembke, R. A., Zunker, J. D., Thelen, D. G., & Adamczyk, P. G. (2020). Wearable Tendon Kinetics. *Sensors (Basel)*, *20*(17), 4805. Advance online publication. doi:10.339020174805 PMID:32858833

Harrison, J. S., & Freeman, R. E. (1999). Stakeholders, social responsibility, and performance: Empirical evidence and theoretical perspectives. *Academy of Management Journal*, *42*(5), 479–485.

Harris, R. (2005). When giving means taking: Public relations, sponsorship, and morally marginal donors. *Public Relations Review*, *31*(4), 486–491. doi:10.1016/j.pubrev.2005.08.006

Harwell, D. (2015). The rise of daily fantasy sports, online betting's newest empire. *Washington Post*. Retrieved from https://www.washingtonpost.com/news/wonk/wp/2015/07/28/how-daily-fantasy-sites-became-pro-sports-newest-addiction-machine/

Harwood, J. (1926). *Wristwatch and Other watch* (Patent No. 1,576,120).

Haugen, T., Säfvenbom, R., & Ommundsen, Y. (2011). Physical activity and global self-worth: The role of physical self-esteem indices and gender. *Mental Health and Physical Activity*, *4*(2), 49–56. doi:10.1016/j.mhpa.2011.07.001

Havens, K. L., Cohen, S. C., Pratt, K. A., & Sigward, S. M. (2018). Accelerations from wearable accelerometers reflect knee loading during running after anterior cruciate ligament reconstruction. *Clinical Biomechanics (Bristol, Avon)*, *58*, 57–61. doi:10.1016/j.clinbiomech.2018.07.007 PMID:30029071

Hawkins, B. (1998). Evening basketball leagues: The use of sport to reduce African American youth criminal activity. *International Sports Journal*, *2*(2), 68–77.

Hawley, J. A., & Noakes, T. D. (1992). Peak power output predicts maximal oxygen uptake and performance time in trained cyclists. *European Journal of Applied Physiology and Occupational Physiology*, *65*(1), 79–83. doi:10.1007/BF01466278 PMID:1505544

He, X., Lau, E. H. Y., Wu, P., Deng, X., Wang, J., Hao, X., Lau, Y. C., Wong, J. Y., Guan, Y., Tan, X., Mo, X., Chen, Y., Liao, B., Chen, W., Hu, F., Zhang, Q., Zhong, M., Wu, Y., Zhao, L., ... Leung, G. M. (2020). Temporal dynamics in viral shedding and transmissibility of COVID-19. *Nature Medicine*, *26*(5), 672–675. doi:10.103841591-020-0869-5 PMID:32296168

Higgs, P., Cunningham, S., & Bakhshi, H. (2008). *Beyond the creative industries: Mapping the creative economy in the United Kingdom*. Retrieved from https://eprints.qut.edu.au/00012166/01/beyond_creative_industries_report_NESTA.pdf

Higgs, P., & Cunningham, S. (2008). Creative Industries Mapping: Where have we come from and where are we going? *Creative Industries Journal*, *1*(1), 7–30. doi:10.1386/cij.1.1.7_1

Hinch, T., & Higham, J. (2011). *Sport tourism development* (2nd ed.). Channel View Publications.

Hing, N., Lamont, M., Vitartas, P., & Fink, E. (2015). Sports-embedded gambling promotions: A study of exposure, sports betting intention and problem gambling amongst adults. *International Journal of Mental Health and Addiction*, *13*(1), 115–135. doi:10.100711469-014-9519-9

Hopwood, M., Skinner, J., & Kitchin, P. (2010). *Sport public relations and communication*. Routledge.

House of Commons. (2021). *Bill C-13*. Retrieved from https://openparliament.ca/bills/43-2/C-13/

Howell, A. M., Kobayashi, T., Hayes, H. A., Foreman, K. B., & Bamberg, S. J. M. (2013). Kinetic gait analysis using a low-cost insole. *IEEE Transactions on Biomedical Engineering*, *60*(12), 3284–3290. doi:10.1109/TBME.2013.2250972 PMID:23475336

Howkins, J. (2002). The creative economy: How people make money from ideas. Penguin UK.; Urbancova, H. (2013). Competitive advantage achievement through innovation and knowledge. *Journal of Competitiveness*, *5*(1).

Hoye, R., Smith, A. C., Nicholson, M., & Stewart, B. (2015). *Sport Management: Principles and Applications*. Routledge. doi:10.4324/9781315733371

Hudson, S. (Ed.). (2003). *Sport and adventure tourism*. Haworth Hospitality Press.

Huggins, M. (2000). *Flat Racing and British Society 1790-1914: A social and economic history*. Frank Cass.

Hullfish, T. J., Qu, F., Stoeckl, B. D., Gebhard, P. M., Mauck, R. L., & Baxter, J. R. (2019). Measuring clinically relevant knee motion with a self-calibrated wearable sensor. *Journal of Biomechanics*, *89*, 105–109. doi:10.1016/j.jbiomech.2019.04.003 PMID:30981425

Humphreys, A. (2014). *Microadventures. Local discoveries for great escapes*. Harper Collins.

Humphreys, B. R. (2021). Legalized sports betting, VLT gambling, and state gambling revenues: Evidence from West Virginia. *Eastern Economic Journal*, *47*(1), 1–20. doi:10.105741302-020-00178-0 PMID:33424046

Hums, M. A., Wolff, E. A., & Siegfried, N. (2020, June 23). Making a case for athlete advocacy: Humanitarians, Olympism, and good governance. *Play the Game*. https://www.playthegame.org/news/comments/2020/1006_making-a-case-for-athlete-advocacy-humanitarians-olympism-and-good-governance/

Hums, M. A., Frederick, E., Pegararo, A., Siegfried, N., & Wolff, E. A. (2020a). What's in a name? Examining reactions to Major League Baseball's change from the Disabled List to the Injured List via Twitter. *Baseball Research Journal*, *49*(2), 22–32.

Hums, M. A., & MacLean, J. C. (2019). *Governance and policy in sport organizations* (4th ed.). Routledge.

Hurkmans, H. L. P., Bussmann, J. B. J., Benda, E., Verhaar, J. A. N., & Stam, H. J. (2006). Accuracy and repeatability of the Pedar Mobile system in long-term vertical force measurements. *Gait & Posture*, *23*(1), 118–125. doi:10.1016/j.gaitpost.2005.05.008 PMID:16260142

Hutchins, B., & Rowe, D. (2012). *Sport beyond television: The internet, digital media and the rise of networked media sport*. Routledge. doi:10.4324/9780203120415

Independent Sport Panel. (2009). The future of sport in Australia. *Independent Sport Panel*. http://www.health.gov.au/internet/main/publishing.nsf/Content/1DDA76A44E5F4DD4CA257671000E4C45/$File/Crawford_Report.pdf

Indiana Pacers. (2019, April 12). CIB approves new 25-year agreement with Pacers Sports Entertainment. *Indiana Pacers*. https://www.nba.com/pacers/news/cib-approves-new-25-year-agreement-pacers-sports-entertainment

Indiana Pacers. (2020). Community relations – Health and wellness. *Indiana Pacers*. https://www.nba.com/pacers/community-relations-health-and-wellness

Informetrics. (2020). Queenstown Lake District Economic Profile. *Informetrics*. https://ecoprofile.infometrics.co.nz/queenstown-lakes+district

Innovation, Science and Economic Development Canada. (2018). *Superclusters in Canada*. Retrieved from Government of Canada website: https://www.ic.gc.ca/eic/site/093.nsf/eng/00017.html#:~:text=Clusters%20are%20dense%20area%20of,secondary%20and%20other%20research%20institutions

INRIX. (2020). Traffic congestion cost UK motorists over £37.7 billion in 2017. *INRIX*. https://inrix.com/press-releases/scorecard-2017-uk/

Institute of Leisure and Amenity Management (ILAM). (1999). *The Contribution of the Arts and Sport to Neighbourhood Renewal and Reducing Social Inclusion*. ILAM.

Internal Revenue Service. (2020). Memorandum no. AM 202042015. *Internal Revenue Service*. Retrieved from https://www.irs.gov/pub/irs-wd/202042015.pdf

International Data Corporation. (2020). *Worldwide Quarterly Wearable Device Tracker*. International Data Corporation. https://www.idc.com/tracker/showproductinfo.jsp?prod_id=962

International Sport and Culture Association & Centre for Economics and Business Research. (2015). *The economic cost of physical inactivity in Europe*. International Sport and Culture Association, & Centre for Economics and Business Research.

International Union for Health Promotion and Education. (2010). *Promoting Health in School from Evidence to Action*. Retrieved from: https://www.iuhpe.org/index.php/en/iuhpe-thematic-resources/298-on-school-health

IOC. (2017). Beijing launches global recruitment programme for volunteers. *IOC*. https://www.olympic.org/news/beijing-2022-launches-global-recruitment-programme-for-games-volunteers

IOC. (2020a). How the IOC funds a better world through sport. *IOC*. https://www.olympic.org/funding

IOC. (2020b). Olympic marketing fact file 2020. *IOC*. https://stillmed.olympic.org/media/Document%20Library/OlympicOrg/Documents/IOC-Marketing-and-Broadcasting-General-Files/Olympic-Marketing-Fact-File.pdf

Isadore, C. (2018). NFL could pocket billions from coming boom in sports gambling. *CNN*. Retrieved from https://money.cnn.com/2018/09/05/news/companies/nfl-sports-gambling-revenue/index.html

Issurin, V. B. (2010). New horizons for the methodology and physiology of training periodization. *Sports Medicine (Auckland, N.Z.)*, *40*(3), 189–206. doi:10.2165/11319770-000000000-00000 PMID:20199119

IUCN. (2017, March 10). The World Now Protects 15 per cent of Its Land, but Crucial Biodiversity Zones Left Out. *IUCN*. Retrieved from https://www.iucn.org/news/secretariat/201609/world-now-protects-15-its-land-crucial-biodiversity-zones-left-out

Jaén-Carrillo, D., Roche-Seruendo, L. E., Cartón-Llorente, A., Ramírez-Campillo, R., & García-Pinillos, F. (2020). Mechanical power in endurance running: A scoping review on sensors for power output estimation during running. *Sensors (Switzerland)*, *20*(22), 1–20. doi:10.339020226482 PMID:33202809

Jamieson, L. M., & Ross, C. M. (2007). Research update: Using recreation to curb extremism. *Parks & Recreation*, *42*(2), 26.

Janssen, I. (2012). Healthcare costs of physical inactivity in Canadian adults. *Applied Physiology, Nutrition, and Metabolism*, *37*(4), 803–806. doi:10.1139/h2012-061 PMID:22667697

Johansson, D., Malmgren, K., & Alt Murphy, M. (2018). Wearable sensors for clinical applications in epilepsy, Parkinson's disease, and stroke: A mixed-methods systematic review. *Journal of Neurology*, *265*(8), 1740–1752. doi:10.100700415-018-8786-y PMID:29427026

Johnson, C., Dowd, T. J., & Ridgeway, C. L. (2006). Legitimacy as a social process. *Annual Review of Sociology*, *32*(1), 53–79. doi:10.1146/annurev.soc.32.061604.123101

Johnson, G., Whittington, R., Scholes, K., Angwin, D., & Regner, P. (2014). *Exploring Strategy*. Pearson Education.

Jones, D. (2006). The representation of female athletes in online images of successive Olympic Games. *Pacific Journalism Review*, *12*(1), 108–129. doi:10.24135/pjr.v12i1.848

Kane, M. J., & Tucker, H. (2004). Adventure tourism: The freedom to play with reality. *Tourist Studies*, *4*(3), 217–234. doi:10.1177/1468797604057323

Kaplanidou, K., & Gibson, H. (2010). Predicting behavioral intentions of active event sport tourists: The case of a small-scale recurring sports event. *Journal of Sport & Tourism*, *15*(2), 163–179. doi:10.1080/14775085.2010.498261

Kaplan, R. S., & Norton, D. P. (2005). The balanced scorecard: Measures that drive performance. *Harvard Business Review*, *83*(7), 172. PMID:10119714

Kaplan, R. S., & Norton, D. P. (2007). Using the balanced scorecard as a strategic management system. *Harvard Business Review*, *85*, 7–8.

Karatsidis, A., Bellusci, G., Schepers, H. M., de Zee, M., Andersen, M. S., & Veltink, P. H. (2017). Estimation of ground reaction forces and moments during gait using only inertial motion capture. *Sensors (Switzerland)*, *17*(1), 75. Advance online publication. doi:10.339017010075 PMID:28042857

Karen, L. (2020). *Fit Cities: My Quest to Improve the World's Health and Wellness—Including Yours*. Penguin Random House Canada.

Kargün, M., Ağaoğlu, Y. S., & Kaya, M. (2020). The economics of sports betting. *European Journal of Physical Education and Sport Science*. doi:10.5281/zenodo.3829624

Kennelly, M., & Toohey, K. (2014). Strategic alliances in sport tourism: National sport organizations and sport tour operators. *Sport Management Review*, *17*(4), 407–418. doi:10.1016/j.smr.2014.01.001

Keough, N., Morrison, B., & Lee, C. (2020, May 27). State of our city 2020: An urgent call for a just transition. *Sustainable Calgary.* https://static1.squarespace.com/static/5ab716b9ee1759b04ca2703e/t/ 5ecd551002f4af1d18d76785/1590514966826/SustainableCalgary_SOOC2020.pdf

Kerber, R. (2019). Online sports betting sites score as NFL season gets underway. *Reuters.* Retrieved from https://www.reuters.com/article/us-usa-gambling-nfl/online-sports-betting-sites-score-as-nfl-season-gets-under-way-idUSKCN1VU2AZ

Kesavan, R., Bernacchi, M. D., & Mascarenhas, O. A. J. (2013). Word of mouse: CSR communication and the social media. *International Management Review*, *9*(1), 58–66.

Ketels, C. H., & Memedovic, O. (2008). From clusters to cluster-based economic development. *International Journal of Technological Learning, Innovation and Development*, *1*(3), 375–392.

Kilgore, A. (2015). Daily fantasy sports web sites find riches in internet gaming law loophole. *Washington Post.* Retrieved from https://www.washingtonpost.com/sports/daily-fantasy-sports-web-sites-find-riches-in-internet-gaming-law-loophole/2015/03/27/92988444-d172-11e4-a62f-ee745911a4ff_story.html

Kilpatrick, D. (2010). *Definitions of public policy and law.* Retrieved from https://www.musc.edu/vawprevention/policy/definition.shtml

King, A., Huseynli, G., & MacGibbon, N. (2018). *Wellbeing frameworks for the Treasury* (No. 18/01). New Zealand Treasury Discussion Paper.

King, A., Huseynli, G., & MacGibbon, N. (2018). *Wellbeing frameworks for the Treasury.* New Zealand Treasury.

Klein, D. (2020, March 31). Indy Parks playgrounds, sport courts closed to enforce social distancing. *WISH-TV.* https://www.wishtv.com/news/local-news/indy-parks-playgrounds-sports-courts-closed-to-enforce-social-distancing/

Koenig, J., Jarczok, M. N., Wasner, M., Hillecke, T. K., & Thayer, J. F. (2014). Heart rate variability and swimming. *Sports Medicine (Auckland, N.Z.)*, *44*(10), 1377–1391. doi:10.100740279-014-0211-9 PMID:24958562

Kram, R., & Taylor, C. R. (1990). Energetics of running: A new perspective. *Nature*, *346*(6281), 265–267. doi:10.1038/346265a0 PMID:2374590

Kuhlman, R. (2010). *Helping Johnny walk to school: Policy recommendations for removing barriers to community-centered schools.* National Trust for Historic Preservation. http://www.bestfacilities.org/best-home/docuploads/pub/214_helping-johnnywalk-to-school.pdf

Kuhlman, R. (2010). *Helping Johnny walk to school: Policy recommendations for removing barriers to community-centered schools.* National Trust for Historic Preservation. http://www.bestfacilities.org/best-home/docuploads/pub/214_helping-johnny-walk-to-school.pdf

Kuipers, H., & Keizer, H. A. (1988). Overtraining in elite athletes. *Sports Medicine (Auckland, N.Z.)*, *6*(2), 79–92. doi:10.2165/00007256-198806020-00003 PMID:3062735

Kurian, S., Sinha, S., & Nanda, N. (2019). Sports and betting: A media intervention. *Journal of Critical Reviews*, *6*(6), 84–88. doi:10.22159/jcr.06.06.12

Kurtzman, J., & Zauhar, J. (1997). A wave in time – the sports tourism phenomena. *Journal of Sport & Tourism*, *8*(1), 35–47. doi:10.1080/14775080306239

Laing, J., & Frost, W. (2014). *Explorer travellers and adventure tourism.* Channel View Publications. doi:10.21832/9781845414597

Lamont, M., Hing, N., & Gainsbury, S. (2011). Gambling on sport sponsorship: A conceptual framework for research and regulatory review. *Sport Management Review*, *14*(3), 246–257. doi:10.1016/j.smr.2011.04.004

Lamont, M., & McKay, J. (2012). Intimations of postmodernity in sports tourism at the Tour de France. *Journal of Sport & Tourism*, *17*(4), 313–331. doi:10.1080/14775085.2012.760935

Landler, M. (2005). Germany still consumed by a scandal. *New York Times.* Retrieved from https://www.nytimes.com/2005/03/23/sports/soccer/germany-still-consumed-by-a-scandal.html

Lawlor, D. A., & Hopker, S. W. (2001). *The effectiveness of exercise as an intervention in the management of depression: Systematic review and meta-regression analysis of randomised controlled trials.* doi:10.1136/bmj.322.7289.763

Lawlor, E. (2014). The pedestrian pound: The business case for better streets and places. *Living Streets.* https://www.livingstreets.org.uk/media/3890/pedestrian-pound-2018.pdf

Lee, H., Lemanski, J., & Jun, J. (2008). Role of gambling media exposure in influencing trajectories among college students. *Journal of Gambling Studies*, *1*(1), 25–37. doi:10.100710899-007-9078-0 PMID:17901930

Lee, I. M., Shiroma, E. J., Lobelo, F., Puska, P., Blair, S. N., & Katzmarzyk, P. T.Lancet Physical Activity Series Working Group. (2012). Effect of physical inactivity on major non-communicable diseases worldwide: An analysis of burden of disease and life expectancy. *Lancet*, *380*(9838), 219–229. doi:10.1016/S0140-6736(12)61031-9 PMID:22818936

Legal Sports Report. (2020). NBA betting 2020. *Legal Sports Report.* https://www.legalsportsreport.com/sports-betting/nba/

Legalsportsreport (n.d.a). Esports betting – overview of the esports gambling vertical. *Legalsportsreport.* Retrieved from https://www.legalsportsreport.com/esports-betting/#:~:text=Esports%20gambling%3A%20Popular%20games%201%20Sports%20betting.%20Sports,3%20Jackpot%20games.%20...%204%20Casino-style%20games.%20

Legalsportsreport. (n.d.b). US sportsbook and casino team sponsorship tracker. *Legalsportsreport*. Retrieved from https://www.legalsportsreport.com/sports-betting-deals/

Legg, D., Emery, C., Konopaki, J., Black, J., Duggan, J., Booke, J., Martin, T., Watson, C., Le May Doan, C., & Swett, C. (2020). Calgary Adapted Hub Lead Assessment and Recommendations Report. *Vivo*. https://ncsra.sharepoint.com/:w:/s/migration/EY7KLW6oiBhIm7H8oN3vr5QB4RyRhat97dvhvy6z9RYcdQ?e=mP1Btr

Lehmann, M., Foster, C., & Keul, J. (1993). Overtraining in endurance athletes: a brief review. Med Sci Sports Exerc., 25(7), 854–862. doi:10.1249/00005768-199307000-00015

Leyden, K. M. (2003). Social capital and the built environment: The importance of walkable neighborhoods. *American Journal of Public Health*, *93*(9), 1546–1551. doi:10.2105/AJPH.93.9.1546 PMID:12948978

Lindsay, O. R., & Fletcher, J. R. (2020). Defining low, medium, and high training loads in men's volleyball using a combination of jump count and jump height. *Proceedings of the Canadian Society for Exercise Physiology Annual General Meeting*, S307.

Liptak, A., & Draper, K. (2018). Supreme Court Ruling Favors Sports betting. *The New York Times*. Retrieved from https://www.nytimes.com/2018/05/14/us/politics/supreme-court-sports-betting-new-jersey.html

Li, X., Dunn, J., Salins, D., Zhou, G., Zhou, W., Schüssler-Fiorenza Rose, S. M., Perelman, D., Colbert, E., Runge, R., Rego, S., Sonecha, R., Datta, S., McLaughlin, T., & Snyder, M. P. (2017). Digital Health: Tracking Physiomes and Activity Using Wearable Biosensors Reveals Useful Health-Related Information. *PLoS Biology*, *15*(1), e2001402. Advance online publication. doi:10.1371/journal.pbio.2001402 PMID:28081144

Lock, S. (2020, March 31). *Tourism worldwide – statistics and facts*. https://www.statista.com/topics/962/global-tourism/

Lockwood, R. I. (2008). The best interests of the league: Referee betting scandal brings commissioner authority and collective bargaining back to the frontcourt in the NBA. *Sports Law eJournal*, *15*, 137.

Lopez-Gonzalez, H., & Griffiths, M. D. (2016). Is European online gambling regulation adequately addressing in-play betting advertising? *Gaming Law Review and Economics*, *20*(6), 495–503. doi:10.1089/glre.2016.2064

Lopez-Gonzalez, H., & Griffiths, M. D. (2018). Understanding the convergence of markets in online sports betting. *International Review for the Sociology of Sport*, *53*(7), 807–823. doi:10.1177/1012690216680602

Lopez-Gonzalez, H., Guerrero-Sole, F., & Griffiths, M. D. (2017). A content analysis of how 'normal' sports betting behaviour is represented in gambling advertising. *Addiction Research and Theory*. Advance online publication. doi:10.1080/16066359.2017.1353082

Lopez-Gonzalez, H., & Tulloch, C. D. (2015). Enhancing media sport consumption: Online gambling in European football. *Media International Australia*, *155*(1), 130–139. doi:10.1177/1329878X1515500115

Lu, G., Yang, F., Taylor, J. A., & Stein, J. F. (2009). A comparison of photoplethysmography and ECG recording to analyze heart rate variability in healthy subjects. *Journal of Medical Engineering & Technology*, *33*(8), 634–641. doi:10.3109/03091900903150998 PMID:19848857

Luo, M. M., Chen, J., Ching, R. K. H., & Liu, C. (2011). An examination of the effects of virtual experiential marketing on online customer intentions and loyalty. *Service Industries Journal*, *31*(13), 2163–2191. doi:10.1080/02642069.2010.503885

Luongo, C. (2020). ESI gambling report: Esports betting, a global lifeline for operators. *Esports Insider*. Retrieved from https://esportsinsider.com/2020/04/esi-gambling-report-esports-betting/

Lupton, D. (2016). *The Quantified Self.* Polity Press.

MacDonald, K., Bahr, R., Baltich, J., Whittaker, J. L., & Meeuwisse, W. H. (2017). Validation of an inertial measurement unit for the measurement of jump count and height. *Physical Therapy in Sport*, *25*, 15–19. doi:10.1016/j.ptsp.2016.12.001 PMID:28254580

Magowan, A. (2020). Gambling in football: Call on Prime Minister to ban betting sponsorship. *BBC*. Retrieved from https://www.bbc.com/sport/football/51638731

Malatests & Associates Ltd. (2014). *2014 British Columbia Problem Gambling Prevalence Study*. Victoria, Canada: Gaming policy and enforcement branch, Ministry of Finance. Retrieved from https://www2.gov.bc.ca/assets/gov/sports-recreation-arts-and-culture/gambling/gambling-in-bc/reports/rpt-rg-prevalence-study-2014.pdf

Maller, C. J., Townsend, M., St. Leger, L., Henderson-Wilson, C., Pryor, A., Prosser, L., & Moore, M. (2008). Healthy parks healthy people: The health benefits of contact with nature in a park context. *Parks Stewardship Forum, 26*(2).

Manuel, D. (2016). *A $4.9 billion decrease in health care expenditure*. Institute for Clinical Evaluative Sciences.

Marsden Jacob Associates. (2018, March 1). Active impacts: The economic impacts of active recreation in Victoria. *Sport and Recreation Victoria.* https://sport.vic.gov.au/__data/assets/pdf_file/ 0026/56537/the20economic20impacts20of20active20recreation20in20victoria_0.pdf

Matijevich, E. S., Branscombe, L. M., Scott, L. R., & Zelik, K. E. (2019). Ground reaction force metrics are not strongly correlated with tibial bone load when running across speeds and slopes: Implications for science, sport, and wearable tech. *PLoS One*, *14*(1), e0210000. Advance online publication. doi:10.1371/journal.pone.0210000 PMID:30653510

Matijevich, E. S., Scott, L. R., Volgyesi, P., Derry, K. H., & Zelik, K. E. (2020). Combining wearable sensor signals, machine learning and biomechanics to estimate tibial bone force and damage during running. *Human Movement Science*, *74*, 102690. Advance online publication. doi:10.1016/j.humov.2020.102690 PMID:33132194

McGee, D. (2020). On the normalisation of online sports gambling among young adult men in the UK: A public health perspective. *Public Health, 184*, 89–94. Advance online publication. doi:10.1016/j.puhe.2020.04.018 PMID:32546295

McMullan, J. L., & Miller, D. (2008). All in! The commercial advertising of offshore gambling on television. *Journal of Gambling Issues*, (22), 230–251. doi:10.4309/jgi.2008.22.6

McMullan, J. L., & Miller, D. (2010). Advertising the "new fun-tier": Selling casinos to consumers. *International Journal of Mental Health and Addiction, 8*(1), 35–50. doi:10.100711469-009-9201-9

Meikle, G., & Young, S. (2011). *Media convergence: Networked digital media in everyday life*. Red Globe Press.

Mercedes Benz Stadium. (2020). Health and safety protocols. *Mercedes Benz Stadium.* https://mercedesbenzstadium.com/health-safety/

Miles, L., & Shipway, R. (2020). Exploring the COVID-19 Pandemic as a Catalyst for Stimulating Future Research Agendas for Managing Crises and Disasters at International Sport Events. *Event Management, 24*(4), 537–552. doi:10.3727/152599519X15506259856688

Miller, D., Capodilupo, J., Lastella, M., Sargent, C., Roach, G., Lee, V., & Capodilupo, E. (2020). *Analyzing changes in respiratory rate to predict the risk of COVID-19 infection*. MedRxiv., doi:10.1101/2020.06.18.20131417

Milner, L., Hing, N., Vitartas, P., & Lamont, M. (2013). Embedded gambling promotion in Australian football broadcasts: An exploratory study. *Communication. Política y Cultura, 46*(2), 177–198.

Milton, J. (2017). History of sport betting. *BigonSports*. Retrieved from https://www.bigonsports.com/history-of-sports-betting/

Ministry of Health. (2019). *Annual Data Explorer 2018/19: New Zealand Health Survey* [Data File]. https://minhealthnz.shinyapps.io/nz-health-survey-2018-19-annual-data-explorer/

Minnesota Public Radio. (2020). College athletic departments cut pay, staff, and teams because of COVID-19. *Minnesota Public Radio.* https://www.marketplace.org/2020/10/19/college-athletics-departments-cut-pay-staff-and-teams-because-of-covid/

Mishra, T., Wang, M., Metwally, A. A., Bogu, G. K., Brooks, A. W., Bahmani, A., Alavi, A., Celli, A., Higgs, E., Dagan-Rosenfeld, O., Fay, B., Kirkpatrick, S., Kellogg, R., Gibson, M., Wang, T., Hunting, E. M., Mamic, P., Ganz, A. B., Rolnik, B., ... Snyder, M. P. (2020). Pre-symptomatic detection of COVID-19 from smartwatch data. *Nature Biomedical Engineering, 4*(12), 1208–1220. Advance online publication. doi:10.103841551-020-00640-6 PMID:33208926

Mitchel, J. (2021). U.S. household income, savings rose at end of last year. *Wall Street Journal.* Retrieved from https://www.wsj.com/articles/consumer-spending-personal-income-coronavirus-december-2020-11611873351

Mitchell, R. K., Agle, B. R., & Wood, D. J. (1997). Toward a Theory of Stakeholder Identification and Salience: Defining the Principle of Who and What Really Counts. *Academy of Management Review*, *22*(4), 853–886. doi:10.5465/amr.1997.9711022105

MLS. (2019a). MLS announces multi-year gaming partnership with MGM Resorts International. *Major League Soccer*. Retrieved from https://www.mlssoccer.com/post/2019/03/19/mls-announces-multi-year-gaming-partnership-mgm-resorts-international

MLS. (2019b). MLS opens up commercial sponsorships to sports betting, spirits categories. *Major League Soccer*. Retrieved from https://www.mlssoccer.com/post/2019/06/26/mls-opens-commercial-sponsorships-sports-betting-spirits-categories

Moir, G. L. (2008). Three different methods of calculating vertical jump height from force platform data in men and women. *Measurement in Physical Education and Exercise Science*, *12*(4), 207–218. doi:10.1080/10913670802349766

Mooney, R., Corley, G., Godfrey, A., Quinlan, L. R., & ÓLaighin, G. (2015). Inertial sensor technology for elite swimming performance analysis: A systematic review. *Sensors (Basel)*, *16*(1), 18. doi:10.339016010018 PMID:26712760

Moore, J. F. (1993). Predators and prey: A new ecology of competition. *Harvard Business Review*, *71*(3), 75–86. PMID:10126156

Moore, S. A., Faulkner, G., Rhodes, R. E., Brussoni, M., Chulak-Bozzer, T., Ferguson, L. J., Mitra, R., O'Reilly, N., Spence, J. C., Vanderloo, L. M., & Tremblay, M. S. (2020). Impact of the COVID-19 virus outbreak on movement and play behaviours of Canadian children and youth: A national survey. *The International Journal of Behavioral Nutrition and Physical Activity*, *17*(1), 1–11. doi:10.118612966-020-00987-8 PMID:32631350

Morgan, J. P. (2020, May 1). Media consumption in the age of COVID-19. *JP Morgan*. https://www.jpmorgan.com/insights/research/media-consumption

Moritz, B. P. (2017). The history of sports journalism (Part 1). *Sports Media Guy*. https://www.sportsmediaguy.com/blog/2017/5/9/the-history-of-sports-journalism-part-1-of-3

Mourot, L., Bouhaddi, M., Tordi, N., Rouillon, J. D., & Regnard, J. (2004). Short- and long-term effects of a single bout of exercise on heart rate variability: Comparison between constant and interval training exercises. *European Journal of Applied Physiology*, *92*(4-5), 508–517. doi:10.100700421-004-1119-0 PMID:15461995

Muller, T., & Cleaver, M. (2000). Targeting the CANZUS baby boomer explorer and adventure segments. *Journal of Vacation Marketing*, *6*(2), 154–169. doi:10.1177/135676670000600206

Mullin, B., Hardy, S., & Sutton, W. (2014). *Sport marketing* (4th ed.). Human Kinetics.

Murfree, J. R., & Moorman, A. M. (2020, May). *An examination and analysis of Division I football game contracts: Legal implications of game cancellations due to extreme weather events* [Conference session]. North American Society for Sport Management Conference, San Diego, CA.

Mutrie, N. (2000). The relationship between physical activity and clinically defined depression. In S. J. H. Biddle, K. R. Fox, & S. H. Boutcher (Eds.), *Physical activity and psychological prosperity* (pp. 46–62). Routledge.

Nachman, C., & Bennett, D. (2011). 14 innovations that changed sports broadcasting forever. *Business Insider.* https://www.businessinsider.com/evolution-how-we-watch-sports-2011-4

National Basketball Association. (2018). MGM Resorts International becomes official gaming partner of NBA. *National Basketball Association.* Retrieved from https://www.nba.com/news/mgm-resorts-international-becomes-official-gaming-partner-nba-official-release?collection=news

National Recreation and Park Association. (n.d.). *Synopsis of 2010 research papers: The key benefits.* https://www.nrpa.org/uploadedFiles/nrpa.org/Publications_and_Research/Research/Papers/Synopsis-of-Research-Papers.pdf

National Recreation and Park Association. (n.d.). *Synopsis of 2010 research papers: The key benefits.* Retrieved from: https://www.nrpa.org/uploadedFiles/nrpa.org/Publications_and_Research/Research/Papers/Synopsis-of-Research-Papers.pdf

NBA Media Ventures. (2020). Local TV and radio listings. *National Basketball Association.* https://www.nba.com/pacers/2020-21-local-tv-and-radio-listings

NBA Media Ventures. (2020). Sponsorships. *National Basketball Association.* https://www.nba.com/pacers/team-sponsorships

NCAA. (n.d.). Finances of intercollegiate athletics. *NCAA.* https://www.ncaa.org/about/resources/research/finances-intercollegiate-athletics

NCAA. (n.d.). Sports Wagering. *NCAA.* Retrieved from https://www.ncaa.org/enforcement/sports-wagering

Ng'etich, E. K., & Auka, D. O. (2019). Influence of advertising on consumer purchase decision of sport betting: A case study of students in Nakuru Town university campuses, Kenya. *International Journal of Business Management and Finance, 3*(2).

Novy-Williams, E. (2018). NBA makes deal with MGM for betting, first for a U.S. league. *Bloomberg.* Retrieved from https://www.bloomberg.com/news/articles/2018-07-31/nba-partners-with-mgm-for-betting-a-first-for-a-u-s-pro-league?sref=2WOTxT1z

Novy-Williams, E. (2018b). If sports betting's going to be legal, major leagues want a cut. *Bloomberg.* Retrieved from https://www.bloomberg.com/news/articles/2018-03-19/if-sports-betting-s-going-to-be-legal-major-leagues-want-a-cut?sref=2WOTxT1z

Obesity Canada. (2020). Obesity in Canada. *Obesity Canada.* Retrieved from: https://obesitycanada.ca/obesity-in-canada/#:~:text=As per cent20a per cent20leading per cent20cause per cent20of,is per cent20directly per cent20attributable per cent20to per cent20obesity

Obesity Canada. (2020). *Obesity in Canada*. Retrieved from: https://obesitycanada.ca/obesity-in-canada/#:~:text=Asper cent20a per cent20leading per cent20cause per cent20of,is per cent20directly per cent20attributable per cent20to per cent20obesity

OECD. (2019). Better Life Index. *OECD*. http://www.oecdbetterlifeindex.org/#/11111111111

Oliver, C. (1990). Determinants of Interorganizational Relationships: Integration and Future Directions. *Academy of Management Review*, *15*(2), 241–265. doi:10.5465/amr.1990.4308156

Oliver, C. (1991). Strategic responses to institutional processes. *Academy of Management Review*, *16*(1), 145–179. doi:10.5465/amr.1991.4279002

Omura, J. D., Carlson, S. A., Brown, D. R., Hopkins, D. P., Kraus, W. E., Staffileno, B. A., ... Undefined, U. U. (2020). Built Environment Approaches to Increase Physical Activity: A Science Advisory From the American Heart Association. *Circulation*, *142*(11). Advance online publication. doi:10.1161/CIR.0000000000000884 PMID:32787451

Onyx, J., & Bullen, P. (2000). Measuring social capital in five communities. *The Journal of Applied Behavioral Science*, *36*(1), 23–42. doi:10.1177/0021886300361002

Organisation for Economic Development and Cooperation. (2021). *Better Life Index*. Retrieved from http://www.oecdbetterlifeindex.org/about/better-life-initiative/

Oxford Economics. (2017). Economic impact of legalized sports betting. *Oxford Economics*. Retrieved from https://www.americangaming.org/wp-content/uploads/2018/12/AGA-Oxford-Sports-Betting-Economic-Impact-Report1-1.pdf

Padrón, N. A. (2020). The Role of Physical Infrastructure on Health and Wellbeing. *Creating a Lifestyle Medicine Center,* 47-56. doi:10.1007/978-3-030-48088-2_6

Panter, J., Heinen, E., Mackett, R., & Ogilvie, D. (2016). Impact of New Transport Infrastructure on Walking, Cycling, and Physical Activity. *American Journal of Preventive Medicine*, *50*(2), e45–e53. Advance online publication. doi:10.1016/j.amepre.2015.09.021 PMID:26585051

Parent, M. M., & Deephouse, D. L. (2007). A case study of stakeholder identification and prioritization by managers. *Journal of Business Ethics*, *75*(1), 1–23. doi:10.100710551-007-9533-y

Parke, A., Harris, A., Parke, J., Rigbye, J., & Blaszczynski, A. (2014). Facilitating awareness and informed choice in gambling. *The Journal of Gambling Business and Economics*, *8*(3), 6–20. doi:10.5750/jgbe.v8i3.971

Parker, R. (2019). The Remarkable Growth of Sport Tourism. *Human Kinetics*. https://humankinetics.me/2019/04/04/the-remarkable-growth-of-sport-tourism/

Parks Canada. (2017). *Parks for All: An Action Plan for Canada's Parks Community* (Rep.). https://static1.squarespace.com/static/57a2167acd0f68183878e305/t/5a79d4b9ec212d1ab6d5ec86/1517933776855/Parks_for_all_Eng_jan31_2018_fnl_web (2).pdf

ParkServe. (n.d.). Retrieved from https://www.tpl.org/parkserve

Parliament of Canada. (2020c). *House Government Bill C-13 An Act to amend the Criminal Code (single-event sport betting).* Parliament of Canada. Retrieved from https://www.parl.ca/LegisInfo/BillDetails.aspx?Language=E&billId=10983057

Parliament of Canada. (2021a). Private Member's Bill C-221. *LEGISinfo.* Retrieved from https://parl.ca/LegisInfo/BillDetails.aspx?Language=E&billId=8092059

Parliament of Canada. (2021b). Hansard – 61. *Ourcommons.ca.* Retrieved from https://www.ourcommons.ca/DocumentViewer/en/43-2/house/sitting-61/hansard#11138272

Parliament of Canada. (2021d). *Private Member's Bill C-218 Safe and Regulated Sports Betting Act.* Parliament of Canada. Retrieved from https://www.parl.ca/LegisInfo/BillDetails.aspx?Language=E&billId=10639805

ParticipACTION. (2019). *Better with Age: Move More Today for a Healthier Tomorrow, ParticipAction Report Card on Physical Activity for Adults.* Retrieved from: https://www.participaction.com/en-ca/resources/adult-report-card

Parung, J., & Bititci, U. S. (2006). A conceptual metric for managing collaborative networks. *Journal of Modelling in Management, 1*(2), 116–136. Advance online publication. doi:10.1108/17465660610703468

Passfield, L., & Doust, J. H. (2000). Changes in cycling efficiency and performance after endurance exercise. *Medicine and Science in Sports and Exercise, 32*(11), 1935–1941. doi:10.1097/00005768-200011000-00018 PMID:11079525

Passfield, L., Hopker, J. G., Jobson, S., Friel, D., & Zabala, M. (2017). Knowledge is power: Issues of measuring training and performance in cycling. *Journal of Sports Sciences, 35*(14), 1426–1434. doi:10.1080/02640414.2016.1215504 PMID:27686573

Paul, R. J., & Weinbach, A. P. (2007). The uncertainty of outcome and scoring effects on Nielsen ratings for Monday Night Football. *Journal of Economics and Business, 59*(3), 199–211. doi:10.1016/j.jeconbus.2006.05.001

Peake, J. M., Kerr, G., & Sullivan, J. P. (2018). A critical review of consumer wearables, mobile applications, and equipment for providing biofeedback, monitoring stress, and sleep in physically active populations. *Frontiers in Physiology, 9*(JUN), 1–19. doi:10.3389/fphys.2018.00743 PMID:30002629

Peppoloni, L., Filippeschi, A., Ruffaldi, E., & Avizzano, C. A. (2014). (WMSDs issue) A novel wearable system for the online assessment of risk for biomechanical load in repetitive efforts. *International Journal of Industrial Ergonomics, 52*, 1–11. doi:10.1016/j.ergon.2015.07.002

Perez, M. V., Mahaffey, K. W., Hedlin, H., Rumsfeld, J. S., Garcia, A., Ferris, T., Balasubramanian, V., Russo, A. M., Rajmane, A., Cheung, L., Hung, G., Lee, J., Kowey, P., Talati, N., Nag, D., Gummidipundi, S. E., Beatty, A., Hills, M. T., Desai, S., ... Turakhia, M. P. (2019). Large-scale assessment of a smartwatch to identify atrial fibrillation. *The New England Journal of Medicine, 381*(20), 1909–1917. doi:10.1056/NEJMoa1901183 PMID:31722151

Peter, J., Schad, T., & Zillgit, J. (2020, November 13). How sports arenas ran up score on 2020 election, hosting hundreds of thousands of voters. *USA Today*. https://www.usatoday.com/story/sports/2020/11/13/how-sports-arenas-ran-up-score-election-thousands-voters/6175568002/

Philadelphia 76ers. (2018). Caesars Entertainment signs deal with HBSE. *Philadelphia 76ers*. Retrieved from https://www.nba.com/sixers/caesars-entertainment-signs-deal-hbse

Pike, H. (2020, July 6). How Parks Canada road closures open opportunities for visitors on two wheels. *CBC*. Retrieved from https://www.cbc.ca/news/canada/calgary/banff-national-park-road-closures-1.5638541

Pitelis, C. (2012). Clusters, entrepreneurial ecosystem co-creation, and appropriability: A conceptual framework. *Industrial and Corporate Change*, *21*(6), 1359–1388. doi:10.1093/icc/dts008

Pivo, G., & Fisher, J. D. (2011). The walkability premium in commercial real estate investments. *Real Estate Economics*, *39*(2), 185–219. doi:10.1111/j.1540-6229.2010.00296.x

Pomfret, G., & Bramwell, B. (2014). The characteristics and motivational decisions of outdoor adventure tourists: A review and analysis. *Current Issues in Tourism*, *19*(14), 1447–1478. doi:10.1080/13683500.2014.925430

Porter, M. E. (1998). Clusters and the new economics of competition. *Harvard Business Review*, *76*(6), 77–90. PMID:10187248

Porter, M. E. (2000). Location, competition, and economic development: Local clusters in a global economy. *Economic Development Quarterly*, *14*(1), 15–34. doi:10.1177/089124240001400105

Porter, M., Bernard, M., Chaturvedi, R. S., Hill, A., Maddox, C., & Schrimpf, M. (2012). *Tennessee Music Cluster. Microeconomics of Competitiveness*. Harvard Business School.

Pradier, P. (2019). Betting on sport: history, regulation, measurement. In J. K. Wilson & R. Pomfret (Eds.), *Historical perspectives on sports economics*. Elgar Publishing., doi:10.4337/9781788977845.00018

Public Health Agency of Canada. (2016, December). How healthy are Canadians? A trend analysis of the health of Canadians from a healthy living and chronic disease perspective. *Public Health Agency of Canada*. https://www.canada.ca/content/dam/phac-aspc/documents/services/publications/healthy-living/how-healthy-canadians/pub1-eng.pdf

Public Health Agency of Canada. (2016, December). *How healthy are Canadians? A trend analysis of the health of Canadians from a healthy living and chronic disease perspective*. Retrieved from: https://www.canada.ca/content/dam/phacaspc/documents/services/publications/healthy-living/how-healthy-canadians/pub1-eng.pdf

Purdhum, D., & Rovell, D. (2018). NBA signs deal with MGM to be gaming partner. *ESPN*. Retrieved from https://www.espn.com/chalk/story/_/id/24245142/nba-first-league-betting-sponsor-deal-mgm

Purdum, D. (2020). New CBA allows owners, players to cash in on stadium sportsbooks. *ESPN*. Retrieved from https://www.espn.com/chalk/story/_/id/28930507/new-cba-allows-owners-players-cash-stadium-sportsbooks

Queenstown, N. Z. (2020). Queenstown Facts and Statistics. *Queenstown NZ.* https://www.queenstownnz.co.nz/insights-and-stats/

Radin, J. M., Wineinger, N. E., Topol, E. J., & Steinhubl, S. R. (2020). Harnessing wearable device data to improve state-level real-time surveillance of influenza-like illness in the USA: A population-based study. *The Lancet. Digital Health*, *2*(2), e85–e93. doi:10.1016/S2589-7500(19)30222-5 PMID:33334565

Raines, P., & Brown, L. (2006). *The economic impact of the music industry in the Nashville-Davidson-Murfreesboro MSA*. College of Business Administration, Belmont University and Nashville Area Chamber of Commerce.

Rajé, F., & Saffrey, A. (2016). The value of cycling. *Cycling Embassy*. Retrieved from http://www.niagaraknowledgeexchange.com/wp-content/uploads/sites/2/2016/04/value-of-cycling.pdf

Raje, F., & Saffrey, A. (2016). The value of cycling. *Department for Transport.* https://assets.publishing.service.gov.uk/government/uploads/system/uploads/attachment_data/file/509587/value-of-cycling.pdf

Randjelovic, D. (2020, June 3). 11 most profitable sports leagues: Their values will surprise you. *Athletic Panda.* https://apsportseditors.org/others/most-profitable-sports-leagues/

Randle, A. (2020, December 23). The insanity, and social necessity, of sports this year. *New York Times*. https://www.nytimes.com/2020/12/23/opinion/COVID-19-sports-nfl.html

Raney, A., & Bryant, J. (2006). *Handbook of sports and media* (1st ed.). Routledge.

Rantala, O., & Rokenses, A. (2018). Is adventure tourism a coherent concept? A review of research approaches on adventure tourism. *Annals of Leisure Research*, *21*(5), 539–552. doi:10.1080/11745398.2016.1250647

Rebula, J. R., Ojeda, L. V., Adamczyk, P. G., & Kuo, A. D. (2013). Measurement of foot placement and its variability with inertial sensors. *Gait & Posture*, *38*(4), 974–980. doi:10.1016/j.gaitpost.2013.05.012 PMID:23810335

Red, C. (2021). Sports gambling partnerships offer MLB new revenue streams, but there are still hurdles to consider. *Forbes*. Retrieved from https://www.forbes.com/sites/christianred/2021/01/12/major-league-baseball-teams-and-a-new-revenue-stream-online-gaming-business-partners/?sh=2a2ce285ef95

Reuters. (2019). Major League Baseball and FanDuel strike sports betting deal. *CNBC*. Retrieved from https://www.cnbc.com/2019/08/15/major-league-baseball-and-fanduel-strike-sports-betting-deal.html

Reuters. (2020, June 12). Commonwealth Games: Athletes to be allowed to take a knee in protest, says Games chief. *Reuters.* https://www.reuters.com/?edition-redirect=br

Rodenberg, R. (2017). Sports betting has an equal sovereignty problem. *Duke Law Journal, 67*(6). https://dlj.law.duke.edu/2017/06/sports-betting-has-an-equal-sovereignty-problem/

Roettgers, J. (2018). The big gamble: Is sports betting really a $7 billion media windfall? *Variety.* Retrieved from https://variety.com/2018/biz/news/sports-betting-media-revenue-forecasts-1202818070/

Rosekind, M. R., Gregory, K. B., Mallis, M. M., Brandt, S. L., Seal, B., & Lerner, D. (2010). The Cost of Poor Sleep: Workplace Productivity Loss and Associated Costs. *Journal of Occupational and Environmental Medicine, 52*(1), 91–98. doi:10.1097/JOM.0b013e3181c78c30 PMID:20042880

Rosenfeld, S. (2005). Industry clusters: Business choice, policy outcome, or branding strategy. *Journal of New Business Ideas and Trends, 3*(2), 4–13.

Ross, P. D. (2000). *The Canadian Fact Book on Poverty.* The Canadian Council on Social Development.

Rothschild, M. (1990). *Bionomics: Economy as Ecosystem.* Henry Holt and Company.

Russ, H. (2018). DraftKings launches mobile sports betting in New Jersey. *Reuters.* Retrieved from https://www.reuters.com/article/us-usa-betting-draftkings-new-jersey-idUSKBN1KM60H

Ryan, G. (2019). I'm a realist: MLB boss Manfred on sports gambling, Disney and Trump. *Boston Business Journal.* Retrieved from https://www.bizjournals.com/boston/news/2019/03/06/mlb-s-boss-on-sports-gambling-disney-and-trump.html

Salaga, S., & Tainsky, S. (2015). Betting lines and college football television ratings. *Economics Letters, 132*, 112–116. doi:10.1016/j.econlet.2015.04.032

Sallis, J. F. (2009). Measuring physical activity environments: A brief history. *American Journal of Preventive Medicine, 36*(4), S86–S92. doi:10.1016/j.amepre.2009.01.002 PMID:19285214

Sanders, D., Myers, T., & Akubat, I. (2017). Training-Intensity distribution in road cyclists: Objective versus subjective measures. *International Journal of Sports Physiology and Performance, 12*(9), 1232–1237. doi:10.1123/ijspp.2016-0523 PMID:28253026

Sand, M., & Gross, S. (2019). Tourism research on adventure tourism – Current themes and developments. *Journal of Outdoor Recreation and Tourism, 28*, 1–5. doi:10.1016/j.jort.2019.100261

Sawalka, V. (2020). 4 stocks to buy on COVID-led e-sports uptick in 2021. *Zacks.* Retrieved from https://www.zacks.com/stock/news/1142863/4-stocks-to-buy-on-covid-led-e-sports-uptick-in-2021#:~:text=The%20global%20e-sports%20betting%20market%20size%20is%20projected,the%-20huge%20video-game%20industry%2C%20it%20is%20growing%20exponentially

Schanzel, H. A., & Yeoman, I. (2015). Trends in family tourism. *Journal of Tourism Futures, 1*(2), 141–147. doi:10.1108/JTF-12-2014-0006

Schlegelmilch, F., & Ollenburg, C. (2013). Marketing the adventure: Utilizing the aspects of risk/fear/thrill to target the youth traveller segment. *Tourism Review*, *68*(3), 44–54. doi:10.1108/TR-03-2013-0010

Schrotenboer, B. (2015). Fantasy sports debate: Gambling or not gambling? *USA Today*. Retrieved from https://www.usatoday.com/story/sports/fantasy/2015/01/11/fantasy-sports-gambling-debate-fan-duel/21612771/

Schultz, L. E., Crompton, J. L., & Witt, P. A. (1995). A national profile of the status of public recreation services for at-risk children and youth. *Journal of Park and Recreation Administration*, *13*, 1–1.

Science, F. (2021). Fatigue risk management system. In The return on investment of fatigue risk management. doi:10.1016/B978-0-323-24288-2.00073-8

Scott, L. (2020). Gambling in football: Bookmakers considering ban of shirt and pitchside advertising. *BBC*. Retrieved from https://www.bbc.com/sport/football/51377202

Scott, W. R., & Davis, G. F. (2015). *Organizations and organizing: Rational, natural and open systems perspectives*. Routledge. doi:10.4324/9781315663371

Scully, D., Kremer, J., Meade, M. M., Graham, R., & Dudgeon, K. (1998). Physical exercise and psychological wellbeing: A critical review. *British Journal of Sports Medicine*, *32*(2), 111–120. doi:10.1136/bjsm.32.2.111 PMID:9631216

Selvaraj, N., Jaryal, A., Santhosh, J., Deepak, K. K., & Anand, S. (2008). Assessment of heart rate variability derived from finger-tip photoplethysmography as compared to electrocardiography. *Journal of Medical Engineering & Technology*, *32*(6), 479–484. doi:10.1080/03091900701781317 PMID:18663635

Senge, P. (2006). *The Fifth Discipline: The Art and Practice of the Learning Organization* (Rev. ed.). Currency Doubleday.

Senge, P. M. (2006). *The fifth discipline: The Art And Practice of The Learning Organization*. Currency.

Shaffer, H. J., LaBrie, R. A., & LaPlante, D. (2004). Laying the foundation for quantifying regional exposure to social phenomena: Considering the case of legalized gambling as public health toxin. *Psychology of Addictive Behaviors*, *18*(1), 40–48. doi:10.1037/0893-164X.18.1.40 PMID:15008684

Shanahan, D. F., Bush, R., Gaston, K. J., Lin, B. B., Dean, J., Barber, E., & Fuller, R. A. (2016). Health benefits from nature experiences depend on dose. *Scientific Reports*, *6*(1), 28551. doi:10.1038rep28551 PMID:27334040

Shapiro, A., Marinsek, N., Clay, I., Bradshaw, B., Ramirez, E., Min, J., Trister, A., Wang, Y., Althoff, T., & Foschini, L. (2020). Characterizing COVID-19 and Influenza Illnesses in the Real World via Person-Generated Health Data. *Patterns*, *2*(1), 100188. doi:10.1016/j.patter.2020.100188 PMID:33506230

Sheerin, K. R., Reid, D., & Besier, T. F. (2019). The measurement of tibial acceleration in runners—A review of the factors that can affect tibial acceleration during running and evidence-based guidelines for its use. *Gait & Posture*, *67*, 12–24. doi:10.1016/j.gaitpost.2018.09.017 PMID:30248663

Shifflet, S., Ostroff, C., & Rivas, A. (2021). How redditors find the next GameStop stock. *Wall Street Journal*. Retrieved from https://www.wsj.com/articles/how-redditors-find-the-next-gamestop-stock-11613644201

Shilbury, D. (2000). Considering future sport delivery systems. *Sport Management Review*, *3*(2), 199–221. doi:10.1016/S1441-3523(00)70086-6

Siegl, A., Kösel, E. M., Tam, N., Koschnick, S., Langerak, N. G., Skorski, S., Meyer, T., & Lamberts, R. P. (2017). Submaximal Markers of Fatigue and Overreaching; Implications for Monitoring Athletes. *International Journal of Sports Medicine*, *38*(9), 675–682. doi:10.1055-0043-110226 PMID:28704885

Silva, J. M., & Stevens, D. E. (2002). *Psychological Foundations of Sport*. Allyn & Bacon.

Silver, A. (2014). Legalize and Regulate Sports Betting. *The New York Times*. Retrieved from https://www.nytimes.com/2014/11/14/opinion/nba-commissioner-adam-silver-legalize-sports-betting.html

Silver, A., Bettman, G., Manfred, R., Garber, D., & Ambrosie, R. (2020). Joint statement from the commissioners of the National Basketball Association, National Hockey League, Major League Baseball, Major League Soccer and Canadian Football League. *Canadiangaming.ca*. Retrieved from http://canadiangaming.ca/wp-content/uploads/Leagues-Joint-Statement.pdf

Silverstein, E. (2020). NFL inches toward stadium sports betting as sportsbook sponsors permitted. *Casino.org*. Retrieved from https://www.casino.org/news/nfl-inches-toward-stadium-sports-betting-as-sportsbook-sponsors-permitted/

Singh, A., Uijtdewilligen, L., Twisk, J. W. R., Van Mechelen, W., & Chinapaw, M. J. M. (2012). Physical activity and performance at school: A systematic review of the literature including a methodological quality assessment. *Archives of Pediatrics & Adolescent Medicine*, *166*(1), 49–55. doi:10.1001/archpediatrics.2011.716 PMID:22213750

Sky Sports. (n.d.). *Skybet*. Retrieved from https://m.skybet.com

Smith, M., & Doherty, B. (2019). Here's everything you need to know about Calgary's $60 million budget haircut. *Star Calgary*. Retrieved from https://www.thestar.com/calgary/2019/07/24/heres-everything-you-need-to-know-about-calgarys-60-million-budget-haircut.html

Smith, D. J., Norris, S. R., & Hogg, J. M. (2002). Performance Evluation of Swimmers - Scientific Tools. *Sports Medicine (Auckland, N.Z.)*, *32*(9), 539–554. doi:10.2165/00007256-200232090-00001 PMID:12096928

SnowFarm NZ. (2020). About Us. *SnowFarm NZ*. https://snowfarmnz.com/about/

Solutions Research Group Consultants Inc. (2014, June 10). *Massive Competition in Pursuit of the $5.7 Billion Canadian Youth Sports Market*. Retrieved from http://www.srgnet.com/2014/06/10/massive-competition-in-pursuit-of-the-5-7-billion-canadian-youth-sports-market/

Sonn, U. (1996). Longitudinal studies of dependence in daily life activities among elderly persons. *Scandinavian Journal of Rehabilitation Medicine. Supplement*, *34*, 1–35. PMID:8701230

Sorensen, M., Smit, J., Barzetti, V., & Williams, J. (1997). *Good practices for urban greening*. Inter-American Development Bank. https://publications.iadb.org/publications/english/document/Good-Practices-for-Urban-Greening.pdf

Spaaij, R. (2012). Beyond the playing field: Experiences of sport, social capital, and integration among Somalis in Australia. *Ethnic and Racial Studies*, *35*(9), 1519–1538. doi:10.1080/01419870.2011.592205

Spangler, T. (2015). ESPN teams with DrafKings as exclusive daily fantasy-sports partner. *Variety*. Retrieved from https://variety.com/2015/digital/news/espn-draftkings-daily-fantasy-sports-1201527028/

Spitz, D. J., & Terry, R. P. (2020). We can handle it: Advocating in support of state legislation of legal sports gambling post-Murphy v. NCAA. *Legal Aspects Sport*, *30*(2), 153–169. doi:10.18060/24366

Sport England. (1999). *The value of sport*. Sport England.

Sport Singapore. (2019). *Live better through sport: Giving back*. Retrieved from https://issuu.com/sportsingapore/docs/for_ebook_190301_sportsg_live_bookl/2?ff&e=29442121/68402603

Sports Betting Dime. (2020). The size and increase of the global sports betting market. *Sports Betting Dime*. Retrieved from https://www.sportsbettingdime.com/guides/finance/global-sports-betting-market/

Sports Khabri. (2020). Sponsorship deals of Indiana Pacers. *Sports Khabri*. https://sportskhabri.com/sponsorship-deals-of-indiana-pacers/

St Leger, L. H. (1999). The opportunities and effectiveness of the health promoting primary school in improving child health—A review of the claims and evidence. *Health Education Research*, *14*(1), 51–69. doi:10.1093/her/14.1.51 PMID:10537947

St. Louis Blues. (2019). Introducing enter the zone – the real-time prediction game. *St. Louis Blues*. Retrieved from https://www.nhl.com/blues/news/introducing-enter-the-zone---the-real-time-prediction-game/c-307326448

Standeven, J., & De Knop, P. (1999). *Sport tourism*. Human Kinetics.

Statista. (2019). *Wearables shipments worldwide 2014-2024*. https://www.statista.com/statistics/437871/wearables-worldwide-shipments/

Statista. (2020). Basketball sports equipment wholesale sales in US from 2007-2019 (in millions). *Statista.* https://www.statista.com/statistics/258582/basketball-sports-equipment-wholesale-sales-in-the-us/#:~:text=In%202019%2C%20wholesale%20sales%20of,about%20181.2%20 million%20U.S.%20dollars

Statistics Canada. (2019, May 21). Sports for fun and fitness. *Statistics Canada.* https://www150.statcan.gc.ca/n1/pub/11-627-m/11-627-m2019039-eng.htm

Staunton, C. E., Hubsmith, D., & Kallins, W. (2003). Promoting safe walking and biking to school: The Marin County success story. *American Journal of Public Health*, *93*(9), 1431–1434. doi:10.2105/AJPH.93.9.1431 PMID:12948957

Sternberg, E. (1997). The defects of stakeholder theory. *Corporate Governance*, *5*(1), 3–10. doi:10.1111/1467-8683.00034

Stieg, C. (2020, July 23). Sports fans have higher self-esteem and are more satisfied with their lives (whether their teams win or lose). *CNBC.* https://www.cnbc.com/2020/07/23/why-being-a-sports-fan-and-rooting-for-a-team-is-good-for-you.html

Stoldt, G. C., Dittmore, S. W., & Branvold, S. E. (2012). *Sport public relations: Managing stakeholder communication.* Human Kinetics.

Stone-Olafson. (n.d.). The New Experience Economy. *Stone-Olafson.* https://www.stone-olafson.com/thenewexperienceeconomy

Street, G., & Ray, J. (2007). *The Relationship between Organized Recreational Activity and Mental Health.* Centre for Behavioural Research in Cancer Control, Curtin University.

Suchman, M. C. (1995). Managing legitimacy: Strategic and institutional approaches. *Academy of Management Review*, *20*(3), 571–610. doi:10.5465/amr.1995.9508080331

Sung, H. H., Morrison, A. M., & O'Leary, J. T. (1997). Definition of Adventure Travel: Conceptual Framework for Empirical Application from the Providers' Perspective. *Asia Pacific Journal of Tourism Research*, *1*(2), 47–66. doi:10.1080/10941669708721975

Svedahl, K., & MacIntosh, B. R. (2003). Anaerobic threshold: the concept and methods of measurement. *Canadian Journal of Applied Physiology = Revue Canadienne de Physiologie Appliquee*, *28*(2), 299–323.

SVG. (2014). NBC's Rotoworld, RotoGrinders ink fantasy sports partnership. *Sports Video Group*. Retrieved from https://www.sportsvideo.org/2014/10/14/nbcs-rotoworld-rotogrinders-ink-fantasy-sports-partnership/

Swarbrooke, J., Beard, C., Leckie, S., & Pomfret, G. (2003). *Adventure tourism – the new frontier.* Elsevier Science.

Tallman, S., Jenkins, M., Henry, N., & Pinch, S. (2004). Knowledge, clusters, and competitive advantage. *Academy of Management Review*, *29*(2), 258–271. doi:10.5465/amr.2004.12736089

Tasker, J. (2020). Federal government to table bill to legalize single-evet sports betting. *CBC*. Retrieved from https://www.cbc.ca/news/politics/legalize-single-event-sports-betting-1.5816059

Taub, D. E., & Greer, K. R. (2000). Physical activity as a normalizing experience for school-age children with physical disabilities: Implications for legitimation of social identity and enhancement of social ties. *Journal of Sport and Social Issues*, *24*(4), 395–414. doi:10.1177/0193723500244007

Taylor, K.-L., Chapman, D. W., Cronin, J. B., Newton, M. J., & Gill, N. (2012). Fatigue Monitoring in High Performance Sport: A survey of current trends. *Journal of Australian Strength & Conditioning*, *20*(1), 12–23.

Taylor, S., Varley, P., & Johnston, T. (2013). *Adventure tourism: Meanings, experience, and learning*. Taylor & Francis. doi:10.4324/9780203120095

The 15-Minute City Project. (n.d.). Retrieved from https://www.15minutecity.com/

The Canadian Press. (2011). Rogers, Bell buy control of MLSE. *CBC Sports*. https://www.cbc.ca/sports/hockey/nhl/rogers-bell-buy-control-of-mlse-1.997655

The Universal Design Project. (2020). Retrieved from https://universaldesign.org/

Thibault, L. (2009). Globalization of sport: An inconvenient truth. *Journal of Sport Management*, *23*(1), 1–20. doi:10.1123/jsm.23.1.1

Thomas, S., Lewis, S., Duong, J., & McLeod, C. (2012). Sports betting marketing during sporting events: A stadium and broadcast census of Australian Football League matches. *Australian and New Zealand Journal of Public Health*, *36*(2), 145–152. doi:10.1111/j.1753-6405.2012.00856.x PMID:22487349

Thompson, J., Wartick, S., & Smith, H. (1991). Integrating corporate social performance and stakeholder management: Implications for a research agenda in small business. *Research in Corporate Social Performance and Policy*, *12*(1), 207–230.

Thompson, W. R. (2021). Worldwide Survey of Fitness Trends for 2020. *ACSM's Health & Fitness Journal*, *25*(1), 10–19. doi:10.1249/FIT.0000000000000631

Thompson, W. R., & Ph, D. (2006). Fitness Trends for 2007. *The Physician and Sportsmedicine*, *10*(6), 7–14. doi:10.3810/psm.2004.01.1627

Thorn, J. (2019). Forget what you know about the Black Sox scandal. *New York Times*. Retrieved from https://www.nytimes.com/2019/10/09/opinion/black-sox-scandal-1919.html

Tourism New Zealand. (2020). *Special Interests. Tourism New Zealand*. https://www.tourismnewzealand.com/markets-stats/sectors/special-interest/

Tremblay, M. S., Warburton, D. E. R., Janssen, I., Paterson, D. H., Latimer, A. E., Rhodes, R. E., Kho, M. E., Hicks, A., LeBlanc, A. G., Zehr, L., Murumets, K., & Duggan, M. (2011). New Canadian physical activity guidelines. *Applied Physiology, Nutrition, and Metabolism*, *36*(1), 36–46. doi:10.1139/H11-009 PMID:21326376

Trendafilova, S., Babiak, K., & Heinze, K. (2013). Corporate social responsibility and environmental sustainability: Why professional sport is greening the playing field. *Sport Management Review*, *16*(3), 298–313. doi:10.1016/j.smr.2012.12.006

TSN. (2020, September). *Morning Coffee: Welcome to The TSN Edge*. Retrieved from https://www.tsn.ca/morning-coffee-welcome-to-the-tsn-edge-1.1522030

Tudor-locke, C., Craig, C. L., Brown, W. J., Clemes, S. A., Cocker, K. De, Giles-corti, B., Hatano, Y., Inoue, S., Matsudo, S. M., Mutrie, N., Oppert, J., Rowe, D. A., Schmidt, M. D., Schofield, G. M., Spence, J. C., Teixeira, P. J., Tully, M. A., & Blair, S. N. (2011). How Many Steps / day are Enough? *For Adults*, 1–17.

Twenge, J. M. (2017). *iGen: Why Today's Super-Connected Kids Are Growing Up Less Rebellious, More Tolerant, Less Happy and Completely Unprepared for Adulthood.* Atria.

Twenge, J. M. (2019). More Time on Technology, Less Happiness? Associations Between Digital-Media Use and Psychological Well-Being. *Current Directions in Psychological Science*, *28*(4), 372–379. doi:10.1177/0963721419838244

United Kingdom. (2005). Gambling Act. *Government of the United Kingdom*. Retrieved from https://www.legislation.gov.uk/ukpga/2005/19/contents

United Nations. (2019). *United Nations Development Index*. Retrieved from http://hdr.undp.org/en/content/human-development-index-hdi

Urbancova, H. (2013). Competitive advantage achievement through innovation and knowledge. *Journal of Competitiveness*, *5*(1), 82–96. doi:10.7441/joc.2013.01.06

Urhausen, A., & Kindermann, W. (2002). Diagnosis of overtraining: What tools do we have? *Sports Medicine (Auckland, N.Z.)*, *32*(2), 95–102. doi:10.2165/00007256-200232020-00002 PMID:11817995

Valuates Reports. (2020). Fantasy sports market by sports yype (football, baseball, basketball, hockey, cricket, and others), platform (website, and mobile application), and Demographics (under 25 years, 25 to 40 years and above 40 years): Global opportunity analysis and industry forecast, 2021–2027. *Valuate Reports*. Retrieved from https://reports.valuates.com/market-reports/ALLI-Manu-1E22/fantasy-sports

Van Alstyne, M. W., Parker, G. G., & Choudary, S. P. (2016). Pipelines, Platforms, and the New Rules of Strategy. *Harvard Business Review*, (April), 54–62.

Van Rompuy, B. & Asser Institute (2015). *The odds of match fixing facts & figures on the integrity risk of certain sports bets*. Brussels: Asser International Sport Law Centre.

Vibar-Bawzon, J. (1997, October). Developing sports as a social deterrence to social deviance: The role of sport on women and girl's lives. Presentation at the *Second Scientific International Conference for Women Sport*, Alexandria University, Egypt.

Viceconti, M., Hernandez Penna, S., Dartee, W., Mazza, C., Caufield, B., Becker, C., Maetzler, W., Garcia-Aymerich, J., Davico, G., & Rochester, L. (2020). Toward a Regulatory Qualification of Real-World Mobility Performance Biomarkers in Parkinson' s Patients Using Digital Mobility Outcomes. *Sensors (Basel)*, *20*(5920), 1–12. doi:10.339020205920 PMID:33092143

Visit Indy. (2020). White River State Park. *Visit Indy.* https://www.visitindy.com/indianapolis-white-river-state-park?utm_source=visitindy

Vuchot, A., Joly, C., & Kawkabani, R. (2020). The Gambling Law Review: France. *The Law Reviews.* Retrieved from https://thelawreviews.co.uk/title/the-gambling-law-review/france

Waddell, D. (2020). Professional sports leagues' commissioner urge federal government to allow single-game betting. *Windsor Star.* Retrieved from https://windsorstar.com/news/professional-sports-leagues-commissioners-urge-federal-government-to-allow-single-game-betting

Wagner, K. (2015). FanDuel acquired esports company AlphDraft, also jumps into competitive video gaming. *Vox.* Retrieved from https://www.vox.com/2015/9/24/11618896/fanduel-acquires-esports-company-alphadraft-also-jumps-into

Wakefield, J. (2016). Manchester City sign first e-sports player. *BBC.* Retrieved from https://www.bbc.com/news/technology-36734518

Warburton, D. E. R., Nicol, C. W., & Bredin, S. S. D. (2006). Health benefits of physical activity: The evidence. *Canadian Medical Association Journal*, *174*(6), 801–809. doi:10.1503/cmaj.051351 PMID:16534088

Washington Center for Equitable Growth. (2020). How the coronavirus recession is impacting part-time US workers. *Washington Center for Equitable Growth.* https://equitablegrowth.org/how-the-coronavirus-recession-is-impacting-part-time-u-s-workers/

Waters, M. (2021). DraftKings goes public after shareholder approval, business combination. *Legal Sports Report.* Retrieved from https://www.legalsportsreport.com/40250/draftkings-vote-going-public/

Weed, M., & Bull, C. (2009). *Sports tourism: participants, policy, and providers* (2nd ed.). Butterworth-Heinemann.

Whitehead, M. (2019). *Physical Literacy Across the World.* Routledge. https://play.google.com/store/books/details?id=6qSbDwAAQBAJ&gl=ca&hl=en-CA&source=productsearch&utm_source=HA_Desktop_US&utm_medium=SEM&utm_campaign=PLA&pcampaignid=MKT-FDR-na-us-1000189-Med-pla-bk-Evergreen-Jul1520-PLA-eBooks_Education&gclid=Cj0KCQiApY6BBhCsARIsAOI_GjbCK-rSj6wx_d8KQw1MNMQnTDQzb-FdVtQhuw9mUjWsomoaqu7SX6EaAnsjEALw_wcB&gclsrc=aw.ds

William Hill. (2020). William Hill annual report and accounts 2019. *William Hill.* Retrieved from https://www.williamhillplc.com/media/13522/ara19_v2.pdf

Williams, K. R. (1985). The relationship between mechanical and physiological energy estimates. *Medicine and Science in Sports and Exercise, 17*(3), 317–325. doi:10.1249/00005768-198506000-00004 PMID:3894868

Williams, P., & Soutar, G. (2009). Value, satisfaction and behavioural intentions in an adventure tourism context. *Annals of Tourism Research, 36*(3), 413–443. doi:10.1016/j.annals.2009.02.002

Winter Games. (2020). Our Story. *Winter Games NZ.* https://www.wintergamesnz.kiwi/our-story

Wolbring, G. (2012). Paralympics vs Olympics coverage: Uneven at best. *The Conversation.* https://theconversation.com/paralympics-vs-olympics-coverage-uneven-at-best-9429

Wolff, E. A., & Hums, M. A. (2020, May 12). The pillars of connection, innovation, and resiliency in and through sport. *Peace and sport.* https://www.peace-sport.org/opinion/the-pillars-of-connection-innovation-and-resilience-in-and-through-sport/

Wong, M. (2020, March 26). *'Out of the question': How the cost of sports excludes low-income kids.* Retrieved from https://theeyeopener.com/2020/03/out-of-the-question-how-the-cost-of-sports-excludes-low-income-kids/

Wood, W. A., Bennett, A. V., & Basch, E. (2015). Emerging uses of patient generated health data in clinical research. *Molecular Oncology, 9*(5), 1018–1024. doi:10.1016/j.molonc.2014.08.006 PMID:25248998

Woodward, C. (2015). DraftKings raises $300m in frenzied fantasy sports land-grab. *Boston. com.* Retrieved from http://www.betaboston.com/news/2015/07/26/draftkings-raises-300m-in-frenzied-fantasy-sports-land-grab/

Woo, J., Ho, S. C., & Yu, A. L. (1999). Walking speed and stride length predicts 36 months dependency, mortality, and institutionalization in Chinese aged 70 and older. *Journal of the American Geriatrics Society, 47*(10), 1257–1260. doi:10.1111/j.1532-5415.1999.tb05209.x PMID:10522962

World Travel & Tourism Council. (2020). *Travel and tourism: Benchmarking trends report 2019.* World Travel & Tourism Council. https://wttc.org/en-gb/Research/Economic-Impact/Benchmarking

World, I. B. S. (2020). Global sports betting & lotteries - Market size 2005-2026. *IBS World.* Retrieved from https://www.ibisworld.com/global/market-size/global-sports-betting-lotteries/

Xue, H., & Mason, D. S. (2011). The changing stakeholder map of formula one grand prix in Shanghai. *European Sport Management Quarterly, 11*(4), 371–395. doi:10.1080/16184742.2011.599205

Zeng, D. (Ed.). (2008). *Knowledge, technology, and cluster-based growth in Africa.* The World Bank. doi:10.1596/978-0-8213-7306-4

Zhu, G., Li, J., Meng, Z., Yu, Y., Li, Y., Tang, X., Dong, Y., Sun, G., Zhou, R., Wang, H., Wang, K., & Huang, W. (2020). Learning from Large-Scale Wearable Device Data for Predicting Epidemics Trend of COVID-19. *Discrete Dynamics in Nature and Society*, *2020*, 1–8. Advance online publication. doi:10.1155/2020/6152041

About the Contributors

David J. Finch is a professor and senior fellow at Mount Royal University's Institute for Community Prosperity. David holds a PhD in management and is an active educator, scholar, and practitioner. He currently holds several academic appointments including as a Professor at Mount Royal University's Bissett School of Business, a Visiting Fellow at the Henley Business School at the University of Reading (UK) and an Adjunct at the Gordon S. Lang School of Business and Economics at the University of Guelph. Dr. Finch has authored over 50 scholarly papers and published in journals such as the Academy of Management Learning & Education, Journal of Business Ethics, Journal of Marketing Management, Journal of Sport Management, and the Corporate Reputation Review. His most recent book, *Implications and Impacts of eSports on Business and Society: Emerging Research and Opportunities* explored emerging themes in esports. Prior to joining academia, Dr. Finch held progressively senior roles in areas of corporate strategy in Canada, the U.S., and the U.K.

David Legg is a Professor and past Chair for the Department of Physical and Health at Mount Royal University in Calgary. He is the Past President of the Canadian Paralympic Committee and past board member for the 2015 Pan Parapan American Games in Toronto. David has also served on the International Paralympic Committee's Sport Science Committee. In June he was elected President of the International Federation of Adapted Physical Activity. Dr. Legg also worked with the Calgary BidCo for the 2026 Olympic and Paralympic Games.

* * *

Richard Opara Ajiee is a Lecturer in Tourism and Event Management at Auckland University of Technology (AUT), New Zealand. His research interest transcend sport management, sport sociology and event management, focusing on sport and integration, sport and migration, sport and social capital, sport for development, event for development, event impacts and legacy and entrepreneurship. Prior to

AUT, Dr Ajiee taught at New Zealand Institute of Sport (NZIS) and Best Pacific Institute of Education. His active involvement in sport transcends three continents; as a player, entrepreneur, manager and coach, with extensive interest in football, basketball, table tennis and boxing. He considers himself an active sport enthusiast. He was the pioneer coach of AUT women's football team and also coached table tennis with the Special Olympics Counties Manukau.

Cheri Bradish is an industry leader and pioneer in sport business education, with areas of expertise in sport business, sport marketing, and female sport leadership. She currently is the Founder and Managing Director of the Future of Sport Lab (FSL) a sport innovation lab and sport tech incubator supported by Maple Leaf Sports and Entertainment (MLSE). She is also the Ted Rogers Director of Sport Business at the School of Management at Ryerson (TRSM), coming from Brock University where she spent sixteen years at the Founding Professor of their Department of Sport Management. In 2019 she became the first Canadian to receive the Academic Achievement in Sport and Entertainment Award from the SEVT Group at the University in South Carolina. She is a proud alumna of Florida State University and the University of Guelph - where she is a proud member of the Gryphon Women's Varsity Volleyball team.

Nick Burton is an assistant professor at Brock University, having spent a year as a post-doctoral fellow at Ryerson University. His research is focused on the nature and strategy of ambush marketing within the sport marketing industry in order to better understand the managerial implications for sport sponsors and partnership relations. His other areas of interest include: sponsorship management and strategy, commercial rights management, athlete branding and celebrity endorsements, international sport business, sport marketing management, consumer behavior, event marketing.

Chris Dawe's experience is rooted in Canada and U.S. leadership and consulting roles within higher education and community, with proactive, upstream wellbeing impacts (recreation, active living, wellness, health promotion, sport, and community-building). Chris is co-chair of the ActiveCITY Collective in the Calgary region. He's also served in industry leadership roles including NIRSA's Board of Directors, the planning committee for NASPA's Wellness and Health Promotion Leadership conference, and the executive committee of the U.S. Health Promoting Campuses Network. Chris is a regular presenter on related industry topics including NIRSA, NASPA, CACUSS, ARPA, and Athletic Business.

Geoff Dickson started his academic career at Central Queensland University before a 14-year tenure at Auckland University of Technology. During his time in

New Zealand, Geoff was a director of Gymnastics New Zealand, Tennis Northern, AFL New Zealand and President of the Sport Management Association of Australia and New Zealand. He has been a visiting professor at universities in Brazil, Portugal, Canada, Germany, Hong Kong and Iran. Now at La Trobe University (Melbourne, Australia) his research interests transcend sport management and event management, usually focusing on interorganisational relationships, network governance, event impacts and legacies, volunteers, sponsorship, ambush marketing and consumer behaviour. He has supervised to completion nearly 30 honours, masters, and PHD theses. He is a keen golfer and describes his ability as 'better than most but not nearly as good as some'.

Mark Dottori, MBA, PhD, APR, is a Mitacs postdoctoral fellow at McMaster University's department of communication studies and media arts in the McMaster Communication Metrics Research Lab. Mark holds an MBA from the Schulich School of Business at York University and a PhD in sport management from the University of Ottawa. His research is primarily focused on sport and political communication, marketing, reputational strategy and metrics. Prior to his doctoral studies, Mark spent almost 20 years working for such organizations as the Canadian Football League, Toronto Raptors, Rugby Canada, Canada Basketball, Callaway Golf, and the Canadian Paralympic Committee. He has also worked as a consultant in data science and digital strategy for offices in the Parliament of Canada. Mark is also an accredited public relations professional by the Canadian Public Relations Society and a member of the board of directors for its foundation.

Mathew Dowling is a Senior Lecturer within the Cambridge Centre for Sport and Exercise Sciences at Anglia Ruskin University. He holds an MSc in Sport Management from Loughborough University and completed his PhD in Physical Education and Recreation (Sport Management) at University of Alberta. He has published widely across a number of leading journals including *Journal of Sport Management*, *European Sport Management Quarterly*, *Sport Management Review,* and *International Journal of Sport Policy and Politics.* He also currently sits on the editorial board of *Managing Sport and Leisure*. His principal research interests include sport policy and governance, organizational theory, professionalization, comparative methodology and government involvement in the not-for-profit sport sector within the UK and Canada.

Jared R. Fletcher is an Assistant Professor in the Department of Health and Physical Education at Mount Royal University and serves as a scientific consultant for Biomechanigg Sport and Health Research Inc. He is also an Adjunct Assistant Professor in the Faculty of Kinesiology at the University of Calgary. He holds a

PhD in applied muscle physiology from the University of Calgary. His research program, which is funded by the Natural Sciences and Engineering Research Council of Canada and the Ehlers-Danlos Society, examines the energetic implications of muscle-tendon interaction during running and walking in health and disease as well as the ability of wearable sensors to monitor training load in recreational and elite athletes. He has published over 20 peer-reviewed publications and is also an Associate Editor for *Frontiers in Physiology*. Prior to academia, Dr. Fletcher was the lead sport physiologist for the Canadian National Para-swimming team, where he helped support swimmers, with the use of wearable devices, to Canadian, Regional and World Record performances.

Mark Hentze, active in design and public engagement for sport and recreation facilities, has led projects in Canada, USA, Germany, and Mongolia serving PBK Architects, CEI Architecture (Partner), and HDR (Vice President), and in collaboration with multiple affiliate firms. He is Chair of IAKS Ice Facilities Experts Circle. A background in collegiate and professional sports gives Mark unique insight into sport facility design. He is a regular presenter at conferences like IAKS, Athletic Business, RFoBC, BCRPA, ARPA, CPRA, RFABC, ORFA, AIBC.

Mary A. Hums, PhD, is a Professor of Sport Administration at the University of Louisville. In 2009, she was named a NASSM Earle F. Zeigler Lecturer, the organization's most prestigious academic honor. In 2014, she received the NASSM Diversity Award. She has worked 4 Paralympic Games, the Olympic Games, and the Para-Pan American Games. Hums co-authored Article 30.5 of the 2006 UN Convention on the Rights of Persons with Disabilities. She has authored over 150 refereed journal articles and book chapters and given over 200 presentations in the United States and abroad. Her research interests are policy development in sport organizations regarding inclusion of people with disabilities and also sport and human rights. Hums is a monogram letter winner in Field Hockey at the University of Notre Dame and a 1996 inductee in the ASA Indiana Softball Hall of Fame.

Christy Lane is a startup Founder, mentor and award-winning exercise scientist with expertise in big data, wearable devices, and lifestyle medicine. Currently, Dr. Lane is the Chair of Health and Physical Education at Mount Royal University. She is also a Visiting Associate Professor in Orthopaedics at Stanford University and a founding member of the Stanford Wearable Health Lab. She is the Founder of Vivametrica, a health tech company that uses data from wearable devices to predict mortality and disease risks, as well as to engage individuals in wellness. Christy has won many international awards for her work in lifestyle medicine and the application of technology in health and speaks often internationally on these topics. She was recently recognized as Top 40 Under 40 in Calgary, 2018 Female Founders of Insuretch Winner and Top 20 Women in Tech 2018. Christy has a PhD in Rehabilitation Medicine from the University of Alberta, as well as an MSc. In Exercise Physiology from Western University. She completed a Postdoctoral Fellowship in Rehabilitation Science at the University of Michigan.

Becca Leopkey is an Associate Professor in the Department of Kinesiology at the University of Georgia, USA. Dr. Leopkey holds a MA and PhD in Sport Management from the University of Ottawa in Canada and has received support for her research from the International Olympic Committee and the Social Sciences and Humanities Research Council of Canada (SSHRC). She has over 35 publications that can be found in a number of leading journals in the field such as *Journal of Sport Management, European Sport Management Quarterly*, and *Event Management*. Dr. Leopkey's main areas of research interest focus on the application of organization theories to better understand sport event organization, event legacy and international sport organizations.

Tracey Martin was part of the founding leadership team that brought Vivo for Healthier Generations to life. She's led the start up of Vivo's Brand and Research and Innovation Arm as well as the original design and engagement of Vivo's multi-million-dollar expansion project. On top of Tracey's worked in municipal government and has led the brand development experience for three major fortune 500 companies. She is also an avid explorer and storyteller presenting about Social Impact at conferences across Canada and internationally, generating proof points, case studies and articles on community-led projects, mentoring millennial leaders and exploring and figuring out what is possible in the world. Tracey believes in being a catalyst for change by co-creating and measuring solutions to raise healthier generations. She hopes Calgary will become the next prototype for a Citizen- Led and Designed City. She wishes for people to be curious and stand up and out for a better tomorrow.

Norm O'Reilly is recognized as one of the leading scholars in the business of sports. He is currently Professor and Assistant Dean of Executive Programs in the Gordon S. Lang School of Business & Economics at the University of Guelph. As Assistant Dean, he leads Lang's two professional programs, the MBA and MA(Leadership) degrees. Dr. O'Reilly is also the founding Director of the International Institute for Sport Business & Leadership at Guelph, a think-tank devoted to improving the sport business globally. He was previously the Richard P. and Joan S. Fox Professor of Business and Chair of the Department of Sports Administration at Ohio University's College of Business. He has authored or co-authored eight books, and more than 120 peer reviewed journal articles. Dr. O'Reilly is the lead researcher on the Canadian Sponsorship Landscape Study, currently in its thirteenth edition. For more than a decade, he has been minority owner and partner consultant Toronto-based agency, T1, where he has worked for clients including Nike, UFC, Nissan, and Canadian Olympic Committee. Dr. O'Reilly was 'Assistant Chef de Mission' for the Canadian Paralympic Team at the 2016 Paralympic Games in Rio, Brazil. In 2017, his work was highlighted publicly in the media as part of the Canadian Hockey League legal case around player compensation. He currently holds visiting/adjunct appointments in Canada, the United States and Australia, and also holds the CGA/CPA Accounting Designation.

Jason Ribeiro is a corporate leader, community advocate, and one of Canada's most awarded social science graduate students. As Director of Strategy at Calgary Economic Development, Jason is responsible for setting and implementing corporate and community vision through the city's new economic strategy, "Calgary in the New Economy." Jason is simultaneously completing his Ph.D. research at the University of Calgary, which is funded by the prestigious SSHRC Joseph-Armand Bombardier Canada Graduate Scholarship and aims to assist organizational leaders in shaping, leading, and sustaining innovation efforts in cross-sector partnerships. He is an active member of the international academic community, and has taught over 600 university students, written 13 scholarly works, delivered over 20 national/international conference presentations, and received over $180,000 in competitive funding. Jason is committed to improving the lives and well-being of Canadians across the country and has represented Canada at the World Bank/IMF Annual Meetings, United Nations Peacekeeping Defence Ministerial, and Young Leaders Program of Atlantik-Brücke. He was recently elected as Curator of the World Economic Forum Global Shapers Calgary Hub for the 2019-2020 year. A passionate leader, Jason currently sits on boards and standing committees within Sport Calgary, EducationMatters, and the Calgary Public Library. Finally, Jason weighs in regularly on civic, national, and international affairs as a commentator on CBC.

Jonathan Robertson is a Lecturer in Deakin Business School's sport management program at Deakin University, Melbourne, Australia, where he is the course director of the Master of Business (Sport Management). His research and teaching interests revolve around the impact of sport on society and primarily focus on social change, social responsibility, and organization theory. He has published in leading journals such as Journal of Sport Management, Sport Management Review, and Annals of Leisure Research as well as various books and conference proceedings.

Alex Sévigny, PhD, APR, is associate professor of communications management and communication studies in the department of communication studies and media arts at McMaster University. Alex is editor-in-chief of the Journal of Professional Communication and co-director of the McMaster Communication Metrics Research Lab. He is currently Chief Accreditation Examiner for the Canadian Public Relations Society. From 2011-19, Alex was director of the Master of Communications Management program, offered in partnership by McMaster and Syracuse Universities. His research examines the intersections between data science, artificial intelligence, communication and reputation strategy, marketing, culture, economics and politics. For 15 years, Alex has been an active consultant to organizations and highly public individuals in the political, public, private and not-for-profit sectors. Alex has served on the board of the Canadian Public Relations Society national society and of its Hamilton chapter, where he has served as professional development chair, accreditation chair and president.

Trevor Tombe is an Associate Professor of Economics at the University of Calgary and a Research Fellow at The School of Public Policy. Prior to joining the University of Calgary in 2012, he was an Assistant Professor of Economics at Wilfrid Laurier University. He received his BBA (Finance) from Simon Fraser University, and his MA and PhD (Economics) from the University of Toronto. His research focuses on a broad range of topics from international trade and public finance to energy and environmental policy. In addition to his academic work, he regularly promotes the public understanding of economics and policy issues through his numerous public policy papers through the School, active social media presence, and general interest writings in various media outlets, including regular contributions to CBC Calgary and other media outlets.

Brian Torrance is the Executive Director with Ever Active Schools, a national charity focussed on the health and wellbeing of school communities. He works alongside associated government ministries, school health partners, and has a focus on fund development, and initiating new innovative projects. Brian enjoys the larger system goals of improved health and wellness and the meaningful collaboration it takes to get there. Prior to joining Ever Active Schools Brian went to the University of Alberta completing a Bachelors in Physical Education and a Master of Science from the Faculty of Medicine and Dentistry. During his post secondary years, Brian competed on the varsity Track and Field and Cross-Country running teams igniting a passion for the power of sport and making lifelong friends along the way. Brian has been honoured with an indigenous name Piitaa meaning Eagle from the Kainai community on the Blood Tribe.

Cynthia Watson is Chief Evolution Officer of Vivo for Healthier Generations Society, a charity on a mission to inspire a wholistic mindset for healthy living. She loves to tinker, test and prototype in the realms of social innovation, service design and social economics to co-create solutions with communities at a systems level. She is happiest leading with heart in a lifelong quest to embolden others to make a bigger difference in the world. In her parallel universe, she Co-chair of the ActiveCITY Collective Transition Team, a group of passionate volunteers leading a sustained, collaborative commitment to citizen well-being through Calgary's emerging active economy sector. She is a graduate of the Royal Roads University Master of Arts in Leadership.

Richard Keith Wright is the leader of the Auckland University of Technology (AUT) Graduate Programme in Sport and Exercise and a Senior Lecturer within the School of Sport and Recreation's Department of Sports Leadership and Management. His teaching, research and industry engagement activities collectively focus on the connection and relationship between sports events and entrepreneurship. He is equally interested in the study of serious leisure as a vehicle for social change and sustainable development. Dr. Wright has published widely within the fields of sport, tourism, events and leisure studies and is an Associate Editor of the International Journal of the Sociology of Leisure and the Annals of Leisure Research. He currently sits on the executive committees of the AUT Centre for Active Ageing, the Australian and New Zealand Association for Leisure Studies (ANZALS) and the Auckland Sunday Football Association. Richard is passionate plogger and the founder of 'Walk on Aotearoa'.

Index

H

I

J

L

M

N

O

P

R

S

T

V

W

www.ingramcontent.com/pod-product-compliance
Lightning Source LLC
LaVergne TN
LVHW060003031026
849161LV00025B/1353